Penn State Bowl Games

Penn State Bowl Games

A Complete History

TOMMY A. PHILLIPS

Foreword by TOM BARR

McFarland & Company, Inc., Publishers

Jefferson, North Carolina

Library of Congress Cataloguing-in-Publication Data

Names: Phillips, Tommy A., 1984– author.
Title: Penn State bowl games : a complete history /
Tommy A. Phillips ; foreword by Tom Barr.
Description: Jefferson, North Carolina : McFarland & Company, Inc.,
Publishers, 2021. | Includes bibliographical references and index.
Identifiers: LCCN 2021021166 | ISBN 9781476685267 (paperback : acid free paper) ∞
ISBN 9781476643502 (ebook)
Subjects: LCSH: Pennsylvania State University—Football—History. |
Penn State Nittany Lions (Football team)—History. |
BISAC: SPORTS & RECREATION / Football
Classification: LCC GV958.P46 P55 2021 | DDC 796.332/630974853—dc23
LC record available at https://lccn.loc.gov/2021021166

British Library cataloguing data are available

ISBN (print) 978-1-4766-8526-7
ISBN (ebook) 978-1-4766-4350-2

Front cover: Penn State Nittany Lions running back Curtis Enis (39)
carries the ball through the Texas Longhorns defense at the Fiesta Bowl
in Sun Devil Stadium in Tempe, Arizona on January 1, 1997
(Penn State University Archives)

Printed in the United States of America

*McFarland & Company, Inc., Publishers
Box 611, Jefferson, North Carolina 28640
www.mcfarlandpub.com*

To my mom, my dad, and my sister:

Mom: For being there even at my very lowest moments, even when it looked like this book would never be written.

Dad: For taking me to my first Penn State game in 2003 against Wisconsin, and making me stay a fan even through the dark days.

Joy: For being my best friend, and playing thousands of hours of NCAA Football with me—you deserved to win the national championship.

Without you three, this book never would have even gotten off the ground. I sincerely thank you and love you with all of my heart.

Table of Contents

Table of Contents

Acknowledgments

I'd like to thank the following people for your help, in one way or another. Even if you never read this book, you still have my gratitude.

- My family: obviously, none of this would happen without you and your financial and moral support. I've thanked you earlier, but I want to do so again here. Mom, you've been my rock, at times the one and only person in the world who I had left. I hope you realize even a fraction of how much you've meant to me, because it's too much to quantify. Dad, you took me to my first Penn State game and basically forced me to stay as a Penn State fan through the dark years between 2011 and 2014. That has now all paid off with this book. Joy, you played thousands upon thousands of games of NCAA Football with me, where I never let you win the national championship. I apologize for that, but I also want to let you know that all those games mean far more to me than you could ever imagine. Andrew and Uncle Rick, you bought my book at Bradley's before the store closed to help me save face, and I thank you so much for that.
- Ben: you are a big reason why I'm a Penn State fan. I still remember us in study hall discussing who Penn State was going to play in the 2001 Final Four after the Lions knocked off #2 North Carolina. Our trips to Penn State football games included a car getting stuck in a ditch (Florida International 2007), not being able to find our car for an hour in the middle of a field of tens of thousands of cars in the pouring rain (Temple 2006), freezing our butts off to the point that our hot chocolate had turned to solid (Michigan State 2010), and of course all the visits to Ponderosa. I wouldn't have wanted them to have been with anyone else.
- Jay: too many reasons to count, but the main one would be taking all my verbal abuse during the 2002 college football season and staying as my friend. Honestly, I'm not worthy of your friendship, but you've kept me around anyway. For that, I thank you with all my heart. And anyone brave enough to go to war twice is the definition of a true legend. But I still have to say, the Insight.com Bowl is not a high-quality bowl.
- Dr. Wang: as I thanked you in my *Great Eighties* book, your perseverance in getting me on the right medication made this all possible. I wouldn't be in the right mindset to write if not for your guidance in getting me the right medication.
- Tom and Carol Barr: for reaching out to me when I asked if there were any Penn State players willing to help me on the book. You were the only one, and I thank you so much for that.

- Greg: for helping me be able to view all the past bowl games, most of which this book would be incomplete without.
- Mrs. Sutherland: I know you passed away over ten years ago, and your family may never know that I wrote this, but I have to thank you again. Your teaching on Shakespeare changed my life. If I didn't have so much fun acting out *Romeo and Juliet* and *Julius Caesar*, I would never written a single story in my life. The first class I had with you, you had us write on the teacher I remember most. If I could rewrite that paper, you would be the subject, for all the right reasons.
- The NTO: I don't think I've ever had as much fun on a 20-degree day in State College than I did with you guys in November 2019. Granted, most of the time when I got Penn State tickets, I picked the first game on the schedule. But we froze our butts off to see the Lions wrap up a New Year's Six berth (though it should have been a Rose Bowl). If they ever play football again, I want to go to another game with you guys.
- Alex: you helped me get Penn State bowl photos, and the book would not be possible without them. You assisted me at probably the hardest time possible for you, because of the shutdowns and quarantine. That means a lot to me.
- Glenn Y., Daniel C., Andrew J., Jim G., Jeanie G., and all of my other anime friends: you have been a friend to me even when I have not been a friend to you. You have shown me grace, while also opening up my mind to possibilities I had never considered. Our time and memories together at conventions is priceless.
- Finally, and most importantly, my Lord and Savior Jesus Christ who made me, died for me, rose again, and will call me home someday.

If I've forgotten anyone, I apologize. In the meantime, all I have to say is … "We are…"

Foreword by Tom Barr

After my last senior high school football game, my focus turned to preparing for playing this game at the next level, Division I, for the Penn State Nittany Lions, under head coach Joe Paterno. My attraction to Coach Paterno and the Lions' program was the lack of names on the jerseys, black shoes, colors blue and white, and student-athlete philosophy. My next four years playing for Penn State shaped me for becoming a high school math teacher and high school football coach, with the influence from four bowl games: the 1979 Liberty Bowl, 1980 and 1982 Fiesta Bowl, and 1983 Sugar Bowl.

Following my Penn State freshman year, I became more aware of the importance of following a practice schedule/routine, rules and guidelines that Coach Paterno put on the team in the next three bowl games. We always flew out a week before the game, and prior to that, we always had our game plan in for the bowl game. Game week consisted of meals, team meetings, position meetings, practice, social events with and without the opponents, and free time. Coach Paterno spoke to us that bowl games are not just preparing for winning the game, but also for us to enjoy the leisure time when not on the field.

Each bowl game had their own special memories. In the 1980 Fiesta Bowl, we defeated Ohio State 31–19 and Heisman Trophy winner Art Schlichter of Ohio State. In the 1982 Fiesta Bowl, we defeated USC 26–10 and Heisman Trophy winner Marcus Allen of USC. In the 1983 Sugar Bowl, for the national championship, my former roommate Gregg Garrity caught the touchdown pass which turned out to be the touchdown that defeated the Georgia Bulldogs and, once again, the Heisman Trophy winner, Bulldogs running back Herschel Walker.

The Sugar Bowl became a very special event which will stay with me for the rest of my life. Besides the game results, I was able to share the experience with my wife. I was the only married player at the time. She was able to fly with the team. She developed friendships with many of my teammates. I will never forget my parents meeting up with me in New Orleans a couple days before the game. Finally, I was on a national championship football team with some outstanding people and players, such as Todd Blackledge, Curt Warner, Gregg Garrity, Bill Contz, Walker Lee Ashley, Kenny Jackson, Mike McCloskey, Mike Zordich, and many more. "We are Penn State."

Tom Barr played fullback for Penn State from 1979 to 1982. He blocked in front of two-time All-American Curt Warner, who rewrote the school record book. During Barr's time in Happy Valley, the Nittany Lions went 4–0 in bowl games, including two Fiesta Bowl wins and a national championship in the Sugar Bowl.

Preface

This book covers Penn State's 50 bowl games, starting from the 1923 Rose Bowl and going all the way to the 2019 Cotton Bowl Classic. It goes through all the important moments and scoring plays of every game. It differs from most books because it describes *how* everything happened; it is not just a summary of statistics. The goal is to tell the story of the games, play by play, allowing the reader to follow along with the action.

While I am a longtime Penn State fan, I only became particularly interested in their bowl games when I traveled to Pasadena to attend the 2017 Rose Bowl. After a historic, record-breaking 52–49 game in which the Nittany Lions came up short, I wanted to go back and view many of the other bowls Penn State has taken part in. Once I collected a few of the programs of the past bowl games, I decided to gather as many as possible. I eventually decided that it would make a good book project.

The format of this book is as follows: summaries of the regular-season games in the seasons the Nittany Lions went to a bowl game; team and player statistics for the whole season; where Penn State was ranked and why they were selected for that particular bowl; the play-by-play story of the bowl game; and finally the aftermath of the win, loss, or tie. This book does not cover seasons in which Penn State did not make it to a bowl, nor does it cover off-the-field issues such as the 2011 scandal involving former defensive coordinator Jerry Sandusky. I will leave the off-the-field stuff to authors like Malcolm Gladwell; this book is only focused on what happened on the field. At the end of the book, I will include several lists about which players had the best performances in bowls and which bowls were the most exciting to watch.

This book is unique amongt Penn State books, the only one that deals specifically with their bowl games. I hope you enjoy this look into Nittany Lions football in a book that is truly unrivaled.

Introduction

Penn State football began on November 12, 1881, exactly 11 years prior to the birth of pro football, and 103 years prior to my own birth. The Penn State team defeated the University of Lewisburg (now known as Bucknell), 9–0. However, that game was forgotten in school annals for nearly 40 years, and the official first game came in 1887. The pink-and-black-wearing team went 2–0 with a pair of wins over Bucknell. After the uniforms were washed many times, the pink faded to white and the black faded to dark blue. Thus Penn State's colors became blue and white, and the football program was underway.[1]

The first Rose Bowl game followed the 1901 season. Until the 1934 season, it was the only bowl game in the country, and it regularly matched teams from the East and the West. Penn State got their first taste of bowl action in 1923, with head coach Hugo Bezdek leading the Nittany Lions to the Rose Bowl not based on their 1922 record, but rather their past successes. There was no shortage of drama in Pasadena for Penn State's game against Southern California, but ultimately the Lions lost, 14–3, in their first taste of post-season action.

Penn State wouldn't go to another bowl until following the 1947 season, by which time there were a handful of bowl games (Rose, Sugar, Orange, Sun, Cotton, Gator). The Lions went undefeated, getting an invite to Dallas for the Cotton Bowl, but told to leave their two black players (Dennie Hoggard and Wally Triplett) at home. After refusing to give in, using the now famous "We are Penn State" phrase, head coach Bob Higgins and the Lions tied Southern Methodist at 13 in a most exciting Cotton Bowl, with Triplett catching the tying score.

Rip Engle took over the team in 1950, and the Lions would pass up an invitation to the Cigar Bowl in 1957 before going to the Philadelphia-based Liberty Bowl following the 1958 season. Penn State defeated Alabama 7–0 for their first bowl victory, then proceeded to win two more bowls in a row in the next couple of seasons.

Once Engle retired following the 1965 season, his assistant Joe Paterno took over the program, where he'd remain for many, many years. His first team to reach a bowl game was his second one, as the 1967 Lions went to the Gator Bowl. That game was best known for an infamous decision by Paterno to go for it on fourth down deep in his own territory, and after they failed, the Lions walked out of Jacksonville with only a tie.

But the floodgates opened after that game. In the next 30 years, the Lions went to 27 bowl games. These included a trio of Orange Bowl wins following undefeated seasons in 1968, 1969, and 1973, none of which yielded a national championship due to various factors (including President Richard Nixon picking a national champion). Running back

John Cappelletti won the Lions' first and only Heisman Trophy in 1973, following the footsteps of great backs such as Franco Harris and Lydell Mitchell.

In 1978, Penn State went undefeated once more, and they received an invitation to their second Sugar Bowl. They came in ranked #1 in the nation, and they would have won their first national championship with a win (or possibly a tie) against Alabama. But the Crimson Tide stuffed the Lions on two tries from the 1-yard line, and Penn State's national title hopes would have to wait after a 13–6 loss.

They wouldn't have to wait long, though. After a poor season in 1979 that ended in a Liberty Bowl win, the Lions went to back-to-back Fiesta Bowls, raising the profile of that up-and-coming bowl. In 1982, the Lions lost one game, but they reached the Sugar Bowl in the #2 spot. They then beat Georgia 27–23 behind the arm of Todd Blackledge and on the legs of Curt Warner, and at long last they were voted as national champions.

After a couple of down years, including a year in 1984 when they missed a bowl altogether, the Lions rebounded in 1985 to another undefeated season. They went into the Orange Bowl against Oklahoma ranked #1 and having every chance to come away with a second national title. But the offense fizzled in Miami, and the Lions lost to the Sooners 25–10.

The pieces were in place for another run, though. Running back D.J. Dozier and a punishing defense led by linebackers Shane Conlan and Pete Giftopoulos led the Lions to a second straight undefeated season in 1986. They went to the Fiesta Bowl ranked #2, where they knocked off #1 Miami 14–10 in the highest-rated bowl game on television of all time, winning their second national title.

Penn State remained a good team but not a great one for the rest of the eighties and early nineties. They reached glory days once more starting with the 1991 team that reached the Fiesta Bowl and defeated Tennessee by a resounding 42–17 margin. In 1994, the Lions had perhaps the greatest offense in college football history, scoring 63 points against Ohio State on their way to the Rose Bowl. But the voters snubbed Penn State once again, and they finished #2 despite quarterback Kerry Collins and running back Ki-Jana Carter leading the Lions to a 38–20 Rose Bowl win.

After another stellar victory in the Fiesta Bowl following the 1996 season with running back Curtis Enis, Penn State fell on hard times. The Lions missed out on bowl games four out of five years starting in 2000. In between, they went to one bowl—the Capital One Bowl—in a season where running back Larry Johnson ran for over 2,000 yards. They lost that bowl without scoring a touchdown, though, and it looked like Paterno had lost his magic.

But in 2005, that all changed. Quarterback Michael Robinson revitalized the Penn State program, having an outstanding season while leading the Lions to a 10–1 record and a berth in the Orange Bowl. The Lions defeated Florida State in triple overtime, and the program had yet another renaissance. Quarterback Daryll Clark took over in 2008 and led the Lions to two big-time bowl games, including a Rose Bowl appearance in his first season as a starter.

In 2011, everything in Happy Valley came to a screeching halt when it was revealed that defensive coordinator Jerry Sandusky was under investigation for abusing young boys. Paterno testified against Sandusky in court, a big reason why Sandusky was charged and later convicted. However, the seriousness of the allegations brought down everyone at Penn State, including Paterno, and the program was banned from bowl games for two years.

After a two-year stint where Bill O'Brien worked wonders with a depleted roster, James Franklin took over in 2014, with the bowl ban removed. After taking baby steps his first two seasons, his team took the big leap once quarterback Trace McSorley and running back Saquon Barkley took over in 2016. They led the team to back-to-back New Year's Six bowls, including a Fiesta Bowl win in 2017.

McSorley stayed around for one more year, as the Lions got to the Citrus Bowl in 2018. He went to the NFL in 2019, leaving the program to Sean Clifford. Under Clifford's guidance, the Lions made it back to the New Year's Six in 2019, winning the highest-scoring Cotton Bowl of all time with a record performance by running back Journey Brown in Penn State's 50th bowl appearance.

But to get to the 2019 Cotton Bowl, we need to first go back and start with the 1923 Rose Bowl, where Penn State's bowl history all began. I hope you enjoy this journey through nearly 100 years of Penn State football.

1922 Season (6–3–1)

At the time Penn State made their first-ever bowl appearance, there was only one bowl in existence: the Rose Bowl. The Nittany Lions got into the Rose Bowl not based on winning a conference or having a great record, but rather based on what they had accomplished prior to the season. As a "tribute to past achievements,"[1] according to the Penn State student newspaper *The Collegian*, the Lions were invited to the 1923 Rose Bowl before the season even began.

Penn State's 1922 opponents are a far cry from the Big Ten schedule of current days. The Lions crushed St. Bonaventure 54–0, William & Mary 27–7, Gettysburg 20–0, Lebanon Valley 32–6, and Middlebury 33–0. All of these were easy victories, with halfback Harry Wilson scoring nine touchdowns and an extra point for a nation-leading 55 points.[2]

The Lions then went to the Polo Grounds to battle Syracuse for the first time ever. Quarterback Mike Palm, tackle Jay McMahon, and center Newsh Bentz were all nursing injuries, hurting Penn State's chances. Palm tried playing through the pain, but he was pulled from the game by the referee in the third quarter. Neither team scored a point, but the tie was seen as a major victory for Syracuse.[3]

Next came Navy, for a game so big that even President Warren G. Harding planned on showing up (later backing out due to his wife becoming ill). Even though he couldn't make it, nearly every big-time college coach attended the game. The Lions had won 30 straight games dating back to 1919 coming into this game, but their streak came to an end with a 14–0 loss.[4] Penn State outgained Navy by a two-to-one margin, but Palm's two dropkick field goal attempts failed, and Navy scored on a fumble return to put the game away.[5]

Wilson helped the Lions bounce back, as he scored another touchdown in a 10–0 home win over Carnegie Tech. Palm made a 30-yard field goal to help seal the victory. The Lions then went on the road to face Penn. The Quakers scored a touchdown and an extra point to go up 7–0 in the third quarter. Palm got the Lions on the scoreboard with a fake field goal pass for a touchdown to Wilson. However, he just barely missed the extra point, and the Quakers held on to win 7–6.[6]

In the most disheartening game of the season, Penn State couldn't get on the scoreboard against Pitt at Forbes Field. Palm missed two field goals in a scoreless first half. The Panthers then scored two second-half touchdowns to win 14–0. The Lions finished the regular season 6–3–1, which was their worst record under head coach Hugo Bezdek. After the season, the Philadelphia Phillies offered Bezdek a job as manager, but he turned it down to stay at Penn State for the next seven years.[7]

1923 Rose Bowl Game

Penn State (6–3–1) vs. USC (7–1)
January 1, 1923, at the Rose Bowl in Pasadena, California

This Rose Bowl, the ninth one, was the first one to be held at the brand-new Rose Bowl stadium, which held about 43,000 people. As such, it was the first Tournament of Roses football game to be officially called the Rose Bowl. It was the first bowl game for each Penn State and USC, and it wouldn't be the last time these two teams met in this stadium.[8]

Rose Bowl program cover, 1923. Author's collection.

This game was most known for what happened before the game started than anything that happened on the field. The Nittany Lions were held up in a traffic jam, following the Tournament of Roses parade. At the time, the city of Pasadena did not have stop signals. With the game scheduled for 2:15 p.m. local time, the Penn State buses did not show up at the stadium until 2:30. Upon arrival, USC head coach Elmer Henderson got into a fight with Bezdek, one that came close to becoming physical. Henderson accused Bezdek of delaying on purpose to avoid playing in the California heat. Bezdek, who refused to let any reporters take pictures of his team during practice, called Henderson a "liar," as the two had to be separated. The game did not start until 3:05 because of the delay. As a result, things got dark before the end of this one. With no lights in the press box, the reporters were forced to strike matches so they could finish writing on the game.[9]

The Lions struck first, with Wilson breaking off runs of eight, ten, and 12 yards down to the USC 15. Palm then dropkicked a 20-yarder to put Penn State up 3–0.[10] USC right tackle Wallace Newman injured his shoulder on the drive, and he had to be replaced by Ralph Cummings.[11] USC got great field position in the second quarter when Palm muffed a punt and Cummings recovered at the Penn State 21. On fourth-and-goal at the 1, Henderson called for a trick play where center Lowell Lindley was to snap the ball almost sideways. His snap ended up hitting a player in the heel and rolled into the end zone, where the Nittany Lions recovered for a touchback.[12]

Left guard Leo Calland intercepted a Penn State pass, before fumbling. His teammate, left tackle Norman Anderson, recovered the fumble at the Penn State 45. After an exchange of punts, the Trojans had the ball at the PSU 35. Fullback Gordon Campbell pounded off the left side for five yards, then halfback Roy Baker ran it off right end for 20 more. Baker then completed a rare pass to quarterback Harold Galloway, getting the Trojans down to the 2. Two plays later, the Trojans ran a double pass play on which Baker threw to Campbell for the one-yard touchdown. Right guard Johnny Hawkins kicked the extra point to put USC up 7–3 at the half.[13]

In the third quarter, Baker took off on a pair of long runs, going 20 and 12 yards. He and Campbell split carries from the Penn State 12, getting the ball down to the 1. Baker then hammered it in for a one-yard touchdown run. Hawkins kicked the extra point, and the Trojans had an 11-point advantage.[14] The Trojans dominated the rest of the game, getting near the goal line twice, only to be stopped each time. Hawkins also missed a field goal from the Penn State 30. USC ended up cruising to a 14–3 win.[15]

Penn State's offense was nearly completely shut down in this game. The Nittany Lions managed just 100 yards of net yardage, all but five of those yards coming on the ground. USC, on the other hand, rushed for 260 yards and passed for another 36. The Trojans doubled Penn State's six first downs. The Lions also threw three interceptions, as opposed to just one for USC.[16]

Baker rushed for 107 yards on 27 carries, while Campbell added another 76 yards on 19 attempts. In 1953, Trojans captain Calland was retroactively named Rose Bowl Most Valuable Player. As for the Lions, Wilson struggled carrying the ball, managing only 48 yards on his 21 carries. Palm had an even worse average, rushing 19 times for a mere 33 yards.[17]

Sixty-two years later, Penn State would finally get back to the Rose Bowl as a member of the Big Ten. They'd also get three more shots at USC in bowl games, two of them in the Rose Bowl. As for this team, they finished 6–4–1, with their most losses since 1917. It may have ended in defeat, but the Tournament of Roses gave Penn State over $21,000 off gains, making the bowl profitable for the school.[18]

Box score[19]:

1923 Rose Bowl	1st	2nd	3rd	4th	Final
Penn State	3	0	0	0	3
USC	0	7	7	0	14

1st Quarter: PSU—Palm 20 FG
2nd Quarter: USC—Campbell 1 pass from Baker (Hawkins kick)
3rd Quarter: USC—Baker 1 run (Hawkins kick)
4th Quarter: No Scoring

1947 Season (9–0)

Penn State started its 1947 season in an unusual location: Hershey, Pennsylvania, against Washington State. The Lions scored a touchdown on a blocked punt to go up 14–0 at halftime. In the second half, halfback Wally Triplett scored on a 15-yard reverse, and fullback Fran Rogel scored on a five-yard dive, as Penn State won their opener 27–6.[1]

Two weeks later, the Nittany Lions had their official home opener against Bucknell. Running back Larry Joe took back the opening kickoff 95 yards for a score, and the rout was on. Tackle John Nolan took back an interception 34 yards for a touchdown, as the Lions picked off an unofficial school-record ten passes in a 54–0 win.[2]

Against Fordham, the Nittany Lions scored an unreal number of points, pouring on 75 at the Polo Grounds. The Lions led 55–0 at halftime, scoring on ten of their 12 possessions. Wingback Jeff Durkota scored four touchdowns—one on a reverse, two on receptions, and another on a pick-six. Running back Ellwood Petchel ran for a 78-yard touchdown on his only carry of the day. Kicker Ed Czekaj made eight extra points to tie a team record.[3]

Penn State then shut out Syracuse 40–0 for their first three-shutout streak since 1940. The PSU defense was overwhelming. Syracuse ran the ball 28 times for a whopping minus-107 yards. While Syracuse did pass for 58 yards, their offensive total of minus-47 set an NCAA record that still stands to this day.[4] West Virginia was next, coming in with a 4–0 record. The Nittany Lions marched 64 yards on ten plays to start the game, and Rogel scored the opening touchdown. In the second half, Petchel threw a 49-yard touchdown pass to Triplett. Head coach Bob Higgins and the Lions escaped with a 21–14 victory.[5]

Colgate provided Penn State yet another chance to record a shutout. This time, the Nittany Lions won 46–0. Durkota scored two touchdowns, from 22 and 24 yards out. Running back Bill Luther ran for another two scores, from 40 and nine yards out. The Penn State rushing offense poured on 390 yards, while the defense allowed just 68 net yards (minus-16 rushing).[6]

The Lions went to Philadelphia to play Temple, a 3–3 team that looked like an easy win. However, they proved a bigger challenge than they thought. Temple used a "hidden ball" play early in the game to pick up a 46-yard gain down to the Penn State 15, but they couldn't punch it in. After a scoreless first half, PSU running back Bobby Williams pounded in a two-yard touchdown at the end of a 16-play, 51-yard drive. The Nittany Lions escaped the Owls with a 7–0 triumph.[7]

Penn State traveled to Baltimore to take on Navy, a 1–5–3 team. Durkota opened

11

the scoring with a 48-yard touchdown run, following the block of end Sam Tamburo from New Kensington. Williams scored to put Penn State back ahead, then Tamburo made another outstanding block to spring Durkota for a 42-yard touchdown. Navy gained 243 yards on Penn State, the most of any opponent in 1947, but the Lions won, 20–7.[8]

The season ended at Pitt Stadium before a crowd of 47,000. Five different Nittany Lions scored touchdowns, including Petchel off a lateral from Rogel for a 40-yard touchdown. Czekaj made two extra points to reach 32 for the season, a new school record. He also kicked his only field goal of the year, a 21-yarder. The Lions allowed just 45 yards by Pitt, while rushing for 276 yards themselves. Penn State fans tore down the Pitt Stadium goalposts after Penn State's 29–0 win wrapped up a perfect regular season.[9]

But when it came to bowl games, the Orange and Sugar Bowls both passed on Penn State because the Lions had two players, Triplett and Dennie Hoggard, who were black. Like those two bowls, the Cotton Bowl also had never allowed a black player to their bowl. But Southern Methodist assistant coach Rod McClean happened to be at the PSU-Pitt game to scout Pitt for next season, and he thought Penn State would be a good opponent. SMU head coach Matty Bell concurred, and they pressured Cotton Bowl officials to allow Penn State to play.[10]

Even so, Penn State was pressured to leave Triplett and Hoggard at home. The Nittany Lions had a game cancelled at Miami the year before because Miami refused to play against black players. This time, though, there would be no cancellation. Captain Steve Suhey and the other players made a statement: "We are Penn State, there will be no meetings" (referring to a meeting to cancel the game or leave Triplett and Hoggard behind). Thus, Triplett and Hoggard came with the team to Dallas, although they were forced to stay at a Naval Air Station 14 miles outside of city limits because no hotel would take them.[11]

That phrase, "We are Penn State," has been shouted millions of times since. But few people realize that the original meaning of that phrase was to resist the racism against black players. Suhey and his teammates wouldn't leave Triplett and Hoggard behind; they stood by them even in the face of extreme discrimination. Every time a Penn Stater yells, "We are Penn State," they are making a stand against racism.

1948 Cotton Bowl Classic

#4 Penn State (9–0) vs. #5 Southern Methodist (9–0–1)
January 1, 1948, at the Cotton Bowl in Dallas, Texas

For Penn State, the key to picking up their first-ever bowl win was to stop Southern Methodist back Doak Walker. He finished third in the Heisman voting after a season in which he ran for 653 yards and 11 touchdowns, while completing 30 of 52 passes for 344 yards and two more scores. They'd also have to put up with the weather, which was close to freezing temperatures with high winds.

Running back Larry Joe took back the opening kickoff to the 39, nearly escaping for an even bigger return. The Lions ended up punting, and SMU took over at their 37. After holding Walker and the SMU offense, Penn State took over at their 47. Fullback Fran Rogel got the Lions down to the SMU 18, but on fourth-and-two, running back Bobby Williams came up short.

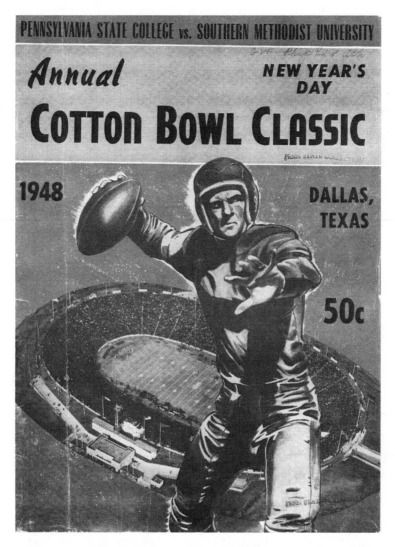

Cotton Bowl program cover, 1948. Photographic vertical files, Athletics, 1855–2009 (01167). Penn State University Archives, Eberly Family Special Collections Library, Penn State University Libraries, Penn State University.

SMU took over on downs, and they moved the ball to the 47. Walker launched a long pass to Paul Page, who caught the pass down the right sideline, escaped a tackle from PSU wingback Jeff Durkota, and easily scored the touchdown. Walker kicked the extra point, and SMU took a 7–0 lead. In the second quarter, SMU kept on moving deep into Penn State territory, but the Lions stayed in the game by making a couple of stops, including one at their own 8. SMU got the ball back at the Penn State 38, and their drive ended with Walker plowing in from three yards away to make it 13–0. Walker missed the extra point, but that seemed to mean little at this point.

However, the Nittany Lions weren't about to roll over. They began a comeback, with running back Ellwood Petchel starting a drive with an 18-yard pass to end Bob Hicks. Petchel then ran for 15 more yards after avoiding tackles, before throwing a short pass to halfback Wally Triplett. With the clock running out in the first half, Petchel stepped back

Chuck Drazenovich and Steve Suhey pursuing Doak Walker in Cotton Bowl, 1948. Players shown, left to right: #37: SMU running back Doak Walker, #66: PSU linebacker Chuck Drazenovich, #62: PSU guard Steve Suhey. Photographic vertical files, Athletics, 1855–2009 (01167). Penn State University Archives, Eberly Family Special Collections Library, Penn State University Libraries, Penn State University.

and threw a bomb down the middle of the field. Back Larry Cooney caught it at the 10 and sprinted into the end zone. Kicker Ed Czekaj made the extra point to pull the Lions within six at the half.

In the third quarter, Penn State forced a punt, and they got the ball back at the SMU 44. They got all the way down to the 1, but Rogel was stuffed shy of the goal line. After a punt which Petchel returned 25 yards to the SMU 9, the Nittany Lions had another chance to score. Petchel went back to pass, rolled to his right, and fired a pass back across the field to Triplett for a touchdown. Czekaj's extra point kick was ruled no good, wide right; however, the kick was so high above the goal posts that it was hard to tell, and PSU players thought it should have been ruled good. As a result of the miss, the score was tied at 13 apiece.

This game had a wild ending. SMU got a couple of interceptions off Petchel, one by Walker, who ran it back to the 50. The Mustangs got the ball down into field goal range, when the holder, Page, picked up the ball and ran with it, avoiding Penn State defenders all the way to the PSU 5. It looked like he had first-and-goal, only to find out that he had stepped out of bounds on the play behind the line of scrimmage, negating the whole run and giving the ball to Penn State.

Petchel to Triplett touchdown, Cotton Bowl, 1948. Players shown: on left, wearing white, standing, PSU quarterback Woody Petchel. On right, in foreground, wearing white, PSU half-back Wally Triplett. Photographic vertical files, Athletics, 1855–2009 (01167). Penn State University Archives, Eberly Family Special Collections Library, Penn State University Libraries, Penn State University.

Penn State got the ball with very little time left. Petchel threw to Hicks for a first down at the SMU 37. The Lions had time for one last play. Petchel rolled to his right, and he fired up a Hail Mary. Dennie Hoggard and Triplett both were in the end zone with a chance to catch the ball. It would have been a perfect ending—one of the two black players scoring the game-winning touchdown in the Cotton Bowl. Alas, the pass bounced off Hoggard, Triplett, and Walker before falling to the ground, incomplete. There was no overtime in the forties; the game ended in a 13-all tie.[12]

Rogel was Penn State's leading rusher with 95 yards on 25 carries. The mighty Penn State defense held Walker in check, allowing him just 66 rushing yards on 18 attempts. Petchel completed seven of his 15 passes for one touchdown. The Nittany Lions outgained the Mustangs 258–206, including a big 165–92 edge in rushing.

The game may have ended in a tie, and Penn State may have needed to wait another twelve years until they finally got their first bowl victory. But the real victory was Triplett and Hoggard breaking the color barrier at the Cotton Bowl. Triplett would go on to become the first black player to be drafted by the NFL.[13] There's no better way to wrap up the story of this undefeated team than with these words: "We are Penn State."

Box score[14]:

1948 Cotton Bowl	1st	2nd	3rd	4th	Final
Penn State	0	7	6	0	13
Southern Methodist	7	6	0	0	13

1st Quarter: SMU—Page 53 pass from Walker (Walker kick)
2nd Quarter: SMU—Walker 2 run (kick missed)
   PSU—Cooney 38 pass from Petchel (Czekaj kick)
3rd Quarter: PSU—Triplett 6 pass from Petchel (kick missed)
4th Quarter: No Scoring

1959 Season (8–2)

The Nittany Lions began the 1959 season playing at Big Eight opponent Missouri. Quarterback Richie Lucas had a great day, completing ten of 11 passes for 154 yards and a touchdown, while also running for 48 yards. The lone Missouri score came very late in the game. The Lions won 19–8 to move to #18 in the country.[1]

They then came back home to play Virginia Military Institute, in a unique matchup—Penn State never played VMI before, and they never would again. The Nittany Lions shut them out in a 21–0 victory. Lucas completed eight of 11 passes for 120 yards and two touchdown passes to end Norm Neff.[2] Against Colgate, head coach Rip Engle's team put up 58 points, the most in his career in a single game. Pat Botula scored two touchdowns, as the Lions defeated Colgate 58–20.[3]

The Nittany Lions headed to West Point to take on Army. Lucas ran for two touchdowns to put Penn State up 17–3 at halftime. Late in the game, Lucas intercepted an Army pass to prevent a score, and the Nittany Lions held on for a 17–11 win, their first over Army since 1899.[4] Next came homecoming against Boston University. It was a close game for much of the day, until the Lions scored at the end of a 73-yard drive in the fourth quarter. Lucas ran for a pair of touchdowns, and the Nittany Lions won it 21–12.[5]

Illinois and Penn State then met at Cleveland Municipal Stadium, where the crowd turned out to be sparse. Lucas threw four interceptions, but he ran for 71 yards and a touchdown, and he helped the Lions pull out a 20–9 win.[6] The Lions leaped out to a 20–0 halftime lead against West Virginia, and they had a 28–3 lead late in the game before giving up a garbage touchdown. Halfback Roger Kochman ran for 111 yards on eight carries, the first Penn State player to go over the century mark for the season. He scored on a 52-yard touchdown, as Penn State beat the Mountaineers 28–10.[7]

#7 Penn State now took on #3 Syracuse. Kochman scored on a 17-yard fourth-down run, giving Penn State the early 6–0 lead. In the fourth quarter, the Lions fell behind by 14, but Kochman returned a kickoff 99 yards for a touchdown to pull PSU within 20–12. The Lions blocked a punt to set up another touchdown, this one by fullback Sam Sobczak from a yard away. They missed the two-point conversion, however, and Syracuse ran out the clock to win it 20–18.[8]

The Nittany Lions bounced back quickly with a blowout win over Holy Cross. Kochman was injured early in this one, but Lucas made up for it. He threw for 176 yards and a touchdown while also running for 40 yards and a score. Lucas went over 1,184 offensive yards for the season, a new Penn State record, as the Lions won 46–0.[9]

The season ended against Pitt, who was having an off season at only 5–4. However, the Panthers set the tone early by tackling Lucas in the end zone for a safety. They took a 16–0 lead into halftime, and they score on the first play of the second half as well. The Lions managed just 107 rushing yards, finishing a great season with a disappointing 22–7 loss.[10]

Two years prior, 6–3 Penn State had refused an invitation to the Cigar Bowl because they couldn't get Texas Christian or Mississippi State to agree to be their opponent.[11] Last year, the Gator Bowl passed on the Nittany Lions despite a 6–3–1 record.[12] This year, though, the Lions were definitely going to a bowl game. It just wouldn't be a glamorous one. The Rose was off limits since Penn State wasn't a member of the Big Ten. The Orange couldn't happen because the Big Eight representative was Missouri, and their officials didn't want a rematch of the regular-season game. The Cotton snatched up Syracuse, and the Sugar was staying away from teams from the East. That left three choices: the Gator Bowl, or one of the two brand-new bowls, the Bluebonnet Bowl in Texas, or the Liberty Bowl in Philadelphia. The Lions ended up picking the Liberty. In turn, Georgia, Georgia Tech, and TCU all passed on the chance to play Penn State, so it was Bear Bryant and #10 Alabama who came in to save the bowl and play the Lions. They'd provide a stiff challenge to Lucas, who came up just short in the Heisman Trophy voting to LSU's Billy Cannon.[13]

1959 Liberty Bowl

#12 Penn State (8–2) vs. #10 Alabama (7–1–2)
December 19, 1959, at Municipal Stadium in Philadelphia, Pennsylvania

The game-time temperature for this one was 42 degrees, with a 20 miles-per-hour wind. That forced both teams into strictly a running game. Alabama head coach Paul "Bear" Bryant also used a lot of quick kicks to try to change field position. On their first possession, Alabama got down to the Penn State 27 and decided to quick kick, with the ball landing at the Penn State 3. Quarterback Richie Lucas led the Lions on an 89-yard drive. However, halfback Roger Kochman fumbled at the Alabama 9, and the first quarter ended with no score.

Lucas had reached 55 yards on nine carries early in the second quarter when he came out of the game with a bruised hip. But the Lions' fortunes changed when lineman Jay Huffman came up with a recovery of an Alabama fumble at the Tide 28. Backup quarterback Galen Hall led the Lions down to the 1. Facing fourth-and-goal, head coach Rip Engle decided to go for it. He threw into coverage, where the pass disappeared in a heap of players, and the game remained scoreless.

The Lions got the ball back late in the first half at the Alabama 22, getting the good field position thanks to the wind being in Alabama's face. The Lions faked two field goals, getting a first down on one, and getting an 18-yard touchdown off a screen from Hall to Kochman on the final play of the first half. Sam Stellatella's extra point gave Penn State a 7–0 lead going into the half.

With such difficult playing conditions, neither team managed to do much in the second half. Alabama fumbled the ball seven times over the course of the game, losing three of them to Penn State. The Nittany Lions also lost four fumbles themselves. In the end, neither Penn State nor Alabama threatened to score after halftime. The Lions got the closest, making a 52-yard drive to the Alabama 10 as the clock ran out, and they had a 7–0 victory.

The Nittany Lions ran for 269 yards and passed for 46. They held Alabama to only 111 on the ground and 27 passing. Lucas led all rushers with 54 despite coming out early. Botula had another 50 yards, and fullback Sam Sobczek ran for 42. Both the Lions and the Tide completed only two passes each. Lucas had a 23-yard completion, and Hall had his 18-yard pass to Kochman for the winning touchdown. Huffman was named Most Valuable Player mainly because of his fumble recovery.

At the time, the polls were finalized before the bowls took place, so there was no chance for Penn State to move up after beating a higher-ranked opponent. They'd finish this season with a 9–2 record and a #12 national ranking, in their first bowl win in school history.[14]

Box score[15]:

1959 Liberty Bowl	1st	2nd	3rd	4th	Final
Alabama	0	0	0	0	0
Penn State	0	7	0	0	7

1st Quarter: No Scoring
2nd Quarter: PSU—Kochman 18 pass from Hall (Stellatella kick)
3rd Quarter: No Scoring
4th Quarter: No Scoring

1960 Season (6–3)

The Nittany Lions started out the 1960 season ranked #20 in the Associated Press preseason poll. Due to pouring rain against Boston University, only about 22,500 showed up to the new Beaver Stadium. The Lions won 20–0, as running back Eddie Caye picked off a pass and ran for a one-yard touchdown. They ran the ball 72 times as opposed to just nine passes, picking up 326 yards on the ground.[1]

Next came Homecoming against Missouri. The #19-ranked Tigers jumped out to a 14–0 lead at halftime. Penn State got on the board when quarterback Galen Hall threw a touchdown and two-point conversion pass to end Henry Oppermann. However, the Lions made too many miscues. They threw three interceptions, lost two fumbles, and had a punt blocked. Missouri went on to win, 21–8.[2]

At West Point, the Lions fell into a 7–0 hole. Halfback Jim Kerr scored on a one-yard touchdown to tie it at seven at the half. Army retook a 13–7 lead, but Hall threw a 25-yard touchdown pass to Kerr and ran for an 11-yard touchdown to give the Lions a four-point lead. Finally, fullback Dave Hayes pounded it in for a game-sealing touchdown, and the Nittany Lions won, 27–16.[3]

The Nittany Lions fell behind Syracuse by a 21–7 margin, caused partially by Hall throwing a 40-yard pick-six in the third quarter. But in the fourth quarter, they began to rally. Hall threw a three-yard touchdown pass to halfback Dick Pae to cut the margin to six. The Lions made it down to the Syracuse 4 with half a minute to go, but Hall lost his shoe and didn't have time to get it back on. He had to throw an off-balance pass on fourth down, and it fell incomplete. The Lions lost, 21–15.[4]

Penn State next went to Illinois. Again they fell behind, this time by a 10–0 margin. In the fourth quarter, the Lions went on a 74-yard drive for a touchdown and a two-point conversion. However, their onside kick came up short, and the Illini ran out the clock. The Lions lost 10–8 to fall to 2–3, with a bowl bid looking unlikely.[5]

Dick Hoak had a great game at quarterback against West Virginia. He threw for two touchdowns, including a 17-yard pass to fullback Buddy Torris, and he also ran for a third, as the Lions won 34–13.[6] On another rainy day at Beaver Stadium, the Nittany Lions had an easy time with Maryland. They started the game with a 17-play, 91-yard drive, capped off by Kerr running it in from eight yards away. Jonas returned a punt 65 yards for a touchdown, while also picking off a pass and scooping up a fumble. The Lions beat Maryland, 28–9.[7]

Penn State headed to Holy Cross next, where five different Nittany Lions scored touchdowns. Hoak was successful on six of his seven passes, completing them for 164 yards and a touchdown, while also running for 54 yards on his seven rushes. The Lions beat Holy Cross 33–8.[8] In the season finale against Pitt, Kerr fumbled the opening kick-off to set up a Panther field goal. The Nittany Lions trailed 3–0 all the way into the fourth quarter, when Hall then threw a 30-yard touchdown pass to Kerr to put Penn State up 6–3. The Lions then scored on a three-yard pass from Hoak to Bob Mitinger to win by a final count of 14–3.[9]

However, despite their 6–3 record, Penn State was having a hard time finding a bowl suitor. The Gator Bowl didn't send a representative to Pitt Stadium for the Nittany Lions' season finale, but Penn State was rescued from a postseason-less fate when a Liberty Bowl representative did. The Penn State players voted to accept a bid to the Liberty Bowl, where they'd play Oregon, who came into Philadelphia with a 7–2–1 record.[10]

1960 Liberty Bowl

#16 Penn State (6–3) vs. Oregon (7–2–1)
December 17, 1960, at Municipal Stadium in Philadelphia, Pennsylvania

Philadelphia was hit with a large snowstorm the week of the bowl, and temperatures were below freezing for game time, with wind speeds of 25 miles per hour. The Ducks scored first, starting their second drive from their own 2, then marching 98 yards in 12 plays to score on a one-yard sneak by quarterback Dave Grosz.

The Nittany Lions then turned things around in the second quarter. Jonas returned a punt 23 yards to set up a touchdown, which he scored from one yard out. Then, Kerr recovered a fumble on the next kickoff to set up another touchdown, scored by fullback Al Gursky from two yards away. Hoak then ran for a six-yard touchdown for the Lions' third score of the second quarter, as Penn State went to the half with a 21–6 lead.

Dave Grayson scored a touchdown for Oregon to start the second half, cutting the Penn State advantage to 21–12. But in the fourth quarter, Hall answered by driving the Nittany Lions 95 yards for a touchdown, scored by Caye from the 1. Hoak would later run for an 11-yard touchdown and throw a 33-yard touchdown pass to Pae. The Lions went on to win by a 41–12 margin.

Hoak was named Most Valuable Player after running for 61 yards and two touchdowns while also completing three of five passes for 67 yards and another score. Oppermann won the award for Most Valuable Lineman. He caught four passes for 49 yards and also kicked four extra points. Jonas ran for 40 yards and a touchdown and also kicked Penn State's final extra point of the game. Hall threw seven passes, completing four for 47 yards.

The Lions thoroughly dominated Oregon, outgaining them 301–187 on the ground and 420–360 overall. The Ducks turned the ball over four times, twice on interceptions and twice on fumbles. Penn State lost just one fumble and did not throw an interception. The Nittany Lions had their second straight Liberty Bowl championship, but they hoped that their next bowl game would be in a warmer climate.[11]

Box score[12]:

1960 Liberty Bowl	*1st*	*2nd*	*3rd*	*4th*	*Final*
Oregon	6	0	6	0	12
Penn State	0	21	0	20	41

1st Quarter: ORE—Grosz 1 run (kick failed)
2nd Quarter: PSU—Jonas 1 run (Oppermann kick)
   PSU—Gursky 2 run (Oppermann kick)
   PSU—Hoak 6 run (Oppermann kick)
3rd Quarter: ORE—Grayson 10 run (pass failed)
4th Quarter: PSU—Caye 1 run (Oppermann kick)
   PSU—Hoak 11 run (kick failed)
   PSU—Pae 33 pass from Hoak (Jonas kick)

1961 Season (7–3)

Penn State started the 1961 season with high hopes at Beaver Stadium against Navy. They surprisingly trailed at halftime by a 10–7 margin. To lead Penn State back, halfback Don Jonas made a pair of field goals, from 31 and 25 yards out, while also running for a six-yard touchdown. Quarterback Don Caum scrambled for a 19-yard touchdown with six minutes to go in the fourth quarter, and the Nittany Lions came away with a 20–10 win. Unfortunately, future Pro Football Hall of Fame defensive end Dave Robinson dislocated his shoulder, putting him out for the next five games.[1]

The Lions then went to Miami. By the time the Nittany Lions finally got on the scoreboard, the Hurricanes were already up 25–0. The Lions went to backup quarterback Pete Liske, who threw a six-yard touchdown pass to Frank Sincek in the final minute, but that was only window dressing in a 25–8 loss.[2]

Liske got the start for the next game against Boston University, in the final time these two teams met on the gridiron. Penn State would roll to over 400 yards of offense. Liske completed seven of 12 passes for 98 yards, while running for 38 yards and a touchdown. Fullback Dave Hayes ran for 90 yards and two touchdowns. Caum completed a 50-yard touchdown pass to running back Harold Powell, as the Nittany Lions rolled to a 32–0 win.[3]

Army came to Beaver Stadium, and after two years of losing at home to the Lions, they got their revenge. Halfback Roger Kochman ran for 55 yards, and Liske threw a 17-yard touchdown pass to Jonas, but it was not enough. The Lions got to the Army 36, but they couldn't advance it further. Army had come out of Happy Valley with a 10–6 victory.[4]

Quarterback Galen Hall came back from an earlier injury to play against Syracuse. He had a big day passes, connecting on ten of his 12 passes for 169 yards. He threw a 48-yard touchdown pass to Kochman and a 13-yarder to end Dick Anderson. Kochman ran for 105 yards on 14 attempts, as the first Penn Stater to rush for more than 100 yards since 1959. Head coach Rip Engle won his 100th game of his career, as the Nittany Lions shut out Syracuse, 14–0.

At Homecoming, the Lions came back from down 10–3 in the first quarter against California. Hall threw two touchdown passes again, this time a 36-yarder to Kochman and a 51-yard pass to Powell. He also scored a touchdown of his own on a sneak. Kochman ran for 107 yards, his second straight 100-yard rushing day. The Nittany Lions defeated California by a 33–16 margin.[5]

With Gator Bowl scouts watching, the Lions fell behind Maryland 21–6 at halftime. The Terrapins then came up with a goal-line stand in the final minutes to hold off Penn

State, 21–17.[6] Against West Virginia, Hall threw a 66-yard touchdown pass to Kochman in the first quarter. Kochman added a touchdown run in the second quarter. Fullback Buddy Torris had a big day, rushing for 108 yards and a touchdown on his 21 attempts. The Nittany Lions won it 20–6, spoiling West Virginia's Homecoming weekend.[7]

The Lions ran all over Holy Cross in their next game. Kochman ran for 133 yards and multiple touchdowns, while Torris rushed for 145 yards and multiple touchdowns of his own. They were the first pair of Nittany Lions to go over the 100-yard mark in the same game since Lenny Moore and Billy Kane did so back in 1954. The Lions won, 34–14.[8] In the final game of the regular season, Penn State headed to Pitt Stadium. Hall set a school record for most passing yards in a game with 256 yards on 11 of 14 attempts, totaling four touchdowns, two passing and two rushing. The Nittany Lions crushed Pitt 47–26.[9]

Kochman led the team with 666 rushing yards on 129 carries, a 5.2 average. He added ten catches for another 226 yards. Hall was the key to the offense, though. He completed 50 of his 97 passes for 951 yards and eight scores, averaging 9.8 yards per pass, while also averaging 2.1 yards per carry.[10]

When it came to bowl selection, the Bluebonnet, Gotham, and Liberty Bowls all were interested in Penn State. The Gotham Bowl in New York City even extended an invitation to the Nittany Lions, but they turned it down. As it turned out, thanks to a loss by Maryland to Virginia, the Gator Bowl dropped the Terrapins and wanted the Lions. Penn State then accepted an invitation to the Gator Bowl in Jacksonville, where the Nittany Lions would face segregation again.[11]

1961 Gator Bowl Classic

#17 Penn State (7–3) vs. #13 Georgia Tech (7–3)
December 30, 1961, at the Gator Bowl in Jacksonville, Florida

Penn State was forced to stay at a military barracks because Jacksonville was a segregated city and one of their star players, end Dave Robinson, was black. When the team went together to the airport for a meal, the restaurant refused to serve them because of Robinson, so the entire team walked out. Karma was smiling on Robinson, though, as he would end up making the play of the game in the Gator Bowl.

Georgia Tech won the toss and elected to receive. They got a few first downs from quarterback Stan Gann and halfback Bob Sheridan. That helped them with field position, as they punted it out of bounds down at the 5. Penn State quarterback Galen Hall then got caught throwing the ball away in his own end zone to avoid a sack. It was ruled intentional grounding and a safety for Georgia Tech, who took a 2–0 lead.

Hall fumbled on Penn State's next possession, and Georgia Tech got the ball at the Penn State 33. But quarterback Pete Liske, playing on defense, picked off a Gann pass, and the game remained 2–0. On Georgia Tech's next possession, Robinson sacked the quarterback and stripped him of the ball, although Georgia Tech recovered. Tech quarterback Billy Lothridge completed a 45-yard pass to halfback Billy Williamson, but this drive ended when Robinson recovered a loose ball. The Lions trailed 2–0 after one quarter.

The Lions got away a 62-yard punt, only to have Tech come right down and score. Running back Joe Auer took a handoff, broke several tackles and eluded some more on his way to a Gator Bowl-record 68-yard touchdown run. But Penn State turned it around quickly. Hall led the Nittany Lions on a ten-play, 78-yard drive, finishing with a pass to halfback Al Gursky for a touchdown. Then, right before the half, Hall led another big drive, this one going 87 yards in seven plays. He fired a 27-yard pass to halfback Roger Kochman in the corner of the end zone. The Lions went to the locker room with a 14-9 lead.

Robinson came out for the second half and made a fantastic play. He jumped over two blockers, getting to Gann, where he stripped him of the ball, and then recovered it himself at the Georgia Tech 35. On their very first play, Hall threw to halfback Harold Powell, who was left wide open. Powell jumped up and down as he ran it into the end zone for a touchdown, putting Penn State up 20-9 at the end of the third quarter.

In the fourth quarter, Tech got lucky on a play where Auer fumbled a pitch but ended up scoring after scooping up the ball and making some great moves to the end zone. Gann tried running for two points, but he was stopped shy of the goal line, and Penn State's lead remained at a tenuous 20-15.

Later in the game, Georgia Tech went for a fake punt deep in their own end. Lothridge's pass fell incomplete, and Penn State took over deep in Tech territory. Don Jonas kicked a 23-yard field goal, and Penn State's lead increased to eight points. Gann then threw an interception to end Jim Schwab, and that ended any chances Tech had at a comeback. Fullback Buddy Torris plunged in from one yard away, and the Nittany Lions won by a final count of 30-15.[12]

Hall was named Most Valuable Player for completing 12 of 22 passes for school bowl-records of 175 yards and three touchdowns. Hall's passing yards record would stand until the 1970 Orange Bowl. His three touchdown passes stood as the record all the way until the 1992 Fiesta Bowl. But a strong case could be made for Robinson as MVP. His team forced six Georgia Tech fumbles, three of which they recovered, and he also caught four passes for 40 yards on offense. To top it off, he did it all in a state where he was not welcome. Robinson went on to reach the Pro Football Hall of Fame as a Green Bay Packer.

Box score[13]:

1961 Gator Bowl	1st	2nd	3rd	4th	Final
Penn State	0	14	6	10	30
Georgia Tech	2	7	0	6	15

1st Quarter: GT—Safety
2nd Quarter: GT—Auer 68 run (Lothridge kick)
    PSU—Gursky 13 pass from Hall (Jonas kick)
    PSU—Kochman 27 pass from Hall (Jonas kick)
3rd Quarter: PSU—Powell 35 pass from Hall (kick failed)
4th Quarter: GT—Auer 14 run (run failed)
    PSU—Jonas 23 FG
    PSU—Torris 1 run (Jonas kick)

1962 Season (9–1)

Coming off their first Gator Bowl victory, the Nittany Lions were ranked #5 in the season-opening Associated Press poll. They began the season at home against Navy. Quarterback Pete Liske completed a 55-yard touchdown pass to halfback Harold Powell. Halfback Al Gursky took back an interception 77 yards for a score, and Powell returned one 48 yards for another. The Lions came away with a resounding 41–7 victory.[1]

Penn State was to play all three service academies this season, as their second game was against Air Force. Liske threw to Kochman for a three-yard touchdown early. They then drove 81 yards in the fourth quarter that ended with a 15-yard touchdown catch by Kochman. That put the finishing touches on a 20–6 win.[2]

Now ranked #4, the Lions took on Rice. Trailing 7–6 at halftime, head coach Rip Engle knew his team needed a spark, so he brought in his third unit, and he began shuffling all three units for the rest of the game. It worked. Liske led a 68-yard drive in ten plays that ended in a three-yard touchdown run by fullback Dave Hayes. Liske picked off another pass and returned it 42 yards, setting up Hayes for a 16-yard touchdown run to finish out an 18–7 win.[3]

Penn State was up to #3 in the nation, and they were six-point favorites headed to West Point. The score was tied at three at halftime. In the third quarter, after a dropped touchdown and an offside penalty, the Lions settled for a field goal to go up 6–3. Powell then fumbled on the Lions' next possession, and Army took advantage by going in for a touchdown. The Lions lost, 9–6, dropping to #14 in the nation.[4]

For Homecoming, a record 48,000 fans showed up for the game against Syracuse. Kochman scored two touchdowns in the first quarter, making it 14–0. Syracuse then battled back to go ahead 19–14, but they made a weird decision that cost them the game. On their third touchdown, head coach Ben Schwartzwalder decided to go for an onside kick, which Penn State recovered. The Lions then went 58 yards for the go-ahead score, a one-yard run by Hayes. Syracuse could have won it on a last-second field goal, but lineman Harrison Rosdahl blocked the kick to preserve a 20–19 victory.[5]

The Lions then visited the West Coast for the first time since 1948. They took a 10–0 lead on California in the second quarter, before Golden Bears head coach Marv Levy put in quarterback Craig Morton. He immediately made a difference. Despite Kochman scoring a one-yard touchdown, Morton led a pair of touchdown drives to pull within three. Liske threw a ten-yard touchdown to Gursky, but then Morton got another touchdown to cut Penn State's lead to two. At the end of the game, Liske intercepted a bomb by Morton to help the Lions escape with a 23–21 triumph.[6]

Penn State came back home into a winter wonderland. The Lions tangled with

Maryland at Beaver Stadium in a steady snowstorm, and their defense led the way for this win. Back Don Caum intercepted two passes, including a 35-yard return which set up a 13-yard touchdown run by Liske, who rushed for 76 yards and two touchdowns in a 23–7 win.[7]

Against West Virginia, the Nittany Lions recorded 38 first downs, breaking a record that had stood for 40 years. They ran for 337 yards and passed for another 193, with Liske throwing a pair of touchdown passes to Powell as part of his three scoring passes in the Lions' 34–6 win. The next week, against Holy Cross, the offense again lit it up. This time they put up 357 rushing yards and another 130 passing yards in a 48–20 triumph. The Lions moved back into the top ten in the AP rankings.[8]

The regular season ended at Pitt Stadium. The only score of the first half was a 26-yard Coates field goal that put Penn State up 3–0. Gursky intercepted a pass in the end zone to start the second half, and Liske threw a 56-yard touchdown pass to Kochman to make it 10–0. Powell intercepted a pass himself, and this one led to an 18-yard touchdown pass from Liske to Gursky. The Lions won 16–0 to finish the regular season 9–1. Liske set three school records for a single season: most touchdown passes with 12, most yards passing with 1,047, and total offensive yards with 1,302. Kochman and end Dave Robinson were named first-team All-Americans.[9]

When it came to bowls, the Orange and Cotton Bowls were interested in the Nittany Lions, but they passed on Penn State for higher ranked teams. The Liberty and Gotham Bowls were also interested in Penn State, but the Nittany Lions ultimately decided on a trip back to Jacksonville for the Gator Bowl. The team was not happy about being passed on by the top bowls, and also having to go back to the place where Robinson had been treated so terribly. They weren't happy about their opponent, a 6–4 Florida team, either. It would be tough for Engle to get his team up to face the Gators.[10]

1962 Gator Bowl Classic

#9 Penn State (9–1) vs. Florida (6–4)
December 29, 1962, at the Gator Bowl in Jacksonville, Florida

The Lions got to visit the White House and meet President John F. Kennedy in the weeks leading up to the Gator Bowl, which was the only positive about this bowl. They again couldn't go down south and practice due to the segregation. The Lions lost three fumbles in the game, the first one by Kochman in the first quarter, which set up a 43-yard field goal by Bob Lyle.

Back Don Caum then muffed a punt at his own 24 in the second quarter. That led to quarterback Tom Shannon throwing to fullback Larry Dupree for a seven-yard touchdown. Jimmy Hall made an extra point to put the Gators up ten. The Lions then went on a 76-yard drive, and quarterback Pete Liske's one-yard run coupled with Ron Coates's extra point made it 10–7 at the half.

In the third quarter, Liske threw an interception at the 50. Florida would move into the red zone, and they capitalized. Shannon threw a 19-yard touchdown pass to halfback Hagood Clarke, making it a ten-point Gator lead. The Lions couldn't do anything on offense in the fourth quarter, running just four plays in the final 15 minutes. They ended up holding the ball for less than 20 minutes for the game, as they lost by a score of 17–7.

Due to all the problems Penn State had to put up with from the southern bowls, the

Nittany Lions voted against going to a bowl in 1964, and it would take until 1967 until they finally went back to another bowl. But there was one positive. End Dave Robinson was named Penn State's most valuable player for the Gator Bowl. Progress was finally being made toward acceptance of black players in college football.[11]

Box score[12]:

1962 Gator Bowl	1st	2nd	3rd	4th	Final
Florida	3	7	0	7	17
Penn State	0	7	0	0	7

1st Quarter: FLA—Lyle 43 FG
2nd Quarter: FLA—Dupree 7 pass from Shannon (Hall kick)
    PSU—Liske 1 run (Coates kick)
3rd Quarter: No Scoring
4th Quarter: FLA—Clarke 19 pass from Shannon (Hall kick)

1967 Season (8–2)

Head coach Joe Paterno took over the team in 1966, going 5–5 in his first season. After having used a 5–3–3 defense in his first season, he switched to a 4–4–3 formation, which had never been used in college football before. In the first game of the season, Penn State visited Navy, where running back Bobby Campbell ran for a seven-yard touchdown early in the second half to put the Lions up 11–10. Later, on a fourth-and-two play, quarterback Tom Sherman hit Campbell for a 20-yard touchdown, putting PSU up 22–17. But Navy drove 78 yards for a touchdown in the final minute, and the Nittany Lions lost their opener, 23–22.[1]

Next, Penn State went to play Miami in the Orange Bowl stadium. The Hurricanes were 11-point favorites, but Sherman threw two touchdown passes, including a 15-yarder to tight end Ted Kawlick and a seven-yarder to fullback Don Abbey. The Lions took a 17-point lead in the fourth quarter off a 28-yard field goal by Abbey, and they held on to beat Miami 17–8.[2]

UCLA came into Beaver Stadium ranked #3, but Campbell ran for an early seven-yard touchdown to put Penn State up 7–0 at the half. However, Campbell had a punt blocked in the third quarter, and the Lions ended up losing, 17–15.[3] Campbell was injured in the UCLA game and would miss the rest of the season. Abbey made up for his absence by rushing for 120 yards and three touchdowns against Boston College, and kicking six extra points. The Nittany Lions picked off three passes and recovered two fumbles to cruise to a 50–28 win.[4]

Homecoming was against West Virginia, and back Charlie Pittman had a big game against the Mountaineers. He returned the second-half kickoff 83 yards for a touchdown to give Penn State a 21–7 lead which they wouldn't surrender. He ran for 137 yards on 24 attempts while also catching a pair of passes for 45 yards, as Penn State won 21–14.[5]

The Lions visited Syracuse next, a place they hadn't won in ten years. Going up against fullback Larry Csonka, the Lions defense kept him in check by only allowing him 112 yards and two touchdowns. Penn State never trailed in the game, going up early on a three-yard run by Pittman. Late in the game, linebacker Dennis Onkotz returned an interception 47 yards for a score to seal a 29–20 win.[6]

The Nittany Lions knocked out Maryland by a 38–3 margin, with Pittman scoring three touchdowns on his 127 yards. Next, Penn State played #3 North Carolina State. Sherman threw an early 18-yard touchdown pass to tight end Ted Kwalick, and Onkotz returned an interception 67 yards to put the Lions up by 13. The defense made a late goal-line stand, and the Lions held on for a 13–8 win.[7]

Onkotz had another return for a touchdown against Ohio. This time, he took back a punt 56 yards for a touchdown, as Penn State won 35–14. The season ended at home against Pitt, where it was no contest. Sherman threw four touchdown passes in the game, a record that would stand for the next 24 years. Abbey scored a pair of touchdowns, as the Nittany Lions won 42–6 for their biggest win over Pitt since 1912.[8]

Tim Montgomery and Onkotz led the team with six interceptions each. Receiver Jack Curry caught 41 passes. Tackle Rich Buzin was ranked as one of the best blockers in the country, along with center Bill Lenkaitis.[9] Sherman set seven offensive records in 1967, including most touchdown passes in a season (13), which he'd hold for ten years.[10]

The Sugar, Orange, and Liberty Bowls all showed interest in hosting Penn State. However, it was the Gator Bowl who leaped in at the last moment to snatch up the Nittany Lions. They agreed to play the winner of the Florida State-Florida game.[11] When the Seminoles defeated the Gators 21–16, the Gator Bowl matchup was set.[12]

1967 Gator Bowl Classic

#10 Penn State (8–2) vs. Florida State (7–2–1)
December 30, 1967, at the Gator Bowl in Jacksonville, Florida

With Florida State having a great passing attack, head coach Joe Paterno made wholesale changes on defense to counter them for the Gator Bowl. He brought in a 3-6-2 defense as well as a 5-5-1. It worked at the beginning of the game. Defensive end Tim Montgomery stuffed FSU on a couple of goal-line plays, and he also picked off a pass and returned it 42 yards. The Lions got a 27-yard field goal from Tom Sherman to take a 3–0 lead after one quarter.

Linebacker Neal Smith made a diving interception in the second quarter near the 50. That set up a drive that seemed to end on a field goal. However, when Sherman missed, the Seminoles had jumped offside. With a second chance now, Sherman threw a ten-yard touchdown pass to receiver Jack Curry, and Penn State took a 10–0 lead. Back Charlie Pittman took a draw 35 yards later in the half. That would lead to Sherman throwing a 12-yard touchdown pass to tight end Ted Kwalick, giving the Nittany Lions a 17–0 halftime lead.

The lead didn't last. The defense stopped the Seminoles on a goal-line stand, and the offense got the ball at their own 5. On third down, Pittman came up half a foot shy of the first down marker. Paterno chose to go for it, despite being at his own 14. Sherman ran a sneak and was stopped short. That led to quarterback Kim Hammond throwing a 20-yard touchdown pass to receiver Ron Sellers. On the ensuing kickoff, Pittman fumbled, and Florida State recovered at the Penn State 23. Three plays later, Hammond took it in from a yard out, and Penn State's lead had been cut to three.

Late in the fourth quarter, Florida State launched a desperation drive. They drove 46 yards from their own 40 to the Penn State 14. The Seminoles had two passes broken up by linebacker Dennis Onkotz and defensive back Bob Capretto. Florida State head coach Bill Peterson settled for a field goal, which kicker Grant Gutherie made to tie the score at 17.

Penn State got one last play with the ball, way back in their own territory. The pass was intercepted, but chaos erupted after the play. It seemed that Penn State players might have given a late hit to the Florida State interceptor. However, after much discussion, the officials waved off whatever flag there was, and the game was declared over. Paterno's first bowl game had ended in a 17–17 tie.

Florida State outgained Penn State 418–244, launching a passing attack that racked up 363 yards. Hammond threw 53 passes, completing 37 of them for 362 yards. Sherman threw for nearly 300 fewer yards than his FSU counterpart. The Lions outgained the Seminoles by 120 yards on the ground. The key was turnovers; Penn State lost a pair of fumbles, and Sherman threw two interceptions. However, the Penn State defense picked off Hammond four times. The result was an even game that ended justifiably in a tie. Paterno would have to wait a year for his first bowl victory.[13]

Box score[14]:

1967 Gator Bowl	1st	2nd	3rd	4th	Final
Florida State	0	0	14	3	17
Penn State	3	14	0	0	17

1st Quarter: PSU—Sherman 27 FG
2nd Quarter: PSU—Curry 9 pass from Sherman (Sherman kick)
  PSU—Kwalick 12 pass from Sherman (Sherman kick)
3rd Quarter: FSU—Sellers 20 pass from Hammond (Gutherie kick)
  FSU—Hammond 1 run (Gutherie kick)
4th Quarter: FSU—Gutherie 26 FG

1968 Season (10–0)

Penn State opened up the 1968 season at home against Navy. Halfback Charlie Pittman broke off a 57-yard touchdown run on his way to a 162-yard day. The defense forced nine turnovers—five interceptions and four fumble recoveries. Linebacker Pete Johnson scored on a 28-yard pick-six, as the Nittany Lions won this one 31–6.[1]

Next, Kansas State came to Beaver Stadium to face the now #4-ranked Lions. Wildcats quarterback Lynn Dickey threw a 56-yard touchdown pass to put K-State up 9–7 at the half. Pittman ran for a five-yard touchdown in the second half to give Penn State back the lead. Linebacker Jack Ham intercepted Dickey to set up a two-yard touchdown run by fullback Tom Cherry, and quarterback Chuck Burkhart threw a 25-yard touchdown pass to receiver Leon Angevine to seal a 25–9 comeback victory.[2]

The Lions were now at #3 in the polls behind just Purdue and USC. They took their first road trip of the year to West Virginia, where tight end Ted Kwalick got them on the board first with a one-yard run. Linebacker Dennis Onkotz picked off a pass to set up Penn State's second touchdown, as Burkhart threw to halfback Charlie Wilson for a 21-yard touchdown. Late in the game, Onkotz scored on a nine-yard pick-six, and Penn State won 31–20.[3]

The next game was at the Los Angeles Memorial Coliseum against UCLA, who played there in those days. Ham blocked a punt early in the game, which linebacker Jim Kates returned 36 yards for the opening score. Burkhart later threw a 76-yard touchdown to Cherry, and Pittman ran for a ten-yard score to put away a 21–6 win.[4]

Against Boston College, the Lions got a 31-yard touchdown catch by Kwalick and an 11-yard scoring run by Cherry to come away with an easy 29–0 win. The defense forced four turnovers, and Ham blocked a punt. Next, the Lions played Army, where halfback Bob Campbell scored an early nine-yard touchdown. Pittman added a five-yard score, and Campbell scored a second touchdown on a two-yard run. Army tried to come back, but Kwalick returned an onside kick 53 yards to seal a 28–24 win.[5]

At #3 in the polls, the Nittany Lions took on Miami at Beaver Stadium. They trailed 7–0 at halftime, but Pittman scored a pair of touchdowns to put the Lions back ahead. Ham recovered a fumble and blocked a team-record third punt to help put away a 22–7 win. The next week against Maryland, the Lions had an easy time, winning 57–13. Burkhart threw for 121 yards by completing 12 of 17 attempts against the Terrapins.[6]

The season concluded at Pitt Stadium, where the Nittany Lions rolled up the most points in the history of their series against the Panthers. Pittman scored three touchdowns, while Campbell rushed for over 100 yards. The Lions put up 618 total yards in a 65–9 blowout. Finally, Penn State wrapped up an undefeated season by beating Syracuse

30–12. Pittman ran for his 14th touchdown, setting a new school record, while Campbell ran for 239 yards.[7]

Campbell averaged nearly six yards per carry during the 1968 season. Pittman rushed for 950 yards, part of a team rushing record of 2,739 yards. Burkhart completed 49 percent of his passes, which was an impressive number in that day. Kwalick made 31 catches, averaging nearly 13 yards per catch, as the Lions poured on 34 points per game and another team record of 4,025 yards of total offense.[8]

At the Miami game at Beaver Stadium, scouts from the Sugar, Cotton, Orange, and Gator Bowls all showed up, with the Cotton and Orange Bowls particularly interested in the Lions. After their victory over Maryland, the Lions accepted a bid from the Orange Bowl to go to Miami to play against Kansas. With the Jayhawks averaging more points than any other team in the country, the Orange Bowl had all the makings of an all-time classic.[9]

1969 Orange Bowl Classic

#3 Penn State (10–0) vs. #6 Kansas (9–1)
January 1, 1969, at the Orange Bowl in Miami, Florida

Coach Paterno with players in locker room at Orange Bowl, 1969. People shown, left to right: #22: quarterback Chuck Burkhart, #51: linebacker Gary Hull, #72: defensive tackle John Ebersole, #14: defensive end Frank Spaziani, head coach Joe Paterno, #68: defensive tackle Mike Reid, #73: offensive tackle Dave Bradley, #63: guard Tom Jackson, #86: tight end Tim Horst. Photographic vertical files, Athletics, 1855–2009 (01167). Penn State University Archives, Eberly Family Special Collections Library, Penn State University Libraries, Penn State University.

There was much more ballyhooed game coming up at the Orange Bowl within two weeks—Super Bowl III between the NFL's Baltimore Colts and the AFL's New York Jets. While that game changed football history, this one was pretty good itself. Unfortunately, it would have no effect on the national championship, which would come down to #1 Ohio State and #2 USC in the Rose Bowl.

Penn State got off to a bad start in this one. Quarterback Chuck Burkhart threw two interceptions in the first quarter, and fullback Don Abbey fumbled the ball away. Kansas took advantage on the second interception, driving 45 yards for a two-yard touchdown by fullback Mike Reeves. The Jayhawks led 7–0 after one quarter.

In the second quarter, the Nittany Lions drove 53 yards for a score. Halfback Charlie Pittman pounded the ball up the middle for a 13-yard scoring run, and kicker Bob Garthwaite added the extra point to tie the game at seven. But the miscues continued, as fullback Tom Cherry fumbled it away deep in Kansas territory. The Lions had a chance to go up right before the half, but Garthwaite missed a chip-shot 21-yard field goal.

Penn State made another long drive to start the second half, a 62-yard drive that reached the Kansas 5. However, Cherry could only get as far as the 1 on three tries, and Pittman got tackled on fourth down to end the drive. Kansas responded by driving back

Bob Campbell scores two-point conversion, Orange Bowl, 1969. Players shown, left to right: #88: PSU receiver Greg Edmonds, #19: Missouri defensive back Dale Holt, #23: PSU halfback Bob Campbell, #83: Missouri defensive end John Zook, #1: Missouri defensive back Dave Morgan, #82: PSU tight end Ted Kwalick, #56: PSU center Warren Koegel, #60: PSU guard Charlie Zapiec. Photographic vertical files, Athletics, 1855–2009 (01167). Penn State University Archives, Eberly Family Special Collections Library, Penn State University Libraries, Penn State University.

down the field, but they missed a 33-yard field goal of their own. The game remained tied at seven through three quarters.

Kansas running back Donnie Shanklin returned a punt 46 yards to the Penn State 7 to start the fourth quarter. Running back John Riggins took over from there, just as he would during his Hall of Fame career with the Washington Redskins. He ran it twice, scoring from a yard out on the second one, and the Jayhawks took a 14–7 lead.

The Nittany Lions were forced to punt again, and Kansas took over at their own 28. They drove the ball 67 yards down to the Penn State 5. On fourth-and-one with ten minutes left in the game, head coach Pepper Rodgers surprisingly decided to go for it instead of putting the game away with a Bill Bell field goal. Riggins ran off tackle, but he was stuffed by linebacker Pete Johnson and defensive back Paul Johnson, and Penn State got the ball back on downs.

Late in the game, the Lions forced a punt. They rushed ten men on the play, and defensive back Neal Smith blocked the kick, which rolled out of bounds at midfield with 1:16 to go. Burkhart made amends for his earlier miscues by throwing long downfield to halfback Bob Campbell to the post. He hauled it in for a 47-yard reception, and Penn State had a first-and-goal at the Kansas 3. On third-and-goal, Burkhart faked a handoff and kept it, running around left end for a touchdown, the first of his career. Penn State had pulled within one point.

Head coach Joe Paterno wanted a win, not a tie. He called for a two-point pass. Burkhart threw to Campbell, but two Kansas defenders broke it up. That seemed to be the end, but umpire Foster Grose caught the Jayhawks with 12 men on the field. That gave

Orange Bowl, team captains with trophy, 1969. People shown: far left, Orange Bowl Committee President James L. Llewellyn; second from left, defensive tackle Mike Reid; second from right, defensive tackle Steve Smear; far right, offensive tackle John Kulka. Photographic vertical files, Athletics, 1855–2009 (01167). Penn State University Archives, Eberly Family Special Collections Library, Penn State University Libraries, Penn State University.

Penn State a second chance. Campbell took a sweep to his left on the second two-point play, and he dived into the end zone for the winning points.[10] The Nittany Lions had won a most thrilling Orange Bowl, 15–14!

Penn State outgained Kansas 361–241 overall and 207–76 in rushing. Campbell led the way with 18 carries for 101 yards and a touchdown, while Pittman added another 58. Burkhart completed 12 of his 23 passes for 154 yards and two interceptions. Tight end Ted Kwalick led in receiving with six catches for 74 yards.[11]

The Nittany Lions finished 11–0, their best record in program history. They ended up #2 in the polls behind #1 Ohio State. Paterno would be named coach of the year by fellow coaches around college football, but he'd pass over a potential coaching job with the Pittsburgh Steelers.[12] It was Paterno's first bowl victory, but he was just getting started.

Box score[13]:

1969 Orange Bowl	1st	2nd	3rd	4th	Final
Kansas	7	0	0	7	14
Penn State	0	7	0	8	15

1st Quarter: KAN—Reeves 2 run (Bell kick)
2nd Quarter: PSU—Pittman 13 run (Garthwaite kick)
3rd Quarter: No Scoring
4th Quarter: KAN—Riggins 1 run (Bell kick)
  PSU—Burkhart 3 run (Campbell run)

1969 Season (10–0)

While the 1994 team's snub for the national championship may be the worst one ever, it was the 1969 team's snub that put Penn State on the map. Never before had the President of the United States chosen the national champion of college football. Given how this particular President's time in office ended, it's safe to say that he was unqualified to even make that decision.

The season started at Navy, where halfback Charlie Pittman scored a pair of touchdowns on 19 carries for 177 yards. Halfback Lydell Mitchell added a 39-yard touchdown run despite losing his shoe on the play. Fullback Franco Harris scored on a six-yard run, and the Nittany Lions went on to a 45–22 win. They moved up to #2 in the rankings after this game.[1]

The Lions then played Colorado for the first time ever. Fullback Don Abbey scored on a 40-yard run, and Harris ran it in on a five-yard sweep to give the Lions a 17–0 halftime lead. They'd go on to win 27–3 after defensive back Paul Johnson returned a kickoff 91 yards for a score. Next, Penn State went to Kansas State where they won only 17–14.[2]

After dropping to #5 in the polls, the Lions defense shut down the powerful Mountaineer rushing attack, not allowing a single point. Quarterback Chuck Burkhart threw a 66-yard pass to Mitchell, setting up a two-yard touchdown run by Harris. The Lions put up nearly 400 yards of offense as they defeated West Virginia, 20–0.[3]

Penn State fell behind Syracuse 14–0 at halftime, and it looked like their winning streak would come to an end. In the fourth quarter, the Lions faced fourth-and-six, where they got bailed out by a pass interference call. That set up a touchdown run by Mitchell. Another penalty on the two-point play gave Harris the chance to run it in to make it 14–8. Later in the game, Harris ran for a touchdown, and guard Mike Reitz kicked the extra point to give Penn State a 15–14 win.[4]

The Nittany Lions easily defeated the Ohio Bobcats, 42–3. The next week, Boston College held the lead over Penn State at halftime, 13–10. But PSU bounced back for a 38–16 win, with Harris, Mitchell, and Pittman all going over 100 yards rushing, only the second time three players did so in the same game in Penn State history.[5]

The Nittany Lions wiped out Maryland, 48–0, with Johnson scoring on a 56-yard punt return, and Mitchell running for a 71-yard score. Next came Pitt, who the Lions beat 27–7. Pittman and Harris both went just over 100 yards rushing, with Pittman scoring a four-yard go-ahead touchdown. The season ended against North Carolina State, who the Lions beat 33–8. Pittman scored his 31st career touchdown and his 186th point, both school records.[6]

Pittman finished up his Penn State career with a 706-yard season, scoring ten rushing touchdowns. He also caught ten passes for 127 yards and another score. Harris and Mitchell were right behind him, each going over 600 rushing yards. Harris had ten touchdowns, while Mitchell had six. Burkhart passed for 805 yards while completing nearly 52 percent of his passes. Notably, Penn State scored just one touchdown through the air in 1969.[7]

But when it came to the national title, the Nittany Lions were robbed. President Richard Nixon declared the winner of the Texas-Arkansas season finale as the national champions. Texas won the game on a late two-point conversion and accepted a championship plaque from Nixon. The President later offered a consolation plaque to Paterno, who was furious over Nixon's declaration.[8]

The bowls were still to come, but both teams were already locked into different bowls. Texas went to the Cotton Bowl as Southwest Conference champions. Penn State passed on a trip to Dallas partially because of civil rights reasons, and also because they never expected #1 Ohio State to lose its finale against Michigan. They figured they'd never have a chance of winning the national championship in the Cotton Bowl; as it turned out, Ohio State lost, and Penn State could have made a #1 vs. #2 game in Dallas. The Lions instead accepted a berth in the Orange Bowl before playing their next-to-last game. They would play against Missouri in Miami, while Texas would go up against Notre Dame in Dallas.[9]

1970 Orange Bowl Classic

#2 Penn State (10–0) vs. #6 Missouri (9–1)
January 1, 1970, at the Orange Bowl in Miami, Florida

Penn State's chances for the national title went by the wayside when Texas defeated Notre Dame in the Cotton Bowl, but there still was the opportunity to make it 30 games without a loss. The weather called for a bit of rain that would mainly manifest at the end of the night. Before that, however, the Nittany Lions and Tigers would play quite possibly the most exciting 10–3 game in the history of football.

Head coach Joe Paterno had the trickery going right from the very start. He had quarterback Chuck Burkhart go back in a punt formation on the first play of the game. It wasn't a quick kick, though; Burkhart threw to running back Franco Harris for six yards. Halfback Charlie Pittman picked up a first down at the 39, before Burkhart almost had a screen picked off and returned all the way. The incompletion brought on a punt that went down to the 16.

Missouri halfback Jon Staggers broke a long run to the 45, only getting tackled by linebacker Jack Ham before going all the way. Quarterback Terry McMillan then completed a pass for a first down to receiver Tom Shryock at the Penn State 38. Halfback Joe Moore added seven more yards and almost broke it, but Ham made another tackle that saved a touchdown. Missouri settled for a 47-yard field goal attempt by Henry Brown, but he missed it short.

Burkhart threw to receiver Greg Edmonds for a pair of first downs, getting to the Missouri 36. He then threw to halfback Lydell Mitchell, who got within a yard of a first down. Pittman picked up a new set of downs from there. Harris made up for a sack with a good run to the 15, and Pittman picked up another first down. Burkhart

Tom Jackson and Steve Smear knocking down Missouri bowling pins in front of Old Main, 1970. Photographic vertical files, Athletics, 1855–2009 (01167). Penn State University Archives, Eberly Family Special Collections Library, Penn State University Libraries, Penn State University.

threw to tight end Pete Johnson in the end zone, but the pass fell incomplete. Mitchell dropped a screen on third down, so the Lions settled for a Mike Reitz 29-yard field goal.

Moore fumbled on the first play of the new drive, and defensive back Paul Johnson recovered for Penn State. Burkhart wasted no time in taking advantage. Under pressure, he threw to Mitchell on the left side, and Mitchell made a fantastic run for a 28-yard touchdown. Reitz kicked the extra point, giving the Lions a 10–0 lead.

The teams exchanged punts. On Penn State's punt, Missouri halfback Jon Staggers made some great moves and nearly went all the way. Harris was there to tackle him at the Penn State 38, saving a touchdown. That tackle proved crucial when McMillan was intercepted on the very next play by defensive end Gary Hull, who returned it to the Missouri 47. The first quarter came to an end with Penn State up by ten.

Both sides would throw interceptions to begin the second quarter. First, Burkhart threw a pick to halfback Lorenzo Brinkley. Then, McMillan threw a second interception, this one to defensive back George Landis. Penn State was forced to punt, and Missouri got a big gain on a McMillan run down to the 10. However, this time Mel Gray fumbled, and defensive end John Ebersole recovered for Penn State.

Later in the half, Bob Parsons had his punt returned by Staggers to the Penn State 20, with only Mitchell's tackle saving a touchdown. Yet again, it proved to be a huge tackle, as

McMillan threw his third interception, this one to linebacker Dennis Onkotz. Penn State got one first down before having to punt again.

Missouri put together a long drive, with the main play being a flare pass from McMillan to Moore to get past midfield. Another pass to Shryock got the Tigers down to the Penn State 12. The Tigers were stymied there, so they called on their kick unit. Brown made a 33-yard field goal, and the teams went to the locker rooms with Penn State up by seven.

Neither team scored in the second half, but that didn't mean it wasn't exciting. McMillan threw a fourth interception to defensive back Neal Smith, and a fifth one to Onkotz. Finally, Missouri head coach Dan Devine had seen enough. He replaced McMillan with Chuck Roper in the fourth quarter. But before he came out, Penn State drove all the way down to the 1, where Reitz missed a chip-shot 17-yard field goal wide to the right after a low snap.

Roper proved to do no better than McMillan, as he threw an interception to Smith. The Tigers sacked Burkhart to force a punt, and Parsons's punt was partially blocked, landing at the Missouri 20. But the Tigers committed pass interference to force themselves into a long field goal situation, and Brown missed the kick wide to the left.

Missouri punted on their next possession, and they'd get one last chance with two minutes to play. Roper threw two passes to receiver John Henley, getting the Tigers down to the 15. As Devine began pondering whether he should go for the win or for the tie on the PAT, all that was blown up when Landis picked off Roper for Penn State's seventh interception of the game. The Lions ran out the clock, and they won the Orange Bowl by a low score of 10–3.

The Lions managed only 57 yards rushing in the game, though a lot of that came from lost yards on sacks. Burkhart completed 11 of 26 passes for 187 yards and a touchdown, while Mitchell led in receiving with five catches for 81 yards and a score. The Nittany defense completely rattled the Missouri passers, who threw more interceptions (seven) than completions (six).[10] The Nittany Lions finished their second straight season undefeated in the Orange Bowl, but a national title was still not to be.

Box score[11]:

1970 Orange Bowl	1st	2nd	3rd	4th	Final
Penn State	10	0	0	0	10
Missouri	0	3	0	0	3

1st Quarter: PSU—Reitz 29 FG
  PSU—Mitchell 28 pass from Burkhart (Reitz kick)
2nd Quarter: MIZZOU—H. Brown 33 FG
3rd Quarter: No Scoring
4th Quarter: No Scoring

1971 Season (10–1)

The Nittany Lions went 7–3 in 1970. The Liberty Bowl showed some interest, and the Peach Bowl even extended an invitation to Penn State, but the players voted it down because they were exhausted from the season.[1] Because of that, the Peach Bowl remains the only "New Year's Six" bowl that Penn State has never played in.

As the Lions moved on to the 1971 season, they entered their opener against Navy ranked #16 in the Associated Press poll. Running back Lydell Mitchell scored five touchdown against the Midshipmen, while quarterback John Hufnagel completed all seven of his passes for 133 yards. Backup Steve Joachim got some playing time, throwing an 86-yard touchdown to running back Jim Scott, in a 56–3 victory.[2]

Penn State played Iowa for the first time since 1930. Mitchell ran for 211 yards and a score, while fullback Franco Harris added another 145 yards and four touchdowns, as the Lions won 44–14. Next came the home opener against Air Force, in which kicker Alberto Vitiello made a 22-yard field goal with four minutes to go to give Penn State a 16–14 win.[3]

Against Army, Hufnagel threw an early touchdown pass to receiver John Skarzynski, as the Lions won 42–0. They then went to Syracuse, where the defense completely shut down the Orange rushing attack. They allowed only 110 yards on the ground in a second straight shutout, this one 31–0.[4]

Penn State put up 66 points against Texas Christian, with the offense rolling up a school-record 633 yards. Mitchell ran for 177 yards and four touchdowns, while Harris ran for another 104 yards. After that 66–14 victory, the Lions headed to West Virginia. Despite a close game for the first two-and-a-half quarters, Penn State pulled away with the help of Mitchell, winning 35–7.[5]

Mitchell, who had already scored the most touchdowns in a season, ran for 209 yards and five touchdowns to set a new points record while also becoming the #1 rusher in school history. The Lions won this one 63–27. They'd move on to Pitt Stadium and demolish the Panthers 55–18. Mitchell added to his records with 181 yards and three more touchdowns.[6]

The Lions were undefeated and ranked #5 going into their season finale against Tennessee. The surprisingly low ranking was because many sportswriters thought their schedule had been soft. Indeed, their schedule did not prepare them for the Volunteers. Hufnagel completed a school-record 19 passes in a futile comeback effort as the Lions lost, 31–11.[7]

Fortunately for Penn State, they had already accepted a bowl bid. They planned on going to the Gator Bowl against Notre Dame, but ND head coach Ara Parseghian decided that the Fighting Irish would stay home for the holiday season. As a result, the Lions chose to play in the Cotton Bowl against Southwest Conference champion Texas.[8]

1972 Cotton Bowl Classic

#10 Penn State (10–1) vs. #12 Texas (8–2)
January 1, 1972, at the Cotton Bowl in Dallas, Texas

After the devastating loss in the season finale, Penn State was written off going into their bowl against Texas. The Longhorns, practically playing at home, were six-point favorites. The Nittany Lions had been sold short by the previous President, Richard Nixon, who awarded the 1969 national championship to Texas; now the previous President, Lyndon B. Johnson, was in attendance to see if Penn State could beat his Longhorns.

Bob Parsons got off a poor 28-yard punt late in the first quarter, leading to an easy 29-yard field goal by Texas's Steve Valek. But in the second quarter, the Nittany defense changed things when linebackers John Skorupan and Tom Hull forced a fumble, which Charlie Zapiec recovered in Texas territory at the 20. That set up a 21-yard Alberto Vitiello field goal, and the Lions tied it at three.

With less than a minute left in the first half, quarterback John Hufnagel threw an interception to linebacker Glen Gaspard, who snagged the ball with one hand. He returned it to the Texas 40. Quarterback Eddie Phillips completed a pair of passes to set up Valek for a 40-yard field goal attempt. Valek made it to set a Cotton Bowl record for the longest field goal, and Texas led 6–3 at the half.

But the Nittany defense came out on fire in the second half. Phillips fumbled on the first drive, which Zapiec recovered on Texas's side of the field at the 41. Running back Lydell Mitchell ripped off a 20-yard run, then Hufnagel fired to Parsons for another 20 yards. Mitchell pounded it in for a one-yard touchdown from there, and Penn State took a 10–6 lead.

Texas quickly punted again, and the Lions got the ball back at their own 35. It took just one play to score. Hufnagel launched a pass to receiver Scott Skarzynski, who caught it for a 65-yard touchdown. Vitiello added a 37-yard field goal shortly afterward, and Penn State led 20–6 at the end of three quarters of play.

To start the fourth quarter, Vitiello kicked another field goal, this one from 22 yards away, setting the Cotton Bowl record for the most field goals with his third. Head coach Joe Paterno then had his offense absolutely suffocate the ball. The Lions held the ball for almost 13 of the final 15 minutes. To end the game, they went on a 64-yard drive, which Hufnagel capped off by running for a four-yard touchdown on fourth down. What appeared to be a tight game had turn into a rout in Penn State's favor. The Nittany Lions won, 30–6.[9]

Hufnagel had a big day, completing seven of 12 passes for 137 yards and a touchdown, while also running for 14 yards and a touchdown. Mitchell ran for 146 yards and a touchdown, ending a spectacular career by being named the Outstanding Offensive Player. Defensive end Bruce Bannon was named the game's Outstanding Defensive Player, as the Lions allowed just 242 yards.[10]

Penn State earned national acclaim for this victory, moving up to #5 in the final Associated Press poll. Their offense school records of 454 points, 3,347 rushing yards, and five yards shy of 5,000 total yards would not be broken until the 1994 juggernaut. Mitchell also had set NCAA records of 28 touchdowns and 174 points in a season. The Lions finished 11–1, finally getting the respect they deserved.[11]

Box score[12]:

1972 Cotton Bowl	1st	2nd	3rd	4th	Final
Penn State	0	3	17	10	30
Texas	3	3	0	0	6

1st Quarter: TEX—Valek 29 FG
2nd Quarter: PSU—Vitiello 21 FG
   TEX—Valek 40 FG
3rd Quarter: PSU—Mitchell 1 run (Vitiello kick)
   PSU—Skarzynski 65 pass from Hufnagel (Vitiello kick)
   PSU—Vitiello 37 FG
4th Quarter: PSU—Vitiello 22 FG
   PSU—Hufnagel 4 run (Vitiello kick)

1972 Season (10–1)

The Nittany Lions opened their 1972 season against the team who had spoiled their last season: the Tennessee Volunteers, at Knoxville. The Lions fell into a 21–0 hole at halftime, before mounting a comeback. Quarterback John Hufnagel launched a 69-yard touchdown pass to receiver Jim Scott, and running back John Cappelletti set up another one to pull within seven, but time ran out on the Lions in a 28–21 loss.[1]

Against Navy, Cappelletti scored a pair of touchdowns, and linebacker John Skork-upan picked off a pass and took it back 32 yards to give Penn State a 21–10 win. Next came Iowa. With three minutes to go and down by three, Hufnagel led an 80-yard drive, culminating with a ten-yard touchdown pass to tight end Don Natale, which gave the Lions a 14–10 victory.[2]

Cappelletti had his first career 100-yard game against Illinois, putting up 124 yards and a 35-yard touchdown. The Lions scored 21 points in the first quarter and went on to beat the Illini 35–17. They then visited West Point, where they destroyed Army 45–0. Hufnagel threw for 152 yards and two touchdowns while also running for 71 yards against the Cadets.[3]

Against Syracuse, the Lions pulled off a second straight shutout, beating the Orange by a 17–0 margin. Cappelletti ran for 162 yards in the win. They then went to West Virginia, which was especially hostile this year. But despite allowing a touchdown on the opening kickoff, the Lions came back to win 28–19 thanks to three Cappelletti touchdowns and 117 yards from running back Walt Addie.[4]

Penn State ripped off consecutive blowout victories over Maryland (46–16) and North Carolina State (37–22), with Hufnagel throwing for a touchdown and running for two more in the latter. Next came Boston College, who the Lions put away with a 77-yard touchdown from Hufnagel to Scott. They won that one 45–26.[5]

Finally, an absolutely terrible Pitt team came to Beaver Stadium only to get completely embarrassed. Penn State had a 42–0 lead in the third quarter before putting in backups. Hufnagel threw three touchdown passes in the victory, which ended up 49–27. Penn State finished the regular season with a 10–1 record, opposite of what Pitt finished at.[6]

Cappelletti became the third 1,000-yard rusher in Penn State history, with only Lydell Mitchell and Lenny Moore reaching that mark before him. Scott caught only 12 passes, but he gained an outrageous 36.1 yards per catch! Hufnagel finished his career at Penn State with a 26–2 record, having begun starting halfway through the 1970 season.[7]

The Cotton, Orange, Gator, and Sugar Bowls were all interested in hosting Penn State. The Cotton wanted a rematch with Texas, while the Orange was looking for a game against either Alabama or Nebraska. In the end, Penn State got the nod for the Sugar Bowl, up against Big Eight foe Oklahoma. It was the only time between 1950 and 1995 that a Southeastern Conference team did not play in the bowl in New Orleans.[8]

1972 Sugar Bowl Classic

#5 Penn State (10–1) vs. #2 Oklahoma (10–1)
December 31, 1972, at Tulane Stadium in New Orleans, Louisiana

Everything was all out of sorts for this Sugar Bowl. The lack of a SEC team was strange enough, but this game was also being played on New Year's Eve instead of on New Year's Day as is customary. Joe Paterno was totally distracted from the game due to the fact that the New England Patriots were pursuing him to become head coach there. Finally, Cappelletti had a fever and had to sit out the game, utterly crippling the Penn State offense.

Oklahoma didn't show any mercy to the Lions. They allowed just 49 rushing yards to the hurting Penn State offense. Minus-25 of that came on sacks of Hufnagel, who was only able to complete 12 of his 31 pass attempts for 147 yards and a pick. The Lions fumbled the ball away four times, but surprisingly Oklahoma lost even more fumbles than that, as they gave it away five times.

Sooners quarterback Dave Robertson threw a 27-yard touchdown pass to receiver Tinker Owens in the second quarter, and kicker Rick Fulcher's PAT gave OU a 7–0 lead. The Nittany Lions couldn't do anything with the ball, and in the fourth quarter, the same combination put the game away. Robertson hit Owens for a pass down to the 1, which the Lions claimed had been trapped. They were right, but there was no instant replay in those days. Fullback Leon Crosswhite scored from there, and Oklahoma won by a count of 14–0.[9]

After the game, Paterno accepted a $1.4 million offer to become head coach of the New England Patriots. But within 24 hours, he changed his mind, and decided to stay with the Nittany Lions. Penn State finished #10 in the final Associated Press poll with a 10–2 record. That was satisfactory, but bigger and better things were to come!

Box score[10]:

1972 Sugar Bowl	1st	2nd	3rd	4th	Final
Penn State	0	0	0	0	0
Oklahoma	0	7	0	7	14

1st Quarter: No Scoring
2nd Quarter: OU—Owens 27 pass from Robertson (Fulcher kick)
3rd Quarter: No Scoring
4th Quarter: OU—Crosswhite 1 run (Fulcher kick)

1973 Season (11–0)

The Nittany Lions began their 1973 campaign out on the West Coast against Stanford. Quarterback Tom Shuman threw a 14-yard touchdown pass to receiver Gary Hayman, and running back John Cappelletti scored a short touchdown to lead the Lions to a 20–6 win.[1] Against Navy, Shuman threw a pair of first-half touchdown passes, and Cappelletti ran for 104 yards, as Penn State cruised to a 39–0 win. The Lions then came home for the first time this season, where they beat Iowa 27–8. Shuman threw three touchdown passes, two in the first quarter, as Penn State got off to a 21–0 lead in the opening frame and never looked back.[2]

Cappelletti took over against Air Force, running the ball 34 times for 187 yards and two touchdowns. The Lions missed two extra points, but still held on to win by a 19–9 margin. At Syracuse two weeks later, Cappelletti was out with a shoulder bruise. Kicker Chris Bahr picked up the slack, making three field goals, including a 50-yarder, in a 49–6 win.[3]

After having played four of their first five games on the road, the Lions closed with five of six at home. Against Army, Cappelletti ran for over 150 yards before hurting his shoulder again. The Lions did fine without him, putting up over 600 yards of offense in a 54–3 win. Similarly, West Virginia proved to be a breeze, especially with Cappelletti back healthy. He ran for four touchdowns against the Mountaineers on 130 yards, with PSU winning by a 62–14 margin.[4]

Hayman took back the opening kickoff 98 yards for a touchdown against Maryland. The Terrapins fought back to tie the game at 22 going into the half, but Shuman threw a trio of touchdown passes to put Penn State back in front. Cappelletti took 37 carries, a school record, gaining over 200 yards, as the Lions won 42–22.[5]

North Carolina State was the team who came closest to knocking off the Nittany Lions. They tied it up at 29 in the fourth quarter, before Cappelletti took off on a game-winning 27-yard touchdown run, his third of the ballgame. After that 35–29 win, the Lions piled up 515 yards of offense against the Ohio Bobcats. Cappelletti scored four touchdowns in the first half, and the Lions cruised to a 49–10 victory.[6]

The season ended at home against Pitt, who took a 13–3 lead into halftime at Beaver Stadium. In the second half, linebacker Tom Hull scored on a 27-yard pick-six, and Shuman threw a 32-yard touchdown to receiver Chuck Herd. The Lions went on to win 35–13 and clinch an undefeated regular season.[7]

Cappelletti had a marvelous year, rushing for 1,522 yards and 17 touchdowns, and adding another six catches for 69 yards as well as a 17-yard pass. He was named Penn State's first (and to this day, only) Heisman Trophy winner.[8] In two seasons, he ran for over 2,639 yards, ranking him second in school history. "Cappy is the best player I have ever been around," head coach Joe Paterno said. "He is a strong, fast, durable, and a great leader. You know he is going to come through for you when you need him."[9]

But in what was becoming a theme, the Lions were robbed by the Associated Press voters. This time, they didn't even have Penn State in the top five. #1 Alabama and #3 Notre Dame played in the Sugar Bowl for the national title, and while the Cotton Bowl showed some interest, the #6 Lions ended up stuck playing #13 LSU in the Orange Bowl. What did the Lions have to do to get some respect? They would have the chance to earn some in Miami against the Tigers.[10]

1974 Orange Bowl Classic

#6 Penn State (11–0) vs. #13 LSU (9–2)
January 1, 1974, at the Orange Bowl in Miami, Florida

Going into this game, Louisiana State's biggest goal was to stop Heisman Trophy winner John Cappelletti. They were willing to throw everything at him and completely sell out to stop the run. They'd end up completely successful in those efforts. However,

Banner—Miami is Lion Country, 1974. Photographic vertical files, Athletics, 1855–2009 (01167). Penn State University Archives, Eberly Family Special Collections Library, Penn State University Libraries, Penn State University.

it was the arm of quarterback Tom Shuman that would prove to be the difference in this game.

LSU got the ball to start at midfield thanks to a great return by defensive back Robert Dow. Using a heavy dose of running back Brad Davis, the Tigers moved the ball right down the field. Davis carried it six times, but he didn't get the honor of scoring the touchdown. That went to running back Steve Rogers, who punched it in from three yards out. Kicker Rusty Jackson made the extra point, and LSU took an early 7–0 lead.

Penn State tried running Cappelletti on the first drive, but he was stopped, and they went three-and-out. On their next drive, it was more of the same. This time fullback Bob Nagle picked up a first down at midfield before the Lions were forced to punt. On their third drive, they went three-and-out despite fantastic field position. But as they walked off the field after the punt, they got some good news: LSU had committed a personal foul, and now the Lions had a first down. They couldn't get any closer, but they were in field goal range. Kicker Chris Bahr made a 44-yard field goal to cut the deficit to four.

LSU went with running back Terry Robiskie on their next drive. He carried the ball five times, and the Tigers got down into field goal range. It was a long one, so they called on their specialist Juan Roca. He tried a 54-yard field goal, but he never had a chance. Defensive end Dave Graf rushed in and blocked it, and fellow defensive end Greg Murphy recovered it for Penn State at the LSU 35.

Shuman went right away to the end zone to receiver Chuck Herd, who came down with the ball touching the end line, so it was ruled incomplete. Penn State ended up having to punt on that drive. They forced a quick three-and-out, though, and they got the ball back after a punt. Shuman went back to Herd on second down. This time Herd made a fantastic one-handed catch, before running the rest of the way for a 72-yard touchdown. With that, Penn State took a 10–7 lead.

The Nittany Lions forced a quick three-and-out, and receiver Gary Hayman returned the punt 36 yards into LSU territory down to the 26. Cappelletti ran for one first down, and Shuman picked up another. Once the Lions got down to the 1, it was obvious who they were going with. Cappelletti dived over the top of the pile for a one-yard touchdown. Bahr missed the extra point off the left upright, but the Lions now had a nine-point advantage.

The Tigers had to punt, but a roughing the kicker penalty gave them a second chance. Having a chance to score before the half, quarterback Mike Miley led the way, completing passes to Davis as well as receiver Ben Jones to get down inside the 10. After burning their final timeout, LSU head coach Charles McClendon eschewed the field goal in favor of a pass with less than half a minute to go. Miley threw complete to Davis in bounds inside the 5, but now the clock was running out. All Miley could do was get up to the line and throw an incompletion, but time was up. LSU had gotten nothing out of the drive, and Penn State was up 16–7 at the half.

But after all that offensive fireworks in the first half, neither offense could get on the board in the second half. Brian Masella went back to punt after Cappelletti went three runs and out. The snap went over Masella's head, and he had to cover it in the end zone for a safety. LSU pulled within seven, but that was the last time either team would score.

On a pitch to Davis, the ball came loose, and linebacker Doug Allen recovered for Penn State. But on the very next play, defensive back Mike Williams picked off Shuman. Three punts ensued, two by LSU. From the 38, Shuman threw a screen to Cappelletti down the right sideline, and he picked up 40 yards. However, the LSU defense wouldn't let him have another inch, stopping him on three consecutive plays. Bahr then missed a 38-yard field goal attempt wide to the right, ending the third quarter with Penn State up by a touchdown.

LSU's last best chance came on their second possession of the fourth quarter. Robiskie again ran the ball a bunch, carrying it four times on the drive. The Tigers got down inside the Penn State 30, where they faced a fourth-and-three. Allen tackled Rogers for a loss on the play, and the Tigers turned it over on downs.

The Tigers got the ball one last time, but they never really threatened to score. Miley hit tight end Brad Boye for 51 yards, and he got out of bounds with less than a minute to go. After a short gain on first down, Miley threw three incompletions in a row. His final pass was way off target, and that was it; Penn State had finished another undefeated season with a 16–9 win.

Cappelletti ran for only 50 yards on 26 carries. That was all okay, though, because the LSU defense keying in on him led to Shuman throwing for 157 yards. The Lions were outgained by nearly 100 yards, and they had only half as many first downs as LSU had. The teams combined for 15 punts and would have had a 16th if Masella had been able to handle that high snap.

The Nittany Lions finished unbeaten at 12–0. However, they'd only move up to #5, passing just Michigan, who didn't play in a bowl game (the Big Ten, who sent Ohio State to the Rose Bowl, only offered one bowl spot at the time). The Lions were hurt in the rankings by the fact that so many teams finished undefeated. Notre Dame, Ohio State, Oklahoma, Michigan, and Miami of Ohio all finished without a loss. They'd have to settle for an Orange Bowl victory; their chance at a national title would have to wait.

Box score[11]:

1974 Orange Bowl	1st	2nd	3rd	4th	Final
LSU	7	0	2	0	9
Penn State	3	13	0	0	16

1st Quarter: LSU—Rogers 3 run (Jackson kick)
    PSU—Bahr 44 FG
2nd Quarter: PSU—Herd 72 pass from Shuman (Bahr kick)
    PSU—Cappelletti 1 run (kick missed)
3rd Quarter: LSU—Safety
4th Quarter: No Scoring

1974 Season (9–2)

Head coach Joe Paterno instituted a Wing-T offense for this season, a brand-new offense in Happy Valley. They faced adversity right off the bat, trailing Stanford 20–17 late in the fourth quarter in their opener. They put together an eight-play, 80-yard drive, which ended with running back Woody Petchel punching it in from a yard away for the winning points in a 24–20 win.[1]

Trailing Navy 7–0, Penn State quarterback Tom Shuman capped off a 59-yard drive late in the fourth quarter with a five-yard touchdown pass to receiver Jerry Jeram, but he misfired on a two-point pass, and the Lions lost 7–6.[2] But Penn State bounced back with an easy win in Iowa. The Nittany Lions held the Hawkeyes to only 100 yards in a 27–0 wipeout. Next, they went to West Point, where they came back from a 14–0 deficit. Running back Tom Donchez pounded in a two-yard touchdown, and Shuman threw an 18-yard touchdown to tight end Randy Sidler. Running back Duane Taylor put the game away with a 19-yard touchdown run in the final quarter, as the Lions won 21–14.[3]

The Nittany Lions had an easy time with Wake Forest, putting up 532 yards of offense and 55 points on the board. Receiver Jimmy Cefalo caught a 57-yard touchdown pass from Shuman, then later scored on a 39-yard run. The Lions shut out the Demon Deacons, making it 13 of the last 14 quarters that they had not allowed a point.[4]

Against Syracuse, the Lions fell into a 14–3 hole early on. Shuman brought Penn State back, running for two touchdowns and throwing a ten-yard touchdown to Taylor in a 30–14 win. Headed to West Virginia next, Shuman threw an early 30-yard touchdown to Jeram. Taylor added an eight-yard run as the Lions went on to win, 21–12.[5]

Defensive back Jeff Hite scored two touchdowns against Maryland. The first came on a 79-yard pick-six, and the second came on a 21-yard return of a lateral that he picked off, to pull out a 24–17 win. The offense's struggles continued against North Carolina State, who needed only two touchdowns to down the Lions. Shuman threw a late touchdown pass, but the Lions lost, 12–7.[6]

Ohio University provided a breather for the tired Lions. Donchez ran for three touchdowns, as Penn State jumped out to a 35–0 lead. Ohio scored a pair of garbage touchdowns to make the score look closer than it was, but PSU still won 35–16. In the season finale, the Lions trailed at Pitt Stadium by a 7–6 margin at the half. Shuman then threw two touchdown passes to receiver Jim Eaise, as the Lions roared back for a 31–10 triumph.[7]

Running back Tom Donchez led the team in rushing with 880 yards and seven touchdowns. Taylor added another 412 rushing yards and five touchdowns. Cefalo, a receiver, ranked third on the team with 328 rushing yards and a score, while also catching six passes for 144 yards and a score. Jeram and Donchez tied for the team lead in receptions, and Jeram paced the team in receiving yards with 259. Shuman completed 53 percent of his passes for 1,355 yards and six touchdowns.[8]

The Cotton Bowl invited Penn State to play in its annual classic following the loss to North Carolina State. The Southwest Conference champions got an automatic bid to face them; however, first-place #5 Texas A&M lost to Southern Methodist, and second-place Texas lost as well. The Baylor Bears ended up with the Southwest title and the trip to Dallas. That meant that Penn State's last two bowls involved the Lions, the Tigers, and the Bears. Could the Lions win for a second time?[9]

1975 Cotton Bowl Classic
#7 Penn State (9–2) vs. #12 Baylor (8–3)
January 1, 1975, at the Cotton Bowl in Dallas, Texas

The Bears got the ball at their own 20 to start the game. Baylor head coach Grant Teaff put the ball in the hands of running back Steve Beaird, who carried the ball five times on the first series. The Bears got as far as midfield before having to punt. Penn State took over with the football after the punt went down to the 26.

Receiver Jimmy Cefalo jumpstarted the Penn State offense with a 23-yard gain on a sweep. Later, quarterback Tom Shuman threw to fullback Tom Donchez for 23 more yards. The Lions got all the way down to the 13 before their drive expired. The usually reliable Chris Bahr missed a 30-yard field goal wide left, though, and the game remained scoreless.

Defensive back Jim Bradley picked off Baylor quarterback Neal Jeffrey, but only two plays later, Donchez fumbled it back to Baylor. Beaird burst for a 19-yard run, then Jeffrey threw to receiver Alcy Jackson for a 21-yard pickup. Beaird took over from there, running the ball six times, and eventually getting it in from the 4. Kicker David Hicks made the extra point, and Baylor led 7–0 after one quarter.

Penn State put together a long drive that resulted in a punt. After getting the ball back on a Baylor punt, Donchez fumbled again, and the Bears recovered at the Penn State 39. Linebacker Chris Devlin made two huge plays, sacking Jeffrey and knocking down a pass. That forced Baylor out of any possible field goal, and they had to punt it back.

On Penn State's next drive, Cefalo got his team's initial first down at the 25. Shuman then hit tight end Dan Natale for a first down at the 42 and Cefalo for another first down past midfield at the 39. Running back Neil Hutton ran for nine yards, then Donchez got another first down. This all set up a 25-yard Bahr field goal, which cut the deficit to four at the half.

Penn State started the second half with the ball at their own 20 after a touchback. Shuman hit Natale for 43 yards down to the Baylor 33, and he later hit Natale again for another first down at the 12. Shuman then handed off to Donchez on four consecutive plays, on the fourth of which Donchez scored from the 1. With kicker George Reihner's extra point, Penn State went up 10–7.

The teams exchanged punts, and Baylor took over at their own 45. The Lions tackled Jeffrey for a loss on second down, but they got flagged for a personal foul for piling on. Two plays later, Jeffrey went to the end zone, where a Penn State player tipped the ball to Baylor receiver Rick Thompson. The 35-yard completion put Baylor back in front, 14–10.

The Lions were greatly helped by the fact that Baylor kicked the ball out of bounds twice in a row. That moved the kickoff back to the 30, and the Lions returned it to just short of midfield. Donchez ran for a three-yard pickup, then Shuman threw a 49-yard bomb down the left sideline to Cefalo. Touchdown! The Lions were now ahead, 17–14.

Baylor punted to end the third quarter. On Penn State's next possession, they gave the ball to Hutton. He plugged away at the Baylor defense, running the ball a bunch of times and earning three first downs, including an 18-yard run. Donchez chipped away at the Baylor defense a little more, then Cefalo took a handoff off the weak side of the line for a three-yard touchdown. Penn State was now up by ten.

The Bears went nowhere on their next possession, and Penn State started their new drive at the 30. Hutton ripped off a 14-yard run, then Shuman connected with Cefalo on a 34-yard pass. Hutton ran it a couple of more times, setting the Lions up in field goal range. Bahr made a 33-yard kick, and the Lions improved their lead to 13 points.

This game was wrapped up when defensive back Mike Johnson intercepted a pass and returned it to the 18. Hutton ripped off a nine-yard run for a first down, and a pass interference call set up first-and-goal at the 1. Two plays later, Shuman snuck it in for a touchdown. The Lions chose to let Bahr kick the extra point instead of going for two, so their lead was now 20.

Baylor got one last chance with the ball, and their drive ended with backup quarterback Mark Jackson throwing an 11-yard touchdown pass to Thompson with only 14 seconds left in the game. The Bears despondently went for two, just trying to make the score look better, and their pass was broken up. On the ensuing kickoff, the Bears tried an onside kick, which Penn State linebacker Joe Jackson timed perfectly to grab and go 50 yards for a touchdown. That made the final count of this Cotton Bowl 41–20, in favor of Penn State.

Penn State may have struggled early, but they ended up dominating this game. Donchez led all rushers with 116 yards, and Hutton and Cefalo both ran for good amounts (79 and 55, respectively). Cefalo also caught three passes for 102 yards and a score. Shuman wasn't bad himself, completing ten passes for 226 yards and a touchdown. The Lions outgained the Bears by nearly 200 yards.

Penn State finished the season 10–2 and #7 in the final rankings, while Baylor dropped slightly to #14. The Lions had now won two Cotton Bowls as well as an Orange Bowl in the seventies, and the decade wasn't even half over. They'd next get a chance at the Sugar and the Gator, a couple of bowls in which they were looking for redemption.

Box score[10]:

1975 Cotton Bowl	1st	2nd	3rd	4th	Final
Penn State	0	3	14	24	41
Baylor	7	0	7	6	20

1st Quarter: BAY—Beaird 4 run (Hicks kick)
2nd Quarter: PSU—Bahr 25 FG
3rd Quarter: PSU—Donchez 1 run (Reihner kick)
   BAY—Thompson 35 pass from Jeffrey (Hicks kick)
   PSU—Cefalo 49 pass from Shuman (Reihner kick)

4th Quarter: PSU—Cefalo 3 run (Reihner kick)

PSU—Bahr 33 FG

PSU—Shuman 2 run (Reihner kick)

BAY—Thompson 11 pass from M. Jackson (pass failed)

PSU—J. Jackson 50 kickoff return (Reihner kick)

1975 Season (9–2)

The Nittany Lions began their season with a real scare against Temple. Despite a 100-yard kickoff return by receiver Rich Mauti, the Lions trailed 23–18 in the fourth quarter. Fullback Duane Taylor scored from three yards away, and quarterback John Andress completed a two-point pass to tight end Mickey Shuler, and the Lions pulled out a 26–25 win.[1]

Against Stanford, receiver Tom Donovan entered the Penn State record books as the first-ever freshman to rush for 100 yards in a game. He gained 113 yards, including a 61-yard touchdown run, as the Lions beat Stanford 34–14. But no one could get it into the end zone against Ohio State, who dominated in a 17–9 win. Taylor ran for 113 yards, but the Lions managed just three field goals in their first loss of the season.[2]

The Lions bounced back against Iowa, with Andress throwing for 195 yards, including two passes of 70-plus yards. They took a 14–3 lead into halftime and breezed to a 30–10 win. There wouldn't be so much offense against Kentucky. Fullback Larry Suhey scored on a one-yard run that proved to be the difference in a 10–3 victory.[3]

The defense proved to be unbreachable in the next three games. While they were shutting out the Mountaineers, kicker Chris Bahr made three field goals and four extra points to set the school record for most kicking points. The Lions won easily over West Virginia, 39–0. In a 19–7 win over Syracuse, Bahr made a 55-yard kick for the sixth field goal of at least 50 yards of his career, an NCAA record.[4]

Penn State finished a stretch of three games having allowed only seven points with a 31–0 win over Army. Petchel ran for two touchdowns and nearly ran for a third; he fumbled near the goal line and Shuler recovered for a touchdown. The Lions blew a 12–0 lead against Maryland, but Bahr made a 40-yard kick with seven-and-a-half minutes left to lift Penn State to a 15–13 win.[5]

The Lions got off to a 14–0 start against North Carolina State, but the Wolfpack came back to take a 15–14 lead. Bahr missed a 46-yard field goal at the end of the game that would have won it. Penn State bounced back from that loss in their season finale, knocking off Pitt at Three Rivers Stadium by a 7–6 score. Running back Steve Geise ran for a 28-yard touchdown with six-and-a-half minutes left to lift PSU to the win.[6]

Petchel and Taylor led a dual rushing attack, combining for nearly 1,200 yards and nine touchdowns on the ground. Andress threw for just shy of 1,000 yards in a very run-oriented offense. Receiver Dick Barvinchak led the team in receiving with 17 catches for 327 yards. Bahr made 18 field goals and 19 extra points, as well as punting 56 times for a 38.6 average.[7]

It looked like Penn State was headed for the Fiesta, Sun, or Gator Bowl after their loss to North Carolina State, but they backed into the Sugar Bowl when Pitt knocked off Notre Dame. Alabama head coach Paul "Bear" Bryant was going to pick Notre Dame as his Sugar Bowl opponent, but when they lost, he went with Penn State instead. With those two defenses, one thing was for sure: there wouldn't be many points in New Orleans.[8]

1975 Sugar Bowl Classic

#8 Penn State (9–2) vs. #4 Alabama (10–1)
December 31, 1975, at the Louisiana Superdome in New Orleans, Louisiana

Alabama was a 13-point favorite to defeat Penn State.[9] The Lions must have used that as motivation, because their offense came out on fire. Quarterback John Andress threw to receiver Jimmy Cefalo for a first down at the 39, and running backs Duane Taylor and Woody Petchel combined for nine more yards. Andress got the first down on the sneak, before Cefalo was held up at the Alabama 45 on the next third down. Head coach Joe Paterno sent out kicker Chris Bahr to try a 62-yard field goal. It came up well short, but college rules at the time put the ball at the 20 and not at the former line of scrimmage, making it worth the gamble.

The Crimson Tide rolled right downfield for a score, though. Quarterback Richard Todd hit receiver Joe Dale Harris at the 35, and he took off for a 54-yard gain all the way down to the Penn State 20. Todd then fired to receiver Ozzie Newsome to get down to the 10. The Tide got as far as the 4, before settling for a 25-yard field goal by kicker Danny Ridgeway. Each team punted on their next drive, and that was the end of the first quarter.

The second quarter was an exercise in futility for both offenses. Neither team managed to get even into field goal range. Linebacker Ron Hostetler picked up a sack and another tackle for loss in stopping one Alabama drive. Receiver Scott Fitzkee had the longest run of the half with a 15-yarder into Alabama territory. The drive ended in failure, though, when Andress saw his pass picked off by defensive back Mark Prudhomme. The Lions went to the locker room down by three.

The two strong defenses kept it up to start the second half. Penn State's defense forced two punts before their offense finally got something going. Andress ran for a 14-yard gain, and he threw to Petchel for another first down to the Alabama 33. Taylor and running back Rich Mauti got the ball as far as the 25, before the drive stalled. Bahr made the 42-yard field goal attempt, and the Lions tied it at three.

Alabama changed field position with a long pass from Todd to Newsome. He picked up 56 yards on the deep ball, and the Tide got down to the 10. Fullback Calvin Culliver fumbled on the next play, but the Tide got lucky and recovered the football for a loss of yards. On the very next play, running back Mike Stock ran for a 14-yard touchdown to make it 10–3 at the end of the third quarter. Imagine how different things might have been had Penn State recovered that fumble!

Running back Steve Geise helped move the ball back down the field, starting with a pitch for 29 yards. He ran it four more times on the drive, getting a pair of first downs to the Alabama 27. Andress threw to tight end Mickey Shuler to get to the 20, but again the Penn State drive stalled. Bahr made his 37-yard field goal, and the Lions pulled within four.

The Tide then just suffocated the clock for the rest of the quarter. Stock ran it a couple of times to get a first down, and Culliver added another first down after a couple of carries of his own. Todd hit Stock for a first down at the 25, and he also found tight end Jerry Brown for a first down inside the 10. While Alabama couldn't punch it in, they got a 28-yard field goal by Ridgeway that put them up by seven with just three minutes to go in the game.

Penn State's last chance started out with a Geise run, then a pass from Andress to Cefalo for a first down at the 30. On the next third down, receiver Dick Barvinchak took an end around to get within one yard on the first down. Paterno had no choice now, he had to go for it. But Mauti was stopped inches short of the first down, and the Lions turned it over on downs. Alabama then ran out the clock for a 13–6 win.

This was a classic defensive struggle, and despite the score, the Lions weren't outplayed by that much. The problem was the passing game. Alabama threw for 210 yards; Penn State had just 57 as well as an interception thrown. Geise led both teams in rushing with 46 yards, but the Lions just couldn't get the ball even near the Alabama red zone. Penn State took a second straight loss in the Sugar Bowl; they'd get a third chance (and a rematch with Alabama) only a few years later.

Box score[10]:

1975 Sugar Bowl	1st	2nd	3rd	4th	Final
Penn State	0	0	3	3	6
Alabama	3	0	7	3	13

1st Quarter: ALA—Ridgeway 25 FG
2nd Quarter: No Scoring
3rd Quarter: PSU—Bahr 42 FG
    ALA—Stock 14 run (Ridgeway kick)
4th Quarter: PSU—Bahr 37 FG
    ALA—Ridgeway 28 FG

1976 Season (7–4)

In their season opener against Stanford, running backs Steve Geise and Matt Suhey both ran for touchdowns, as Penn State took a 15–0 lead. The defense held on to the lead for a 15–12 win.[1] But the Lions were unable to get on the board until only six minutes to go. The Buckeyes got a couple of touchdowns and held on to defeat Penn State 12–7.

The ensuing game against Iowa was more of the same. The Lions didn't score until the fourth quarter again. This time, kicker Herb Menhardt missed a game-winning 25-yard field goal in the final minute for a 7–6 loss. Penn State then lost a third straight game, marking the first three-game losing streak in head coach Joe Paterno's career. This one wasn't even close, as Kentucky dominated on their way to a 22–6 win.[2]

The Lions turned things around with a big win over Army, though. The offense exploded, with Geise and running back Mike Guman each running for over 100 yards in their 38–16 win. Against Syracuse, Guman ran for two touchdowns on 88 yards, while Geise added another 98. The Lions breezed to a 27–3 win to move back to .500 for the season.[3]

West Virginia proved to be a pushover. Fusina threw for 261 yards and two touchdowns, while the defense completely dominated in a 33–0 shutout. It was Penn State's 18th straight win over West Virginia. In a shootout with Temple, Fusina threw for 219 yards and two touchdowns, but the Owls kept coming back. Penn State held on to win 31–30 after Temple missed a two-pointer at the end.[4]

Geise and Guman both went over 100 rushing yards again in their game against North Carolina State. Geise had a 64-yard touchdown run, and Guman had a 46-yard scoring run. The Lions crushed the Wolfpack 41–20. At Miami, Fusina threw for 212 yards and two touchdowns, and the Lions held the Hurricanes to under 79 rushing yards in a 21–7 win.[5]

Fusina threw a touchdown pass in the first quarter of the season finale at Three Rivers Stadium, and it looked like the Lions might pull off an upset over the #1 Pitt Panthers. But Panther running back Tony Dorsett was too much for the Lions defense, running for 224 yards on the way to a 24–7 Pitt win.[6]

The Lions had a three-headed running attack, with a trio of running backs all over 450 yards but all under 600. Geise led with 560 and three touchdowns, Suhey had 487 and five touchdowns, and Guman rushed for 470 and six scores. Tight end Mickey Shuler led in receptions with 21, finishing only 14 yards behind receiving yards leader Jimmy Cefalo, who had 295.[7] Fusina took the quarterback job from John Andress, who got hurt early on in the fourth game of the season. Fusina's 1,260 passing yards were the sixth-most in Penn State history.[8]

The Fiesta, Sun, Liberty, and Peach Bowls were all interested in Penn State. But Notre Dame ended up deciding the Lions' postseason fate. They were headed to the Gator Bowl, and they insisted on playing Penn State instead of Nebraska. The Fighting Irish hadn't played the Nittany Lions since 1928, which was a big reason they picked PSU. So, the Lions were off to Jacksonville to play in their fourth Gator Bowl, where they were 1–1–1.[9]

1976 Gator Bowl Classic

#20 Penn State (7–4) vs. #15 Notre Dame (8–3)
December 27, 1976, at the Gator Bowl in Jacksonville, Florida

Penn State may have been ranked only five spots lower than Notre Dame, but there was a clear gulf in talent between the two clubs. The Nittany Lions were a year away from being really good. The pieces were in place for a dynasty to begin, but for now, they were going through growing pains. The Fighting Irish would take full advantage of those in the first half.

The game started out pretty well for the Lions. They forced a three-and-out, then moved the ball right down the field. Receiver Jimmy Cefalo took a reverse 15 yards, and running back Steve Geise picked up the next first down on a couple of carries. Fullback Bob Torrey gained the team's next first down, before they were stopped just past the 10. Tony Capozzoli made a 26-yard field goal, and Penn State took an early 3–0 lead.

However, the whole game changed when Notre Dame running back Terry Eurick returned the ensuing kickoff 65 yards to the Penn State 35. Quarterback Rick Slager got a first down on a third-down sneak, then running back Al Hunter picked up another one on a fourth-down play. Hunter later scored from the 1, on a drive that took ten plays and a ton of time off the clock.

As the second quarter began, the Irish were on another drive. Hunter ran for 17 yards, and running back Vagas Ferguson ran for another one to the 27. Slager then found tight end Ken MacAfee for 17 yards, setting up first-and-goal. The Irish got as far as the 3, where they faced fourth-and-goal. Head coach Dan Devine chose to go for it, but Slager's pass for MacAfee fell incomplete.

Running back Mike Guman fumbled away a reception on Penn State's next drive, and defensive back Jim Browner recovered it for Notre Dame at the Lions 23. Slager threw to receiver Dan Kelleher for 12 yards, setting up another first-and-goal. The Irish couldn't punch it in again, but this time Devine went for the field goal. Kicker Dave Reeve made a 23-yard attempt to make it 10–3.

Penn State went three-and-out, and Notre Dame moved it right downfield again. They started at the 49 after a short punt, and a pass to MacAfee picked up 13 yards. Hunter ran it down to the 2, setting up first-and-goal. He then pounded it in to the end zone off right tackle, and the Fighting Irish went up by a score of 17–3.

On Penn State's next punt, defensive back Ted Burgmeier returned it all the way to the Penn State 13, but the return got called back on a clipping call. The teams exchanged punts again, and Penn State got called for fair catch interference on the next kick. Slager found Kelleher for a 26-yard gain to put the Irish in field goal range, then Reeve made a 23-yard kick to put Notre Dame up 20–3 at the half.

The wide lead by the Irish made the second half nothing more than a formality. Penn State had a long way to go, and they just couldn't mount a comeback. Fusina completed passes of 12 yards to Cefalo and 21 yards to receiver Rich Mauti, getting the Lions inside the 35. But on a fourth-down play, Fusina threw incomplete for tight end Mickey Shuler, and the Lions turned it over on downs.

Notre Dame drove it to the edge of field goal range, where Reeve missed a 55-yard field goal short. Fusina then led the Lions down the field again. A pass interference call gave the Lions one first down, then Geise ran for 12 yards and another one. Fusina passed to receiver Tom Donovan for 11 more yards, and the Lions reached the 10. But Fusina threw an interception to Browner, and the Lions still trailed 20–3 after three quarters.

About midway through the fourth quarter, Penn State finally got the break they needed. Linebacker Bruce Clark blocked a punt, and the Lions took over at the Notre Dame 8. Two plays later, fullback Matt Suhey caught a pass on the right side for a touchdown. Head coach Joe Paterno chose to go for two, but the play call was very unimaginative. It was a simple fullback dive by Torrey, who was stopped for no gain. The Lions still trailed, 20–9.

The Irish ran more time off the clock, but Penn State got the ball back at their own 12 with a slight chance at a comeback. Torrey ran for a first down to the 23, and Suhey got the next first down by inches. Suhey ran for ten more and caught a pass beyond midfield. Fusina threw to Shuler at the 40, and then ran the ball down to the 25. Torrey ran for nine more yards, and Penn State was in the red zone, threatening to score. But Burgmeier picked off Fusina's next pass, and the Irish ran out the clock. The Nittany Lions had come up short, 20–9.

Fusina threw for 118 yards and a touchdown but also two interceptions. The Lions outrushed the Irish, but Hunter was the leading rusher on the day with 102 yards and two touchdowns. Torrey led Penn State's rushers with 63 yards. Cefalo had a great game, catching five passes for 60 yards and rushing three times for 18 yards. The teams finished just one yard apart, but the key statistic was turnovers: three by Penn State, none by Notre Dame. The Nittany Lions finished the season out of the top 20 with a 7–5 record.

Box score[10]:

1976 Gator Bowl	1st	2nd	3rd	4th	Final
Notre Dame	7	13	0	0	20
Penn State	3	0	0	6	9

1st Quarter: PSU—Capozzoli 26 FG
    ND—Hunter 1 run (Reeve kick)
2nd Quarter: ND—Reeve 23 FG
    ND—Hunter 1 run (Reeve kick)
    ND—Reeve 23 FG
3rd Quarter: No Scoring
4th Quarter: PSU—Suhey 8 pass from Fusina (run failed)

1977 Season (10–1)

Penn State began the 1977 season at Giants Stadium trying to end the longest winning streak in the nation. That's right, the Rutgers Scarlet Knights, of all teams, came into this game with a 18-game winning streak.[1] In the first half, running backs Matt Suhey and Mike Guman each ran for two touchdowns, including a 51-yard score by Suhey. Quarterback Chuck Fusina threw a 31-yard touchdown pass to receiver Bob Bassett, and the Lions cruised to a 45–7 victory.[2]

Houston came to Beaver Stadium for the home opener. The stadium was a year away from being renovated to add more seats, so the crowd of over 62,500 was a stadium record. The Lions got off to a good start, with Guman running for a first-quarter touchdown, and Fusina adding a 29-yard pass to receiver Scott Fitzkee. Running back Ed Guthrie ran for a 14-yard score and caught a two-point pass from Fusina, putting away a 31–14 win.[3]

Against Maryland, Fusina came out firing in the second half, finding receiver Jimmy Cefalo for a 58-yard touchdown, and then going to Guman for a 20-yard score in a 27–9 victory.[4] Kentucky next came to Beaver Stadium, where the Lions got off to a 10–0 start thanks to a 75-yard punt return by Cefalo. Fusina threw a 29-yard touchdown pass to Guman, giving Penn State a 20–14 halftime lead, but Kentucky put up ten points in the third quarter to pull out a 24–20 upset.[5]

For Homecoming, Penn State scheduled Utah State as their opponent. Running back Steve Geise rushed for a five-yard touchdown. Defensive lineman Randy Sidler later intercepted a pass and returned it to the USU 17. Running back Booker Moore went in from two yards to give Penn State a 16–7 win.[6] Geise ran for two first-quarter touchdowns against Syracuse, and Fusina hit Bassett for a 12-yard touchdown. Syracuse clawed back from their 21-point deficit, scoring two fourth-quarter touchdowns to make it close, but the Lions escaped with a 31–24 victory.[7]

Against West Virginia, linebacker Matt Millen returned a blocked punt seven yards to open the scoring. Fusina threw a pair of touchdown passes, and Cefalo returned a punt 57 yards for a score, as the Lions waltzed to a 49–28 triumph.[8] Miami (Florida) proved to be an even bigger pushover. Fusina threw a 56-yard touchdown pass to Guthrie in the first quarter, and Suhey ran for three short touchdown runs in the second quarter. Fitzkee added a 72-yard reception off a Fusina pass, and the Lions won 49–7.[9]

The Lions then visited North Carolina State, where they had a back-and-forth battle. Fusina threw two touchdown passes and Suhey ran for a score to win it, 21–17. Along the way, Fusina set Penn State records for passing yards (315) and completions (22).[10] In their home finale, the Nittany Lions blew out Temple, 44–7. Linebacker Rick Donaldson returned a blocked punt 22 yards for a score in the first half, and Fusina threw three touchdown passes, two of them to Cefalo and one to Guthrie.[11]

The season finale came at Pitt Stadium. The special teams were key to this game. Kicker Matt Bahr kicked three field goals, and Guman returned a punt 52 yards. Penn State took a 15–7 lead into the final seconds, when Donaldson, Millen, and defensive end Joe Diange combined for a stop on the two-point try to seal the 15–13 victory.[12]

Fusina threw for 2,221 yards, the most in Penn State history, while tying the Nittany Lion record with 15 touchdown passes. The carries were equally split between Suhey and Geise; Suhey led the team with 638 rushing yards and eight touchdowns, while Geise added another 550 yards and five touchdowns. Shuler was the team's leading receiver with 33 catches for 600 yards; Cefalo added another 507 receiving yards and five touchdowns.[13]

Penn State finished the regular season ranked #8 in the Associated Press poll. That would have ordinarily given them a berth in one of the major bowls: the Orange, Sugar, or Cotton. The dominoes started to fall when Michigan defeated Ohio State in "The Game" to claim win the Big Ten and claim a spot in the Rose Bowl. SEC champion Alabama head coach Paul "Bear" Bryant then pushed for Ohio State as his team's opponent in the Sugar Bowl. Notre Dame came on strong at the end of the season, making them a no-brainer to be invited to the Cotton Bowl to face Southwest champion Texas.[14]

That left just one spot: a berth in the Orange Bowl to face Big 8 champion Oklahoma. But the Nittany Lions were hurt by the fact that they pushed their game against Pitt back a week. In the meantime, Arkansas blew out Southern Methodist 47–7 to move up to #6 in the rankings. The Orange Bowl then decided to invite Arkansas to play Oklahoma, while Pitt worked out a deal with the Gator Bowl.[15] Penn State was left in the lurch.

After the Nittany Lions beat Pitt, the up-and-coming Fiesta Bowl chose them to play against Western Athletic champion Arizona State. The Fiesta Bowl was at the time a big disappointment for Penn Staters; it paid out $100,000 less than even the Gator Bowl, and it was played in December and not the prestigious January 1 date.[16] But the reputation of the Fiesta Bowl was soon to change dramatically, and all because of the Nittany Lions themselves.

1977 Fiesta Bowl

#8 Penn State (10–1) vs. #15 Arizona State (9–2)
December 25, 1977, at Sun Devil Stadium in Tempe, Arizona

The Sun Devils had won the Western Athletic Conference in their final season as members of that league. In 1978, they and the Arizona Wildcats were moving from the WAC to the Pacific-8 Conference, which would become the Pac-10. Arizona State was playing in its fifth Fiesta Bowl, having won all four of their previous appearances.

Penn State got the ball first, and fullback Matt Suhey took the first handoff for four yards. Running back Steve Geise got a further two, before quarterback Chuck Fusina fired to tight end Mickey Shuler for a first down at the 33. Suhey took a draw for nine yards, and Geise took it for another first down. That was the way Penn State moved the ball; slowly, but surely. But after getting as far as the 45, the drive stalled with a couple of incompletions. Scott Fitzkee, both a receiver and the punter, kicked the ball 50 yards out of bounds down at the 5.

Arizona State quarterback Dennis Sproul completed his first pass to receiver Ron

Washington for 13 yards. He'd hit running back Newton Williams for four more, before firing incomplete on third down. The Sun Devils were forced to punt, but they never had a chance. Defensive end Bill Banks blocked the punt, and Joe Lally rushed in to pick it up and return it 21 yards for a touchdown. The Lions had the early 7–0 lead.

On ASU's first play of their next possession, Williams fumbled, having the ball knocked from his hands by defensive tackle Matt Millen. Linebacker Tom DePaso picked it up, and Penn State had great field position. Geise then touched the ball on six of the next eight plays, picking up two first downs and getting down to the 3. Fusina then went play action, and he fired to his left to fullback Bob Torrey for a touchdown. This was too easy; Penn State was up 14–0.

Sproul was injured on the next Arizona State drive, and backup Fred Mortensen had to come in for a few plays. After shaking off the injury, Sproul came back in, but he threw a long pass that was intercepted by defensive back Gary Petercuskie. Penn State would go three-and-out, though, and Sproul would start a new drive. He threw to receiver Chris DeFrance for 25, then kept it for eight more. After the change of sides for the second quarter, fullback Mike Harris ran for a pair of first downs to get to the 12. Two plays later, Sproul hit running back Arthur Lane for an 11-yard touchdown pass, cutting the Penn State lead to 14–7.

Things changed in Arizona State's favor, with Penn State going three-and-out after a sack by defensive tackle Bob Pfister. The Sun Devils got the ball back at the Penn State 44. Sproul found DeFrance for a first down at the 25, then he got a first down on a sneak after a pair of runs by Harris. It looked like ASU had first-and-goal at the 5 after a pass to DeFrance, but they got called for illegal motion. They settled for a 37-yard field goal attempt by Steve Hicks, but he missed it badly to the right.

Penn State nearly lost the ball on a Fusina fumble, but guard Eric Cunningham came up with a clutch recovery. Fusina then followed by throwing to Fitzkee for a first down at the 33. The Lions would be forced to punt, but Fitzkee at least got the ball out to the ASU 40. The Penn State defense forced a quick three-and-out. Receiver Jimmy Cefalo went back to return the punt, and he ripped off a long one. In fact, if not for punter Mark Jones making the tackle, he would have gone all the way. He returned it 67 yards down to the ASU 10, setting up a 23-yard field goal by kicker Matt Bahr to make it 17–7.

The Nittany Lions forced a three-and-out, but when they went for another punt block, they ran into Jones and got flagged for a penalty. It was a big one, as Sproul threw to Washington for 21 yards, then went to DeFrance to get down to the 13. He then found Washington open in the corner of the end zone, and Arizona State had pulled within 17–14 at halftime.

The offenses cooled down to start the third quarter. The first five drives of the second half all ended in punts, three by Arizona State and two by Penn State. But the field position game was tilting in Penn State's favor, especially after the third ASU punt which Cefalo fair caught at the 41. It took the Lions just four plays to score from there. Suhey and Geise alternated carries, with Suhey gaining 32 on one carry, and Geise taking it 18 yards into the end zone. The Lions went up 24–14 with his touchdown run.

On the kickoff, the ball bounced off an Arizona State player's foot, and defensive back Tom Wise recovered it for Penn State at the 44. The Lions wouldn't get a first down, but that was okay; head coach Joe Paterno was playing the field position game. After pinning Arizona State down deep, the Lions forced a three-and-out, and Cefalo fair caught the next punt at the ASU 43. Fusina took over from there, and although he hurt his hand on an incomplete pass, he came back in and found Cefalo for his first catch of the game at the 33. Geise ripped off a run down inside the 15, and Torrey got it down to the 7. On the first play of the fourth quarter, Suhey plowed in on the left side of the line for a three-yard touchdown, and Penn State took a 31–14 lead.

With a 17-point advantage and only 15 minutes to go, anyone would expect that the game was now over; however, it was only beginning. Things got wild in this final quarter, starting on Arizona State's next drive. Sproul threw to receiver John Jefferson for nine yards, and Harris picked up a first down. Sproul went to Jefferson again to get a first down at the 34, before keeping it on an option down to the 30. He then fired for the end zone to Washington, completing it for a 30-yard touchdown and cutting the deficit to ten points.

Torrey ripped off a 24-yard run to get near midfield, and Arizona State got called for a facemask penalty. Fusina fired to Cefalo for a first down at the 23, and Torrey further took it down to the 17. Geise came up short on a third-down run, so Bahr was back on to try a 32-yard field goal. He made the kick, and Penn State took a 34–21 lead.

The Nittany Lions got called for pass interference on a third-down pass, keeping Arizona State's next drive alive. Sproul then threw an interception to linebacker Rick Donaldson, but the Lions were called for pass interference again, and the drive kept going. Sproul ran it for a first down, then went to tight end Marshall Edwards for another first down at the 15. After an incompletion to the end zone, Edwards caught another pass down to the 2. Three plays later, running back George Perry pounded it in, and suddenly Arizona State was down by just six points.

With four minutes to play, Fusina gunned it to Cefalo on a third-down play to pick up a first down at the 44. Torrey then ripped off a 53-yard run down the middle of the field, getting all the way down to the 2. Suhey dived in for a touchdown, making it 40–28. Fusina's two-point conversion pass fell incomplete, but the Sun Devils were called for pass interference. Given a second chance, Geise took a pitch in for two points, and the Nittany Lions led 42–28 with 3:10 to go.

Sproul led a desperation drive for the Sun Devils, starting with a pair of passes to Jefferson for first downs. DeFrance hauled one in for a first down at the Penn State 32, and Edwards caught one at the 21. Facing third down a few plays later, Sproul hit Edwards down at the 3 with two minutes remaining. The Sun Devils would have another third down, but this time they couldn't convert. Sproul threw an interception to defensive back Joe Diminick, and the Lions had the ball inside their own 5. It appeared that it was all over.

But this wild fourth quarter wasn't quite over yet. After running the ball on three plays in a row, the Lions took the clock down to 20 seconds. With a 14-point lead, Paterno figured that the only hope Arizona State had was a blocked punt returned for a touchdown, an onside kick, and a Hail Mary. His idea was to take that possibility out of the equation, so he had Fitzkee take the punt snap and run out of his own end zone for a safety. That gave Arizona State two points, and they took the ball back after a fair catch at their own 40 with 14 seconds left. Sproul then threw a Hail Mary to DeFrance, who caught it down at the 24. The Sun Devils rushed downfield, trying to punch it in, but Sproul's final pass fell incomplete. The Nittany Lions could finally breathe; they had won it, 42–30.

After the wild and woolly fourth quarter, Penn State got the victory, while Sproul got the Most Outstanding Player award on offense. Millen was recognized as the Most Outstanding Player on defense, as he forced Arizona State's only fumble. Geise led in rushing with 111, and Torrey was right behind with 107. Suhey had 76 and two touchdowns. The passing offense was particularly inept in this game; Fusina's amazing season ended with a dud, as he had only 83 yards passing. It didn't matter, though; the running game was more than enough to carry the team.

Penn State had their first of many Fiesta Bowl victories. They finished #5 in the final Associated Press rankings, and #4 in the UPI coaches' poll. The only teams finishing higher than them were Cotton Bowl and national champion Notre Dame, Sugar Bowl champion Alabama, Orange Bowl champion Arkansas, and Cotton Bowl runner-up Texas. With so many players coming back, the Lions were hungry for their first national title in 1978.

Box score[17]:

1977 Fiesta Bowl	1st	2nd	3rd	4th	Final
Arizona State	0	14	0	16	30
Penn State	14	3	7	18	42

1st Quarter: PSU—Lally 21 blocked punt return (Bahr kick)
  PSU—Torrey 3 pass from Fusina (Bahr kick)
2nd Quarter: ASU—Lane 11 pass from Sproul (Hicks kick)
  PSU—Bahr 23 FG
  ASU—Washington 13 pass from Sproul (Hicks kick)
3rd Quarter: PSU—Geise 18 run (Bahr kick)
4th Quarter: PSU—Suhey 3 run (Bahr kick)
  ASU—Washington 30 pass from Sproul (Hicks kick)
  PSU—Bahr 32 FG
  ASU—Perry 1 run (Hicks kick)
  PSU—Suhey 2 run (Geise run)
  ASU–Safety

1978 Season (11–0)

To start this magical season, Penn State played Temple, who used an unusual strategy where they punted on third down for the majority of the game. The quick kicks kept getting the Lions into bad field position.[1] Kicker Matt Bahr made a game-winning 22-yard field goal to help Penn State escape with a 10–7 win.[2]

Against Rutgers, Penn State jumped out to a ten-point lead in the first quarter, and they led 13–3 at the half. Backup quarterback Dayle Tate went down with an injury, thus cementing Chuck Fusina as the leader of this team the rest of the way.[3] The Lions ended up winning 26–10, but it was not nearly as easy as the score made it look.[4]

The Lions went to Columbus next to take on the Buckeyes. Running back Matt Suhey ended up with 96 rushing yards on 25 attempts. Fusina completed half his passes for just over 150 yards.[5] Ohio State turned the ball over eight times, and Penn State came away with a 19–0 victory.[6] Bahr kicked another four field goals against Southern Methodist, all coming in the first half. Penn State rallied from a nine-point deficit with two second-half touchdowns, including a 16-yard pass from Fusina to receiver Scott Fitzkee, winning 26–21.[7]

There would be no such struggles the next week against Texas Christian. Running back Booker Moore ran for a nine-yard touchdown, and Penn State cruised to a 58–0 win.[8] The Lions made it back-to-back shutouts with a 30–0 win at Kentucky. Getting revenge on the one team who beat them a year before, Penn State got off to a 17–0 start in the first half. Fusina completed nine of his first 16 passes for 139 yards and a touchdown.[9]

Penn State found all sorts of ways to score against Syracuse. Fusina threw to Fitzkee for a 65-yard pass to set up a nine-yard catch by running back Mike Guman, putting the Lions up 21–9. Linebacker Mickey Urquhart then blocked a punt which defensive tackle Matt Millen recovered in the end zone for another touchdown. The Lions ended up winning 45–15, their third straight blowout win.[10]

At West Virginia, the Nittany Lions fell into a 14–0 hole, but special teams got them out of it. Defensive end Joe Lally blocked a punt, and Guman took back a punt 85 yards. Fusina threw a couple of touchdown passes in a 49–21 win.[11] Against Maryland, the Lions took a 13–3 lead as Bahr broke his brother Chris's record for most kicking points in school history. Fusina found receiver Tom Donovan for a 63-yard touchdown, and the Lions eased to a 27–3 victory.[12]

Bahr had his third four-field goal game of the season against North Carolina State, tying the NCAA record for the most field goals in a single season with 21. Suhey returned a punt 43 yards for a touchdown in the fourth quarter, giving the Lions a 19–10 win.

When #1-ranked Oklahoma fell to Nebraska 17–14, Penn State moved into the #1 spot in the Associated Press poll for the first time in school history.[13]

The Nittany Lions ended the season at home against #15 Pitt. They trailed 10–7 to the Panthers in the fourth quarter, when they faced a fourth-and-two situation at the Pitt 4. Guman took a toss and scored a touchdown, putting Penn State ahead by four. The Lions finished off the Panthers by a 17–10 score, and for the first time ever, the Nittany Lions would have the chance to be named national champions.[14]

But which bowl? The Orange Bowl looked like it would be Penn State's destination, as the Nebraska Cornhuskers were ranked #2. But when Nebraska lost to Missouri 35–31, the Orange Bowl was off the table. Alabama then beat Auburn 34–16 in the "Iron Bowl" to clinch the SEC title and a spot in the Sugar Bowl. Paterno jumped at the shot to play #2 Alabama for all the marbles, so Penn State and its Heisman runner-up Fusina[15] were headed to New Orleans for the Sugar Bowl.[16]

1979 Sugar Bowl Classic

#1 Penn State (11–0) vs. #2 Alabama (10–1)
January 1, 1979, at the Louisiana Superdome in New Orleans, Louisiana

This game is best known for the most famous goal-line stand in college football history. What gets lost and forgotten are all the other chances Penn State had, before and after they got stopped on the 1. Timeout mismanagement, having too many players on the field, and dropped interceptions were all involved in Penn State's failure to win its first national championship.

Alabama got the ball first and punted after one first down. Penn State took over deep in their own territory. Quarterback Chuck Fusina had the ball knocked from his hands by defensive lineman Curtis McGriff, but running back Mike Guman recovered. The Nittany Lions had to punt as well, and Alabama got the ball at the 44.

Quarterback Jeff Rutledge fired to fullback Steve Whitman, and he got about nine yards. He then pitched to running back Tony Nathan to pick up the first down. Running back Major Ogilvie got the ball as far as the 33, before the Alabama drive was stopped. Kicker Alan McElroy tried a 51-yard field goal, but it came up well short, and the game remained scoreless.

Fusina threw to receiver Bob Bassett for 18 yards to start the next series. Two plays later, he threw an interception to defensive back Murray Legg. That began a long line of fruitless possessions and punts. Throughout the rest of the first half, both teams punted the ball four times each, with Penn State having horrible field position and Alabama having great field position. Despite all of Penn State's struggles on offense, they were holding their own in a scoreless tie.

Late in the first half, Rutledge had a pass deflected and intercepted by linebacker Rich Milot. He returned it 55 yards to the Alabama 37, giving Penn State its best field position of the day. Defensive tackle Byron Braggs sacked Fusina, though, and the Lions were forced to punt. Scott Fitzkee's kick went into the end zone for a touchback.

There was just about a minute to go in the half. Alabama went with a simple handoff to Ogilvie, and head coach Joe Paterno called timeout. He wanted the ball back before the half. Rutledge threw a short pass to Nathan, and Paterno called another timeout with 49 seconds left. The Crimson Tide looked ready to just go into the locker room with no points. But on third down, Whitman got the first down, so head coach Paul "Bear" Bryant decided to speed things up. Nathan ripped off a long run down to the Penn State 37, and Alabama called timeout. Nathan took a pitch for seven more, and Bryant stopped the clock again. Rutledge then fired down the middle of the field to receiver Bruce Bolton for a 30-yard touchdown. Alabama went to the locker room with a 7–0 lead. Paterno had to be kicking himself for calling those timeouts, which led to the Tide scoring that touchdown.

The teams traded punts to start the second half, with Penn State missing out on a good opportunity when defensive back Karl McCoy dropped an interception. Fusina started his next drive with an interception to defensive back Jim Bob Harris, who returned it 22 yards but had most of it wiped out by a clipping call. Whitman ran for a first down, and the Tide got as far as the 19. After getting stopped, Bryant sent out McElroy to try a 40-yard field goal. He missed it wide to the right, and the lead remained at seven.

After another Penn State punt, defensive back Pete Harris made one of the biggest plays of the game for the Nittany Lions. He intercepted a Rutledge pass, setting up the Lions with great field position. Fusina then threw to Guman for 24 yards, and he got the ball down into the red zone. Two plays later, Fusina fired to the back of the end zone to Fitzkee, who got one foot in bounds with possession. His 17-yard touchdown had tied the game at seven.

The teams exchanged punts again, but it was what Alabama did with the punt that mattered. Running back Lou Ikner got some good blocks, and he took back Fitzkee's punt 62 yards down the left sideline to the Penn State 11. After runs by Rutledge and Nathan, Ogilvie took a pitch eight yards into the end zone for a touchdown to put Alabama up 14–7 after three quarters.

Again, both teams punted the ball, but this time the special teams miscue came from Alabama. Punting from the Penn State 40, their kick only went nine yards, giving Penn State great field position. Running back Booker Moore ran for a first down at the 46, and Fusina found Guman for a first down at the Alabama 47. He then fired to tight end Brad Scovill for a first down at the 29. The Lions looked ready to tie the game, but Fusina's pass for the corner of the end zone was intercepted by defensive back Don McNeal.

The Lions got a big break when Rutledge made a bad pitch on an option play. The ball came loose, and defensive end Joe Lally recovered it at the Alabama 19. Suhey immediately got the ball to the 8 on a run up the middle, and Guman then took it to the 6. On second down, Fusina gunned it to Fitzkee, who would have had the touchdown if he simply had reached the ball over the goal line. Instead, Fitzkee gripped the ball tight as McNeal hit him out of bounds inches shy of the goal line.

It was third down and goal from inside the 1. Penn State's running game had been terrible all day long. In fact, they'd finish the game with a grand total of 19 yards rushing. With two cracks at the end zone from a yard away, a play action pass or a bootleg or even an option should have been on the table. But this was not Paterno's greatest game coaching. He had called timeouts at the wrong time before, and now he got super conservative on his play calls. For the third-down play, Suhey tried diving over the pile, but he was stopped short. Penn State called timeout to talk it over, and Paterno wasn't sending on kicker Matt Bahr. He called for a run by Guman right up the gut. Linebacker Barry Krauss stopped Guman in his tracks, and he never had a chance at crossing the goal line. The Lions turned the ball over on downs.

With six minutes to go, the Lions forced a three-and-out, and they figured to get excellent field position. But on the punt play, Penn State somehow had 12 men on the field. In those days, the "too many men" penalty was five yards if you had someone rushing to get off the field, but 15 yards if no one tried to get off. The Lions got charged with the latter, and the Tide got a big first down. They'd run the clock down to three minutes to play before punting it back to Penn State.

Somehow, despite getting totally dominated all game long, the Nittany Lions still had a chance to come away with a tie (or even a win). To start their fateful drive, they got called for a delay of game. Fusina made up for it with a pass to Fitzkee for a first down to the 31. He then threw short to Guman for six yards, before going back to Guman a couple plays later for the first down. Guman then caught a third pass in four plays, this one for 14 yards. Scovill caught one at the Alabama 41, setting up second-and-seven with just under two minutes left.

This was it. The Lions needed to pick up a first down or it was curtains on their national title hopes. Fusina threw it away on second down. On third down, he threw a bomb for Scovill in the end zone, but he overshot him and threw it too far. That brought up fourth down. Fusina aimed for receiver Bob Bassett, but defensive back Murray Legg broke up the pass, and the Lions turned it over on downs.

Penn State got the ball back at their own 32 with 12 seconds left, but Fusina's desperation pass was intercepted by defensive back Mike Clements. The Crimson Tide had won the game, 14–7. Krauss was named Most Valuable Player for his key stop on fourth-and-goal. Alabama had outgained Penn State by over 100 yards, but the Lions were in it until the bitter end.

The Nittany Lions fell to #4 in the final Associated Press poll rankings. Alabama leapfrogged them to reach #1 in the AP poll, but Rose Bowl champion USC was ranked #1 in the coaches' poll. (This was because USC had beaten Alabama during the regular season.) Penn State got no piece of the split national championship, but they had gotten a taste of what it was like to be #1. The next time Paterno had a shot at winning it all, he wouldn't make the same mistakes. The Nittany Lions were just a few years away.

Box score[17]:

1979 Sugar Bowl	1st	2nd	3rd	4th	Final
Penn State	0	0	7	0	7
Alabama	0	7	7	0	14

1st Quarter: No Scoring
2nd Quarter: ALA—Bolton 30 pass from Rutledge (McElroy kick)
3rd Quarter: PSU—Fitzkee 17 pass from Fusina (Bahr kick)
    ALA—Ogilvie 8 run (McElroy kick)
4th Quarter: No Scoring

1979 Season (7–4)

To start the season, freshman running back Curt Warner ran for 100 yards, returned kickoffs for 109 yards, and caught passes for 71 more against Rutgers, scoring three touchdowns. The Nittany Lions picked up two safeties in the second half on their way to a 45–10 win.[1] The Texas A&M Aggies came to Beaver Stadium next, nursing an 0–2 start to their season. Despite a touchdown run by running back Booker Moore and a touchdown catch by running back Matt Suhey in the fourth quarter, the Aggies beat Penn State 27–14. It was head coach Joe Paterno's first-ever loss to a Southwest Conference team.[2]

At Nebraska, the Lions got off to a 14–0 lead in the first quarter. Quarterback Dayle Tate threw a 19-yard touchdown pass to tight end Brad Scovill, and defensive back Tom Wise took back an interception 30 yards for a score. Then everything fell apart, with the Nebraska offense roaring to 28 second-quarter points. Penn State lost by a 42–17 margin.[3]

The Lions got off to a 17–0 halftime lead at Maryland. Suhey ran for a 14-yard touchdown in the first quarter. Moore added two short scoring runs in the second and third quarters, and Penn State went on to win, 27–7.[4] Suhey had the game of his life at Homecoming against Army. He rushed for 225 yards, the fourth-most in Penn State history. He scored on 17- and 61-yard runs, while Moore ran for 103 yards and a touchdown of his own. That gave Penn State two 100-yard rushers for the first time since the 1977 Fiesta Bowl, as the Lions put up 324 total rushing yards. The Lions won 24–3, allowing fewer than 200 total yards.[5]

The Nittany Lions next went to Giants Stadium to take on Syracuse. The Orange decided that they wouldn't let Suhey or Moore beat them, so they loaded up the box to try to contain the Penn State rushing attack. Tate completed 14 of his 18 attempts for 199 yards and three touchdowns, and the Lions won, 35–7.[6]

The Moore-Suhey combo came together for another big performance against West Virginia. Moore rushed for 166 yards and three touchdowns, including a 52-yard run in the second quarter. Suhey added another 124 yards. The Lions won it 31–6, and that poor 1–2 start had turned into a 5–2 record.[7]

But freshman quarterback Jim Kelly and the Miami Hurricanes came into Beaver Stadium next, and they took no prisoners. Kelly threw for 280 yards and three touchdowns, absolutely torching the Penn State defense. They beat the Lions 26–10.[8] Against North Carolina State, the Penn State offense couldn't get in the end zone. But kicker Herb Menhardt kicked three field goals, including a 54-yarder on the final play of the game, to beat N.C. State 9–7.[9]

Menhardt kicked three more field goals against Temple, on a day when Tate was injured early. Frank Rocco came on to replace him, throwing for 54 yards but keeping the ball away from the Owls. The Lions rushed for 270 yards, and Rocco had 60 of those. Suhey rushed for 87 yards and two touchdowns, as Penn State beat the Owls 22–7.[10]

What had been a disappointing season only became more so when Penn State allowed Pitt to come to Beaver Stadium and beat them 29–14. Suhey ran for a 65-yard touchdown in the first quarter, before the avalanche of Pitt scores began. Pitt quarterback Dan Marino threw a 50-yard touchdown pass in the fourth quarter, and Penn State freshman quarterback Jeff Hostetler was unable to lead the Lions back.[11]

Tate had a quiet year passing, throwing for 1,179 yards and eight touchdowns along with 11 interceptions. Scovill was the leading receiver with just 26 catches for 331 yards and three touchdowns. The Nittany Lions' bread-and-butter was the running game. Suhey led the team with 973 yards on the ground. Moore put up 555 and led in rushing touchdowns with nine. Warner rushed for 391 yards, caught ten passes, and put up nearly 500 kickoff return yards. His story was just beginning.[12]

The top eight teams were in the major bowls (Rose, Sugar, Orange, and Cotton), and fierce rival #10 Pitt earned a spot in the steadily improving Fiesta Bowl. The Sun Bowl matched two top-13 teams, while #9 Brigham Young went to the Holiday Bowl. With little choice left, Penn State jumped at the shot to face #15 Tulane in Memphis for the Liberty Bowl. The Lions would be slight favorites over the Green Wave, who were in their first bowl since the 1973 Bluebonnet Bowl.[13]

1979 Liberty Bowl

Penn State (7–4) vs. #15 Tulane (9–2)
December 22, 1979, at the Liberty Bowl in Memphis, Tennessee

If a berth in the Liberty Bowl was a disappointment, there was an even bigger letdown by the Nittany Lions offense in this game. They simply failed to show up in Memphis. The defense brought their A-game, as did kicker Herb Menhardt. But neither team managed to score a touchdown in this game, which said a lot about Penn State's injury-ravaged defense, and even more about their offense.

Tulane got the ball first and went three-and-out. Fullback Matt Suhey went back to catch the punt, but he muffed it, and Tulane recovered at the Penn State 38. Quarterback Roch Hontas simply had nowhere to go against the mighty Penn State defense. He was sacked by defensive end Larry Kubin on third down, and the Green Wave had to punt. Defensive tackle Leo Wisniewski blocked the punt, and lineman Greg Jones recovered it at the Tulane 23. But Penn State got nothing out of it, as Suhey fumbled for a second time.

Neither team scored for the remainder of the first quarter, and to be honest, neither team got even close to doing so. As the second quarter began, Suhey looked to make amends for his fumbles. He first ran for a first down to the 28, then he took off on a 30-yard run. He and running back Booker Moore split carries, and along with quarterback Frank Rocco, they picked up a pair of first downs. Rocco got sacked on third down by linebackers Marty Wetzel and Jeff Roberts, so Menhardt came on to try a field goal. He made his 33-yard attempt, and Penn State led 3–0.

Kubin picked up two sacks in three plays, and Tulane punted again. This time, running back Curt Warner provided a spark. He ran for a first down to the 38, and he got some more yards on a couple more carries. Rocco threw to tight end Brad Scovill for a first down, and Suhey took off on a 25-yard run. The Lions got as far as the 10 before having to settle for another field goal attempt. Menhardt converted his 27-yard try, and the Nittany Lions led 6–0.

The Penn State defense forced another quick three-and-out, and the offense got the ball back before the half. Suhey ran for five yards to the 48, and Rocco found Scovill down at the 33 with very little time left. He threw incomplete on the next play, so Paterno called on the kick team. Menhardt's 50-yard attempt fell far short and to the right, keeping the Lions' lead at just six at the half.

So far, the Penn State offense had not been great, but you couldn't argue they were playing bad. However, in the second half, they became completely inept, starting with their first series, where Suhey was stopped on a fourth-down run shy of the first down. Fortunately, the Tulane offense wasn't going anywhere. When Hontas completed a pass to receiver Darrel Griffin, it was the first time Tulane got a first down since the first quarter. They and the Lions continued to play a field position game, and the rest of the third quarter was all punts. Penn State entered the final quarter with no offense whatsoever, but at least a six-point lead.

Hontas finally got a drive going in the beginning of the fourth quarter. He threw to receiver Alton Alexis for 17 yards, then found him again at midfield. His next two passes went to tight end Rodney Holman, who got two first downs to the Penn State 25. He then got the ball to Alexis, and the Green Wave had first-and-goal at the 9. But Penn State linebacker Lance Mehl came up with a clutch sack, forcing a field goal. Kicker Ed Murray made a 26-yard attempt to cut the deficit to three points.

Rocco got a first down on a pass to receiver Tom Donovan, and Warner took a run across the midfield stripe for another first down. However, Rocco's next pass was intercepted by defensive back Nolan Gallo. The Green Wave couldn't score off the turnover, but they managed to change field position, and they got the ball after an exchange of punts at the Penn State 46.

Hontas fired to running back Terry Harris, who took the ball all the way down to the Penn State 21. However, Tulane was called for holding on the play. Hontas made up for it, throwing to Griffin for 21 yards, then hitting receiver Marcus Anderson for a first down at the Penn State 33. He further moved the ball closer to the goal line, finding Holman for a first down at the 21, and completing to Griffin for another new set of downs at the 8. The Penn State defense held strong there, keeping Tulane out of the end zone. Murray came back out and kicked a 26-yard field goal, so with 2:40 left in the game, the score was tied at six apiece.

The Tulane kickoff trickled down the sideline and went into the end zone for a touchback. Penn State had one last chance to win the game with a drive that could break the tie. Warner ran for eight yards, and Suhey picked up a first down. Moore ran for another first down at the 42, then Rocco threw to Scovill for four more yards. Warner got the ball to midfield, but the Lions now faced third down with about a minute to play.

As Hontas was being announced as Liberty Bowl MVP, Paterno threw a wrench into his celebration by calling a trick play. He had Rocco pitch to running back Joel Coles to the left side. Coles then stopped and fired a pass downfield. It was the old halfback option play! Coles found a wide-open Donovan for a huge gain. He wasn't tackled until he reached the Tulane 11. Warner and Suhey ran the ball a couple of times to get down to the 3, then Menhardt converted a 20-yard field goal to win the game. Yes, it was ugly, but Penn State had won it, 9–6.

Suhey ran for 112 yards over the course of the game, making up for his two early fumbles. Rocco had a rough go at it, completing only half of his ten passes for 56 yards and getting picked off twice. But the Lions defense had an outstanding game, giving up just 202 total yards of offense. That included minus-eight yards rushing. Tulane only mustered ten first downs. Penn State's 8–4 season may have been disappointing, but they still finished ranked #20 in the final Associated Press poll.

Box score[14]:

1979 Liberty Bowl	*1st*	*2nd*	*3rd*	*4th*	*Final*
Penn State	0	6	0	3	9
Tulane	0	0	0	6	6

1st Quarter: No Scoring
2nd Quarter: PSU—Menhardt 33 FG
   PSU—Menhardt 27 FG
3rd Quarter: No Scoring
4th Quarter: TUL—Murray 26 FG
   TUL—Murray 26 FG
   PSU—Menhardt 20 FG

1980 Season (9–2)

Penn State opened against Colgate, where running back Curt Warner dominated. He rushed for two touchdowns in the first quarter, then returned a kickoff 89 yards for a touchdown in the second. By the end of the game, he had 149 rushing yards on only ten attempts. The Lions won this one easily, 54–10.[1]

At Texas A&M, Lions ran the ball 63 times for 277 yards, including 79 by Warner and 62 by Booker Moore. The Lions blocked a punt out of the end zone in the second quarter, going on to win 25–9.[2] Nebraska then came to Beaver Stadium and completely shut down the Nittany offense. The Lions managed just one touchdown, and quarterback Todd Blackledge threw three interceptions while completing just six passes. The Cornhuskers, meanwhile, pounded the ball for 287 yards rushing, beating Penn State 21–7.[3]

Penn State played Missouri for the first time since their Orange Bowl meeting. The Nittany Lions turned the ball over five times, while forcing four from the Missouri offense. In the fourth quarter, Blackledge took an option play off the left side for a 43-yard touchdown to seal a 29–21 victory.[4]

The Lions piled up 293 rushing yards at Maryland, making up for an impotent passing game. Moore ran for a 55-yard touchdown, and Blackledge threw the go-ahead touchdown pass to receiver Kenny Jackson in a 24–10 win.[5] Against Syracuse, the Nittany Lions didn't allow any offensive points. Warner ran for a three-yard touchdown in the first half as part of his 76 rushing yards, and Moore ran for 100 yards, and the Lions pulled away for a 24–7 win.[6]

Warner returned a kickoff 88 yards for a touchdown against West Virginia. The Lions held on to win, 20–15, keeping head coach Joe Paterno perfect against the Mountaineers.[7] The offense was firing on all cylinders against Miami, rushing for 283 yards and throwing for 176 more. One hundred thirty of those passing yards came from Blackledge, while running back Joel Coles threw an option pass to Jackson for a 25-yard touchdown. Warner ran for 146 yards, and the defense forced five turnovers. Blackledge's 25-yard pass to tight end Vyto Kab put away a 27–12 win.[8]

North Carolina State continued to provide exciting games against Penn State in 1980. The Nittany Lions led 14–0 after the first quarter, with Moore rushing for a touchdown and Blackledge throwing a 39-yard scoring pass to Jackson. Coles rushed for 151 yards on only 12 carries, as Penn State won, 21–13.[9]

Blackledge struggled in the first half against Temple, fumbling a pair of times and throwing an interception. In came Hostetler to save the day. He ran for two touchdowns and passed for 111 yards, completing 70 percent of his passes. His performance turned a 12–7 lead into a 50–7 rout.[10]

The trip to Arizona would be a bit bittersweet, however, as the #5 Nittany Lions lost a close game to the #4 Pitt Panthers in their season finale at Beaver Stadium. Both defenses played well, but the Panthers played just a tad better. Trailing 14–3 in the third quarter, Blackledge hit Jackson for a 13-yard touchdown, but the Lions missed the two-point conversion. On the final drive of the game, with a chance to win it, Blackledge threw an interception to defensive back Carlton Williamson, and the Lions lost 14–9 to Pitt.[11]

Blackledge led the team in passing with 1,037 yards and seven touchdowns. Disappointed by his lack of playing time, Hostetler—who threw for 247 yards and accounted for four touchdowns—transferred to West Virginia. Rocco, last year's starter in the Liberty Bowl, completed just one pass in 1980. After the musical chairs at quarterbacks in 1980, Blackledge would be firmly entrenched as starter in 1981.[12]

Warner rushed for 922 yards and six touchdowns, while also catching 13 passes and returning two kicks for touchdowns. Moore was second in rushing with 707 yards and four touchdowns. Coles added another 406 yards and a score. Jackson ended up the team's leading receiver with 21 catches for 386 yards and five touchdowns. This year's offense wasn't spectacular, but it was sowing seeds for a bigger and better offense in the years to come.[13]

When it came to the big bowls, the Sugar Bowl took #7 Notre Dame as Southeastern Conference champion #1 Georgia's opponent. The Orange Bowl snatched up #2 Florida State to play Big Eight champion #4 Oklahoma. The Cotton Bowl went with #9 Alabama to go up against Southwest Conference champion Baylor. That left only a handful of spots in big bowls, namely the Gator, Sun, and Fiesta. With the Sun taking #8 Nebraska and the Gator taking #3 Pitt, Penn State was headed back to the Fiesta Bowl for the second time in four years. This time, though, they'd be facing a big-time opponent in #11 Ohio State. It may have still been a December bowl, but the Fiesta was fast closing in on the other major bowls, with this major matchup continuing to propel them toward the top.[14]

1980 Fiesta Bowl

#10 Penn State (9–2) vs. #11 Ohio State (9–2)
December 26, 1980, at Sun Devil Stadium in Tempe, Arizona

The matchup looks odd on paper, Penn State vs. Ohio State in a bowl game. Of course, at the time, Penn State was an independent, so this wasn't an all-Big Ten matchup. They had played each other seven times coming into Fiesta Bowl X, six of those coming in Columbus, where Penn State was 5–1. In all those meetings, only twice did Penn State reach the 20-point plateau, and Ohio State never did. The 1980 Fiesta Bowl would thus be a scoring bonanza for these clubs.

Ohio State went three-and-out to start the game. Penn State running back Curt Warner took the first handoff and burst down the middle for 64 yards and a touchdown, not even two minutes into the game. The Nittany Lions drive lasted just 11 seconds, and they took a 7–0 lead very early. The Buckeyes didn't flinch. Running back Calvin Murray ran for 26 yards, then quarterback Art Schlichter threw a pair of passes for first downs to receiver Gary Williams. Murray took another handoff for a first down to the 19, before Penn State defensive tackle came up with a sack. Schlichter immediately bounced back with a pass into the end zone to receiver Doug Donley for a 23-yard touchdown. Kicker

Vlade Janakievski missed the extra point wide left, but the Buckeyes had at least pulled within one.

Penn State quarterback Todd Blackledge scrambled for a pair of first downs on the next drive. After getting to the Ohio State 35, the drive stalled, and punter Ralph Giacomarro put it into the end zone for a touchback, only 15 net yards. The Buckeyes had their next series end on an offensive pass interference call, which carried loss of down in those days. Penn State got a first down on a 12-yard run by fullback Mike Meade, but they had to punt a second time, down to the Ohio State 14.

Schlichter fired to Williams for a 23-yard gain, then the Bucks lost ten yards on a fumble which running back Victor Langley alertly fell on. Schlichter got all the yards back and then some with a 21-yard throw to Williams. But on the first play of the second quarter, linebacker Ed Pryts picked Schlichter off, returning the interception to the Ohio State 44.

Penn State went three-and-out on its next two possessions, wiping out any gains from their good field position. Ohio State took over after the second of those two punts at their own 16. They got downfield quickly, with Williams catching one at the 25, and Schlichter picking up the first down on a run. Schlichter then threw to running back Jim Gayle for nine yards and to Donley for another 24. He ran for six on the next play, before firing a 33-yard touchdown pass to Williams. The Buckeyes failed to get two points when Case forced a fumble on the conversion try, but they still took a 12–7 lead.

Buckeyes defensive back Todd Bell forced a fumble by fullback Booker Moore, and linebacker Ben Lee recovered. Schlichter then threw to Williams for seven yards, before running for 13 more. He then found his fast target Donley for a 36-yard gain to the 21. On the next third down, he yet again went to Donley, this time 19 yards for a touchdown. This time Ohio State head coach Earle Bruce opted for the kick, and backup kicker Bob Atha, who was on for an injured Janakievski, made the extra point to go up 19–7.

After a sack by linebacker John Epitropoulos, the Nittany Lions faced third-and-long. Blackledge converted it, however, with a 13-yard pass to tight end Brad Scovill. He then fired to receiver Kevin Baugh for 17 more yards, as the clock hit one minute to go in the first half. Meade took the ball to the Ohio State 45, then Warner ran for 17 more yards. After three incompletions, head coach Joe Paterno sent out the kick team. But it was a fake! Kicker Herb Menhardt stood all alone, while backup quarterback Jeff Hostetler took the snap from a bizarre formation. He ran for a first down to the 16. Hostetler's trick play set up Menhardt for an easier field goal, from 38 yards, which he made. The Lions went to halftime trailing 19–10.

Penn State started the second half with the ball at their 25. Blackledge threw a third-down pass to Baugh over the middle for a big gain to the Ohio State 38. He then found tight end Mike McCloskey for 21 more yards. Warner made a spin move for seven yards, then running back Jon Williams got a first down at the 6. Two plays later, Blackledge ran a bootleg off the right side for a three-yard touchdown, and Penn State pulled within two.

The Nittany Lions forced a three-and-out and got the ball back at their own 44. On second down, they ran a reverse to Warner, who picked up a first down at the OSU 45. Moore took the next run for seven, before running back Joel Coles bounced it outside for a pickup of nine yards. The drive ended when Blackledge was sacked by linebacker Marcus Malek. Menhardt then had his field goal attempt blocked by defensive back Vince Skillings.

Ohio State punted on their next two possessions, the second one after consecutive sacks by defensive tackle Pete Kugler and linebacker Matt Bradley. Williams returned that second punt to the Ohio State 37. Blackledge then found Scovill wide open in the middle of the field for a 26-yard gain. Two plays later, Williams ran it in for a four-yard touchdown, and Penn State was back on top, 24–19.

Now the Buckeyes needed a drive to take back the lead. Gayle ran for a first down, and fullback Tim Spencer ran for nine more. Gayle got the next first down, before Murray broke off a 14-yard run to the outside. Schlichter scrambled for another six, then dumped the ball off to Gayle for a first down. Case picked up a sack of Schlichter on second down, so when Schlichter found Gayle for 15, he was still short of the first down. Bruce called timeout to talk it over, then he had the offense go out on fourth-and-three instead of the field goal team. The play ended up as a total disaster when Schlichter couldn't escape the oncoming rush, and defensive lineman Greg Jones sacked him for a loss of 20.

Penn State now had the chance to put things away. Warner spun for a first down to the 43, and more time ticked off the clock. On a third down, Blackledge went to Scovill but short of the first down. After calling timeout, Paterno sent out the offense to go for it on fourth down. He ran a toss to Williams, and he was stopped for a loss, giving the Buckeyes great field position.

But the Penn State defense forced a quick three-and-out, and they got the ball back after a punt with four minutes to play. A few plays later, the Buckeyes sacked Blackledge, only to have the play called back on a facemask penalty, offsetting a Penn State holding call. The Lions ran the clock down to two minutes, at which point Coles broke into the open field for 34 yards. The Buckeyes used their final timeout after the next run. Two plays later, Moore escaped into the open field and couldn't be caught. He scored a 37-yard touchdown, sealing the 31–19 win for Penn State.

Warner ran for 155 yards, a Penn State bowl record at the time. He was named Outstanding Offensive Player of the Game. Case, who was in the backfield all day long, got named Outstanding Defensive Player as well as winning the Sportsmanship Award.[15] Blackledge only completed eight passes, but they went for 117 yards, and he also ran for a touchdown.

Penn State finished the season ranked #8 in the Associated Press poll, but ranked six spots behind archrival Pitt. For the Nittany Lions to reach the big time, they needed to knock out Pitt and keep them down. That would be the theme of a very promising 1981 season.

Box score[16]:

1980 Fiesta Bowl	1st	2nd	3rd	4th	Final
Ohio State	6	13	0	0	19
Penn State	7	3	7	14	31

1st Quarter: PSU—Warner 64 run (Menhardt kick)
    OSU—Donley 23 pass from Schlichter (kick missed)
2nd Quarter: OSU—Williams 33 pass from Schlichter (run failed)
    OSU—Donley 19 pass from Schlichter (Atha kick)
    PSU—Menhardt 38 FG
3rd Quarter: PSU—Blackledge 3 run (Menhardt kick)
4th Quarter: PSU—Williams 4 run (Menhardt kick)
    PSU—Moore 37 run (Menhardt kick)

1981 Season (9–2)

The Nittany Lions opened up the 1981 season with a blowout win over Cincinnati. Running back Curt Warner ran for three touchdowns in the first half on his way to a 122-yard game. The Lions never let up, scoring at least ten points in every quarter, and going on to a 52–0 victory.[1] The next week, down a point at Nebraska, quarterback Todd Blackledge threw a 33-yard touchdown pass to receiver Kenny Jackson. Blackledge later led his team on a 61-yard scoring drive capped off by a two-yard touchdown run by Coles, helping the Lions win, 30–24.[2]

The Lions came back home to dominate Temple. Warner ran for two more touchdowns in the first half, as he ran for 117 yards. Blackledge ran for a one-yard touchdown and threw a five-yard scoring pass to Jackson. The Penn State offense outgained the Owls by over 100 yards, while forcing three turnovers in a 30–0 win.[3] For Homecoming, Penn State hosted the Boston College Eagles. Warner ran for a touchdown in the first quarter and two touchdowns overall for the third time in four games. Blackledge threw a 39-yard touchdown pass to Jackson, and the Nittany Lions roared out to a 24–0 lead, going on to win 38–7.[4]

Warner had an unbelievable game against Syracuse. He ran the ball 26 times for 256 yards, breaking a 70-year-old school record. He reached 341 all-purpose yards, another Penn State record. All of that obscured the fact that Blackledge also had a great game, totaling three touchdowns. The Nittany Lions beat Syracuse 41–16 to improve to 5–0.[5]

Against West Virginia, Warner would get zero yards, as he pulled his hamstring before the game and couldn't play. Running back Jon Williams took his place and ran for 140 yards and a first-half touchdown. Blackledge threw for 118 yards and an 11-yard touchdown to Jackson in a 30–7 win.[6] But Miami was a completely different animal. The #1-ranked Nittany Lions fell behind 17–0, before Blackledge led a furious comeback. He threw a 13-yard touchdown pass to McCloskey and a screen pass to Williams for a score, but the Lions turned the ball over on both of their final two possessions, and they lost, 17–14.[7]

Trailing North Carolina State 9–7 in the third quarter, head coach Joe Paterno called for a fake punt. Ken Kelley, who was lined up as the punt protector, took a direct snap and threw to Harry Hamilton, who went 51 yards for a touchdown. The special teams came up big again on the next series, when defensive back Giuseppe Harris blocked a punt out of the end zone for a safety. The Lions went on to win 22–15, staying in the national title race at 7–1.[8]

Beaver Stadium was packed to the tune of over 85,000 fans, a new Penn State home record. But the blue-and-white faithful had nothing to cheer about in the first half, as the Lions eventually lost 31–16.[9] Penn State then took on Notre Dame. In the fourth quarter, trailing by four, defensive tackle Greg Gattuso picked off a pass deep in Penn State territory. Blackledge then led the Lions on an 82-yard drive for the game-winning touchdown, which he snuck in from a yard away to win it 24–21.[10]

The next game was one of the most famous ever in the Penn State–Pitt rivalry. The Panthers were ranked #1 in the nation, meaning that a victory would give them the chance to win the national championship in their Sugar Bowl game against Georgia. After quarterback Dan Marino threw two first-half touchdown passes to receiver Dwight Collins, it looked like they were well on their way to doing so, with a 14–0 lead. But after that, it was all Penn State. Blackledge threw for 262 yards and two touchdowns, while also running for an eight-yard score. Jackson caught five passes for a school-record 158 yards and two scores. Warner rushed for 104 yards. The Lions forced seven turnovers, including a fumble recovery in the end zone by defensive lineman Sean Farrell, and a 91-yard interception return for a score by defensive back Mark Robinson. It was a crushing defeat for Pitt, who has never had a chance at the national title since. The Nittany Lions emerged from Pittsburgh with a 48–14 victory, their first win over a #1-ranked team since 1964 (vs. Ohio State).[11]

Warner rushed for over 1,000 yards despite his injuries, scoring eight touchdowns. Williams was a solid second option, running for 667 yards and six touchdowns of his own. Fullback Mike Meade ran for 475 yards and five scores, while fellow fullback Tom Barr ran for 157 yards on 29 carries. Blackledge may have thrown only 12 touchdowns as opposed to 14 interceptions, but he passed for over 1,500 yards, and also ran for five touchdowns. His favorite receiver was Gregg Garrity, who caught 23 passes for 415 yards. Jackson was the home-run threat, going for 440 yards and six touchdowns on his 19 catches. McCloskey added another 308 yards and three touchdowns.[12]

Again, though, the Nittany Lions were left out of the three biggest bowls (Orange, Sugar, and Cotton, with the Rose being off-limits to independents). The Orange Bowl selected #1 Clemson as the opponent to automatic qualifier Big Eight champion Nebraska. The Sugar Bowl went with one-loss Pitt to play Georgia, who qualified as SEC champion. And the Cotton Bowl took 9–1–1 Alabama to play against its automatic qualifier, Southwest champion Texas.

But the Nittany Lions wouldn't be left out of the New Year's Day picture. For the first time, the Fiesta Bowl was held on January 1. They selected the two highest-ranked eligible teams remaining, #7 Penn State and #8 USC. The Fiesta Bowl Board of Directors predicted that this game would propel their game into the big-time, and they were right. In 1986, it would host its first national championship game. Early in the next decade, the Fiesta Bowl would supplant the Cotton Bowl as the fourth bowl in the "Big Four." And it would also get to host the first Bowl Championship Series national championship game. Penn State was a big part of helping the Fiesta Bowl make that leap, starting on January 1, 1982.[13]

1982 Fiesta Bowl

#7 Penn State (9–2) vs. #8 USC (9–2)
January 1, 1982, at Sun Devil Stadium in Tempe, Arizona

Penn State had not played USC since the infamous 1923 Rose Bowl where the two head coaches almost came to blows. USC running back Marcus Allen won the Heisman

Trophy in 1981 by rushing for an NCAA-record 2,342 yards and 22 touchdowns. He set 12 records this season, as the Trojans averaged just a hair under 300 yards rushing per game as a team.[14]

But in this game, he lost control of the ball on the very first play, without even being hit. Defensive back Roger Jackson came up with the loose ball for Penn State. After an incompletion, quarterback Todd Blackledge handed off to running back Curt Warner, who repeated his feat from a year ago of scoring on his first carry in the Fiesta Bowl. He went 17 yards for a touchdown, and Penn State took the early 7–0 lead.

Allen finally got in gear on the next drive, rushing for 19 yards, and another first down after that. But quarterback John Mazur threw to running back Todd Spencer short of the first down, and the Trojans had to punt. The next two possessions both ended in turnovers. First, Warner fumbled, and defensive back Joey Browner recovered for USC. On the very next play, Mazur threw long into double coverage, and defensive back Mark Robinson came down with the ball. He returned it 31 yards.

Warner then went down with a temporary injury, and he had to come out. Running back Jon Williams made up for his absence by catching a screen and going for a first down. Warner came back in and ran it to the USC 39. Blackledge then threw a dangerous pass that his tight end Vyto Kab came down with for 29 yards. That set up a 36-yard field goal attempt for kicker Brian Franco, but he missed it wide left.

Allen ran for seven yards on first down, then caught a pass for another 15. The Trojans ended up having to punt, but they pinned Penn State down at their own 9. Three plays later, facing third-and-long, Blackledge made a huge mistake, throwing an interception to linebacker Chip Banks. He returned it 20 yards for a touchdown, and the Trojans tied it at seven at the end of the first quarter.

Each team punted on their next possession. Penn State took over at their own 30 after USC's punt. Fullback Mike Meade plowed up the middle for 12 yards. Warner then caught a pass and took a carry to get to the 48. That set up the play action. Blackledge used a great play fake to throw a bomb to receiver Gregg Garrity for a 52-yard touchdown. The Nittany Lions were back in front, 14–7.

USC went three-and-out inside their own 20 thanks to a mishap on the kickoff. Receiver Kevin Baugh returned the punt to the Trojan 39. Jackson then dropped the ball on a reverse, but picked it up for a gain of four. Meade plowed ahead for a first down at the 29. The Lions couldn't get the ball to the red zone, though, and Franco missed his 37-yard field goal attempt wide left.

Allen fumbled away the ball again, and Leo Wisniewski recovered for Penn State. With great field position, head coach Joe Paterno put the ball in the hands of Warner, who touched the ball on the next four plays. He got the Lions down to the 9, and Williams further reached the 4. Again the drive stalled, however, so Franco came on to try a 21-yard field goal. He made this one, and Penn State went ahead by ten.

USC got the ball back at their 30. Allen ran for 11 yards, then Mazur dumped the ball off to Spencer for a first down at the Penn State 44. On the play, he was injured, so backup Sean Salisbury came into the game. Over the next nine plays, the two teams combined for seven flags, mostly by USC. The Trojans got backed up into a third-and-21, and Salisbury threw an interception to linebacker Ed Pryts. He returned it 23 yards to the 45 with 36 seconds left in the half.

Blackledge threw complete to Jackson for a first down at the USC 35. He got the Lions to the line quickly, and he handed off to Meade on a draw. He got 12 yards, and

Penn State called their first timeout with 17 seconds to go. Blackledge then found Jackson again, this time down at the 4 for a 19-yard gain. Warner took a toss down to the 1, but Penn State had just five seconds left after using a timeout. Paterno opted to go for the touchdown instead of getting the sure three points. He called for an option play, but Blackledge was stuffed short of the goal line, in shades of the 1979 Sugar Bowl. Penn State went to the half with just a ten-point lead.

Penn State started the second half with the ball after a touchback. Warner took his first carry of the half for 13 yards down the left side. Blackledge then found Kab on a third-down play for 14 more. Two plays later, he went play action to Jackson, getting 15 more yards. Tight end Mike McCloskey caught a pass for seven yards, and Meade picked up a first down. Warner then took a run down the right sideline, speeding 21 yards for a touchdown. The Nittany Lions took a 24–7 advantage.

Before this game could get out of control, the Trojans made a drive for points of their own. Mazur was back in the game, and he pitched to Allen on second down for nine yards and a first down. Facing third-and-11, Mazur found receiver Jeff Simmons for 18 yards and a first down. He then faked a handoff and scrambled for 13 yards. Allen got another first down, setting up a 37-yard field goal by kicker Steve Jordan to cut the deficit to 14.

The umbrellas came out as the overcast Arizona sky turned to rain. Warner got one first down on a 12-yard run off the right side, before the Nittany Lions had to punt. The Trojans rushed everyone, and they didn't get the punt, but they did get the punter. That meant 15 yards and an automatic first down. Williams then touched the ball five times on the next six plays, getting two first downs. The Lions were back in field goal range, but they quickly vacated it with an 11-yard loss on a reverse to Jackson, and a Blackledge third-down interception to linebacker Keith Browner.

The Lions forced a quick three-and-out, mainly due to a sack of Mazur for a loss of four yards on third down. USC was punting from their own 19, and Penn State sent everyone after the kick. Defensive tackle Dave Paffenroth got through and blocked the punt. The ball sailed backwards into the USC end zone and over the end line for a safety. Penn State's lead increased to 16 as the third quarter came to an end.

Penn State managed just one first down after the free kick, and they punted it down to the 13. It was now or never for the Trojans on their next drive. Mazur threw to receiver Timmie Ware for 20 yards, and Spencer ran for another first down to the 45. Allen ran for a pair of further first downs, and Mazur completed a fourth-down pass to Simmons for a first down. But the USC drive fell apart on consecutive sacks by the Penn State defense. Defensive back Walker Lee Ashley got the first one, and defensive tackle Dave Opfar got the second one for a huge loss of 21. Jordan then tried a 54-yard field goal, but it was well short, and Penn State maintained their 16-point lead with six minutes to go.

The Lions simply ran the ball three times and punted it back to USC. Mazur's very first pass of the next series was intercepted by linebacker Ken Kelley. On USC's last chance, Penn State sacked Mazur twice. First, Ashley and defensive end Rich D'Amico combined for a sack for seven yards lost. Then, on third down, defensive tackle Joe Hines sacked Mazur again. The Trojans cried uncle, and the Lions won the game, 26–10.

Warner had another outstanding effort in a bowl game. He rushed for 145 yards, meaning he totaled 300 rushing yards in the last two bowl games. Meade rushed for 60 yards himself. Blackledge threw for 175 yards and a touchdown, though he did have the two interceptions. Meanwhile, Allen was held to just 85 yards on 30 carries. It was with that closing flourish that Penn State finished the season ranked #3 in the nation, and ready for something bigger and better in 1982.

Box Score[15]:

1982 Fiesta Bowl	1st	2nd	3rd	4th	Final
Penn State	7	10	9	0	26
USC	7	0	3	0	10

1st Quarter: PSU—Warner 17 run (Franco kick)
   USC—Banks 20 interception return (Jordan kick)
2nd Quarter: PSU—Garrity 52 pass from Blackledge (Franco kick)
   PSU—Franco 21 FG
3rd Quarter: PSU—Warner 21 run (Franco kick)
   USC—Jordan 37 FG
   PSU—Safety
4th Quarter: No Scoring

1982 Season (10–1)

Head coach Joe Paterno came into the 1982 season still searching for that first national championship. Oh, he had finished undefeated before. Three times, in fact. None of those seasons, topped off with Orange Bowl wins, earned Penn State the mythical national championship created by the media and the coaches. Unfortunately, Paterno had to play by their rules, despite the fact that he was one of the earliest advocates for a play-off system. His idea was for a four-team playoff to be played *after* the bowl games.[1] It may take until midway through the 2020s for such an idea to finally get realized.

Paterno's 1982 team began with an offensive flourish against Temple. Quarterback Todd Blackledge threw three touchdown passes in the first quarter, on his way to a 203-yard, four-touchdown day. Running back Curt Warner didn't break any records like he had on opening days in the past, but he still gained 101 yards from scrimmage. The Nittany Lions went on to win, 31–14.[2]

The game against Maryland turned out to be a seesaw affair. It was Blackledge against Maryland quarterback Boomer Esiason in a tug-of-war through the air. Esiason threw two touchdown passes amongst his 276 passing yards, but the Penn State defense also intercepted him twice. Blackledge threw for 262 yards and four touchdown passes. Kicker Massimo Manca made four field goals, as the Lions held on for an exciting 39–31 victory.[3] Against Rutgers, defensive back Mark Robinson took back a first-quarter punt 92 yards for a touchdown, the second-longest punt return in Nittany Lions history. Blackledge again had a big game, throwing four touchdown passes amongst his 213 yards, and the Lions won 49–14.[4]

The Nittany Lions next went up against Nebraska at Beaver Stadium. Penn State put up 505 yards, while Nebraska had 472. Blackledge threw for 295 yards and three touchdowns. Trailing 21–17 with 1:18 to go, he led a nine-play, 65-yard drive. The most memorable play was a 15-yard catch by tight end Mike McCloskey, who caught it out of bounds. The officials didn't see it, and they ruled it a catch down at the 2.[5] Blackledge then found tight end Kirk Bowman in the end zone for the winning points in a 27–24 classic.[6]

Nothing went right against Alabama, though. The Nittany Lions trailed 21–7 at the half in Birmingham, with a 69-yard touchdown pass from Blackledge to Warner being the only points. The Lions pulled within 27–21 in the fourth quarter, but after Paterno sent punter Ralph Giacomarro on to kick, defensive back Mike Suter accidentally blocked his own team's punt. The Crimson Tide rolled from there, getting two touchdowns and winning 42–21.[7]

The Nittany Lions bounced back with a win over Syracuse on Homecoming Weekend. The Lions went back to playing ground-and-pound offense, after five weeks of airing it out. It worked to perfection, as they piled up 225 rushing yards. One hundred forty-eight of them came from Warner, who ran for two touchdowns. Blackledge snuck into the end zone twice for scores, as the Lions beat Syracuse 28–7.[8]

In one of the most amusing box scores you'll ever see, West Virginia outgained Penn State 382–343, yet didn't just lose—they were shut out! Former PSU quarterback Jeff Hostetler threw for 250 yards, but he was picked off twice. One of those was grabbed by linebacker Scott Radecic, who took it back 85 yards for a touchdown, giving Penn State a 24–0 victory.[9]

There would be no sluggishness offense against Boston College. The Nittany offense put up the same number of yards passing and rushing, 309 each. That gave them 618 yards, 243 of them coming from the arm of Blackledge. For the second straight week, the Lions were outgained by their opponent, yet came away with a resounding victory. Warner ran for 183 yards, and receiver Kenny Jackson caught four passes for 104 yards, as the Nittany Lions won 52–17.[10]

After the BC win, Paterno declared the final three weeks to be a "playoff" for the national championship.[11] Against North Carolina State, the Lions defense gave up just 183 yards, recovering four fumbles. Warner rushed for 106 yards and two touchdowns, and Blackledge threw for 192 yards. Jackson had a big game with seven catches for 122 yards, as Penn State finished off the Wolfpack 54–0 for their second shutout in three weeks.[12]

The final two games were tough ones—Notre Dame and Pitt. Penn State got off to a 13–7 first-half lead over Notre Dame with Blackledge sneaking for a score and kicker Nick Gancitano making a pair of field goals. In the fourth quarter, trailing by one, Blackledge threw a 48-yard touchdown pass to Warner. The Lions then got a safety when defensive end Walker Lee Ashley tackled Pinkett in the end zone, and Penn State beat Notre Dame, 24–14.

Pitt wasn't just playing spoiler in the final game of the season. They had national title aspirations of their own. Both teams were 9–1, with Penn State at #2 and Pitt at #5. The Lions trailed Pitt 7–3 at halftime, but then Blackledge threw a 31-yard touchdown pass to Jackson, and Warner ran for 118 yards. The Nittany Lions won it 19–10, finishing the regular season 10–1 and again ruining Panthers quarterback Dan Marino's national championship hopes.[13]

Paterno was named coach of the year by the UPI, while defensive back Mark Robinson, Warner, and Jackson were all named as first-team All-Americans. Blackledge rewrote the team's record book with 22 touchdown passes and 161 completions. Jackson also set marks of most touchdown receptions (seven) and yards (697). The Lions also set the NCAA record for consecutive non-losing seasons at 44.[14]

Blackledge threw for 2,218 yards, finishing sixth in the Heisman voting. Running behind the blocking of fullback Tom Barr, Warner rushed for 1,041 yards and eight touchdowns while also catching five touchdown passes on his way to 335 receiving yards. He finished tenth in the Heisman vote. Jackson led the team in receiving yards with 697, but Garrity also had 32 catches for 509 yards and three touchdowns.[15]

The Nittany Lions had their pick of the litter when it came to bowl games. They were ranked #2 in the nation following the regular season. The Lions had their choice between two undefeated teams: the #1-ranked 11–0 Georgia Bulldogs, SEC champions in the Sugar Bowl, or the #4-ranked 10–0–3 Southern Methodist Mustangs, Southwest champions in the Cotton Bowl. Penn State had no interest in playing the #3-ranked, one-loss Cornhuskers in the Orange Bowl. They instead chose to play #1 Georgia, who had an automatic bid to the Sugar Bowl as SEC champions. For the second time in five seasons, the Nittany Lions would have a chance to win the national championship in New Orleans.[16]

1983 Sugar Bowl Classic

#2 Penn State (10–1) vs. #1 Georgia (11–0)
January 1, 1983, at the Louisiana Superdome in New Orleans, Louisiana

The Nittany Lions got the ball to start out this national championship game against Georgia. Running back Curt Warner began with a four-yard run and a catch for a first down. Quarterback Todd Blackledge threw play action to tight end Mike McCloskey for a first down at the Georgia 37. He then hit receiver Gregg Garrity for another first down all the way down to the 10. After a pass to McCloskey got the Lions to the 2, Warner took a handoff into the end zone, and Penn State took the early 7–0 lead.

The Bulldogs responded with a drive of their own. Fullback Chris McCarthy ran for his team's initial first down, and running back Herschel Walker got one as well. Quarterback John Lastinger then threw off play action over the middle for a first down to tight end Clarence Kay. Walker got another first down at the 21, and Lastinger ran it himself for the next first down at the 11. On second down from there, Kay was "so alone he was lonesome" in the end zone, according to ABC announcer Keith Jackson.[17] But Lastinger overthrew him! The Bulldogs were forced to settle for a 27-yard field goal by kicker Kevin Butler, making it 7–3.

The defenses had struggled on the first drives, but they settled in after this. Each team punted twice in a row, with Blackledge getting sacked a couple of times. He fumbled once, but fullback Jon Williams recovered to prevent great field position for Georgia. PSU punter Nick Gancitano got away one 55-yard punt, and the first quarter ended with the Lions up 7–3.

Receiver Kenny Jackson began his team's next drive with a great effort. "Oh, what a catch that was!" Keith Jackson exclaimed, as Penn State got a first down at the Georgia 45.[18] Warner then followed a block by tackle Ron Heller and made it all the way down to the 21. That set up a 37-yard field goal by kicker Nick Gancitano, and Penn State extended their lead to 10–3.

The Bulldogs got a couple first downs before having to punt it back. Receiver Kevin Baugh returned punter Jim Broadway's kick 65 yards to the Georgia 28, a spectacular return that nearly went all the way. But the Lions went backwards with an illegal procedure call and couldn't get a first down. Gancitano then missed his 47-yard field goal try wide left. Baugh's great return had gone for naught.

McCarthy fumbled on Georgia's next possession, but they were lucky to get it back. They ended up punting, and this time Baugh only returned it to the 34. But Blackledge moved them quickly, hitting Garrity down the sideline for a first down at the Georgia 30. Williams broke off runs of 12 and seven, each time getting a first down. Warner then scored on an eight-yard run, and Penn State went up 17–3.

Running back Keith Montgomery muffed the kickoff out of bounds at the 8, and Georgia had terrible field position. They went three-and-out, and Baugh returned the punt to the Georgia 44 with just over a minute left in the half. Blackledge completed a pass to McCloskey for a first down, but Penn State couldn't get any farther. Gancitano came on for a 45-yard field goal attempt, which he made to extend the lead to 17 points.

It looked like Georgia was dead in the water, but they refused to go down. Walker returned the kickoff to the 34, and Lastinger threw to Kay for a first down to the midfield stripe. After a timeout, Lastinger hit receiver Herman Archie for another first down. Lastinger threw his next pass to receiver Kevin Harris, who immediately lateraled the ball to Walker. He got out of bounds at the 10. Lastinger then went to the left corner of the end zone to Archie for a touchdown. Georgia's score with just five seconds left in the half had cut the deficit to ten points as the teams went to their locker rooms.

Georgia kept things going on the first drive of the second half. Lastinger fired to Harris for a first down at the Penn State 45. Walker ran for five more, then Lastinger went back to Harris for a first down at the 30. Walker ran it three times in a row, getting a first down at the 17. McCarthy ran it down to the 1, and Walker pounded it in for a touchdown to reduce the Bulldogs' deficit to just three points.

The Penn State offense began to struggle. They got one first down before having to punt. Defensive back Mark Robinson picked off a deep ball by Lastinger, and he returned it to the Georgia 37. But again, the Nittany Lions couldn't move the ball. They got flagged for clipping, before Blackledge was sacked on third down. After their punt, both teams

Lions stuff Herschel Walker, Sugar Bowl, 1983. Players shown, left to right: #97, PSU linebacker Scott Radecic; #41, PSU defensive end Steve Sefter; #34, Georgia running back Herschel Walker; #86, PSU defensive end John Walter. Photographic vertical files, Athletics, 1855–2009 (01167). Penn State University Archives, Eberly Family Special Collections Library, Penn State University Libraries, Penn State University.

went three-and-out again. Lastinger threw a second long ball that was intercepted by Robinson, and Penn State had the ball back at their own 26 at the end of the third quarter.

Williams ran for a first down, and Warner picked up another first down past midfield. Blackledge and Garrity then made the play of the game. Blackledge launched the long bomb down the left sideline, and Garrity got under it for a 47-yard touchdown to put Penn State up, 27–17. The ten-point lead appeared to be enough to get Penn State a national championship at long last.

Penn State's swarming defense shut down Georgia and forced a three-and-out. Blackledge then ran some clock by completing a third-and-14 pass to Jackson. Williams got another first down at the Georgia 40, but he was stopped later on a third down. Head coach Joe Paterno eschewed a long field goal try, and Giacomarro punted it for a touchback with seven minutes to play.

The Nittany defense forced another three-and-out, capped off by a third-down sack by defensive end Walker Lee Ashley. On fourth-and-17, Georgia head coach Vince Dooley chose to punt. The game would have been all but over had Baugh just caught it, but he didn't. His muff gave the ball to Georgia in great field position. Lastinger then hit Harris for a first down at the Penn State 27. Kay caught a nine-yard pass, and Walker took a toss for another first down. Three plays later, Lastinger hit Kay for a nine-yard touchdown to cut the Penn State lead to just four.

This is where the math got interesting. At the time, there was no overtime in college football; a game knotted up at the end of the fourth quarter went into the books as a tie. Earlier in the day, at the Cotton Bowl, #3 Southern Methodist had defeated Pitt 7–3. That meant that a tie would likely doom both Penn State *and* Georgia, and SMU would win the national title in that case. So, Dooley went for two. The Penn State defense stopped Walker short of the end zone, and the score remained 27–23.

Georgia pinned Penn State down at their own 13 on the kickoff. It was now up to the Penn State offense to run out the clock. Warner ran it twice to get nine yards, and Blackledge picked up the first down on a sneak. Williams ran it a couple times to take the clock under two minutes, setting up a huge third down. Georgia called timeout before the play to stop the clock. Blackledge audibled as he came to the line, then threw to the left sideline to Garrity. Complete! Penn State had a first down, and the opportunity to run down the clock almost all the way. They ran it three times, and Georgia used their last timeout. The Lions ended up with fourth-and-long with only six seconds left. Paterno sent on Giacomarro, and the Georgia special teams sent all 11 men. But they couldn't get the block, Giacomarro's punt bounded into the end zone, and Penn State won the Sugar Bowl, 27–23!

Blackledge threw for 228 yards and the iconic touchdown pass to Garrity. Warner rushed for 117 yards and two touchdowns. Garrity led Penn State's receivers with four catches for 116 yards and the touchdown. The Lions forced two turnovers while only giving it up once, on the punt muff. They slightly outgained the Bulldogs, 367–326. "This is the greatest, greatest team I have played on in my life," Blackledge said after the game.

The Nittany Lions were finally national champions. Both polls ranked them at #1 over SMU, so Paterno at last had his elusive title. Blackledge had gotten the Nittany Lions into the promised land, and his teammates carried Paterno off the field. "Being number one is important to our fans and our kids, but not to me. Next year let there be a playoff," Paterno said. "This year, let's vote."[19]

Box score[20]:

Football players on trailer during victory parade, 1983. Players shown, left to right: #67: defensive tackle Dave Opfar; in jacket, center Mike Dunlay; #14: quarterback Todd Blackledge. Penn State University Archives, Eberly Family Special Collections Library, Penn State University Libraries, Penn State University.

1983 Sugar Bowl	1st	2nd	3rd	4th	Final
Penn State	7	13	0	7	27
Georgia	3	7	7	6	23

1st Quarter: PSU—Warner 2 run (Gancitano kick)
   UGA—Butler 27 FG
2nd Quarter: PSU—Gancitano 38 FG
   PSU—Warner 9 run (Gancitano kick)
   PSU—Gancitano 45 FG
   UGA—Archie 10 pass from Lastinger (Butler kick)
3rd Quarter: UGA—Walker 1 run (Butler kick)
4th Quarter: PSU—Garrity 47 pass from Blackledge (Gancitano kick)
   UGA—Kay 9 pass from Lastinger (run failed)

1983 Season (7–4–1)

Coming off their first national championship, the Nittany Lions had to start over, with so many players gone to the NFL. They started the 1983 season against Nebraska at Giants Stadium in the first-ever Kickoff Classic in late August. The Cornhuskers embarrassed the Nittany Lions in a 44–6 rout, with PSU's only score coming on a 39-yard touchdown pass from quarterback Dan Lonergan to receiver Sid Lewis.[1]

The Nittany Lions couldn't punch the ball in the end zone even once against Cincinnati. Receiver Kevin Baugh muffed a punt in the first half, leading to a Cincinnati touchdown. He then fumbled again on the next kickoff. The Lions lost 14–3 for one of the most embarrassing defeats in school history.[2] The offense finally got going against Iowa, though it also turned the ball over three times. Quarterback Doug Strang threw for 254 yards and three touchdowns, as the teams combined for 1,079 yards, the most in Beaver Stadium history, but Penn State lost 42–34.[3]

At 0–3, even Temple proved to be a challenge for the Nittany Lions. Penn State got off to a 20–3 lead in Philadelphia, thanks mainly to running back D.J. Dozier piling up 107 yards and fullback Tony Mumford adding another 85. But the Owls came back, scoring a pair of touchdowns to make a game of it. The Lions got a late field goal to hold off Temple and wins its first game, 23–18.[4] The Nittany Lions were back to Giants Stadium for a game against Rutgers. Dozier ran for a Nittany Lion freshman-record 196 yards. Penn State piled up over 300 rushing yards in all. Strang threw a 31-yard touchdown pass to Baugh, boosting the Lions to a 36–25 win.[5]

The #3-ranked Alabama Crimson Tide visited Beaver Stadium to take on the 2–3 Nittany Lions. Strang threw an 80-yard touchdown pass to tight end Dean DiMidio, as well as a 38-yard touchdown to Baugh. Dozier later scored on a one-yard touchdown run, and the Lions went up 34–7 on the Tide! But Alabama wouldn't go down without a fight, and they scored 21 unanswered points.[6] In the game's final moments, Alabama had an apparent touchdown pass ruled incomplete, and the Nittany Lions held on to win, 34–28.[7]

At the Carrier Dome, Penn State trailed 6–0 in the third quarter to Syracuse after gaining only six first downs and less than 100 yards of offense in the first half. But Dozier scored on a short run, and the Lions used a 19-play drive to chew up nearly nine minutes, getting a field goal to clinch a 17–6 win.[8] The next week, former Penn State quarterback Jeff Hostetler led the undefeated, #5-ranked West Virginia Mountaineers into Beaver Stadium next, but Penn State beat them 41–23. Running back Jon Williams ran for 106 yards, while the Lions put up 220 yards passing for the day.[9]

The five-game winning streak ended at Boston College, where the Eagles got off to a 21–0 halftime advantage. Quarterback Doug Flutie and the Eagles outgained Penn State by over 240 yards in the first half. The Lions made a game of it in the second half, but they still fell by a 27–17 margin.[10] The next week against Brown, Paterno's alma mater, the Lions got off to a 17–0 lead, with Strang running one in from six yards away, and Williams running for a 61-yard score. Receiver Kenny Jackson scored on a 55-yard reverse, while Dozier ran for a 44-yard touchdown. The big plays helped put away a 38–21 win.[11]

The Fighting Irish came to Happy Valley for a shootout. Trailing by three, Strang threw a 36-yard pass to DiMidio to put Penn State in scoring range. He then ran it in from 13 yards away with just 19 seconds left, and Penn State won, 34–30.[12] The Nittany Lions finished the season against Pitt. Down by three, Strang completed a 26-yard pass to Dozier on third-and-21, getting the Lions got into field goal range. Kicker Nick Gancitano's 32-yard field goal with no time left salvaged a 24–24 tie.[13]

Strang was highly efficient for the Lions throughout the season. He threw 19 touchdowns as opposed to just seven interceptions, and he finished just shy of 2,000 yards passing. He averaged 14-and-a-half yards per completion. His favorite receiver was Baugh, who caught 36 balls for 547 yards and five touchdowns. Jackson caught another 28 for 483 yards and a team-high seven touchdowns.[14]

As for the running game, Dozier became a star, rushing for over 1,000 yards and seven touchdowns. He also caught 19 passes for 355 yards and three scores. Williams was coming off knee surgery, limiting his participation, but he still managed 590 yards. Running back Tony Mumford added another 331 yards and a touchdown.[15]

With only a 7–4–1 record, Penn State was passed on by all the major bowls, and even some of the other high-quality bowls such as the Florida Citrus and the Gator. They were forced to settle for a bid in the brand-new Aloha Bowl in Hawaii. Their opponent would be the Washington Huskies, who missed out on the Rose Bowl thanks to a loss to archrival Washington State in the Apple Cup. Both disappointed teams headed to Honolulu looking to salvage a lost season.[16]

1983 Aloha Bowl

Penn State (7–4–1) vs. Washington (8–3)
December 26, 1983, at Aloha Stadium in Honolulu, Hawaii

The Huskies got the ball to start this game, and disaster almost struck immediately. Running back Cookie Jackson couldn't handle the ball on the kickoff, and he ended up bobbling it out of bounds at his own 4. Washington got out of the hole with a run by and a pass to running back Sterling Hinds, who took the ball to the 25. The Huskies committed an illegal motion penalty a couple plays later, and they were forced to punt. Penn State got the ball at the 44.

Fullback Jon Williams started with an eight-yard run. Running back D.J. Dozier followed him by plowing up the middle for a first down. Dozier caught a pass and took a toss to get another first down at the 30. Quarterback Doug Strang scrambled for a first down on third-and-long, getting 14 yards plus extra yards on a personal foul call. The Nittany Lions got a 23-yard field goal by kicker Nick Gancitano, and they took the early 3–0 lead.

Washington got the ball into Penn State territory, where they were stopped on a fourth-down play. As the second quarter began, Penn State forced a Washington three-and-out, and receiver Kevin Baugh took the punt back to the Washington 49. Strang threw to tight end Dean DiMidio for eight yards, but couldn't convert on a third down. The Lions punted it back to Washington, who got the ball at the 31 after a fair catch interference call on PSU.

After forcing a Washington punt, the Lions took over at their own 20. Strang found himself sacked by defensive tackle Ron Holmes, and Penn State had to punt from deep in their own end. Their ensuing punt was returned 57 yards for a touchdown by receiver Danny Greene. The Huskies had gone ahead, 7–3.

The game was turning into a defensive struggle, as both teams punted back and forth. Washington got the ball back before the half at their own 12 after a 53-yard kick. Jackson ran for about nine yards, then caught a pass a few plays later to get to the 40. Quarterback Steve Pelluer threw to tight end Tony Wroten, and the Huskies called timeout. He then found receiver Mark Pattison for 38 yards down to the 21. Kicker Jeff Jaeger kicked a 39-yard field goal, and the Huskies went to the locker room with a 10–3 score and a 175–62 lead in total yards.

Things did not get better for the Penn State offense in the third quarter. Strang had a pass go through the hands of his receiver Kenny Jackson and into the arms of linebacker Tim Meamber. The Lions then punted on their next two possessions. Their defense was holding strong, but at the end of three quarters, they still trailed by seven.

The Lions finally got something going after punter Thane Cleland got away a punt of only 14 yards. Jackson took a reverse for a first down to the 40, then the Lions got a break when a flag for intentional grounding was waved off. Williams took a draw to the 30, and Strang found DiMidio down at the 22 for a new set of downs. A couple plays later, another flag was thrown, presumably for pass interference. It too got waved off. The Lions settled for a 49-yard field goal from Gancitano, and they pulled within four.

Penn State's defense forced two more punts, and they again got good field position. This drive they started at their own 49. Dozier caught a pass for nine yards, then Williams picked up the first down at the 38. Facing third down a few plays later, Strang scrambled for a first down to the 24. The Lions got called for offensive pass interference on a throw to the end zone, but Williams quickly made up for it by hauling in a pass for 19 yards. Strang then found Baugh for a first down at the 4. After the Huskies jumped offside, Dozier took a toss two yards into the end zone for a touchdown, and Penn State went ahead by three.

With Washington's offense completely stymied by the Penn State defense, that lead looked good to hold up. The Huskies got a reprieve after a third-down pass came up short of the sticks, as the Lions were called for holding. They had two minutes to go at this point, but Pelluer fired four incomplete passes in a row, and Penn State took over on downs. The Nittany Lions had won the Aloha Bowl, 13–10.

There wasn't much to write home about from Hawaii. Williams was Penn State's leading yard-getter with 72 yards from scrimmage. Dozier had another 59 scrimmage yards and the Lions' only touchdown. Strang completed only 14 of his 34 passes for 118 yards. In an unusual move, punter George Reynolds was named Outstanding Defensive Player for averaging 46.8 yards on his eight punts. The Lions finished the year 8–4–1, but searching for answers.[17]

Box Score[18]:

1983 Aloha Bowl	1st	2nd	3rd	4th	Final
Washington	0	10	0	0	10
Penn State	3	0	0	10	13

1st Quarter: PSU—Gancitano 23 FG
2nd Quarter: WASH—Greene 57 punt return (Jaeger kick)
   WASH—Jaeger 39 FG
3rd Quarter: No Scoring
4th Quarter: PSU—Gancitano 49 FG
   PSU—Dozier 2 run (Gancitano kick)

1985 Season (11–0)

Coming off two extremely disappointing seasons, including a 6–5 1984 season where Penn State missed a bowl for the first time since 1970, the Nittany Lions began their 1985 schedule at Maryland, getting out to a 17–0 advantage in the second quarter. Linebacker Michael Zordich took back a pick 32 yards for a touchdown not even a minute into the game. Maryland came back to go up 18–17, but Massimo Manca made a 46-yard field goal to give Penn State a 20–18 victory.[1] Penn State survived another close one at home against Temple. They got off to a 24–10 lead at halftime. Quarterback John Shaffer threw for 220 yards and a touchdown.[2] Fullback Steve Smith rushed for 96, and the Lions held on for a 27–25 win.[3]

Against East Carolina, the Lions jumped out to a 14–3 halftime lead. Helped by punter John Bruno averaging over 44 yards per kick, the Lions managed to stave off the Pirates for a 17–10 win.[4] The defense forced five fumbles, three of which they recovered. Shaffer passed for 174 yards and a touchdown, and fullback Tim Manoa led in rushing yards with 73.[5]

The Lions got two long runs against Rutgers, with running back David Clark ripping off a 76-yarder, and Smith scoring on a 63-yard run.[6] Again, it was a great defensive effort to defeat the Scarlet Knights; the Lions allowed only three points until the final two minutes when Rutgers got a touchdown. By rushing for 248 yards, Penn State pulled out a 17–10 win.[7]

Manca kicked four field goals against Alabama, including a 50-yarder. Backup quarterback Matt Knizner came into the game after Shaffer got hurt, and he threw his only pass of the game 11 yards to tight end Brian Siverling for a touchdown.[8] The Lions again gave up a touchdown at the very end of the game, but by recovering Alabama's onside kick, they held on for a 19–17 victory.[9]

After getting off to a 14–0 start at Syracuse, the Lions fell behind 20–17 in the fourth quarter. Penn State managed just 11 first downs, so it was the defense that had to pick them up.[10] Defensive end Bob White forced a fumble which fellow defensive end Don Graham recovered at the Syracuse 42, setting up an eight-yard touchdown pass to Smith with two minutes remaining to give Penn State a 24–20 win.[11]

All of Penn State's victories thus far had been close ones. But now, midway through the season, they started posting impressive wins. The Lions recorded their first shutout since 1982.[12] Shaffer threw two touchdown passes to receiver Ray Roundtree. Dozier ran for 125 yards and a score, and the Nittany Lions finished off a 27–0 win.[13]

The Lions fell into a 12–3 hole against Boston College. Shaffer led an eight-play, 74-yard drive in the third quarter, capped off by a one-yard sneak to pull the Lions within two. In the fourth quarter, defensive tackle Mike Russo picked off a pass and returned it 21 yards for a touchdown.[14] The Lions managed a 16–12 win despite just 12 first downs while committing ten penalties.[15]

After a pick-six put Cincinnati up 10–7, the Nittany Lions rallied to post an impressive road win. Defensive back Ray Isom picked off a pass in the end zone to turn things around. Shaffer threw two touchdown passes and also ran for one. Dozier rushed for 112 yards and a score.[16] The Lions won 31–10, and they moved to #1 in the polls.[17]

Up to this point, it could be argued that Penn State had gotten by on smoke and mirrors for much of the season. Seven games were decided by seven points or less. But in the final two games, the Nittany Lions made a statement that they were indeed the best team in the country. In their home finale against Notre Dame, Manca tied the school record by kicking five field goals. Shaffer threw for 126 yards, Dozier ran for 75, and the Nittany Lions crushed Notre Dame 36–6.[18]

The only thing sweeter than an Orange Bowl invitation was a shutout of Pitt. The Nittany Lions scored 21 points in the second quarter, including a 60-yard touchdown run by Manoa. Graham forced a fumble off Pitt quarterback John Congemi, and linebacker Pete Giftopoulos recovered it in the end zone for a touchdown.[19] The Penn State defense held Pitt to under 250 yards, as they won 31–0 to finish an unbeaten regular season at #1.[20]

Shaffer threw for 1,366 yards during the course of the 1985 season. Dozier led the team in rushing yards with 723. Smith added another 421, and Manoa and Clark both went over 300 yards. The Lions managed to win all these games without a single receiver going over 15 catches or 300 receiving yards. Roundtree was the best with just 15 catches for 285 yards and two touchdowns, leading the team in all categories. It was the defense that was the heart and soul of this team, picking off 18 passes and returning them 200 yards for the year.[21]

This time, there was little drama over where Penn State would go when it came to bowl season. As an independent, Penn State had their choice of the bowls. The Sugar Bowl's automatic qualifier was #8 Tennessee, the Cotton Bowl's automatic bid went to #11 Texas A&M, and the Orange Bowl had the winner of the Big Eight, #3 Oklahoma. The Sooners had lost only one game, to Miami, in which starting quarterback Troy Aikman went down with a season-ending injury. It was only natural to pick the highest-ranked opponent, so the Lions went to Miami to play the Sooners.[22]

1986 Orange Bowl Classic

#1 Penn State (11–0) vs. #3 Oklahoma (10–1)
January 1, 1986, at the Orange Bowl in Miami, Florida

A great misconception about this game is the idea that it wasn't competitive, that Penn State never had a chance. In reality, the Nittany Lions were in this one up until about three minutes left in the contest. Unfortunately, quarterback John Shaffer had the worst game of his career, and things would get out of hand in the final two minutes.

When Penn State won the coin toss (an unusual ceremony where the referee tossed three coins instead of just one), head coach Joe Paterno chose to defer. His plan worked out to perfection, as his defense forced a quick three-and-out. The Lions took over at their own 38 after the punt. They got their initial first down on a pass interference call. Fullback Steve Smith ran it a couple of times, getting a first down. Shaffer then found receiver Eric Hamilton for gains of 12 and 14. Two plays later, fullback Tim Manoa plowed in from a yard away, and the Lions took the early 7–0 lead.

Early on, the Lions were having their way with the Oklahoma offense. Linebackers Shane Conlan and Michael Zordich tackled Oklahoma quarterback Jamelle Holieway for a 13-yard loss to start the next drive. Holieway ran for 17 yards on third down, but it was not enough. The Sooners punted the ball back to Penn State, who took over at their 15.

For the rest of the game, the Lions would struggle on offense. They went three-and-out on their next series, and after a lateral on the punt return, Oklahoma took over at the Penn State 45. Holieway

Orange Bowl button, 1986. Author's collection.

completed a 13-yard pass to tight end Keith Jackson, and fullback Lydell Carr ran it for ten more yards. The Sooners got a 26-yard field goal from kicker Tim Lashar, cutting the Penn State lead to four early in the second quarter.

Penn State went three-and-out again, and OU receiver Derrick Shepard had his punt return to the 42 called back on a personal foul penalty. The Sooners quickly made up for it, with running back Spencer Tillman ripping off a 12-yard run. Holieway then threw up a bomb, which Jackson ran under and collected for a 71-yard touchdown. Oklahoma now had a 10–7 lead.

The Oklahoma defense was swarming, and the Nittany Lions had no answers. They went three-and-out again. After forcing a quick OU punt, the Lions did get a first down after a 15-yard pass to tight end Dean DiMidio and a run by Smith. However, Shaffer threw his next pass into tight coverage, which was intercepted by defensive back Sonny Brown. He returned it 22 yards. The Sooners then got a 31-yard Lashar field goal to go up by six.

It was déjà vu for the Lions on the next drive. Shaffer was sacked by defensive end Troy Johnson, before throwing into tight coverage again. This time the pass was tipped and picked off by defensive back Tony Rayburn. He took back the pick 34 yards inside the Penn State 10. The Nittany Lion defense held, but OU got another field goal from Lasher. This one was from 21 yards out, and now the Sooners led by nine.

Penn State punted again after a three-and-out, and Oklahoma got the ball back at their own 13 with a minute to go in the half. Head coach Barry Switzer should have had Holieway just take three knees and punt, because Penn State wasn't about to drive 70 yards in a minute, or even 40 yards into field goal range. At first it looked like he was doing that, as Holieway just ran it up the middle a couple of times. Paterno called two timeouts, and OU had third down with just 15 seconds left. Taking a knee would end the half, but instead Holieway tried a run, and he had the ball punched out of his hands by defensive end Bob White. Conlan recovered it deep in OU territory, setting up a 27-yard field goal by kicker Massimo Manca to cut the deficit to 16–10 at the half.

Paterno's plan to defer seemed to be working again when the Lions drove the ball downfield on the first drive of the second half. Smith ran for a first down, and receiver Michael Timpson took a reverse for 21 yards. Shaffer threw a third-down pass to DiMidio for 12 yards, then he ran for a first down on the next third down. The Lions were down to the Oklahoma 21, but Shaffer threw his next pass into double coverage. Brown picked it off for his second interception of the game at the 1-yard line.

The Lions defense was doing everything it could to stay in the game. They forced a three-and-out inside the Oklahoma 5, and punter Mike Winchester came on to kick. His punt was caught by receiver Jim Coates, but Coates had the ball punched out of his hands by defensive end Mike Mantle. Defensive tackle Jodie Britt recovered the loose ball at the 42. The Sooners offense now had great field position to work with. Holieway ran for a 13-yard gain, and Carr picked up a pair of first downs, including a 17-yarder. From there, Lashar made his fourth field goal of the game, an Orange Bowl record. This one was from 22 yards out, and it gave Oklahoma a nine-point lead at the end of the third quarter.

Shaffer was ineffective, but Paterno stuck with him for the moment. On Penn State's next series, he did complete one pass for a first down to Hamilton, and running back David Clark got a first down at the midfield stripe. But Paterno's patience with Shaffer was limited, as seen by the fact that he had running back D.J. Dozier throw the first pass of the fourth quarter. His halfback option pass fell incomplete, and Penn State punted again.

On Oklahoma's next series, linebacker Bob Ontko punched the ball out of Holieway's hands, and the Nittany Lions recovered. However, not even this turnover could save Penn State and their impotent offense. Linebacker Dante Jones sacked Shaffer, and the Lions went three-and-out again. They punted away with nine minutes to play, and Paterno said enough was enough. Backup quarterback Matt Knizner started warming up on the sideline.

Penn State's defense forced one more three-and-out, and they gave Knizner a legitimate shot at making the comeback. He started by handing off to Dozier for ten yards. He then threw a shovel pass to Smith, who picked up 15 yards, only to have them all taken away on a late hit after the play. Knizner got the yards back and then some on passes to tight end Brian Siverling for 18 and 13. Knizner ran the ball down to the 10, but the Lions were held on third down. Paterno figured that since he needed two scores anyway, he might as well take the sure three points. He sent Manca out to try a chip-shot 26-yard field goal. However, Manca missed it wide to the left! Manca thought his kick was good, but perhaps because of the shorter goal posts at the time, the officials couldn't tell.

Manca's miss was the final straw for the Lions. Oklahoma needed to do nothing more than run out the clock. They proved to do more than that, starting with a ten-yard run by Tillman on second down. Two plays later, Carr broke a long one, and he wasn't stopped until he had gone 61 yards to the end zone. Lasher missed the extra point wide left, but Oklahoma now had a 25–10 lead with 1:42 to go.

Starting inside his own 10 due to a clipping penalty on the kickoff, Knizner tried leading one last drive. He completed a fourth-down pass to DiMidio for a new set of downs, as well as another pass for a first down to receiver Darrell Giles. But all Penn

State hopes were extinguished when defensive back Ledell Glenn picked off Knizner and returned it deep into Lion territory. The Lions' undefeated season was no more.

It is an indictment on Shaffer that Knizner threw for more yards than he did despite playing only half a quarter as opposed to three-and-a-half quarters. Knizner completed eight of 11 passes for 90 yards and a pick, while Shaffer completed just ten of 22 for 74 yards and three picks. Dozier was the team's leading rusher with just 39 yards. It was a disastrous day for the Penn State offense overall.

But Shaffer's story didn't end here, nor did Dozier's. The Nittany Lions weren't going away. This Orange Bowl loss just fueled them on their quest for #1 in 1986. The Lions finished #3 in the Associated Press poll for the 1985 season. The Sooners, helped out by a 35–7 loss by #2 Miami to Tennessee in the Sugar Bowl, ended up as national champions. Both major bowl losers Penn State and Miami would rebound in 1986, and set up a never-seen-before showdown for the ages.

Box score[23]:

1986 Orange Bowl	1st	2nd	3rd	4th	Final
Penn State	7	3	0	0	10
Oklahoma	0	16	3	6	25

1st Quarter: PSU—Manoa 1 run (Manca kick)
2nd Quarter: OU—Lashar 26 FG
    OU—Jackson 71 pass from Holieway (Lashar kick)
    OU—Lashar 31 FG
    OU—Lashar 21 FG
    PSU—Manca 27 FG
3rd Quarter: OU—Lashar 22 FG
4th Quarter: OU—Carr 61 run (kick missed)

1986 Season (11–0)

Penn State's only undefeated national championship season began with the first-ever night game at Beaver Stadium against Temple. Quarterback John Shaffer, who had been heavily criticized following the Orange Bowl loss, started out the season by completing 12 of 18 passes for 194 yards and three scores, the most touchdown passes of his career. Fullback Tim Manoa broke off a 51-yard run and ended up with 89 rushing yards. The Lions won 45–15 for their most opening-day points since 1981.[1]

The next week, Shaffer went to Schaefer Stadium to play Boston College. He only completed a third of his 21 passes for 95 yards, but his backup Matt Knizner was no better, throwing two interceptions and four incompletions on his six passes.[2] It was running back D.J. Dozier who bailed out the Lions, rushing for 78 yards and a touchdown. Linebacker Shane Conlan recorded 11 tackles, a sack, and an interception, in helping the Lions pull out a 26–14 victory.[3]

Next came East Carolina, who threw an interception on the second play of the game to defensive back Ray Isom. The Lions defense allowed the Pirates just 20 yards in the first half. In the second quarter, Shaffer threw a seven-yard touchdown pass to receiver Eric Hamilton, while running back Blair Thomas ran for a seven-yard touchdown. The Lions blew open the game when receiver Ray Roundtree scored a pair of touchdowns, one receiving and one rushing, going on to win, 42–17.[4]

The Penn State defense completely shut down Rutgers, who went one-for-16 on third downs while punting ten times. Shaffer threw for 187 yards and rushed for another 33, while Dozier was the leading rusher with 54 yards.[5] Roundtree ran for another touchdown, this one from 34 yards out. The Lions outrushed the Scarlet Knights 287–45 in this 31–6 victory.[6]

The perfect season was almost ruined by Cincinnati, who took a 17–14 lead in the fourth quarter. On a third-and-ten play, Shaffer threw to Thomas for 32 yards to keep the drive alive. Thomas later broke off a 27-yard run, which set up running back David Clark's six-yard touchdown run to give Penn State the lead. Conlan then blocked a punt out of the end zone for a safety to ensure the Lions' 23–17 triumph.[7]

Against Syracuse, the Nittany Lions piled up 434 rushing yards, the fifth-most since head coach Joe Paterno took over in 1966. Thomas led the way with 132 yards on just three carries, including a 92-yard run from his own 7 to the Syracuse 1 that marked the longest non-scoring run in school history. He later scored on a 38-yard run, and the Lions poured it on in a 42–3 victory.[8]

Next, the Nittany Lions headed to Tuscaloosa to take on undefeated #2 Alabama. Shaffer had the most accurate game of his career, completing 13 of 17 passes for 168 yards and no interceptions. Dozier ran for a 19-yard touchdown, and Thomas added a three-yard score. The Crimson Tide managed just 216 total yards and one field goal, as Penn State blew them out, 23–3.[9]

The Lions went to West Virginia next, where they didn't allow a touchdown for the third game in a row. In this one, they allowed only 134 total yards in shutting out the Mountaineers. Shaffer threw a 23-yard touchdown pass to Dozier that proved to be more than enough points to win it. Kicker Massimo Manca connected on four of his school-record six field goal attempts, in a 19–0 win.[10]

Against Maryland, defensive tackle Pete Curkendall made the play of the game, picking off a pass and returning it 82 yards to the 9. Like Thomas a few weeks earlier, his run came up short of the end zone, but it was the longest non-scoring interception return in school history. Dozier took it into the end zone from there. The Terrapins came back, though, scoring a touchdown with 13 seconds left to pull within two. Penn State defensive back Duffy Cobbs knocked away the tying two-point pass, and the Lions escaped with a 17–15 victory.[11]

The Lions had another tense game at Notre Dame. Shaffer completed nine of his 13 passes for 162 yards and a 37-yard touchdown pass to Roundtree, while also sneaking it in from a yard away for a score. Penn State led 24–19 with a minute left, when the Fighting Irish drove to the 6-yard line. Isom picked up a sack, and defensive tackle Bob White and linebacker Don Graham combined on another. The Lions held the Irish out of the end zone, holding on for a 24–19 win.[12]

To finish off a second straight undefeated regular season, the Nittany Lions needed to defeat Pitt. The Panthers scored a touchdown in the first quarter to take a 7–3 lead, but Thomas returned the ensuing kickoff 91 yards for a touchdown. Dozier added a 26-yard touchdown run in the second quarter. Knizner threw an 82-yard touchdown pass to Hamilton in relief of an injured Shaffer, and the Lions went on to win by a 34–14 margin.[13]

Dozier rushed for 811 yards and ten touchdowns, with Manoa coming in second in rushing yards with 546. Thomas had another 504 yards and five touchdowns, on only 60 carries. Shaffer threw for over 1,500 yards and nine touchdowns, remaining undefeated in his regular-season career. His top receiver in yards was Hamilton, who caught 19 passes for 387 yards and four touchdowns.[14]

After Penn State defeated Alabama, the Fiesta Bowl committee saw a golden opportunity. The #1 team in the nation, the Miami Hurricanes, and the #2 team, Penn State, were both independents. That meant that neither of them was locked into one of the "Big Four" bowl games—the Big Ten and Pac-10 champions to the Rose, the SEC champions to the Sugar, the Big Eight champions to

Fiesta Bowl button, 1987. Author's collection.

the Orange, and the Southwest champions to the Cotton. If Penn State and Miami could both make it to the end of the season without a loss, the Fiesta Bowl could invite both teams for a #1 vs. #2 game that would not just decide the national title—it would springboard the Fiesta Bowl into the big time.[15]

The Fiesta Bowl got the money from NBC to offer $2 million to each Penn State and Miami. But as they did, ABC gave the Citrus Bowl a similar sum to try to convince the two teams to go to Orlando instead. Fortunately for the Fiesta, the Orange Bowl committee talked Miami into turning down the Citrus, as such a game would turn the Orange (played in Miami's home stadium) into the second-best bowl in the state of Florida. Once Miami and Penn State finished undefeated, the Fiesta Bowl extended its invitations, and the matchup was set. The brash, cocky Hurricanes against the buttoned-up, close-to-the-vest Nittany Lions. It was a match made in football heaven.[16]

1987 Fiesta Bowl

#2 Penn State (11–0) vs. #1 Miami (11–0)
January 2, 1987, at Sun Devil Stadium in Tempe, Arizona

There was incredible hype leading up to this Fiesta Bowl. NBC, the broadcast of this game, not only had Tom Brokaw delivering news from Sun Devil Stadium, they also had a long interview with President Ronald Reagan. The Miami Hurricanes famously arrived in Arizona wearing military fatigues, while the Nittany Lions were wearing suits and ties. NBC had a perfect narrative: the bad guys, the favorites, Miami, against the good guys, the underdogs, Penn State. As a result, the ratings were off the charts.

Head coach Joe Paterno came out aggressive. When Penn State won the toss, he chose to receive. He had quarterback John Shaffer drop back to pass on the first play. But defensive tackle Dan Sileo and defensive end Dan Stubbs were there to greet him, and he was sacked for a huge loss. Two plays later, defensive end Bill Hawkins rushed in to sack him. The Nittany Lions punted, but Miami wasted a shot at good field position by holding on the return.

Miami quarterback Vinny Testaverde, the Heisman Trophy winner, fired his first pass to receiver Michael Irvin for a gain of 12. Facing third down a few plays later, he'd go to tight end Charles Henry for ten yards and a first down. Two plays later, he hit running back Alonzo Highsmith for ten yards, but it was short of a first down due to a delay of game call. On fourth-and-four, the Canes went for it, but linebacker Pete Giftopoulos tipped the pass, which fell incomplete.

Penn State got one first down on a ten-yard run by fullback Steve Smith. Running back D.J. Dozier picked up ten, but again it was not enough for a first down due to an earlier penalty. The Lions had to punt from near midfield. Punter John Bruno got off a yard 50 kick that linebacker Keith Karpinski downed at the 2.

Testaverde got the Hurricanes out of trouble with a 12-yard pass to running back Melvin Bratton. Karpinski then forced a Highsmith fumble, but Henry recovered for Miami. On the very next play, Irvin made a catch and got blasted by defensive back Ray Isom. He fumbled, and defensive back Duffy Cobbs recovered for the Lions.

Penn State went three-and-out, and Miami took over at their own 9. Linebacker Don Graham picked up a sack of Testaverde, pushing the Canes very close to their own goal line. But on third down, Testaverde made a fantastic play, scrambling out of the back of his own end zone for 21 yards. He'd complete a 14-yard pass to Highsmith and a 13-yarder to receiver Brett Perriman. But shortly after the first quarter ended, he threw an interception to Cobbs, who returned it to the Penn State 30.

The teams exchanged punts, although the Miami drive lasted ten plays and the Penn State drive only three. Dozier ripped off a 19-yard run on Penn State's next possession to get to the 33. Two plays later, however, defensive tackle Jerome Brown hit Shaffer and knocked the ball out of his hands, right into the arms of Hawkins. Miami would score four plays later on a Bratton one-yard run and a Greg Cox extra point, and they took a 7–0 lead.

The Nittany Lions then went on a championship drive. Dozier started it off with a nine-yard run, and he picked up the first down on third down. On the next third down, Shaffer went over the middle to receiver Eric Hamilton, and he picked up 23 yards. Fullback Tim Manoa ripped off a 20-yard run, and he later caught a 12-yard pass down to the 5. With two minutes left in the half, Manoa fumbled his next carry, but receiver Darrell Giles was there to cover it. Shaffer took the next snap, rolled to his right, then dived for the pylon. Touchdown! The Lions tied the game at seven.

Testaverde tried leading a late drive, starting with a pass for a first down to Perriman. He then found receiver Brian Blades for 20 yards, and he got out of bounds at the Penn State 45. He fumbled on the next play, but a teammate picked it up,

Fiesta Bowl button and ribbon, 1987. Author's collection.

and Miami called timeout with 21 seconds left. Two plays later, Testaverde hit Irvin for a gain to the Penn State 34, and out trotted the field goal team. Before they could line up, they realized there was a flag on the play for an ineligible man downfield. Now the field goal was gone, so Highsmith took a simple carry for 18 yards to end the half.

The second half started out slowly. The Hurricanes punted twice, and Penn State went three-and-out on their first try. On their next drive, Shaffer threw a pass that was tipped and intercepted by defensive back Selwyn Brown. He returned it 18 yards to the Penn State 40. But Testaverde returned the favor. He threw an interception to linebacker Shane Conlan, who had open field to run before he slipped to the turf at his own 25.

Manoa fumbled for a second time, and linebacker Winston Moss recovered this one for Miami. Testaverde then went for the home run ball to Irvin, and he drew a pass interference flag on Isom. The Canes couldn't get another first down, however. Kicker Mark Seelig tried a 28-yard field goal, but he missed badly to the right. After a Penn State punt, the third quarter came to an end with the score still tied at seven.

Testaverde started a nightmarish fourth quarter by throwing an interception to Giftopoulos. He returned the pick to the Miami 36, but again the impotent Penn State offense went three-and-out. Kicker Massimo Manca came out to try a 50-yard field goal. His kick was well short of the uprights. With no overtime in college football at the time, the Lions were essentially trailing in their fight for the #1 ranking.

Miami would then make sure that Penn State was officially trailing. Testaverde threw to Bratton for a first down, and Highsmith ripped off runs of eight and 21 yards before going down with an injury. Those runs set up Seelig for a second chance. This time, he made the field goal from 38 yards out, and the Canes took a 10–7 lead.

The Lions went three-and-out yet again, but Bruno got away a 48-yard kick to put the ball down at the 21. Bratton helped get the Canes out of the hole with a 13-yard run. But two plays later, Testaverde threw his fourth interception of the game. Conlan picked off this one for his second theft of the game, and he returned it to the Miami 5. Two plays later, Dozier pounded up the middle for a six-yard touchdown, and Penn State took their first lead of the game.

The Hurricanes got it out near midfield, before tight end Alfredo Roberts fumbled away a reception to Penn State linebacker Trey Bauer. Surprisingly, Paterno had Shaffer go back to pass on two of the next three plays, and one of them he completed to tight end Brian Siverling. His third-down pass fell incomplete, though, so Penn State punted. The teams would exchange three-and-outs, and Miami got the ball back one last time at their own 22 with 3:18 to go.

Testaverde now needed to lead a drive for a touchdown to win the national title. He started with a four-yard scramble, before throwing incomplete twice. On fourth-and-six, head coach Jimmy Johnson chose to go for it, and Testaverde fired to Blades down the left sideline for 32 yards. He went back to Blades for seven, then he got the first down on a pass to Perriman. A pair of passes to Irvin picked up another first down with a minute to go.

Miami now had first-and-goal at the 10. It was at this point that defensive coordinator Jerry Sandusky "choked," in his own words, not able to make any defensive calls.[17] His defense bailed him out anyway. On first down, Testaverde threw to Irvin for a third straight play, but he was tackled in bounds. The clock ran under 30 seconds, and defensive tackle Tim Johnson sacked Testaverde on second down. Miami called timeout after the sack, and coming out of the break, Testaverde threw incomplete. That set up fourth and the ballgame with 18 seconds left. Testaverde fired to his left, but he was picked off by Giftopoulos again. It was the second pick for Giftopoulos and the fifth for Testaverde, and this one meant everything. After Shaffer took a knee, the Nittany Lions had won 14–10, for their second national championship!

The numbers told a story of Miami dominance. Miami had 22 first downs, Penn State only 8. Miami had 445 yards of offense, Penn State only 162. Shaffer completed only five of 16 passes for 53 yards, while Testaverde threw 50 passes for 285 yards. Dozier led Penn State in rushing with 99 yards, but Highsmith beat that with 119 yards.

The number that mattered was turnovers. Penn State turned it over three times, but Miami turned it over a whopping seven times. That was the difference between the teams on this day. "I think our defense played about as great a college football game as I've ever seen," Paterno said after the game. Paterno was carried off the field after the victory, being crowned national champion after quite possibly the greatest bowl game of all time.

Box score[18]:

1987 Fiesta Bowl	1st	2nd	3rd	4th	Final
Miami	0	7	0	3	10
Penn State	0	7	0	7	14

1st Quarter: No Scoring
2nd Quarter: MIA—Bratton 1 run (Cox kick)
    PSU—Shaffer 4 run (Manca kick)
3rd Quarter: No Scoring
4th Quarter: MIA—Seelig 38 FG
    PSU—Dozier 6 run (Manca kick)

1987 Season (8–3)

Coming off their second national championship, the Nittany Lions played Bowling Green in Week 1, after both North Carolina State and Arizona State decided not to come to Beaver Stadium. The Nittany Lions beat Bowling Green 45–19 for head coach Joe Paterno's 200th career win, scoring four second-quarter touchdowns.[1]

Alabama next came to Beaver Stadium, and the rain poured down for this nationally televised game. Crimson Tide running back Bobby Humphrey ran for 220 yards, the fourth-most ever for an opposing running back. Penn State's starting quarterback Matt Knizner got knocked out of the game in the first quarter, forcing backup Tom Bill in. He threw a 21-yard touchdown pass to receiver Ray Roundtree, but it was not enough, as the Lions lost 24–13.[2]

Running back Blair Thomas ran for 154 yards and a touchdown, and fellow running back John Greene ran for 124 yards on only 11 carries in Penn State's 41–0 win over Cincinnati. The Lions ran for 374 yards total, the ninth-most since Paterno took over. The defense forced four sacks, recovered a fumble, and only allowed 117 passing yards.[3]

Thomas ran for 164 more yards against Boston College. He ran for a 17-yard touchdown, while also catching a 40-yard touchdown, giving the Lions an early 17–0 lead. In the second half, kicker Eric Etze kicked a career-long 46-yard field goal, and Greene scored from four yards away to wrap up a 27–17 win.[4]

Thomas set a new career-high with 167 yards against Temple. His 259 all-purpose yards ranked him eighth in Penn State history, and he scored two touchdowns. Knizner had the first 200-yard passing game of his career. The Lions defense held Temple running back Todd McNair to just 88 yards on 34 attempts, and they won it 27–13.[5]

For Homecoming, Penn State took on Rutgers. Thomas scored a pair of first-half touchdowns to put the Lions up 14–7. Knizner had his best game of the year, throwing for 215 yards. Thomas ran for 116 yards, while Roundtree hauled in four passes for 107 yards. Despite a furious passing attack from the Scarlet Knights, Penn State held on to win, 35–21.[6]

Now ranked #10 in the country, the Nittany Lions headed to the Carrier Dome to take on #13 Syracuse. This game ended up as a complete disaster. The Lions gave up an 80-yard touchdown pass on the first play of the game to Syracuse receiver Rob Moore, and it only got worse from there. Syracuse held a 41–0 lead at one point, before Penn State made the score look a bit more respectable at 48–21.[7]

The Lions fell into a 21–10 hole against West Virginia in the fourth quarter. Thomas helped the Lions come back, rushing for 181 yards, and scoring a one-yard touchdown to pull within 21–18. Running back Gary Brown then scored on a 19-yard run, and the Lions pulled out a 25–21 win.[8] Thomas then crossed 1,000 yards for the year with a 138-yard performance against Maryland. The "bend but don't break" defense held Maryland to just one touchdown on five trips to the red zone.[9] Linebacker Pete Giftopoulos made a key interception in the fourth quarter, helping the Nittany Lions win, 21–16.[10]

But nothing went right at Pitt Stadium. Kicker Ray Tarasi had two field goal attempts blocked, and tight end Paul Pomfret dropped a wide-open 44-yard touchdown pass. Knizner had a terrible game, completing just a quarter of his 28 passes for 128 yards and two interceptions. The Lions defense held tough, but they still ended up losing, 10–0.[11]

The Nittany Lions were now unranked. Up against #7 Notre Dame, Thomas ran for 214 yards, the most of his career. The Fighting Irish trailed 21–14 late in the fourth quarter, when their fullback Anthony Johnson ran for a one-yard touchdown to pull within one. The Irish went for the two-point conversion to try to win it, but linebacker Keith Karpinski and defensive tackle Pete Curkendall made the stop on an option play, allowing the Lions to hold on for a 21–20 victory.[12]

Thomas ran for 1,414 yards on 268 carries, catching 23 passes for 300 yards and scoring 80 points over the course of the season. His performance was key, as he ran for almost as many yards as the Lions had passing all season. Fullback John Greene helped the Lions reach nearly 2,400 yards rushing, as he ran for 473 yards to help supplement Thomas.[13] The Nittany Lions were selected to their first-ever Florida Citrus Bowl, to play against 9–2 Clemson.[14]

1988 Citrus Bowl

#20 Penn State (8–3) vs. #14 Clemson (9–2)
January 1, 1988, at the Florida Citrus Bowl in Orlando, Florida

Running back Blair Thomas injured his right knee in a practice a month before the Citrus Bowl.[15] He'd miss the game as a result. The Nittany Lions offense was doomed without him. But he wouldn't be the reason Penn State lost this game. No, it was the defense that completely imploded in this game, giving up the most points in a bowl in school history.

Clemson running back Wesley McFadden returned the opening kickoff 42 yards to the 44. Quarterback Rodney Williams threw to receiver Keith Jennings, who was left wide open, on the first play of the game for a 24-yard pickup. McFadden ran for six more, then fullback Tracy Johnson ran the ball for a pair of first downs. McFadden got the ball down to the 2 on a pitch, earning a first down, before getting tackled for a loss on the next play. Johnson ran it twice from there, and he scored from seven yards out to put Clemson up 7–0.

Quarterback Matt Knizner had struggled mightily during the regular season, and the beginning of this game proved to be more of the same. On third-and-long, he threw a pass that was so far away from its intended receiver that it almost hit Joe Paterno on the sideline. The Lions had to punt, but the defense forced one of their own by Clemson to get the ball back at the 32.

Penn State got its biggest pass play of the game from backup quarterback Darin Roberts. He took a pitch, then threw downfield to receiver Michael Timpson for a 46-yard pickup. Knizner completed to Timpson to the 6, and running back Gary Brown got the ball down to the 3. But on a reverse play, Brown fumbled it away, and defensive lineman

Tony Stephens recovered for Clemson.

As the second quarter began, the Lions got a stop, and Timpson returned it to the Clemson 45. Knizner then threw a third-down interception to defensive back Donnell Woolford, but Clemson was offside on the play. Given a reprieve, Knizner found receiver Michael Alexander open down the left sideline for a 39-yard touchdown, tying the game at seven.

Clemson took over at their own 24. Williams threw to receiver Gary Cooper for a first down at the 39. He then threw to Jennings, who

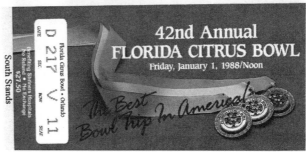

Florida Citrus Bowl tickets, 1988. Author's collection.

dragged Penn State tacklers all the way to the Lions 34. Running back Terry Allen took a pitch for 22 yards, then Johnson pounded the ball twice. On his second attempt, he scored from six yards out, and the Tigers went up 14–7.

The Lions offense couldn't do anything on offense on their next two possessions. Clemson got the ball back right before the half, and they moved it downfield. Williams fired to Jennings for a first down at the 35, then he went to receiver Ricardo Hooper and tight end James Coley for a couple more first downs. That set up future Denver Broncos kicker David Treadwell for a 28-yard field goal, but he somehow missed wide to the right. The Tigers had held the ball for nearly 21 minutes in the first half, yet they went to the locker room only up by seven.

Penn State started the second half with the ball at the 39. Brown came out on fire, ripping off a couple of great runs, including a 21-yarder. Knizner also completed a pass for a first down to tight end Paul Pomfret. The Lions got as far as the 10 before their drive stalled. Kicker Eric Etze made a 27-yard field goal, cutting the deficit to four.

They couldn't stop Clemson's offensive attack, however. Williams threw for first downs to Jennings and Cooper. Allen took the ball on an option pitch and went 21 yards down to the 8. Johnson then got the rock on three straight plays. He scored on the third of them, and the Tigers now had a 21–10 lead. That was Johnson's third touchdown run of the game.

The key play of the entire game happened on the next drive. Running back Leroy Thompson had done a spectacular job getting the Lions down inside the 10, ripping off five runs of at least seven yards (including a 24-yarder). Facing third-and-goal, Knizner tried going to the end zone, but his pass was way off the mark, and it was intercepted by linebacker Dorian Mariable. Penn State would never threaten again for the rest of the game.

Clemson got the ball back to start the fourth quarter after the teams exchanged punts. The Tigers had great field position to start, and it took little time for them to get the ball in the end zone. Williams found Jennings for a first down, then Johnson scampered for another fresh set of downs. A huge hole opened up on the next play, from which Allen took it 25 yards for a touchdown. The score was 28–10, and Penn State was now just playing for pride.

The Nittany Lions punted on their next possession, then they had one last chance to score points. Knizner threw to tight end Bob Mrosko for 25 yards, getting to the Clemson 45. But the Lions soon faced fourth-and-seven. Knizner threw the ball up for grabs, and Woolford intercepted it in the end zone. It would have made more sense for him to simply knock down the ball, but at this point that didn't matter.

If all this wasn't bad enough, Clemson tacked on another score in the closing minutes. Johnson and Allen ran for first downs, and running back Joe Henderson ripped off a 42-yard scamper down to the 8. Three plays after that, Henderson scored from four yards out. The Nittany Lions had lost 35–10, their worst-ever loss in a bowl game.

Knizner threw for 148 yards and a touchdown, but two interceptions, including the costly one when the Lions were only down by 11. Thompson led the way rushing with 55 yards, while Timpson was the leading receiver with four catches for 81 yards. The Lions defense just could not stop the run, as Clemson ran for 285 yards.

The Nittany Lions finished off a good but still disappointing season with an 8–4 record. They were knocked out of the final polls with this result. Coming off a national championship, anything seems bad by comparison, but the bowl loss and the defeat to Pitt loomed large. The next season, they wouldn't even make it to a bowl game, before things turned around in 1989.

Box score[16]:

1988 Citrus Bowl	1st	2nd	3rd	4th	Final
Clemson	7	7	7	14	35
Penn State	0	7	3	0	10

1st Quarter: CLEM—Johnson 7 run (Treadwell kick)
2nd Quarter: PSU—Alexander 39 pass from Knizner (Etze kick)
    CLEM—Johnson 6 run (Treadwell kick)
3rd Quarter: PSU—Etze 27 FG
    CLEM—Johnson 1 run (Treadwell kick)
4th Quarter: CLEM—Allen 25 run (Treadwell kick)
    CLEM—Henderson 4 run (Treadwell kick)

1989 Season (7–3–1)

Coming off their first non-winning season (5–6) since 1966 (5–5), the Nittany Lions were ranked surprisingly high at #11 in the preseason poll.[1] That lofty ranking wouldn't last for long, though. The Lions managed just a pair of field goals against Virginia, but they had a chance to tie the game in the final minute of the game. They got as far the Cavaliers 26 before turning it over on downs.[2] The 14–6 loss knocked Penn State completely out of the top 25.[3]

The Nittany Lions didn't take long to score against Temple, as quarterback Tom Bill threw a 75-yard touchdown pass to receiver David Daniels on the first play of the game. Bill ended up throwing for 192 yards and two touchdowns, both to Daniels, who had 126 yards receiving. Running back Blair Thomas ran the ball 21 times for 138 yards and scored two touchdowns. Linebacker Andre Collins blocked a punt in the 42–3 win.[4]

Boston College came to Beaver Stadium and completely shut down the Penn State passing offense. Quarterback Tony Sacca completed just four passes for 64 yards. Thomas made up for the lack of an air game with 118 yards on the ground, but the Lions trailed 3–0 with four minutes left. On fourth-and-eight, head coach Joe Paterno passed up a tying field goal and kept the offense out there. Sacca picked up 13 yards on a scramble to set up first-and-goal. Facing fourth down again, Sacca faked a handoff to Thomas and kept the ball himself on a bootleg for the game-winning one-yard touchdown in a 7–3 final.[5]

The Nittany Lions next traveled to Austin to take on the Texas Longhorns. Sacca threw a 33-yard touchdown pass to Daniels in the first quarter to open the scoring. On a fourth-quarter Texas punt, Collins rushed in to block the kick, and defensive back Leonard Humphries returned it two yards for the game-winning touchdown. The Penn State defense shut down Texas for the rest of the game to hold on to a 16–12 win.[6]

Giants Stadium hosted a battle between Penn State and Rutgers. The defense continued to dominate, shutting out the Scarlet Knights to make it four weeks with just 18 total points given up. Sacca threw a 23-yard touchdown pass to receiver Terry Smith in the first half, and fullback Brian O'Neal closed the scoring with a six-yard run, as the Nittany Lions came out of New Jersey with a 17–0 victory.[7]

The Lions stayed on the road to take on Syracuse at the Carrier Dome. Receiver O.J. McDuffie returned a punt 84 yards on his way to 203 all-purpose yards. He caught two passes for 40 yards and rushed twice for 48 more, plus all his return yardage (115 yards). Thomas ran for a 38-yard touchdown in the first quarter, as Penn State took a 10–6 lead into the half. Sacca fired a seven-yard touchdown pass to tight end Dave Jakob to put the finishing touches on a 34–12 triumph.[8]

On a five-game winning streak, Penn State had climbed back up to #14 in the Associated Press poll.[9] They now took on #6 Alabama at Beaver Stadium for a chance to climb higher. Thomas had a big day, rushing 35 times for 160 yards. Sacca threw a 19-yard touchdown pass to McDuffie as part of his 91 yards. Late in the game, trailing by one, the Lions rode Thomas down to the 1 to set up a game-winning 18-yard field goal attempt. But the Tide blocked kicker Ray Tarasi's kick, and Penn State lost 17–16.[10]

Next Penn State took on West Virginia. With Thomas rushing for 150 yards, and the defense holding WVU to just one touchdown, Sacca didn't have to do much. In fact, he completed only two of his 13 passes, but one of them went for a 31-yard touchdown to Jakob. Collins blocked an extra point and recovered two fumbles. The Lions fell on top of five of WVU's 11 fumbles, as they went on to a 19–9 victory.[11]

Penn State was back up to #13 in the poll as they went to Baltimore to take on Maryland. Sacca struggled again, throwing for only 45 yards, so Paterno put in Bill, who threw for 119. Fullback Leroy Thompson ran for a seven-yard touchdown, and Thomas picked up 125 yards on the ground. However, Maryland quarterback Neil O'Donnell threw a touchdown pass and led his team to two drives for fourth-quarter field goals. The second one tied the game at 13, and the Terrapins were more than thrilled to come away with a tie.[12]

The Nittany Lions scored their most points since the Syracuse game in a battle with Notre Dame, but they surrendered 425 rushing yards in a 34–23 loss. The PSU passing game continued to struggle, as neither quarterback reached 60 yards throwing. Bill did provide 76 yards on the ground, and coupled with Thomas's 133 yards and two touchdowns, the Lions went over 200 rushing yards, but it was not enough.[13]

The season ended at Pitt Stadium, where the Lions jumped out to a 10–0 lead in the first quarter. Sacca threw a 19-yard touchdown pass to Daniels, while Bill also threw for 137 yards. Pitt quarterback Alex Van Pelt brought the Panthers back to tie the game at 13 in the fourth quarter. Bill then converted two third-and-ten plays to move the ball into field goal range. Tarasi converted the 20-yard field goal, and the Nittany Lions came out with a 16–13 win over their most bitter rivals.[14]

The rotating quarterbacks produced just under 1,300 passing yards for the season. Sacca led with 694 yards and six touchdowns, while Bill had 605 yards and three scores. Daniels led the Nittany Lions in receiving with 22 catches for 362 yards and four scoring catches. Thomas ran for over 1,300 yards and five touchdowns.[15] On defense, the Nittany Lions gave up just 13 offensive touchdowns all season, with only Notre Dame crossing the goal line twice against the Penn State D.[16]

BYU received an automatic bid in the Holiday Bowl by virtue of winning the Western Athletic Conference, making it their eighth trip to San Diego. The Holiday Bowl Team Selection Committee wanted a team from the east to raise the bowl's profile, and they got their wish with Penn State. It was the first trip to the Holiday Bowl for the Nittany Lions, who finished the regular season ranked #18.[17]

1989 Holiday Bowl

#18 Penn State (7–3–1) vs. #19 Brigham Young (10–2)
December 29, 1989, at San Diego Jack Murphy Stadium in San Diego, California

Two of the last three Holiday Bowls had seen at least 70 points combined. It figured that if this game made it three in four years, it would be good for Brigham Young.

Quarterback Ty Detmer and the explosive BYU offense could score at will. But it also figured that if this game was a low-scoring affair, that would benefit Penn State, which liked to run the ball and control the clock. As it turned out, all those assumptions would be wrong.

BYU won the toss, which used a special one-dollar coin commemorating the 200th anniversary of the founding of Congress. They chose to receive, and they started from their own 16. Detmer threw his first pass to receiver Jeff Frandsen for 26 yards, then completed his second pass to receiver Brent Nyberg for another first down. On his third pass, he launched it deep for Nyberg, who came down with it for a touchdown. The Cougars had proved how potent their offense was, but this one wouldn't count, as they got called for having an ineligible man downfield. Detmer managed to get a first down on a pass to receiver Matt Odle, before a couple of penalties set BYU back. On fourth-and-12 from the Penn State 32, head coach LaVell Edwards chose to go for it, but Detmer's pass for Frandsen fell incomplete.

Penn State looked to play ball-control on their first drive. Running back Blair Thomas ran for eight yards on his first carry, then picked up a first down from there. Quarterback Tony Sacca found receiver David Daniels for a first down at the BYU 45. Thomas used a great cutback to gain another first down at the 32. Two more runs by Thomas set up a fourth-and-one, and head coach Joe Paterno also chose to go for it. There wasn't anything fancy about this offense; it was simply Thomas running the ball again, and he got the first down. He set up a 30-yard field goal by kicker Ray Tarasi. The Penn State drive took 13 plays and lasted nearly five minutes.

Defensive back Sherrod Rainge intercepted Detmer on his next drive. Only three plays later, Sacca returned the favor, throwing an interception to defensive back Tony Crutchfield. BYU took advantage, with running back Fred Whittingham running for a first down, and Detmer beating a blitz with a 21-yard pass to receiver Andy Boyce down to the 1. The Cougars couldn't punch it in from there, though, and they settled for a 20-yard field goal by kicker Jason Chaffetz. The first quarter came to an end with the game tied at three.

The Nittany Lions started their next drive at their own 38. Sacca completed a third-down pass to receiver O.J. McDuffie to the BYU 43. Thomas took a pitch and gained seven more yards, then Sacca hit receiver Terry Smith for a first down at the 32. The Lions ran a little misdirection, with Sacca handing to McDuffie for a pickup of seven. Sacca then fired to his left to Smith, who was left wide open for a 24-yard touchdown. Tarasi missed the extra point wide to the right, but Penn State led 9–3.

BYU answered with a time-consuming drive. Detmer started it with a six-yard scramble. On third down, he pump-faked twice before finding tight end Chris Smith for a first down at the 44. Two of his next three passes went to Nyberg, both picking up first downs, and the second one for 24 yards. He then went back to Smith to get down to the 1. On second-and-goal, he faked a handoff, then ran it into the right side of the end zone. Chaffetz's extra point gave BYU a 10–9 lead.

Back came the Nittany Lions, with a drive almost completely composed of runs. Thomas and running back Leroy Thompson split carries, with Thomas carrying it five times and Thompson four. Sacca also completed a pass to McDuffie for a first down in the middle of the drive. He was sacked by linebacker Bob Davis later in the drive, which forced a field goal attempt. Tarasi made the 36-yard field goal to give Penn State a 12–10 lead.

It took only one play for BYU to get back into field goal range. Detmer launched one for running back Matt Bellini, who hauled it in for 50 yards. He then found Smith at the 13 for another first down, before going to Whittingham at the 4. With 20 seconds left in the half, BYU called timeout to talk it over before their third-down play. Detmer couldn't find anyone open, so he threw it away. The Cougars got a 22-yard field goal from Chaffetz, and they went to the locker room with a 13–12 lead.

McDuffie took the opening kickoff of the second half all the way out to the 49. Thomas carried it twice from there, getting a first down. He and Thompson each got another carry, but on third down Sacca couldn't connect with Thomas for a new set of downs. Tarasi came on for a 51-yard field goal attempt, and he managed to get just enough distance to squeeze the ball over the bar. The Lions again led by two.

"This game looks like it's going to be a field goal game," ESPN announcer Vince Dooley commented.[18] But after a BYU punt, the floodgates opened. McDuffie took the punt back to the 46. Sacca then hit tight end David Jakob for 12 yards. After a holding penalty set Penn State back, Thomas gained all the yards back and then some with a great cutback for 19. Thompson then took a carry to his right, broke a tackle, and ran it into the end zone for a 16-yard touchdown. The Lions' lead expanded to nine.

Rainge got called for a personal foul early in the next drive, and that penalty helped spark the drive. Detmer hit Frandsen on three passes, two of them getting first downs, and the third a fantastic catch by the receiver down at the 1. Detmer again ran play action at the goal line, juking out a defender to run it in for his second touchdown. The extra point was low and ended up being blocked, but BYU pulled within three.

McDuffie took the next kickoff to the 34. Thomas received a toss from Sacca, made another nice cutback, and gained a first down at the BYU 44. After a pair of incompletions from Sacca, the Nittany Lions seemingly had to punt, but Paterno pulled a fast one. He put Terry Smith back to "punt." In reality, all he did was just take the long snap, then fire a pass to his right to defensive back Tisen Thomas, who picked up a first down. The Cougars got called for a personal foul on the next play, before Thompson burst up the middle for a 14-yard touchdown. The Nittany Lions were now up 29–19.

The seesaw continued on BYU's next drive, which started after a kickoff return by fullback Scott Charlton to the 43. Detmer threw a fade to Nyberg for a first down at the PSU 40, and Whittingham burst through a hole for nine more yards. The Lions jumped offside to give BYU another first down, then Detmer fired to Bellini for another new set of downs at the 13. Boyce then hauled in a touchdown pass, and the Cougars pulled within 29–26 as the third quarter came to an end.

Facing third down at his own 31, Sacca threw to Thomas, who broke several tackles on a sensational play that got Penn State all the way to the BYU 39. On the next third down, the Cougars brought a blitz, but Sacca got the ball away in time to Thomas for a first down at the 19. Thompson and Thomas split the next four carries, with the final carry going to Thomas for seven yards and a touchdown. While the extra point ended up being aborted due to a mishandled snap, the Lions led again by nine.

The Penn State defense had been gashed for much of this game, but now they made a couple of big plays. First, linebacker Richard McKenzie and defensive tackle Todd Burger combined on a sack. Then, Rainge intercepted a Detmer pass, returning it to the Penn State 40. Thomas ran for a good gain on first down, then Sacca threw a bomb down the right sideline to receiver David Daniels. In an effort that looked like Lynn Swann in Super Bowl X, Daniels bobbled the ball before catching it while lying on his back in the end zone. The 52-yard touchdown pass put the Lions up 41–26, even though Sacca's two-point pass fell incomplete.

It took BYU just four plays to respond. They started at their own 41, and Detmer hit Bellini on the first play for 19 yards. He then threw to Nyberg two times in a row, and the combined 30 yards of the passes got BYU down to the 10. From there, Whittingham pounded the ball for a touchdown, and the Cougars pulled back within eight.

Penn State punted for the first time in the game on their next drive, with punter Doug Helkowski nailing down the Cougars at their own 10. Of course, with Detmer, field position didn't matter much. Detmer found a wide-open Boyce for 36 yards on the first play of the drive. Boyce caught two more passes for first downs, and Chris Smith hauled one in at the 10. The Cougars got a first down on a pass interference call on the Lions, then Detmer hit Nyberg for a three-yard touchdown, making it a two-point game.

Edwards called timeout for the Cougars to talk it over. There was just under three minutes left in the ballgame, so BYU obviously had to go for two. On the play, Detmer threw over the middle, trying to find Smith. However, linebacker Andre Collins hopped in front of the pass and picked it off two yards deep in the end zone. He then sprinted down his right sideline, with no one on the Cougars able to catch him. That's right, a linebacker returned an interception 102 yards without having to pitch the ball to anyone. Not only did Penn State stop BYU, but they got two points of their own, so they now led 43–39.

With little time left, Edwards chose to go for the onside kick. Penn State recovered the kick at the BYU 46, so now it was up to the Cougar defense. Some curious play calling by Paterno led to a quick punt. On second down, he ran an end around, which McDuffie was tackled on for a ten-yard loss. With BYU now having used up all their timeouts, a run seemed in order on third-and-18, but instead Penn State went play action. Sacca had no one to throw to, and he was being chased, so he stepped out of bounds. That gave BYU over two minutes after the punt that went down to the 12.

Detmer got the ball 88 yards from paydirt and a victory. He completed his second pass to Nyberg for 14 yards. Penn State was called for holding, before Detmer threw a short pass to Bellini. His next pass went to Smith, who got across midfield to the 46. He then found Boyce for eight more yards, and a huffing and puffing Penn State defense had to call timeout to catch its breath. Rainge broke up Detmer's next pass, leaving 57 seconds for BYU. On the fateful play, defensive back Gary Brown came in on a blitz, and he ended up running up behind Detmer. He didn't strip Detmer as much as he just stole the ball right out of his hand. He snatched the ball, then ran it 53 yards for the game-clinching touchdown. The Lions had won it, 50–39, after a most incredible defensive play.

The Nittany Lions won despite Detmer throwing for 576 yards, the most in any bowl in the history of the NCAA. Altogether, the teams totaled over 1,100 yards of offense in this wild shootout. Two hundred six of those came on the arm of Sacca, who threw for two touchdowns. Thompson ran for 68 yards and two touchdowns, but it was Thomas who won Player of the Game honors (along with Detmer) for his 186 rushing yards, a Penn State bowl record. The Lions finished the season ranked #15 in the nation with a mark of 8–3–1.[19]

Box Score[20]:

1989 Holiday Bowl	1st	2nd	3rd	4th	Final
Penn State	3	9	17	21	50
Brigham Young	3	10	13	13	39

1st Quarter: PSU—Tarasi 30 FG

BYU—Chaffetz 20 FG

2nd Quarter: PSU—T. Smith 24 pass from Sacca (kick missed)

BYU—Detmer 1 run (Chaffetz kick)

PSU—Tarasi 36 FG

BYU—Chaffetz 22 FG

3rd Quarter: PSU—Tarasi 51 FG

PSU—Thompson 16 run (Tarasi kick)

BYU—Detmer 1 run (kick blocked)

PSU—Thompson 14 run (Tarasi kick)

BYU—Boyce 12 pass from Detmer (Chaffetz kick)

4th Quarter: PSU—Thomas 7 run (PAT aborted)

PSU—Daniels 52 pass from Sacca (pass failed)

BYU—Whittingham 10 run (Chaffetz kick)

BYU—Nyberg 3 pass from Detmer (Collins 102 interception return for two points for PSU)

PSU—Brown 53 fumble return (Tarasi kick)

1990 Season (9–2)

The Nittany Lions began 1990 with a bang against Texas, as running back Gary Brown returned the opening kickoff 95 yards to the Longhorns 3. Running back Leroy Thompson scored from there, and Penn State had an early 7–0 lead. Then things fell apart, as kicker Henry Adkins missed a pair of field goals, and Texas got a long kick-off return of their own to set up a touchdown.[1] Trailing by four, quarterback Tony Sacca's Hail Mary fell incomplete, and Penn State lost its opener, 17–13.[2]

The Lions headed to Los Angeles to play #6 USC the next week. Trailing by five, line-backer Keith Goganious dropped a pass he should have intercepted and returned for a touchdown.[3] Later, Sacca had a fourth-down pass intercepted, and Penn State lost 19–14 for their first 0–2 start since the Aloha Bowl season of 1983.[4]

The Lions then wouldn't lose again for the rest of the regular season. Thompson ran for four touchdowns in the first half against Rutgers, and he set up one of those short runs with a 36-yard catch. The Lions led by 28 points at halftime.[5] The Lions defense recorded six sacks and an interception as they preserved the 28–0 shutout.[6]

For Homecoming against Temple, the Lions offense put up almost 600 yards of offense. Brown returned a kickoff 82 yards to put fullback Sam Gash in range to score a touchdown. Sacca threw long touchdown passes to receivers Terry Smith (33 yards) and David Daniels (26 yards). Thompson rushed for 125 yards, and Brown added another 105.[7] The Nittany Lions won 48–10 for their 20th straight win over the Owls.[8]

Penn State had decided to end its series with Syracuse as they moved into the Big Ten within the next three years. Gash ran for 78 yards and also caught three passes for 33 yards. He scored on a two-yard run and put the game away with a late 35-yard run. Defensive back Willie Thomas picked off a pass, and linebacker Andre Powell forced a fumble on a kickoff which defensive back Greg Fusetti recovered, as Penn State won 27–21.[9]

Running back Shelly Hammonds rushed for a Penn State freshman-record 208 yards against Boston College.[10] Playing because both Thompson and Brown had gone down with injuries, Hammonds's total could have been even more amazing, as he had a 58-yard touchdown run called back on a clipping foul. As it stood, his 191 second-half yards were the second-best in school history, and Penn State had a 40–21 victory.[11]

The defense came up big in Tuscaloosa. They forced six turnovers, allowed only six yards rushing (Alabama's worst ever), and shut out the Crimson Tide 9–0. It wasn't a pretty game offensively, as Penn State failed to reach the end zone, and they had to settle for three field goals by kicker Craig Fayak.[12] But the Lions came away with the first shut-out at Bryant-Denny Stadium in 35 years, as another rivalry series came to an end.[13]

Sacca continued to struggle in the next game against West Virginia, so Paterno put in backup Tom Bill. He threw a touchdown pass while scoring his first career rushing touchdown. Defensive back Darren Perry had a pick-six, and running back Gerry Collins ran for a 19-yard touchdown.[14] The Nittany Lions came out of Morgantown with a 31–19 win.[15]

Against Maryland, defensive back Leonard Humphries picked off a pass and returned it 74 yards for a touchdown. With the game tied at 10 in the third quarter, Paterno replaced Bill with Sacca. He threw a 30-yard touchdown pass to Daniels on fourth-and-21. Thompson added a ten-yard run as part of his 132 rushing yards, and Penn State beat the Terrapins, 24–10.[16]

The Nittany Lions improved to #18 in the nation, but their next game was in South Bend against the #1-ranked Notre Dame Fighting Irish. It didn't look good early, as Notre Dame jumped out to a 21–7 halftime lead. In the third quarter, linebacker Mark D'Onofrio picked off a pass and returned it 38 yards, setting up a touchdown pass from Sacca to tight end Rick Sayles. In the fourth quarter, Sacca threw a 14-yard touchdown pass to tight end Al Golden. With the game tied, Perry picked off a pass and returned it 31 yards into field goal range. Fayak then made a 34-yard attempt with no time left, and Penn State came away with a 24–21 win. The Irish's national title hopes were gone, while Penn State vaulted to #11 in the Associated Press poll.[17]

The season ended at home against 3–6 Pitt. Sacca put up 300 yards of total offense against the Panthers, who nearly pulled out the upset. One hundred thirteen of those yards came on the ground, the first 100-yard game rushing for a Penn State quarterback since way back in 1946.[18] Humphries and defensive back Derek Bochna each picked off passes from Panthers quarterback Alex Van Pelt in the fourth quarter to preserve a 22–17 win.[19]

The 9–2 Nittany Lions finished 1990 exactly one yard shy of 2,000 rushing for the season. Thanks mainly to Sacca, who had 1,866 yards and ten touchdowns, their passing performance actually topped that, as the Lions threw for 2,134 yards for the year.[20] Thompson led the team with 573 rushing yards and eight touchdowns. Daniels was the top receiver, with 31 catches for 538 yards and four scores.[21]

The Nittany Lions were courted by seven bowls: the Sugar, Fiesta, Cotton, Citrus, Gator, Hall of Fame, and Blockbuster. The Hall of Fame, now known as the Outback, was ruled out once Penn State came away with the huge victory over Notre Dame, as it was a lower-tier bowl. The Fiesta was also ruled out due to political controversy in Arizona. The Sugar passed on Penn State before the Notre Dame game, only to come back begging to Paterno after the upset. Paterno refused, and he selected the brand-new Blockbuster Bowl. The #7 Nittany Lions would meet the #6 Florida State Seminoles in Miami for the first edition of this enticing bowl game.[22]

1990 Blockbuster Bowl

#7 Penn State (9–2) vs. #6 Florida State (9–2)
December 28, 1990, at Joe Robbie Stadium in Miami Gardens, Florida

The Blockbuster Bowl? What was that? To the college football fan of the 2020s, they probably have no idea what bowl this was, where it was played, or why it was sponsored by a now-defunct company. The Blockbuster Bowl was originally known as the Sunshine

Football Classic, a game to be played at Joe Robbie Stadium, now Hard Rock Stadium. At the time, the Orange Bowl was still played in the Miami Orange Bowl stadium. The Sunshine Classic had Joe Robbie to itself, and before the first game was played, Blockbuster Video President H. Wayne Huizenga (part-owner of the Miami Dolphins) gave the game a sponsor. Blockbuster's support made this bowl game one of the highest-paying of the season, as well as one of the most highly attended.[23]

For its first few seasons, the Blockbuster Bowl was one of the top bowls in the nation. But once the Orange Bowl game moved to Joe Robbie, and the Blockbuster's attendance went down, the game fizzled out and turned into one of the low-quality bowls. It eventually moved to Orlando to become the sister game of the Citrus Bowl. The bowl changed its name frequently, only getting a "real" name as the Tangerine Bowl for a few years. It is now known as the Cheez-It Bowl, not to be confused with the former Cheez-It Bowl in Arizona. Just like the company who sponsored the bowl at the beginning, the fortunes of the Blockbuster Bowl spiraled downward and crashed.

For this year, though, this bowl was one of the best. In fact, almost all the experts labeled the Blockbuster as the third-best bowl of the season, behind only the Orange Bowl and Cotton Bowl.[24] It had the #6 and #7 teams, and the two winningest coaches in the game, Joe Paterno and Bobby Bowden. Due to the fact that #1 Colorado had a loss and a tie and #2 Georgia Tech had a tie, the winner of this game had an outside shot at the national championship. They would need Colorado to lose the Orange Bowl and Georgia Tech to lose the Citrus Bowl, though.[25]

Penn State won the toss, and Paterno chose to defer to the second half. The Seminoles immediately marched downfield, with quarterback Casey Weldon hitting tight end Reggie Johnson for a 30-yard gain on his first pass of the game. The Nittany Lions then got called for pass interference on a third down. Weldon completed a short pass to running back Amp Lee, then ran to within two yards of the first down. On third down, he threw to receiver Lawrence Dawsey, who was wide open. He dropped an easy catch. FSU settled for a 41-yard field goal by kicker Richie Andrews to go up 3–0.

The Lions went three-and-out, and punter Doug Helkowski came on to kick it away. His kick was fielded by defensive back Terrell Buckley, who ran backwards nearly 20 yards trying to find a seam. He found it, and he sprinted down the right sideline all the way to the Penn State 15. It was a huge risk that paid off with a huge reward. Weldon then ran it down to the 2, and Lee scored from a yard away to put Florida State up 10–0.

Penn State got a first down on a reverse by receiver Terry Smith, who picked up 13 yards. After that, false start penalties doomed their drive. They punted it away, and then Florida State had penalty problems of their own. FSU was called for intentional grounding and holding, and they were forced to kick. Punter John Wimberly's kick went for a touchback.

The Lions made quick work to get downfield. Quarterback Tony Sacca threw to receiver David Daniels for 19 yards, and running back Gary Brown picked up five more. Sacca then went play action, and he fired downfield for tight end Al Golden. In a broken play, Daniels ended up in the same area as Golden, and he stole the reception from the tight end. Florida State defenders crashed into each other in the confusion, and Daniels went all the way for a 56-yard touchdown. The Lions had pulled within three at the end of the first quarter.

Florida State marched downfield for another score. Running back Edgar Bennett caught a dump-off for 17 yards, and later, Weldon hit Dawsey on a pass pattern down to the Penn State 13. Johnson hauled in a tipped pass, then Lee took a pitch seven yards for a touchdown. The Seminoles went back in front by ten points.

Sacca threw an interception to linebacker Howard Dinkins on his next drive. Florida State had the ball near midfield, but Penn State defensive back Darren Perry made an interception of his own. He returned it to the FSU 46. Brown ran for six yards, then Sacca took off on a 20-yard run of his own. Brown took a toss for five more, and Sacca got the first down on another run. But the drive stalled, and kicker Craig Fayak's 22-yard field goal was blocked by FSU defensive back Tommy Henry.

Linebacker Eric Ravotti picked up a sack of Weldon, and the Nittany Lions forced a punt. They took over with great field position at the Florida State 49. Sacca found Daniels for a big gain down to the 18, before Brown had a run down to the 5 taken off the board thanks to a holding call. On the next play, Sacca threw an interception to defensive back Leon Fowler. The Lions went to the half trailing, 17–7.

Penn State defensive back Leonard Humphries picked off a Weldon pass early in the second half. Sacca threw to Daniels for a first down at the 29, then he went to receiver Tisen Thomas for another new set of downs at the 45. Smith hauled in a pass for a first down and picked up more yards thanks to a tackle by the facemask. Daniels caught a pass to get down to the 15, but that was as far as Penn State went. Fayak this time made his 32-yard attempt, and the Lions pulled within a touchdown.

For some reason, the Lions decided to go with the squib kick on the ensuing kickoff. The Seminoles picked it up and got to their own 42, getting outstanding field position. Weldon found Dawsey for a gain of 23, and Bennett hauled one in and got down to the 5. Two plays later, Weldon ran it in off the right side for a five-yard touchdown, and the Seminoles went up by 14.

The Nittany Lions punted on their next possession, and that was the end of the third quarter. They then got the ball back at the Florida State 40 after a terribly shanked 15-yard punt. Brown ran for five yards on first down, but Sacca was sacked on third down, and the Lions had to punt again. That would be the last we would see of Sacca for this game.

Thomas returned the next FSU punt to the 38, and into the game stepped backup quarterback Tom Bill. He immediately gave Penn State a spark, throwing over the middle to Daniels for 22 yards. Running back Leroy Thompson ran for a few more yards, then Bill launched one down the middle to Smith for a 37-yard touchdown. In only three plays, Bill had revitalized the Penn State offense, and the Lions now trailed by only a touchdown.

The Lions defense forced another punt, and they got the ball back at their own 20 after a touchback with five minutes to go. Bill threw to Smith for 25 yards, but that would be his only completion on the drive. The Lions punted again, and Helkowski put the ball down at the 10. The Nittany defense forced a quick three-and-out, and the offense would get one last try with three minutes to play.

While the Raycom announcers discussed whether Penn State should go for the tie or for the win should they score a touchdown, Bill threw a pair of incomplete passes. He ran it on third down and came up short of the marker. On fourth down, he decided to launch the long bomb. It was way off target, and defensive back John Davis foolishly intercepted it at the 1 instead of just knocking it down. That gave Florida State horrible field position, but Bennett got them out of the hole. They were able to run the clock and hold on to beat Penn State 24–17.

On paper, it was an even game. Each team had accumulated exactly 400 yards. Both of them did so mainly through the air. Sacca threw for 194 yards and a touchdown but two interceptions; Bill threw for 84 yards on only seven passes, getting a touchdown and throwing an interception. Daniels had a monster game, catching from both quarterbacks. He set school records in both receptions (seven) and receiving yards (154). Despite the loss, the Lions finished the year ranked a respectable #11 in the Associated Press poll with a 9–3 record.[26]

Box score[27]:

1990 Blockbuster Bowl	1st	2nd	3rd	4th	Final
Penn State	7	0	3	7	17
Florida State	10	7	7	0	24

1st Quarter: FSU—Andrews 41 FG
    FSU—Lee 1 run (Andrews kick)
    PSU—Daniels 56 pass from Sacca (Fayak kick)
2nd Quarter: FSU—Lee 7 run (Andrews kick)
3rd Quarter: PSU—Fayak 32 FG
    FSU—Weldon 5 run (Andrews kick)
4th Quarter: PSU—Smith 37 pass from Bill (Fayak kick)

1991 Season (10–2)

Penn State began the 1991 season at Giants Stadium for the Kickoff Classic against Georgia Tech, the defending coaches' poll national champions. This one proved to be no contest, as the Nittany Lions raced to a 13–3 lead at halftime, and extended their lead to 24–3 after three quarters. Quarterback Tony Sacca set a new school record by throwing for five touchdowns. Receiver O.J. McDuffie caught two of those scoring passes, as the Lions roared to a 34–22 win.[1]

Against Cincinnati in the home opener, Penn State rolled to an 81–0 victory, scoring their most points since 1926. The Lions rushed for 484 yards, as part of a 706-yard day. Sacca threw for 190 yards and two touchdowns, both to tight end Kyle Brady. Running back Shelly Hammonds and fullback Sam Gash each scored two touchdowns.[2]

The Nittany Lions were now ranked #5 in the nation, but they had to travel to Los Angeles to take on the USC Trojans. Penn State had not won in L.A. since 1968, and it stayed that way, as they lost 21–10. The Nittany Lions fumbled seven times, bringing their number for the season to an astonishing 16 in just three games. Sacca was sacked five times in the loss. One bright spot was receiver Terry Smith, who caught ten passes for 165 yards, both school records.[3]

Quarterback Ty Detmer of Brigham Young poised a challenge coming into Beaver Stadium. Having won the Heisman Trophy the year before, he was the first defending Heisman winner to come to Happy Valley since Navy's Roger Staubach in 1964. Despite all that, the Lions held him to just 158 yards passing, the fewest of his career. They also came up with six sacks and an interception. Sacca outplayed Detmer by throwing for 187 yards and a touchdown, and Penn State won easily, 33–7.[4]

Next came Boston College into State College. The Eagles surprisingly led 7–6 at the half. But PSU defensive back Darren Perry intercepted three passes of BC quarterback Glenn Foley, including one he returned 45 yards for a touchdown. That was part of a 22-point second half, in which Sacca scored on a five-yard touchdown run and a two-point rush. The Lions took a 28–7 lead, and despite a late scare, they escaped with a 28–21 win.[5]

In Philadelphia, the Nittany Lion defense held Temple to just one touchdown in a 24–7 win. Sacca completed 15 of his 21 attempts for 211 yards and a pair of touchdowns. Again, it was Perry who provided the big play that put the game away. This time, with the lead at just ten points in the fourth quarter, he picked off a pass and returned it 41 yards for the game-sealing score.[6]

The Nittany Lions were headed to the Orange Bowl—not the bowl game, but the stadium—to face the #2-ranked Miami Hurricanes. This proved to be a back-and-forth battle, in which Miami took a 26–20 lead late. On the final drive, Sacca got the Lions down to the Miami 44. He put up a Hail Mary, but it was intercepted, and the Hurricanes held on to win by six.[7]

Things got sloppy against Rutgers. The Nittany Lions committed 15 penalties, which would have been crippling on most days. However, the Scarlet Knights matched them with 16 of their own! The 314 penalty yards were the most in Beaver Stadium history. Smith caught his 43rd pass of the season, setting a new school record, as the Lions beat Rutgers 37–17.[8]

West Virginia came to Happy Valley only to get creamed. Sacca threw three touchdown passes and also ran for one, and the Lions rolled to a 51–6 win. Penn State was up 24 points before West Virginia got their lone touchdown on the board. Running back Richie Anderson ran for 100 yards and a touchdown, and fullback J.T. Morris scored on a 66-yard run.[9]

Sacca reached career milestones against Maryland, setting school records for passing yardage and completions, as Penn State rolled to a 47–7 victory. Smith also broke a record, going over 700 receiving yards for the season and setting a new school mark in that category. McDuffie returned a punt 60 yards for a touchdown, while Anderson ran for 96 yards and two touchdowns.[10]

Up against Notre Dame, Anderson scored two first-quarter touchdowns, and Penn State got out to a 21-point lead. McDuffie had an enormous day, going for 143 all-purpose yards, including 86 receiving yards and three total touchdowns. Sacca passed for 151 yards and two scores, while Anderson ended up with 136 rushing yards. The final score ended up 35–13 in Penn State's favor, in their final home game of the season.[11]

The season finale was at Pitt Stadium. Anderson ran for 167 yards and two touchdowns, and Fayak kicked four field goals. Meanwhile, the defense picked off five passes by Panthers quarterback Alex Van Pelt, who was forced to throw the ball 64 times in a comeback effort. The Lions closed the season with a 32–20 win over Pitt, earning their tenth victory of the season.[12] It was Paterno's 239th in his career, moving him into fourth place all-time in college football history.[13]

Sacca threw for 2,488 yards in 1991, as the Nittany Lions passed for more yards than for which they rushed for the first time since 1982.[14] Smith led the team with 55 catches for 846 yards and eight touchdowns. McDuffie was right behind him with 46 receptions for 790 yards and six scores. Anderson ended up with 779 yards on the ground and ten rushing touchdowns.[15]

The Citrus, Fiesta, and Sugar Bowls all showed interest in the Lions. At one point, it looked like the Sugar Bowl would invite the winner of the Penn State–Notre Dame game, but ultimately the Fighting Irish were too tempting for the Sugar executives to pass up.[16] The Lions were instead invited to the Fiesta Bowl, where despite being outgained in all four previous games, they were 4–0.[17]

1992 Fiesta Bowl

#7 Penn State (10–2) vs. #10 Tennessee (9–2)
January 1, 1992, at Sun Devil Stadium in Tempe, Arizona

The game couldn't have started out any better for Penn State. Tennessee defensive back Dale Carter went back to return the opening kickoff, but he lost the ball in the sun.

He muffed the return, and Penn State defensive back Geff Kerwin recovered it near the Tennessee 10. Three plays later, quarterback Tony Sacca hit fullback Sam Gash on a play action pass over the middle for a ten-yard touchdown, and the Lions led 7–0 early.

After settling in, the Volunteers proved themselves to be a formidable opponent. Their defense locked down the Nittany offense, completely constricting them for the remainder of the first half. Penn State went three-and-out on each of its next three possessions in the first quarter. Meanwhile, Tennessee had no trouble. Quarterback Andy Kelly completed passes to receivers J.J. McCleskey and Carl Pickens for first downs, and running back James Stewart capped off the drive with a one-yard touchdown run. That tied the game at seven apiece.

Stewart carried the ball five times on Tennessee's next possession. Receiver Lloyd Kerr broke wide open to catch a pass down at the 15, and Stewart got half the distance remaining. However, the Tennessee drive ended there, so kicker John Becksvoort was called on to try a 24-yard field goal. He made it, and Tennessee led Penn State 10–7 after one quarter.

Penn State had been outgained 199–10 in yardage in the first quarter. The second quarter wasn't much better. They got lucky when Becksvoort missed a 37-yard field goal attempt wide right. They only got one first down on each of their next two possessions before having to punt. If not for the defense, this game would be over. On one drive, Tennessee went for it on fourth down deep inside PSU territory late in the second quarter. Lions defensive tackle Tyoka Jackson and linebacker Keith Goganious stuffed Volunteers running back Mose Phillips, and Tennessee turned the ball over on downs. That kept the Vols' lead at just 10–7, even though they outgained Penn State 324 to 59 in yards in the first half.

Things didn't immediately get better for the Lions. Kelly threw to receiver Craig Faulkner for eight yards, and fullback Mario Brunson picked up the first down. On the next play, it looked like Penn State had a sack, but an inadvertent facemask call wiped out the big defensive play. Tennessee took advantage, as Kelly fired to receiver Cory Fleming for a 44-yard touchdown reception on which Fleming skillfully avoided several tackles. The Volunteers had now stretched their lead to ten.

After yet another Penn State punt, Tennessee head coach Johnny Majors tried some trickery on a punt of his own. He had punter Tom Hutton try running the ball on a fake punt, but linebacker Reggie Givens brought him down short of the first down marker. While Penn State punted even on the next possession, it did at least stop Tennessee from making things even worse.

The Lions forced another Tennessee punt, and they finally got the break they needed. Receiver O.J. McDuffie returned Hutton's punt 39 yards, weaving through Volunteers to get inside the Tennessee 35. Getting a free play due to an offside penalty, Sacca threw to McDuffie for a 27-yard gain. On the next third down, Sacca rolled to his left, then fired a pass to receiver Chip LaBarca in the end zone. Touchdown! Kicker Craig Fayak made the extra point, and Penn State now only trailed by three.

That was when the floodgates opened. The Nittany Lions defense would completely take over the game. First, Jackson sacked Kelly on a second-down play, forced a fumble, and recovered it, all while Tennessee got called for holding on the play. On the very next play, Sacca rolled right, then threw it back across the field to tight end Kyle Brady on his left. He ran it the rest of the way for a 13-yard touchdown, and the Lions had their first lead since early in the first quarter.

Kelly turned the ball over on his second play for the second straight drive. This time, he threw a pick to Givens. Sacca came on and fired over the middle to receiver Troy Drayton for 18 yards. Anderson ran it twice from there, getting down to the 2. He then punched it in for a two-yard touchdown. Penn State now had a 28–17 lead briefly into the fourth quarter.

On the next drive, the Vols wouldn't even hold the ball for one play. Defensive back Derek Bochna came on a corner blitz and slammed Kelly, knocking the ball out. Givens picked it up and returned it 23 yards for a touchdown. The game had been turned on its ear; suddenly Penn State had an 18-point lead!

It only got better from there for the Lions. They were the ones forcing a three-and-out, and McDuffie had another nice return inside the Tennessee 48. Anderson ran it three times to start the drive, and he picked up a first down on the third carry. Two plays later, Sacca found McDuffie for a 37-yard touchdown, and Penn State led 42–17. The Lions had astonishingly scored five touchdowns in the last eight minutes.

Tennessee never mounted a threat from there, and Penn State had its fifth Fiesta Bowl victory in five tries. Penn State had been outgained by over 200 yards, yet they won by 25 points! McDuffie was named the offensive MVP for the Lions, while Givens was named the defense's best player. Sacca had a good performance as well, throwing for four touchdowns despite completing only 11 passes. Penn State finished at #3 in all the polls, behind only Miami and Washington, who shared the national title.[18]

Box Score[19]:

1992 Fiesta Bowl	1st	2nd	3rd	4th	Final
Penn State	7	0	14	21	42
Tennessee	10	0	7	0	17

1st Quarter: PSU—Gash 10 pass from Sacca (Fayak kick)
    TENN—Stewart 1 run (Becksvoort kick)
    TENN—Becksvoort 24 FG
2nd Quarter: No Scoring
3rd Quarter: TENN—Fleming 44 pass from Kelly (Becksvoort kick)
    PSU—LaBarca 3 pass from Sacca (Fayak kick)
    PSU—Brady 13 pass from Sacca (Fayak kick)
4th Quarter: PSU—Anderson 2 run (Fayak kick)
    PSU—Givens 23 fumble return (Fayak kick)
    PSU—McDuffie 37 pass from Sacca (Fayak kick)

1992 Season (7–4)

The Nittany Lions began the season in Cincinnati, where running back Richie Anderson ran for 83 yards and a touchdown, and fullback Brian O'Neil rushed for 46 yards and two scores. The passing game struggled, however, mainly due to an injury to starting quarterback John Sacca. He had only completed one pass for nine yards when he came out. True freshman Wally Richardson replaced him and completed half his ten passes for 35 yards. Despite their 44-yard performance through the air, the Lions managed to pull out a 24–20 win.[1]

Richardson showed much improvement in his second game against Temple, completing ten of 19 passes for 164 yards and a touchdown, along with a pair of two-point passes. His main receiver was O.J. McDuffie, who caught six passes for 118 yards and both two-point passes. Anderson led the way in rushing yards again with 103, along with two scoring runs. The Nittany Lions beat Temple easily, 49–8.[2]

The Lions dominated again against Eastern Michigan. Running back Ki-Jana Carter ran for 73 yards and two touchdowns, while Anderson added another 65 yards and two scores. Sacca returned from injury and had a good game, completing ten of his 17 passes for 153 yards and two to McDuffie, who had 79 yards on four receptions. The Lions went up 28–0 in the first quarter and eased to a 52–7 win.[3]

Anderson had yet another big game against Maryland. In this one, he ran for 138 yards and three touchdowns, while also catching a 26-yard touchdown. He was the first Nittany Lion to score four touchdowns in a game since Leroy Thompson in 1990. McDuffie added 89 yards on six catches and a touchdown. Penn State won 49–13 and didn't allow a touchdown until the final quarter.[4]

Sacca had a career game against Rutgers in a neutral site game at Giants Stadium. He completed 21 of 37 passes for 303 yards and three touchdowns. McDuffie caught eight passes for 129 yards, as the Nittany Lions won 38–24.[5] The next week, Penn State played at home against #2 Miami. They outgained the Canes 370–218 and beat them in nearly every major offensive category. The problem was, they made too many miscues. Sacca threw two interceptions, and kicker Craig Fayak missed two field goals, including a chip-shot 20-yarder. The Lions fell to the Hurricanes by a 17–14 margin.[6]

Boston College quarterback Glenn Foley came to Beaver Stadium and torched the Nittany Lion defense, throwing for 344 yards and four touchdowns, as the Eagles went up 35–16. But Sacca rallied the Lions, passing for 288 yards and a touchdown. Nearly all those throws were to McDuffie, who caught 11 passes for 212 yards to set school records in both categories. Sacca brought the Lions back to within 35–32 before leaving with an injury. Backup Kerry Collins came in, and he got Penn State near midfield with a minute to go, before throwing an interception that sealed a three-point loss.[7]

Collins started the next game at West Virginia. He threw for 249 yards and two touchdowns, completing half his 30 passes. Drayton led in receiving with four catches for 95 yards and a touchdown. Anderson ran for 133 yards and a whopping three touchdowns. Linebacker Phil Yeboah-Kodie scored late on a 23-yard pick-six to seal the 40–26 victory.[8]

At Provo, Utah, Brigham Young surprised the Nittany Lions with a potent running game. They ran for 241 yards in the game in jumping out to a 30–3 lead. Collins battled back, setting school records with 28 completions and 54 attempts. His 317 passing yards were the second-most in school history, but the Lions lost by a 30–17 margin.

The next game was the infamous "Snow Bowl" at Notre Dame Stadium. Collins struggled in the snow, completing only a quarter of his 28 passes for 131 yards and an interception. The Lions had a 16–9 lead late in the fourth quarter, but Notre Dame quarterback Rick Mirer threw a three-yard touchdown pass to running back Jerome Bettis with just 20 seconds left, and he then found Reggie Brooks in the end zone for two points. The Lions lost a heartbreaker, 17–16.

There was still a lot to play for; the season finale was against Pitt at Beaver Stadium. This game was all Penn State. O'Neal ran for 105 yards and four touchdowns, matching Anderson's season-high mark against Maryland. McDuffie led the way in receptions with eight for 112 yards and a touchdown. Defensive tackle Tyoka Jackson blocked a Pitt extra point which defensive back Lee Rubin returned for two points. The Lions ended 1992 with a bang, beating the Panthers 57–13 to finish the season at 7–4.[9]

Anderson led the team in rushing with exactly 900 yards and 18 touchdowns. O'Neal had another 458 yards and seven touchdowns, while the young Carter rushed for 264 yards and four scores. Passing the ball, it was a three-man affair; Sacca led in yards with 1,118 and in touchdowns with nine. Collins threw for 925 yards and four touchdowns, while Richardson passed for 312 yards and two scores. McDuffie blew all other receivers out of the water with his 63 catches for 977 yards and nine touchdowns. No other Penn Stater caught more than one touchdown pass.

The bowl situation was very sticky. College football had begun something called the Bowl Coalition. This coalition was designed for the purpose of matching up the top two teams in the polls for a "national championship game." It was a reaction to the fact that both 1990 and 1991 had ended in split national champions. The Coalition had two "tiers" of bowls. The first tier included the Sugar, Orange, Cotton, and Fiesta. The second tier had the Gator, John Hancock (Sun), and Blockbuster. The top-tier bowls were reserved to champions of the Big Eight, Southwest, Big East, ACC, and SEC. The Big Ten and Pac-10 were off doing their own thing with the Rose Bowl.

As a result of this Coalition, independent schools like Penn State were in a supreme disadvantage. The Coalition was designed to help those five conferences, with everyone else on the outside looking in. Because of this, Penn State decided to accept a bowl invitation before the season had even begun! Head coach Joe Paterno agreed that the Lions would go to the Blockbuster Bowl for the second time in three years. All Penn State needed to do was to win six games, and they did so. That earned them a trip back to Miami, where they would take on Stanford.[10]

1993 Blockbuster Bowl

#21 Penn State (7–4) vs. #14 Stanford (9–3)
January 1, 1993, at Joe Robbie Stadium in Miami Gardens, Florida

This was the final game under the "Blockbuster" name. Following this game, the name would be changed to the Carquest Bowl, and it'd go through a myriad of name changes for the next three decades. The loss of sponsorship by Blockbuster coincided with this bowl being left out of the Bowl Coalition the next season. As it was, attendance had dropped considerably between Penn State's first Blockbuster Bowl and this one just two seasons later.

Stanford running back Glyn Milburn returned the opening kickoff to the 28. Quarterback Steve Stenstrom fired his first pass to receiver Mike Cook for 14 yards. His next one went to tight end Ryan Wetnight for a first down at the Penn State 38. Milburn ran the ball three times on the next four plays. On the one play he didn't carry it, Stenstrom hit Wetnight for 29 yards. After getting down inside the 5, Stenstrom went play action and threw to Wetnight again, this time for a three-yard touchdown to put Stanford up early.

Kerry Collins started at quarterback for Penn State, and his first drive was a good one. He threw to receiver O.J. McDuffie for big gains of 21 and 37, each one coming on a third down. However, on the next third down, Collins settled for a dump off to running back Richie Anderson, who came up far short of the first down. With starting kicker Craig Fayak injured, backup V.J. Muscillo was called on for a 33-yard field goal. He made it, and Penn State cut the Stanford lead to four.

Each team punted on their next possession. Stenstrom tried going long to start his team's third drive, but he had his pass picked off by defensive back Lee Rubin. The Lions got a pair of first downs on runs by fullback Brian O'Neal. McDuffie uncharacteristically dropped a pass, and tight end Troy Drayton's third-down catch came up short. The Lions punted it away, ending the first quarter down 7–3.

Defensive back Marlon Forbes got an interception of Stenstrom around the midfield stripe, but the Penn State offense continued to struggle. They went three-and-out and punted it back. On their next drive, O'Neal ran to midfield for a first down, and Collins found McDuffie for 15 yards. But the Lions soon faced a fourth-and-eight at about the Stanford 33. Head coach Joe Paterno chose to go for it. Anderson took a reverse off the left side, but he was tackled a yard shy of the first down.

The teams exchanged punts, and Stanford got the ball back at their own 35. Fullback Ellery Roberts ripped off a 34-yard run off the right side, and Stenstrom found Wetnight for 17 more yards. After a run each by Roberts and Milburn, fullback J.J. Lasley took the ball the rest of the way for a touchdown (five yards). The Lions couldn't get into scoring range on their final drive of the half, so Stanford went to the half up 14–3.

From Penn State's point of view, the entire second half was a waste of time. The offense was so impotent that it didn't matter what Stanford did with the ball. On their first three drives of the third quarter, the Penn State offense managed just one first down, and that one was a fluke since it came off a dead ball personal foul call. They just kept punting and punting.

Meanwhile, the Stanford offense added on to their lead. They started a drive back at their own 21, then marched nearly the length of the field into scoring range. Their drive lasted ten minutes and took off a ton of time. Kicker Eric Abrams finished off the drive with a 28-yard field goal, and Stanford increased its lead to 17–3.

Stanford's next possession, coming after a Penn State three-and-out, was even more successful. They started at their own 31, where Stenstrom got them going with a pair of second-down passes to Cook for first downs, gaining 17 and 11 yards. He'd convert on the next second down as well, this one being a swing pass to Milburn, who sprinted down the right sideline for a 40-yard touchdown. Stanford led 24–3 after three quarters.

Collins threw an interception to defensive back Ron Redell, on the only drive of the third quarter that didn't end in a punt for Penn State. The Nittany Lions then went three-and-out on their first three possessions of the fourth quarter. Paterno tried putting in backup quarterback Wally Richardson to get a spark.

On the next drive, it looked like Penn State had something going, with Richardson hitting fullback Brian Moser for a first down at the four-minute mark. Running back Ki-Jana Carter ran for five yards, and Richardson's next two passes fell incomplete. On fourth-and-five, the Lions went for it, but Richardson was picked off by defensive back Vaughn Bryant. There would be no Nittany Lion touchdown today, as Penn State lost 24–3.

The Nittany Lions managed just 263 total yards of offense, over 100 fewer than Stanford. Collins threw for 145 yards and an interception, while Richardson completed only one of his eight passes. To top it off, third-stringer John Sacca threw two incompletions at the very end of the game. The Lions' leading rusher was Anderson with just 40 yards. McDuffie did have a good game, catching six passes for 111 yards. He was the lone bright spot on a difficult day.

The Blockbuster Bowl name became synonymous with poor Penn State performances. Two seasons ago, they laid an egg against Florida State, but this one was even worse. Penn State finished the year unranked in the Associated Press poll, but better days were ahead.

Box score[11]:

1992 Blockbuster Bowl	1st	2nd	3rd	4th	Final
Stanford	7	7	10	0	24
Penn State	3	0	0	0	3

1st Quarter: STAN—Wetnight 3 pass from Stenstrom (Abrams kick)
　　PSU—Muscillo 33 FG
2nd Quarter: STAN—Lasley 5 run (Abrams kick)
3rd Quarter: STAN—Abrams 28 FG
　　STAN—Milburn 40 pass from Stenstrom (Abrams kick)
4th Quarter: No Scoring

1993 Season (9–2)

The year 1993 was Penn State's inaugural season in the Big Ten. They'd get to play four opponents they had never faced before: Minnesota, Michigan, Indiana, and Northwestern.[1] Quarterback John Sacca won the starting quarterback job over Kerry Collins and Wally Richardson, and he got off to a good start. He threw for 274 yards and four touchdowns, all to receiver Bobby Engram, who set a team record for scoring catches in a game. Running back Ki-Jana Carter rushed for over 100 yards for the first time in his career, going for 120 yards and a touchdown. The Nittany Lions led 31–13 at the half, and they breezed to their first Big Ten victory, 38–20.[2]

Next came a non-conference battle with old foe USC. Penn State led 21–7 at the half thanks to two touchdown runs by fullback Brian O'Neal and a four-yard touchdown pass from Sacca to running back Mike Archie. Carter and Archie each ran for over 100 yards, the 24th such occurrence in school history. Down 21–20 in the final seconds, the Trojans chose to go for two after a touchdown. Their pass fell incomplete, and the Nittany Lions survived to win by one.[3]

In Iowa City, it was a lot easier. The Penn State defense kept Iowa off the board, marking the first shutout of the Hawkeyes at home since 1978. They came up with nine sacks, their most since 1987. Running back Stephen Pitts rushed for two touchdowns, and Carter rushed for 144 yards, his third 100-yard rushing game in a row, as the Nittany Lions came away with a 31–0 victory.[4]

Penn State's next two games came against future Big Ten teams Rutgers and Maryland. (That meant that USC was the lone opponent on Penn State's 1993 regular-season schedule who does not currently play in the Big Ten.) First came Rutgers, who the Lions crushed 31–7. Head coach Joe Paterno decided to switch quarterbacks, and Collins got the start over Sacca. He threw for four touchdown passes and 222 yards. Tight end Kyle Brady caught two of those touchdowns, while Engram went over 100 receiving yards.[5]

The first sign that Penn State was going to dominate on offense came in their game at Maryland. By halftime, the Lions had 46 points, and they were only getting started. Carter rushed for 159 yards and three touchdowns, his fourth 100-yard game of the season. Archie also went over 100 yards, gaining 120 and a touchdown. O'Neal scored two touchdowns as well in a 70–7 victory, Paterno's second-largest in his career.[6]

After two weeks against the two (future) Big Ten teams that the Nittany Lions always beat, next came the two teams who seem to always have Penn State's number, Michigan and Ohio State. The Lions led the Wolverines 10–0 at Beaver Stadium, and they looked to be in good shape in the 1,000th game in school history. But despite Carter going over 100 yards for the fifth time in six games, Penn State fell to Michigan, 21–13.[7]

126

At Ohio Stadium, the Nittany Lion offense failed to even get in the end zone. Kerry Collins had a rough game, throwing four interceptions and completing only one-third of his passes. Carter once again went over 100 yards, outgaining Collins's passing total by a yard. Meanwhile, Ohio State had little trouble on offense, as they breezed to a 24–6 win over the Lions.[8]

It was Homecoming week, and the Hoosiers and Nittany Lions would play one that went down to the wire. Penn State led 17–3 at the end of the first quarter, thanks to two touchdown runs by Carter, who had 138 for the game. But Indiana tied the game at 31 in the fourth quarter. Collins answered by throwing a 45-yard touchdown pass to Engram. Indiana's last gasp was picked off by defensive back Tony Pittman, and the Lions won 38–31.[9]

Carter would not go over 100 yards against Illinois; after suffering a hip pointer against Indiana, he pulled a calf muscle against the Illini. That was okay, however, because Penn State just plugged in Archie, and off he ran. He carried the ball 30 times in Carter's absence, piling up 134 yards and two touchdowns. The Lions roared out to a 28–0 lead and cruised to a 28–14 victory.[10]

In the final first-time battle of the season, the Nittany Lions put up 43 points against Northwestern. Archie ran for 173 more yards and two scores, while O'Neal and fullback Brian Milne also scored. Collins bounced back by throwing for 278 yards and a touchdown pass to Engram, who caught eight of his passes for 132 yards. Penn State ripped off 30 points in a row at one point, and they won 43–21.[11]

In the final game of the season, it was Penn State vs. Michigan State for a spot in the Citrus Bowl. It looked for sure like Sparty had reservations for Orlando when they took a 37–17 lead in the third quarter. However, Collins battled back, throwing for 352 yards. He hit Engram for touchdowns of 40 and 52 yards in the second half, and Penn State secured its spot in Orlando with a 38–37 victory.[12]

Engram set a team record with 13 touchdown catches. He ended up catching 48 balls for 873 yards, while also gaining over 400 yards on punt returns. Carter led the team in rushing with 1,026 yards, and tying for the team lead with O'Neal by scoring seven rushing touchdowns. Archie had a great year as well, rushing for 766 yards and six touchdowns. Sacca, the starter to begin 1993, passed the torch on to Collins this season. Collins threw for 13 touchdowns on 1,605 yards, though he also threw 11 interceptions.[13]

Going into the Citrus Bowl, the Nittany Lions were big underdogs. Their opponents, the Tennessee Volunteers were ranked #5 and had lost only one game. Penn State's last bowl win had come over Tennessee, but this time the Volunteers had an NFL-caliber quarterback in Heath Shuler. It would not be easy to end this first season in the Big Ten on a high note.[14]

1994 Citrus Bowl

#13 Penn State (9–2) vs. #6 Tennessee (9–1–1)
January 1, 1994, at the Florida Citrus Bowl in Orlando, Florida

The Nittany Lions won the coin toss, and head coach Joe Paterno chose to defer to the second half. From the start, it looked like it'd be all Tennessee, who was a ten-point favorite. Quarterback Heath Shuler completed his first pass of the game, a screen to receiver Billy Williams that went for seven yards. Running back Charlie Garner picked up a first down on the left sideline on the game's initial third down. Shuler then tried another screen, and receiver Cory Fleming picked up eight yards. Garner took off on a 17-yard run, and the Volunteers were in field goal range. Kicker John Becksvoort converted a 46-yard kick, and Tennessee had an early three-point lead.

Penn State went three-and-out to start the game, and Vols defensive back Shawn Summers took the punt back to the 46. Tennessee head coach Phillip Fulmer went with some trickery, as Williams took a pitch on a reverse and gained 38 yards deep into Penn State territory. Three plays later, Shuler threw over the middle to Fleming for a 19-yard touchdown, and the Vols led by the ten points they were favored to win by.

But that would prove to be the high point of the day for Tennessee. After a kick-off that went out of bounds, Penn State started at their own 35. Running back Mike Archie ran for six yards, then quarterback Kerry Collins threw a screen to receiver Bobby Engram on a play that went 36 yards. Running back Ki-Jana Carter ran for another four yards, then fullback Brian O'Neal plunged up the middle for a first down at the 19. Archie took a screen for another five yards, and Carter got a first down at the 6. Collins found Engram down at the 2, then Carter pounded up the middle for a two-yard touchdown, cutting the Tennessee lead to three.

Shuler had the Vols back in Penn State territory with a 27-yard pass to Fleming. The Nittany Lions snuffed out that drive when defensive tackle Tyoka Jackson tipped a Shuler pass, and defensive back Lee Rubin snatched it out of the air. The Lions couldn't score on the ensuing drive, but they went to the second quarter only down by three.

Linebacker Phil Yeboah-Kodie stopped a Tennessee drive by tackling receiver Joey Kent two yards short of a first down. Engram took the ensuing punt back to the 42, and Penn State was in business. Collins threw to Engram for 16 yards, then Engram took a reverse all the way down to the Tennessee 7. While the Nittany Lions couldn't punch it in, they did get a 19-yard field goal by kicker Craig Fayak, tying the game at ten.

Penn State forced another punt, and Engram took this one back 11 yards to the mid-field stripe. Unfortunately, the drive only lasted two plays, with Collins throwing a long pass that got picked off by defensive back Jason Parker. The Vols then put together a time-consuming drive. Garner ripped off runs of 19 and 17 yards, as he carried the ball seven times on the drive. On a third-down run, he ended up short of the first down, but referee Mike Pereira called a facemask penalty on the Lions, giving Tennessee a first down. With just over a minute left in the first half, Becksvoort made a Citrus Bowl-record 50-yard field goal, and the Volunteers went back up by three.

The next Penn State drive was the stuff of legends. They started at their own 35 after another kickoff out of bounds, but with only about a minute to work with. Archie ran off the left side for 13 yards, then Collins hit Engram for a 17-yard gain. Carter took a draw, getting to the Tennessee 32, and Penn State called timeout with 43 seconds left. Collins then threw a shovel pass to O'Neal, and he got to the 26. The Lions hurried to the line, then Collins went play action to O'Neal for 12 yards, and he got out of bounds at the 14. Collins tried going to the end zone, but his pass fell incomplete for receiver Chip LaBarca. With only ten seconds left, Paterno called for the ultimate trick play: a draw to Carter. No one on the Tennessee side saw it coming, and Carter took the draw play into the end zone with three seconds left in the half. The Lions took a 17–13 lead into the locker room thanks to that most unusual scoring play in such a situation.

Defensive back Shelly Hammonds returned the opening kickoff of the second half to the 40. The red-hot offense took over there, with Archie taking his first handoff for 19 yards. On a third down, Collins found receiver Freddie Scott for a first down at the 30. Archie ran for five more, and LaBarca hauled in a pass for a first down. Carter got the Lions down to the 7, then tight end Kyle Brady then broke wide open on the right side of the end zone, catching Collins's pass for a seven-yard touchdown to put his team up by 11.

Nose guard Eric Clair sacked Shuler to end the next Tennessee possession. While Penn State went three-and-out afterward, the defense stepped up again and came up with a stop. Engram then returned the next punt across the midfield stripe. Collins found Scott at the Tennessee 40, then fullback Brian Milne pounded his way for ten more yards. After the change of sides for the fourth quarter, Collins fired to Engram for 12 yards. He followed that by going play action right back to Engram for a 15-yard touchdown. The heavy underdog Nittany Lions now had a 31–13 lead!

Tennessee faced fourth-and-three on their next drive. This time, Rubin made a fantastic open-field tackle of Garner short of the first down marker, and Penn State took over on downs. On the next Volunteer possession, Lions linebacker Eric Ravotti sacked Shuler for an eight-yard loss, then knocked down a pass. The Vols were forced to punt again. They got one final chance, when Penn State punter V.J. Muscillo had to field a bad snap, and his punt ended up going minus-four yards. But Rubin made a good tackle of Garner, and the defense forced three incompletions. There was no coming back for the Vols on this day.

Engram was named the most outstanding offensive player of the game for the Nittany Lions. He caught seven passes for 107 yards and a touchdown. Some consideration for the award had to be given to Carter, who ran for 93 yards and two touchdowns. As for defense, Rubin won the defensive player of the game award, who had one interception and five tackles.

The Nittany Lions ended up finishing #7 in the major polls with this win, their first-ever Citrus Bowl victory. Paterno moved into a tie with Paul "Bear" Bryant for the all-time most bowl wins by a head coach, with 15. He made it clear that his team felt disrespected by the media, who made Tennessee a ten-point favorite and even had one writer predict a 48–14 Vols victory. "I never said we were a great team, but that's a lot of points," Paterno said.[15] "I'm sure that rankled some of the kids." It wouldn't be the last time the media disrespected the Lions.

Box Score[16]:

1994 Citrus Bowl	1st	2nd	3rd	4th	Final
Penn State	7	10	7	7	31
Tennessee	10	3	0	0	13

1st Quarter: TENN—Becksvoort 46 FG
    TENN—Fleming 19 pass from Shuler (Becksvoort kick)
    PSU—Carter 3 run (Fayak kick)
2nd Quarter: PSU—Fayak 19 FG
    TENN—Becksvoort 50 FG
    PSU—Carter 14 run (Fayak kick)
3rd Quarter: PSU—Brady 7 pass from Collins (Fayak kick)
4th Quarter: PSU—Engram 15 pass from Collins (Fayak kick)

1994 Season (11–0)

Penn State began their signature season of the nineties in the Hubert H. Humphrey Metrodome. Running back Ki-Jana Carter began his Heisman Trophy campaign by rushing for 210 yards and three touchdowns against Minnesota. It was the first 200-yard game for a Penn State running back since 1990. Carter scored three touchdowns in the first half, including an 80-yard run. Quarterback Kerry Collins also had a great start to his season. He threw three touchdown passes, including a 26-yard pass to receiver Freddie Scott, who caught seven passes for 133 yards. Tight end Keith Olsommer made the first catch of his career in the second quarter for a four-yard touchdown, making it 35–3 at the half. Collins completed 14 passes in a row, setting a school record, and his 82.6 percent completion percentage was the best of his career. The Lions rolled up 689 yards, almost perfectly balanced between rushing (345) and passing (344), as they cruised to a 56–3 win over Minnesota.[1]

Up against the USC Trojans, Carter ran for 119 yards, part of Penn State's 286 rushing yards in a 38–14 romp. Collins threw for 248 yards and two touchdowns, and five different Lions scored touchdowns in the first two quarters. Collins also went over 3,000 career passing yards, becoming just the sixth Penn State quarterback to do so.[2]

There were more first-half fireworks against Iowa. The Lions rolled up 35 points in the first quarter, and they led 45–0 in the second quarter before the Hawkeyes had even gotten on the scoreboard. Running back Mike Archie ran for two touchdowns and caught a ten-yard scoring pass, while Carter rushed for 89 yards and two touchdowns of his own. Defensive back Brian Miller blocked a punt which linebacker Phil Yeboah-Kodie recovered for a touchdown in the end zone. The Lions let up at halftime, but they still ended up going over the 60-point mark in a 61–21 win.[3]

Rutgers was not yet a member of the Big Ten, but they put up more of a fight than most Big Ten teams did during the 1994 season. Carter ran for three first-half touchdowns, as the Lions went to the locker room with a 34–20 lead. Collins then put this one to rest by hitting Scott on an 82-yard touchdown pass, the third-longest pass in school history. He'd later throw a 15-yard touchdown pass to receiver Bobby Engram, who put up 200 receiving yards, second-most in Penn State history. With Scott also going over the century mark, it was only the second regular-season game in PSU history that two receivers had accomplished the feat. The Nittany Lions ended up pulling away for a 55–27 victory.[4]

For their second road game of the season, the Nittany Lions found themselves down 6–0 at the end of one quarter at Temple. The offense then exploded in the next two quarters, putting up 48 points and crushing the Owls. Collins threw three touchdown passes in the second quarter, two to Scott and one to tight end Kyle Brady. Scott ended up with three touchdown catches in the game on his way to 115 yards, but he didn't even lead the team in receiving; that honor went to Engram, who had 136 yards. The Lions won it, 48–21.[5]

The Nittany Lions headed to Michigan Stadium for the first time in school history, where the crowd of 106,832 was the third-largest in the history of college football. The Lions went up 10–0 in the first quarter, with Collins throwing a three-yard touchdown pass to Olsommer. They had a 16–0 lead in the second quarter before the Wolverines came roaring back to take a one-point lead. Collins then led the Lions on an 86-yard drive, punctuated by a nine-yard pass to Jon Witman for a score. He hit Scott for two points, and Penn State led 24–17. Collins led the offense for another touchdown, this one a 16-yard pass to Engram with three minutes left. Miller then intercepted a Todd Collins pass with just over a minute to go, and Penn State held on for a 31–24 victory, moving them to #1 in the polls.[6]

Can you imagine Ohio State losing a game 63–14? Because that's exactly how bad the Lions beat the Buckeyes the following week at Beaver Stadium. Penn State rolled up 33 first downs, most in head coach Joe Paterno's career. Carter ran for 137 yards and four touchdowns, the most of his career. Collins threw for 265 yards and two first-half scores. The Nittany Lions put up exactly 286 yards both rushing and passing; the Buckeyes managed just 214 total yards for the game. Ohio State threw three interceptions, two of them to Miller; Penn State's quarterbacks threw just six incompletions. Ohio State suffered their worst loss in nearly 50 years.[7]

The next game for the Lions should have been just a footnote. Penn State raced out to a 35–14 lead against Indiana, with Carter rushing for 192 yards and a touchdown. Collins threw for 213 yards and two scores. The Lions had a 21-point lead late in the fourth quarter, so Paterno eased up. Bad move. Indiana scored two touchdowns in the final two minutes, including a 40-yard Hail Mary coupled with a two-point conversion. Because the Nittany Lions won the game by just six points, the pollsters took the opportunity to move Nebraska ahead of them in the rankings.[8]

Now ranked #2, the Nittany Lions had a real letdown at Illinois, where they fell behind 21–0 in the first quarter. They were all but left for dead, until Collins led them back. He took them on a 99-yard drive for their first touchdown. Down by ten and facing fourth-and-one on a fourth-quarter drive, Collins found Engram for 17 yards. The drive ended with Milne plunging in from five yards away, and the deficit narrowed to three with just eight minutes left. Collins got the ball back one last time at his own 4, and he completed all seven passes he threw on the drive. The 96-yard drive ended with Milne scoring on a two-yard plunge, and Penn State escaped with a 35–31 win. It was the biggest comeback in Paterno's career.[9]

The Lions had locked up a berth in the Rose Bowl with two games to play, but they weren't finished winning. At home against Northwestern, the Lions turned four turnovers into 28 points in the first half, as they jumped out to a 38–3 lead at halftime. Carter scored three times on 107 yards rushing, as Penn State won it 45–17.[10]

Finally, the Nittany Lions completed an undefeated, untied regular season by scoring at least ten points in all four quarters of a 59–31 win over Michigan State. Carter ran for 227 yards and a whopping five touchdowns for his ninth game over the century mark of the season. Both Engram and Scott went over 100 yards yet again, this time Engram with 169 and Scott with 145. Collins threw for 289 yards, as the Lions coasted to a 28-point win and an 11–0 regular season finish.[11]

The only reason Penn State didn't take home its second Heisman Trophy in 1994 was because their two best players split the votes. Carter finished second in the voting, while Collins finished fourth. As a result, Colorado running back Rashaan Salaam got enough votes to win the trophy. But at the end of the season, it was clear who had the nation's best offense; Penn State led the nation in yards and points. Collins led the NCAA in passing efficiency, and Carter led the nation in yards per carry. To sum it up, this was perhaps the greatest offense in NCAA history.[12]

But none of that mattered in the eyes of the pollsters. Perhaps it was because Penn State had a couple of close calls. Perhaps it was Nebraska was one field goal from winning the previous year's national championship in the Orange Bowl against Florida State. Perhaps it was to reward Nebraska head coach Tom Osborne, because of all his close calls. Or perhaps it was just another classic case of the media hating Penn State. Whatever the reason, Penn State was only ranked #2 at the end of the regular season.

At the time, the Big Ten and Pacific-10 champions were locked into playing each other in the Rose Bowl. That meant that, no matter what, Penn State couldn't play Nebraska head-to-head to decide the national championship. Penn State's only shot at the national title was for Nebraska to lose the Orange Bowl to Miami, and of course also for the Lions to beat Pacific-10 champion Oregon in the Rose Bowl Game.[13]

Many Penn State fans do not know that even had Nebraska lost the Orange Bowl to Miami, Penn State would have gotten no better than a split national title (assuming they won the Rose Bowl). The Bowl Coalition (a forerunner to the Bowl Championship Series) tried to match up the #1 and #2 teams in a bowl that doubled as a national championship game, using something called the "Bowl Poll." But the Bowl Coalition did not include the Rose Bowl, since the Tournament of Roses refused to release the Big Ten and Pacific-10 champions to play in the Bowl Coalition national championship game. So, the Bowl Coalition was forced to have #1 Nebraska play #3 Miami in the so-called "national championship game." Since Nebraska was Big Eight champion, and Big Eight champions always went to the Orange Bowl, that meant that the Orange Bowl would be the site for the national title game. The coaches were obligated to give their votes to the winner of that game, so #3 Miami would have won a national championship over Penn State in the one poll if they beat the Huskers. Penn State could still have won a share by being ranked #1 in the non-obligated AP Poll. For now, though, the Nittany Lions could do nothing but watch the Orange Bowl on New Year's night and hope that Miami could pull off the upset of Nebraska.[14]

1995 Rose Bowl

#2 Penn State (11–0) vs. #12 Oregon (8–3)
January 2, 1995, at the Rose Bowl in Pasadena, California

By kickoff of the 81st Rose Bowl Game in Pasadena, California, the Nittany Lions' fate had already been sealed. #1 Nebraska had defeated #3 Miami in the Orange Bowl on New Year's night, giving them the Bowl Coalition national championship. As for the Associated Press poll, Nebraska was already ranked number one, and no #1 team had ever fallen out of the top spot after winning their bowl game. As unfair as it was, due to the Rose Bowl's position outside the Bowl Coalition, Penn State was playing for second.

Head coach Joe Paterno had a few milestones that were possible, though. If the Lions could beat Oregon to finish undefeated, it would be the fourth consecutive decade in which Paterno had a team go without a loss. (Of course, most of those teams had been snubbed from the national championship, too.) Paterno could pass Paul "Bear" Bryant for the most wins all-time in bowl games, with his 16th.[15] Finally, he could become the first-ever coach to win every major bowl game—Rose, Orange, Sugar, Cotton, and Fiesta.

Oregon began the game with the ball, and Ducks head coach Rich Brooks made it clear that his team was going to throw the ball early and often. Quarterback Danny O'Neil completed a third-down pass to receiver Dameron Ricketts for a first down at the 34, then he found tight end Josh Wilcox just one yard shy of another first down. After picking up the first down on another pass to Ricketts, though, the Ducks offense bogged down, and they were forced to punt.

The Penn State offense had been hyped up quite a bit going into this game, but never would anyone expect them to make this much of a statement. On their first play of the game, running back Ki-Jana Carter took off on an 83-yard run right up the middle, breaking several tackles before finding daylight. "He's gone," ABC announcer Keith Jackson said.[16] "Goodbye." It was the second-longest run in Rose Bowl history, as well as the longest Penn State run of the season, and it put the Nittany Lions up 7–0.

But this Ducks team wasn't about to back down. O'Neil threw to Wilcox on the first play of the next possession, and he picked up a first down. On the play, Penn State defensive back Chuck Penzenik went down with an injury. Luckily for the Lions, he'd be back. In the meantime, O'Neil found running back Dino Philyaw for a first down inside the Penn State 35, before hitting Wilcox in the corner all the way down to the 1. Two plays later, O'Neil hit Wilcox on a one-yard touchdown pass, and the Ducks tied it up at seven.

Penn State got one first down on a run by fullback Brian Milne before having to punt it back to the Ducks. O'Neil had the Ducks right back in PSU territory, as he threw a five-yard pass to receiver Cristin McLemore, then passes to running back Ricky Whittle as well as Wilcox to get down inside the 35. But O'Neil's next pass was a poor one, a ball that popped right up and into the hands of Penzenik. His interception stopped a promising drive for the Ducks.

The Nittany Lions offense stumbled for the second straight drive, and Oregon got the ball back near midfield. O'Neil threw a screen to Philyaw, who got a big gain down to the 15. The Penn State defense rose up and stopped Philyaw on a third-down run, forcing the Ducks to settle for a field goal attempt. Kicker Matt Belden came out to try a 23-yard field goal, but he missed it wide to the right, and the game remained tied at seven.

Lions quarterback Kerry Collins threw to receiver Bobby Engram, getting a first down, and also getting 15 extra yards on a roughing the passer call. Carter ran it to the Oregon 45, then picked up a first down two plays later. Collins fired to tight end Kyle Brady for a few yards, as the first quarter came to a close. He then found Engram again for a first down at the 28. The offense was clicking now, but a surprising foe tripped it up, quite literally: the Rose Bowl grass. Both Carter and Collins slipped on consecutive plays, ending the Penn State drive early. Kicker Brett Conway came out to try a 46-yard field goal attempt, but he missed it short and wide, and the game stayed knotted up.

The next three drives produced three punts: two by Oregon, one by Penn State. On that possession that ended with a punt for Penn State, Carter fumbled, but guard Jeff Hartings fell on top of the loose ball. However, on Penn State's next drive, Carter was not so lucky. Oregon defensive back Chad Cota knocked the ball out of Carter's hands, and defensive end Troy Bailey recovered it for the Ducks.

Penn State defensive end Todd Atkins sacked O'Neil for a seven-yard loss on the first play of the new drive. While O'Neil completed a third-down pass to receiver Pat Johnson for 13 yards, it was not enough for a first down. Belden came out to try his second field goal of the game, from 44 yards out, but he missed this one too wide to the right. The score was still tied, with less than four minutes left in the half.

Now the Penn State offense got rolling. Collins threw consecutive passes to Engram for first downs. Facing third-and-long, he then went long down the left sideline for Joe Jurevicius, a punter who was now getting time at receiver. Jurevicius made the catch down at the Oregon 1, setting up a one-yard plunge by Milne for a touchdown, which put Penn State up 14–7.

Oregon had a chance to score right before the half. O'Neil threw to Wilcox, McLemore, and Johnson, all three passes getting first downs, as the clock ticked under a minute. Ricketts made a catch and avoided a few tacklers as he got a first down at the 24. O'Neil then hit Wilcox for a first down at the 11, and he spiked the ball to save a timeout. On the next play, he threw to McLemore for a short gain, and the Ducks had to call their final timeout. O'Neil now needed to throw into the end zone, because his team had no timeouts and there was not enough time to spike the ball. Instead, he threw short to McLemore, who was tackled in bounds. The half ended with Penn State still up by seven.

Each team went three-and-out to start the second half. On Penn State's second drive of the half, Collins found receiver Freddie Scott for a first down at midfield. Running back Mike Archie then took a screen down to the Oregon 33 for another first down. That set up Conway for a second field goal attempt, but he too missed it wide to the right, leaving Penn State's lead at a tenuous seven points.

Oregon again went three-and-out, and Penn State took over at their 21. Collins fired over the middle to Brady for a first down, then he went to Jurevicius for another fresh set of downs. Archie caught a pass to get into Oregon territory, but then disaster struck. Collins threw an interception to linebacker Reggie Jordan, who escaped down the sideline all the way to the PSU 17. Two plays later, O'Neil lobbed a pass to McLemore, who caught it in the front corner of the end zone for a touchdown, and the Ducks tied it at 14.

But just when the Ducks thought they had the Lions on the ropes, they'd find themselves to be wrong. Running back Ambrose Fletcher was Penn State's surprise hero. He caught the kickoff and returned it all the way to the Oregon 21-yard line, nearly breaking it for a touchdown. From there, Carter needed only two carries to hit paydirt. His second run went 17 yards off left tackle for a score, and Penn State grabbed the lead back again at 21–14.

Two plays into Oregon's next drive, O'Neil threw another bad pass which was picked off by Penzenik. He returned it to the 14, setting up the PSU offense for another easy touchdown. Archie tried a trick play where he took a pitch and threw back to Collins. It didn't work, as Collins only picked up a modest gain. But Carter then took over. He ran the ball down to the 3 for a first down, then he bounced off left tackle for a three-yard touchdown. The Lions had a solid 28–14 lead at the end of three quarters.

Brooks had O'Neil throwing on nearly every play at this point. He completed a pair of passes each to Whittle and McLemore to get his team down into field goal range again. Penn State defensive back Marlon Forbes knocked down a third-down pass attempt, and the Ducks were forced to try a 45-yard field goal. Belden missed this one too, as his kick hit the right upright, making him zero-for-three for the game.

Penn State punted on their next two possessions, and Oregon got one more chance at making a game of it. The Ducks got the ball down to the PSU 31. This time, linebacker Willie Smith helped thwart the Ducks' plans with a sack of O'Neil. On third down, linebacker Terry Killens knocked down a pass. Finally, on fourth-and-14, O'Neil's pass to McLemore fell incomplete and Oregon's threat had expired.

Milne ran the ball three times, getting a first down, then Archie ran for a first down inside the 35. Collins threw to Scott for an eight-yard gain, but Archie was stopped short on a third-down pass reception. Conway came on to try a 43-yard field goal. His kick was true, marking the only time a kicker from either team made a field goal in this game. Penn State now led by 17.

Oregon had no choice on their next possession; they had to go for it on fourth down from deep in their own territory. Linebacker Phil Yeboah-Kodie sacked O'Neil on fourth down at the Oregon 13, and Penn State took over there. Two runs later, fullback Jon Witman pounded his way into the end zone, and backup kicker Michael Barninger made the extra point. Penn State had an unassailable 38–14 lead.

While the Ducks got a garbage touchdown late in the game (and missed the ensuing two-point conversion), the Nittany Lions had completed an undefeated season with their 38–20 victory. Collins threw for 200 yards, completing passes to seven different receivers. Carter rushed for 156 yards and three touchdowns in earning co-Player of the Game honors with O'Neil. Despite being outgained by over 70 yards, the Nittany Lions won this game quite handily.[17]

After the game, Paterno praised the Ducks for their fine effort. "I thought it was a great college football game, and I think college football won today," he said.[18] As for the national championship, which Penn State was unable to win, Paterno proved to be a prophet. "I've always wanted a playoff, that's nothing new with me," he said.[19] Twenty years later, college football would finally get a playoff. For now, the Nittany Lions had to settle for being #2.

Box Score[20]:

1995 Rose Bowl	1st	2nd	3rd	4th	Final
Penn State	7	7	14	10	38
Oregon	7	0	7	6	20

1st Quarter: PSU—Carter 83 run (Conway kick)
   ORE—Wilcox 1 pass from O'Neil (Belden kick)
2nd Quarter: PSU—Milne 1 run (Conway kick)
3rd Quarter: ORE—McLemore 17 pass from O'Neil (Belden kick)
   PSU—Carter 17 run (Conway kick)
   PSU—Carter 3 run (Conway kick)
4th Quarter: PSU—Conway 43 FG
   PSU—Witman 9 run (Barninger kick)
   ORE—Whittle 3 run (pass failed)

1995 Season (8–3)

After an undefeated season in 1994, the Nittany Lions came crashing down to earth in the first half of their season opener against Texas Tech. The Red Raiders came out on fire in this game, and Penn State trailed 20–7 at the half. But quarterback Wally Richardson threw only one incompletion in the second half, and kicker Brett Conway then made a 39-yard field goal with four seconds left, and the Nittany Lions escaped with a 24–23 home victory.[1]

After that heart-stopping victory, Happy Valley needed a more relaxing victory. They got it when the Nittany Lions blew out Temple 66–14. The Owls managed just ten first downs, as opposed to 36 by the Lions. Richardson threw three touchdown passes, gaining 198 yards. Freshman running back Curtis Enis ran for three second-half touchdowns, while fullback Brian Milne added a pair of one-yard plunges.[2]

At Giants Stadium, Rutgers proved to not be quite as much of a pushover. The Nittany Lions just could not put them away. Receiver Bobby Engram caught three touchdown passes as part of his eight catches for 175 yards. He also scored a fourth touchdown by picking up a fumble and taking it 58 yards for a score. Despite a furious Rutgers comeback, the Lions came out on top, 59–34.[3]

Penn State was now on a 20-game winning streak, but all good things must come to an end. Wisconsin came to Happy Valley and jumped out to a ten-point lead. Richardson completed 33 passes, a school record, in trying to lead the Lions back. Receiver Freddie Scott caught 13 of those passes, also breaking a school record. But the Lions lost, 17–9, for the first time since a 24–6 defeat to Ohio State in 1993.[4]

Witman scored three touchdowns against Ohio State, but a six-yard touchdown run by running back Eddie George allowed the Buckeyes to defeat the Lions 28–25.[5] The Lions ended their two-game losing streak with a comeback win against Purdue. The Boilermakers had a 23–19 lead, but Richardson, who passed for 281 yards, threw a 16-yard touchdown pass to running back Mike Archie to win it 26–23. Engram ended up with 203 yards on nine catches, the second-most receiving yards in school history.[6]

Richardson and Engram led Penn State to a 41–27 win over Iowa. Richardson found Engram twice in the final seven minutes for touchdowns, including a 43-yarder that put the contest away. Engram ended up with 150 of Richardson's 202 yards for the game.[7] Linebacker Terry Killens had a killer day in the Lions' win the next week against Indiana. He came up with four sacks, a forced fumble, and a blocked punt which he returned for a touchdown, as the Nittany Lions defeated the Hoosiers 45–21.[8]

Northwestern had its finest season in 60 years in 1995. They went 8–0 in the Big Ten, 10–1 overall, and they defeated Penn State 21–10.[9] After a big snowfall during the week, the Nittany Lions played Michigan at a cold Beaver Stadium. Richardson threw two touchdown passes, to Archie and Engram, but the Lions were only up by three. Then Stephen Pitts took off on a 58-yard run, setting up a field goal attempt. But Joe Paterno pulled a fast one! He ran a fake field goal, which holder Joe Nastasi ran in from two yards away for a touchdown to help Penn State pull out a 27–17 win.[10]

With a berth in a New Year's Day bowl on the line, Penn State went up against Michigan State at Spartan Stadium. Trailing 17–10 in the fourth quarter, Richardson threw a 53-yard pass to Engram to tie the score. Late in the game, Richardson threw a screen to Engram, who evaded tacklers on his way to the winning touchdown, and Penn State won 24–20.[11]

Engram set practically every receiving record there was at Penn State. In 1995, he had the most receptions (63) and yards (1,084) for any receiver in school history (tying O.J. McDuffie in the first category). He ended up with 167 receptions, 3,026 receiving yards, and 31 receiving touchdowns, all school records. He had back-to-back 1,000-yard seasons in 1994 and 1995, the only player to ever go over the 1,000-yard mark at Penn State at the time. He was a Penn State legend, one of the greatest ever to wear the blue and white.[12]

#3 Northwestern got the Rose Bowl bid as Big Ten champions, while #4 Ohio State was passed over by the Orange Bowl in favor of popular Notre Dame (the rest of the spots in the Orange, Fiesta, and Sugar Bowls were filled by automatic qualifiers in the Bowl Alliance). That dropped Ohio State into the Florida Citrus Bowl, which also dropped Penn State a spot. The Nittany Lions were invited to the newly-renamed Outback (née Hall of Fame) Bowl to face Auburn.

1996 Outback Bowl

#15 Penn State (9–3) vs. #16 Auburn (8–3)
January 1, 1996, at Tampa Stadium in Tampa, Florida

Auburn head coach Terry Bowden, the son of Florida State's legendary head coach Bobby Bowden, planned an all-out passing attack for his team's game plan.[13] However, that playbook had to be thrown out the window when he arrived at the stadium. Tampa Stadium had turned into a pit of mud thanks to a downpour of rain that started early in the morning, and it would not let up until the fourth quarter of this game.

Penn State won the toss and chose to receive. After the kickoff went out of bounds, the Nittany Lions put together a 13-play drive. Quarterback Wally Richardson found tight end Keith Olsommer for the team's initial first down at the 46. Auburn then committed pass interference on a throw intended for receiver Bobby Engram. Running back Stephen Pitts followed with an 11-yard run. Richardson then hit Olsommer down at the 16 for a first down. On the next third down, running back Curtis Enis picked up a new set of downs. However, the Lions were stopped inches short of the goal line, and head coach Joe Paterno chose to take the points. Kicker Brett Conway made a 19-yard field goal, and the Nittany Lions took a 3–0 lead.

Running back Stephen Davis took off on a 20-yard run to start Auburn's day, but the Tigers couldn't get another yard, and they had to punt. After taking over at the 28, Penn State fullback Brian Milne took off on a run all the way across midfield. Richardson then hit receiver Freddie Scott for a first down at the 29. Before the Lions could start thinking touchdown, though, Milne was tackled behind the line on two straight plays, and now they couldn't even think field goal. Punter Darrell Kania came on and put Auburn down at their own 3.

Auburn responded with their first good drive of the first half. It almost didn't happen, as Nittany Lions linebacker Aaron Collins knocked the ball out of Davis's hands. The Tigers got a big break when receiver Tyrone Goodson fell on it for a first down. Davis then took off for runs of 28 and 13 yards. Auburn faced fourth down a bit later, and fullback Fred Beasley got a first down when Penn State was caught with just ten men on the field. Davis burst for another big run, getting 24 yards down to the 3. The Tigers ended up having to try a field goal when change-of-pace backup quarterback Dameyune Craig slipped to the ground attempting a play action pass on third down. Penn State defensive tackle Brandon Noble partially blocked kicker Matt Hawkins's 26-yard field goal attempt, and the kick went wide to the left.

The Tigers got the ball right back when defensive back Dell McGee intercepted a Richardson pass that Scott tipped right to him. It took Auburn just five plays to score from there. Starting quarterback Patrick Nix completed his team's first pass of the game to receiver Willie Gosha. Running back Harold Morrow ran for a first down, then Nix completed a third-down pass to receiver Robert Baker for a touchdown. Auburn had their first lead of the game, 7–3.

The teams exchanged three-and-outs, both struggling in the mud. Penn State started their next drive at their own 49, and Pitts took off on a 44-yard run down the left sideline to the Auburn 7. While the Nittany Lions couldn't get the ball into the end zone, they did get another short field goal by Conway, this one from 22 yards out, making it 7–6.

Auburn went three-and-out again. Richardson then opened the next drive with a 37-yard pass to Engram, made even more spectacular by the fact that the Tigers were called for pass interference on the play. Running back Mike Archie followed with a seven-yard run, and Milne picked up a first down afterward. That put the Nittany Lions within range for a short field goal, but Conway missed the 29-yard attempt wide to the left.

Defensive back Mark Tate and linebacker Jim Nelson each tipped away an Auburn pass, and the Lions forced another Auburn punt. Starting at the 42, Milne ran for an 18-yard gain into Auburn territory. Pitts took off on a 12-yard run, and the Lions got into the red zone for a fourth time. But this drive, like the three others before it, also ended shy of the goal line. Penn State settled for a 38-yard field goal by Conway, and they took a tenuous 9–7 lead.

In the final seconds of the first half, Nix threw an ill-advised pass that was picked off by defensive back Kim Herring. Richardson immediately took advantage, throwing deep for receiver Joe Jurevicius. He hauled in the pass for a 43-yard gain, and Penn State had first-and-goal with 12 seconds left. On the next play, Richardson found Archie for an eight-yard touchdown. Paterno then chose to go for two, but the conversion was taken off the board when the Nittany Lions were called for illegal motion. Paterno was furious about the call, throwing a towel in frustration. The Lions settled for an extra point, and they went to the half with a 16–7 advantage.

The Lions quickly took control of the game in the second half. After forcing an Auburn punt, they went on an 80-yard drive. Pitts started it with a seven-yard run, and Milne followed by getting the first down. Richardson threw to Scott for seven more yards, and Pitts got the next first down. Richardson now went for the bomb to Engram, and he caught it down at the 12. Three plays later, Richardson fired to Engram again for a nine-yard touchdown. The Lions' lead expanded to 16 points.

Auburn was backed up deep in their own end after a holding call on a kickoff that went for a touchback. On the third play of their drive, defensive end Terry Killens made a tackle on Davis, and defensive lineman Brad Scioli knocked the ball out. Herring recovered it in Auburn territory, and Penn State was in business. Milne ran for a 22-yard gain, then Richardson found Pitts for a four-yard touchdown. A bad snap botched the extra point, which ended with an incompletion on a desperation pass, but Penn State now led 29–7.

Herring continued having an outstanding game, as he intercepted a Nix pass on Auburn's next drive. It was his third turnover of the game, and it put Penn State back in Auburn territory. Archie burst down the right sideline for a 30-yard gain, and the Lions were now down to the 5. Richardson handed off to Enis on four straight plays, and on the fourth-down carry, Enis got in for a one-yard touchdown. The game was getting out of hand, PSU up by 29.

But the blue-and-white snowball kept rolling. Nix threw three incompletions, one of which was almost intercepted by Herring for a third time. Archie made a fair catch of Auburn's punt at the Tigers 45. Richardson handed off to Milne, who was hit out of bounds late, and that gave Penn State 15 more yards. Pitts ran the ball down to the 20, then Richardson gunned it to Engram for yet another touchdown. It was Richardson's fourth touchdown pass of the game, and Engram's second such catch. Penn State led 43–7 with three minutes to go in the third quarter, and it was safe to say, this one was in the bag.

While Auburn would get a fourth quarter 12-yard touchdown run by fullback Kevin McLeod, the final period was otherwise mop-up duty for all the backups. The Nittany Lions ended up with a 43–14 win, their third bowl victory in a row, and this one by the most points of any of the wins. Engram was named Most Valuable Player of the game for his four catches for 113 yards and two touchdowns, and Penn State finished the season ranked #13 in the Associated Press poll.[14]

Box Score[15]:

1996 Outback Bowl	1st	2nd	3rd	4th	Final
Auburn	0	7	0	7	14
Penn State	3	13	27	0	43

1st Quarter: PSU—Conway 19 FG
2nd Quarter: AUB—Baker 25 pass from Nix (Hawkins kick)
   PSU—Conway 22 FG
   PSU—Conway 38 FG
   PSU—Archie 8 pass from Richardson (Conway kick)
3rd Quarter: PSU—Engram 9 pass from Richardson (Conway kick)
   PSU—Pitts 4 pass from Richardson (pass failed)
   PSU—Enis 1 run (Conway kick)
   PSU—Engram 20 pass from Richardson (Conway kick)
4th Quarter: AUB—McLeod 12 run (Hawkins kick)

1996 Season (10–2)

The Nittany Lions opened up their season at Giants Stadium in the Kickoff Classic against USC. Running back Curtis Enis backed up his fine finish to the 1995 season with a huge performance. He rushed for 241 yards and three touchdowns, as Penn State won 24–7.[1] Then, in their home opener against Louisville, the Nittany Lions won by the same score. Enis rushed for 104 yards and the game's opening touchdown, while quarterback Wally Richardson threw a touchdown to fullback Aaron Harris in leading the Lions to a 14–0 first-quarter lead. Later, linebacker Eric Sturdifen blocked a punt, and defensive back Shino Prater recovered it for a touchdown.[2]

The defense continued its strong play against Northern Illinois, a game that proved to be no more than a scrimmage. Defensive back Mark Tate returned a fumble 21 yards for a touchdown, and running back Chafie Fields ran for 68 yards and two touchdowns in the absence of Enis, who was suffering with strep throat. Penn State went up 35–0 at halftime before putting it on cruise control in the second half, on their way to a 49–0 victory.[3]

In a scheduling quirk, the Nittany Lions went back to Giants Stadium for their fourth game, meaning they had played the same number of games there that they had at home up to this point. This "home away from home" saw Penn State win 41–0 against Temple. Enis came back and ran for 90 yards and a touchdown. The Lions again led big at halftime—31–0—then ended up with a second straight shutout.[4]

For the 700th win in school history, the Lions went to Madison and beat Wisconsin, a team they had never beaten before. Enis ran for 115 yards and two first-half touchdowns, as Penn State took a 20–10 halftime lead. Later, with the score tied, Richardson led the Lions on a drive for a 25-yard field goal by kicker Brett Conway, putting PSU up 23–20. Wisconsin had one last chance at the buzzer, a 58-yard field goal attempt, but it went wide left, and the Nittany Lions held on for the 23–20 win.[5]

As usual, though, Penn State's Big Ten hopes would be ended by Ohio State. While the Lions never turned the ball over, the defense that had been so good ended up being gashed for 565 yards. Penn State's 211 yards of offense in the 38–7 loss were their fewest since 1990.[6] For Homecoming, the Nittany Lions flipped the script, and this time they led 24–0 over Purdue at halftime. Enis rushed for three touchdowns as part of his 177 all-purpose yards, and Harris added another 88 on the ground. Receiver Chris Campbell returned a punt 59 yards for a touchdown in the second quarter, and Penn State rolled to a 31–14 victory.[7]

The Lions outgained Iowa by 63 yards, allowing them to pick up just eight first downs. Harris ran for 152 yards and a touchdown, while Enis gained 100 all-purpose

The Fiesta Bowl trophy, 1997. Photographic vertical files, Athletics, 1855–2009 (01167). Penn State University Archives, Eberly Family Special Collections Library, Penn State University Libraries, Penn State University.

yards and caught a touchdown pass. None of that mattered, as the Hawkeyes came out of Happy Valley with a 21–20 win. It wouldn't be the last time Iowa ended Penn State's big-picture hopes with a one-point victory.[8]

Perhaps feeling a hangover effect of that loss, the Nittany Lions trailed Indiana, of all teams, 20–10 at halftime. Enis and Richardson both left the game early, replaced by Chris Eberly and Mike McQueary, respectively. McQueary ended up throwing two touchdown passes, while Eberly rushed for 110 yards and scored two touchdowns, as the Lions ended up running away with a 48–26 win thanks to four fourth-quarter touchdowns.[9]

Defending Big Ten champion Northwestern came to Happy Valley with an undefeated record in the conference. But before they could get to another Rose Bowl, Penn State completely dominated them. Enis was back and better than ever, rushing for 167 yards and a touchdown. Richardson was also back, and he threw for over 200 yards and two touchdowns. The Wildcats saw their Rose Bowl dreams evaporate in the Happy Valley snow, as PSU beat them 34–9.[10]

Michigan proved to be a bigger challenge. The Wolverines took a 17–13 lead, but the Penn State defense forced five turnovers of their own, as well as blocking a punt that linebacker Ahmad Collins returned for a touchdown. Enis finished things off with a 38-yard touchdown run in the fourth quarter, giving himself 114 yards for the game, and giving the Lions a 29–17 victory at the Big House.[11]

A major bowl berth all came down to whether the Lions could beat Michigan State on Senior Day. Richardson threw a 49-yard touchdown pass to Harris in the first quarter, and the Lions went up 14–13 at the half. In the fourth quarter, Richardson led a last-minute drive for the second straight year against Sparty. Conway kicked a 30-yard field goal with 12 seconds left, and Penn State came away with a 32–29 victory.[12]

Richardson threw for 1,732 yards and seven touchdowns for the season, as the Lions kept the ball on the ground a lot. Enis carried the ball 224 times for 1,210 yards and 13 touchdowns, while Harris ran it another 105 times for 587 yards and nine scores. Jurevicius led the team in receiving with 41 catches for 869 yards and four scores. Herring led the team with seven interceptions on defense.[13]

Ohio State and Northwestern tied for the Big Ten conference crown, with the Buckeyes getting the invitation to Pasadena. Northwestern had a 9–2 record as opposed to Penn State's 10–2; thus, the Wildcats were passed over by the Bowl Alliance and selected for the Citrus Bowl. The new Bowl Alliance offered automatic bids in the Sugar, Orange, and Fiesta Bowls to the champions of the brand-new Big 12 as well as the SEC, Big East, and ACC. Two at-large bids were left after those spots were taken. The Orange Bowl took #6 Nebraska, the Big 12 runner-up, and the Fiesta Bowl took #7 Penn State, while higher-ranked #5 BYU was shuffled off to the non–Alliance Cotton Bowl.[14] That meant that the Nittany Lions were in their sixth consecutive New Year's Day bowl. They were also headed to Tempe, Arizona for the sixth time, trying to remain undefeated in Fiesta Bowls.[15]

1997 Fiesta Bowl

#7 Penn State (10–2) vs. #20 Texas (8–4)
January 1, 1997, at Sun Devil Stadium in Tempe, Arizona

The Texas Longhorns received a berth in the Tostitos Fiesta Bowl by winning the inaugural Big 12 Championship Game over Nebraska. Despite losing four games, only two of those losses came in conference play, and their 6–2 mark was good enough to win the Big 12 South Division. In that championship game, head coach John Mackovic went for it on fourth down from his own 28 with three minutes to play; after converting it there, he'd try the same trick against the Nittany Lions.[16]

Penn State won the coin toss, and head coach Joe Paterno chose to defer. The Longhorns held the ball for only two plays; quarterback James Brown threw an interception to defensive back Mark Tate, and the Lions took over at the Texas 26. Running back Curtis Enis took Penn State's first play for a 15-yard run down inside the 15. Fullback Jason Sload carried the ball a couple of times, then quarterback Wally Richardson found Enis in the right side of the end zone for a four-yard touchdown. Only a couple minutes into the game, the Nittany Lions had a 7–0 lead.

Much like the previous bowl games of the decade, the Lions struggled for much of the first half after getting that one turnover. On the next Texas drive, Brown completed a 17-yard pass to receiver Matt Davis, and future NFL star running backs Ricky Williams and Priest Holmes split carries, as the Longhorns got down inside the 10. Kicker Phil Dawson, another future NFL prospect, made a 28-yard field goal, and Texas pulled within four.

Penn State went three-and-out on their next two possessions, and the first quarter ended with the Lions up 7–3. As the second quarter began, the Longhorns went on another drive. Again it was Williams and Holmes splitting carries, as well as Brown passing to receiver Wane McGarity for 15 yards. The Longhorns again got into field goal range, and the distance for Dawson's field goal try was exactly the same, 28 yards. This

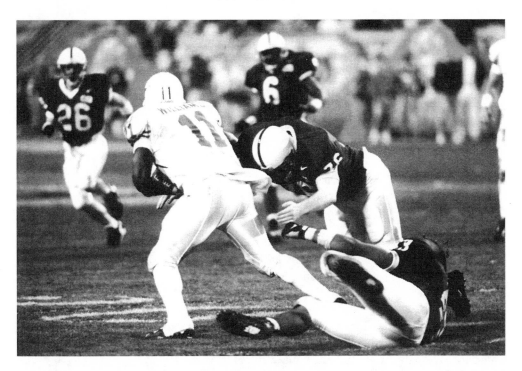

Lion defense harassing the RB, 1997. Players shown, left to right: #26: PSU linebacker Matt Joyner; #11: Texas running back Ricky Williams; #6: PSU linebacker Aaron Collins; #76: PSU defensive tackle Mike Buzin;, #43: PSU linebacker Brandon Short. Photographic vertical files, Athletics, 1855–2009 (01167). Penn State University Archives, Eberly Family Special Collections Library, Penn State University Libraries, Penn State University.

time, Dawson slipped and fell on the relatively tame Sun Devil Stadium turf, but his kick knuckleballed through the uprights, and Texas cut the Penn State lead to one.

Richardson completed a pair of sizable passes on Penn State's next drive, as he found receiver Joe Jurevicius for 18 yards and tight end Cuncho Brown for another 20. However, the drive ended shortly afterward, and punter Darrell Kania put the ball in the end zone for a touchback. The Lions would go three-and-out the next time they got the ball. Tate then made a big play for the defense, knocking the ball out of running back Shon Mitchell's hands, and defensive back Kim Herring fell on it before sliding out of bounds. But the offense struggled again, with only one 12-yard pass to Enis before yet another punt.

With little time left in the first half, Brown fired to receiver Mike Adams for 25 yards, then to Davis for another 19. He scrambled for a first down at the Penn State 18, then Tate got called for pass interference on a pass to the end zone. Williams capped off the Texas drive with a seven-yard touchdown run, but Mackovic got a little too greedy. He went for two points in the first half, far too early. Brown was chased down by defensive end Brandon Short before throwing incomplete, and the Texas lead was just 12–7 at the half.

Paterno was well-known as the master of halftime adjustments, but sometimes the best adjustments are simpler than a change of scheme. Receiver Kenny Watson turned the game on its head by returning the opening kickoff of the second half right down the middle for 81 yards. Fullback Aaron Harris took over from there, catching a pass and running the ball three times. On his third carry, he went off right tackle for a five-yard touchdown. Richardson followed by throwing a two-point pass to Enis, and Penn State took a 15–12 lead.

Brown converted a third-and-long on the next Texas drive, throwing to Davis for a 17-yard gain. Williams caught Brown's next third-down pass, but he was stopped short of the first down. With shades of the Big 12 Championship Game, Mackovic went with a fake punt. Defensive back Cody Danaher took a direct snap and fired it downfield to another defensive back, Bryant Westbrook. He hauled it in for a 33-yard gain. That set up a 48-yard field goal by Dawson, who tied the game at 15, while setting a Fiesta Bowl record for most field goals in a game with three.

But from there, Penn State took over the game like an avalanche. Enis ran for gains of 13 and 12 to start the drive. Richardson threw a three-yard pass to receiver Chris Campbell, then Enis ran right over two tacklers on his way to another first down. Cuncho Brown hauled in a pass for a first down at the 18, then running back Chris Eberly took a pitch down to the 5. Two plays later, Enis leaped over the top of the line for a touchdown, and Penn State took a 22–15 lead.

Texas got only one first down before having to punt again. Penn State took over way back at their own 13, but they'd take little time getting downfield. Running back Chafie Fields took a reverse, coming from the right side and sprinting down the left sideline. No Texas player was able to get him until he reached the 5-yard line, and he ended up with an 84-yard gain, the longest run in Penn State bowl history. Two plays later, fullback Anthony Cleary pounded it in for a one-yard touchdown, and Penn State took a 28–15 lead. Kicker Brett Conway, who had made over 100 straight extra points, pulled this one wide left, leaving the Lions' lead at 13 at the end of three quarters.

The Nittany Lion defense forced another punt, and Campbell returned this one 32 yards. Richardson threw a pass to Harris, then he dumped off a screen to Eberly, who got

Curtis Enis heading for paydirt, 1997. Photographic vertical files, Athletics, 1855–2009 (01167). Penn State University Archives, Eberly Family Special Collections Library, Penn State University Libraries, Penn State University.

13 more yards. A personal foul set the Lions back, but Richardson threw to Eberly again to pick up the first down. Cleary ran it down to the 10 for another new set of downs, but the Lions could not punch it in. Conway came on to make a 23-yard field goal, giving Penn State a 16-point lead.

Short forced a Brown fumble on the next drive, and while the Lions didn't recover, they did force a huge loss. Texas then got called for offensive pass interference, and they were pushed back into a third-and-30. Defensive tackle Matt Fornadel tackled Williams for a loss on a screen play, and the Lions got the ball back after a punt in good field position.

This drive would wrap up the victory for Penn State. Eberly ran for ten yards, then Cleary took it a couple of times to get a first down across midfield. Eberly proved himself almost impossible to tackle, as he shook off tacklers on both of his next two runs, getting to the 17, then down to the 1. Enis followed by taking it into the end zone on a draw. Penn State now had a commanding 38–15 lead, and the competitive portion of the ballgame was over, as was the scoring.

Enis was named player of the game for his 110 scrimmage yards and three touchdowns. He also had a two-point conversion, giving him 20 points on the day. What's more, is that on Cleary's touchdown run, Enis had actually carried the ball past the goal line on the previous play, but the officials ruled him inches short. Had they ruled it correctly, Enis would have had four touchdowns plus a two-point conversion for 26 points. As it stood, he still beat the Longhorns by himself.

"Punching it across the goal line," 1997. Player with ball is Penn State fullback Anthony Cleary. Photographic vertical files, Athletics, 1855–2009 (01167). Penn State University Archives, Eberly Family Special Collections Library, Penn State University Libraries, Penn State University.

About the halftime adjustments that turned the game around, Paterno said that there weren't any. "We didn't tell them anything, really," he said after the game. "Everybody played well, I'm very, very proud." Penn State had its fourth consecutive bowl victory, and they finished #7 in the final polls. Moreover, the 1996 senior class finished 42–7 for their careers, the best record by one class in school history, winning bowls in all four years. Richardson was the quarterback of the last two of them, and he had proven himself to be a surefire winner.[17]

Box Score[18]:

1997 Fiesta Bowl	1st	2nd	3rd	4th	Final
Texas	3	9	3	0	15
Penn State	7	0	21	10	38

1st Quarter: PSU—Enis 4 pass from Richardson (Conway kick)
    TEX—Dawson 28 FG
2nd Quarter: TEX—Dawson 28 FG
    TEX—Williams 7 run (pass failed)
3rd Quarter: PSU—Harris 5 run (Enis pass from Richardson)
    TEX—Dawson 48 FG
    PSU—Enis 2 run (Conway kick)
    PSU—Cleary 1 run (kick missed)
4th Quarter: PSU—Conway 23 FG
    PSU—Enis 12 run (Conway kick)

Curtis Enis scoring, 1997. Photographic vertical files, Athletics, 1855–2009 (01167). Penn State University Archives, Eberly Family Special Collections Library, Penn State University Libraries, Penn State University.

1997 Season (9–2)

Penn State began the year in perfect position: #1 in the nation and with a blow-out win over their archrivals from Pittsburgh. Quarterback Mike McQueary, a fifth-year senior, completed 21 of his 36 passes and set a school record with 366 passing yards. The Nittany Lions beat Pitt 34–17 in front of a Beaver Stadium record 97,115 fans.[1]

In the next two games, the Lions put up over a hundred points combined. First, they beat Temple 52–10 for their 22nd win in a row over the Owls. Receiver Chafie Fields ran for two long touchdowns on reverses, from 43 and 47 yards out. Then, the Nittany Lions went to Louisville and destroyed the Cardinals, 57–21. Fifty of those points came in the first half, marking Penn State's most points in a half since 1947. McQueary threw for 219 yards and three touchdowns. Receiver Joe Jurevicius caught four passes for 150 yards and three scores.[2]

Headed to Champaign, McQueary threw another three touchdowns in a 41–6 win over Illinois. He completed 13 of 21 passes for 266 yards. Jurevicius caught three of those passes for 87 yards and two scores. Fields put up 185 all-purpose yards. Running backs Curtis Enis and Chris Eberly combined for nearly 200 rushing yards, with Enis picking up 108 and two scores, and Eberly running for 87.[3]

Next came a fantastic struggle with Ohio State in a battle of unbeatens. The Lions blew a 10–0 lead, as Ohio State roared back to take a 27–17 lead in the third quarter. Needing a spark, Penn State turned to fullback Aaron Harris, who broke three tackles on his way to a 51-yard touchdown run. Enis then ran for a 26-yard touchdown in the fourth quarter, and Penn State won, 31–27.[4]

The next pair of Big Ten games were close calls. Enis ran for two touchdowns in the fourth quarter against Minnesota, on his way to a 112-yard day. The Lions came from behind to beat the Golden Gophers, 16–15. They then went to Northwestern, where Enis had another big day. He ran for 153 yards, while McQueary threw for 222 yards and ran for an 11-yard touchdown. The Lions escaped with a 30–27 win, moving to 7–0 headed into a big clash with undefeated Michigan.[5]

The Lions' nation-best 12-game winning streak came to an end at home against Michigan. The Wolverines held them to just 169 total yards of offense, their least in a game since 1988. Enis ran for 108 of those yards, going over 100 for their fifth straight game, while also scoring a touchdown and a two-point conversion. However, that was the only positive for Penn State, who lost this one 34–8.[6]

Against Purdue, linebacker Maurice Daniels scored on a pick-six, as the Lions bounced back with a 42–17 win. Enis picked up a career-best 269 all-purpose yards, including 186 on the ground. That put him over 3,000 career rushing yards and gave him his second 1,000-yard season. He scored three touchdowns, two on the ground, and Penn State beat the Boilermakers 42–17.[7]

McQueary threw only three incompletions against Wisconsin, which was also the same number of touchdown passes he threw. He completed his first 12 in a row on his way to 269 yards. Enis had another big game, running for 138 yards and scoring two touchdowns. Jurevicius caught two of McQueary's touchdown passes and totaled 101 yards, as Penn State wiped out the Badgers, 35–10.[8]

The season ended in East Lansing against Michigan State. Enis ran for 106 yards to set a new school record with eight 100-yard games rushing in a row. It was his 17th career 100-yard game, ranking him second in Penn State history. He finished his Nittany Lion career with 3,256 rushing yards, third in school annals. That was all nice, but Penn State got wiped out by the Spartans, 49–14. The score was tied at 14 in the third quarter before Michigan State rolled to five straight touchdowns.[9]

McQueary threw for 2,211 yards and 17 touchdowns, while throwing only nine interceptions. That ranked him fifth in school history for passing yards in a season. Enis also finished the season with the fifth-most in Penn State history in rushing yards, as he ran for 1,363 of them while scoring 20 touchdowns, and was named Big Ten Offensive Player of the Year. Jurevicius led the team in receiving with 39 receptions for 817 yards and ten touchdowns.[10]

However, neither Enis nor Jurevicius would participate in the bowl game. Enis got in trouble for accepting free clothing worth $1,100. Jurevicius skipped too many classes, and head coach Joe Paterno cut him from the team. These dismissals hung a giant black cloud over the Penn State program headed into the Citrus Bowl. It was a consolation prize for the Nittany Lions, who were going to be invited to the Sugar Bowl had they defeated Michigan State. Instead, they were headed to Orlando to face off against the #6 Florida Gators.[11]

1998 Citrus Bowl

#11 Penn State (9–2) vs. #6 Florida (9–2)
January 1, 1998, at the Florida Citrus Bowl in Orlando, Florida

The Nittany Lions had lost this Citrus Bowl long before the Gators scored the first of their three touchdowns. When receiver Joe Jurevicius and running back Curtis Enis were dismissed from the team, Penn State lost over half its total of scrimmage yards for the season. There was no way of replacing them on the fly. The Lions wouldn't reach the end zone, and if not for their defense, they might not have even reached the *red* zone.

Florida head coach Steve Spurrier ran a unique offense where two quarterbacks rotated in and out, but the passing game wasn't his focus today. The Gators started out by simply handing the ball off to running back Fred Taylor. He ripped off runs of eight, seven, and 12, before quarterback Doug Johnson threw to receiver Travis McGriff and tight end Erron Kinney for a pair of first downs. Their other quarterback, Noah Brindise snuck it in from the 1 to give Florida a 7–0 lead.

Penn State quarterback Mike McQueary completed his second pass of the game to tight end Cuncho Brown for a first down. His next pass, however, was intercepted by defensive back Fred Weary. It took Florida just one play to capitalize. Johnson went long to the left corner of the end zone, where receiver Jacquez Green caught the ball off a deflection for a 35-yard touchdown. It was 14–0 in the blink of an eye, and there was no chance this depleted Lion offense could catch them.

The Lions punted on their next two possessions. Fred Taylor then led the Florida offense down into scoring range. Brindise completed a flea flicker to receiver Travis Taylor as well, and the Gators were set up to potentially score again. However, on a fourth down from no man's land, Penn State linebacker Jim Nelson picked off Brindise to end the Gator drive. The first quarter ended with Florida up by 14.

Penn State punted again, but they got the ball back when defensive back Shawn Lee intercepted a pass and returned it to the Florida 30. McQueary found Brown for a first down across the 20, then running back Chris Eberly burst for a 13-yard gain. The Lion drive would end when defensive tackle Reggie McGrew sacked McQueary on third down, but kicker Travis Forney made a 42-yard field goal to get Penn State on the board.

After punting on their next possession, the Lions got the ball back when linebacker Brandon Short sacked Johnson, forced a fumble, and recovered the fumble himself. Deep in Florida territory, McQueary hit Brown down at the 1. On fourth-and-goal from inches away, head coach Joe Paterno kept the offense out there. The Gators stuffed Eberly in the backfield, and the Lions came away with nothing.

Fred Taylor was nearly tackled in his own end zone for a safety, but he broke free and managed to get the Gators out of trouble. The Lions forced a Florida punt before the half, and running back Kenny Watson returned the kick all the way to the 6. It was another perfect opportunity to score, but again they faced fourth-and-goal from the 1. This attempt ended in failure as well, when McQueary threw an interception to defensive back Mike Harris. While the Lions went to the half down 14–3, they could take solace in the fact that they were only a couple yards from actually having the lead going into the locker room.

Getting the ball to start the half, McQueary's first pass was so far off the mark that it nearly hit Paterno on the sideline. However, he quickly recovered, finding receiver Joe Nastasi for a first down at the 41. A screen to Watson got a first down at the Florida 47, and Eberly then ran for his team's next two first downs. The drive ended in a Forney 30-yard field goal, and the Nittany Lions were now within one possession.

The teams traded punts, and Florida took over at their own 24. Taylor picked up nine yards on two carries, then Johnson got a first down. Two plays later, Johnson tried scrambling, and he was hit hard by defensive end Justin Kurpekis. He came out of the game with a shoulder injury. Taylor fumbled on the next play, but guard Cheston Blackshear recovered, getting a first down in the process. Taylor ran it a couple more times, including a 12-yard run. Spurrier had gone to third-string quarterback Jesse Palmer to rotate with Brindise, and it was Palmer who had the honor of throwing a touchdown pass. He threw to Green, who made an incredible catch for a 37-yard touchdown. The Gators now had a 15-point lead, and the game was all but over.

The Lions got backed into a third-and-22 on the next drive before having to punt. The Gators came back out and fed Taylor the ball. He ended up carrying the football 43 times for a Citrus Bowl-record 234 yards. The Penn State rushing defense, which had struggled against the two teams from Michigan, couldn't do anything to stop him. Taylor got the Gators down into field goal range, but kicker Collins Cooper missed a 26-yard field goal that would have iced the game.

With one last shot at making a game of it, McQueary came back on the field. He launched a long one for receiver Titcus Pettigrew, but it ended up just a little too far. Two plays later, he threw an interception to defensive back Elijah Williams. The Nittany Lions would lose this one 21–6, but it was a valiant effort in the face of the dismissals.

McQueary had no help on this day, which excuses the fact that he completed only ten of 32 passes for 92 yards and three picks. His leading receiver in yards was Nastasi with just 26. Eberly ran the ball 14 times for 53 yards, as the Lions totaled just 139 yards on offense for the day. After starting the season ranked #1 in the Associated Press poll, the Nittany Lions would finish ranked #16 with a 9–3 record.

Box score[12]:

1998 Citrus Bowl	1st	2nd	3rd	4th	Final
Penn State	0	3	3	0	6
Florida	14	0	0	7	21

1st Quarter: FLA—Brindise 1 run (Cooper kick)
    FLA—Green 35 pass from Johnson (Cooper kick)
2nd Quarter: PSU—Forney 42 FG
3rd Quarter: PSU—Forney 30 FG
4th Quarter: FLA—Green 37 pass from Palmer (Cooper kick)

1998 Season (8–3)

Penn State started the season at home against Southern Mississippi. The defense completely dominated the Golden Eagles, allowing them a mere nine yards on the ground while coming up with three sacks. Running back Cordell Mitchell ran for just a yard short of 100 yards on 16 attempts, while receiver Joe Nastasi caught four passes for 73 yards. The Nittany Lions won easily, 34–6.[1]

The following week, head coach Joe Paterno recorded his 300th victory of his career. He was the fastest coach to ever reach 300, and he did so in a 48–3 rout over Bowling Green. The Lions led 21–0 in the first quarter, before cruising to an easy victory. Paterno joined five other coaches in the 300-win club.[2] At Pitt Stadium, the Nittany Lions got a win over a Pitt team coming off its best season in ages. The Lions picked up five sacks in the fourth quarter, helping them hold on for a 20–13 win.[3]

There's a theme that this season and many others had: losses to both Ohio State and Michigan, the two teams Penn State just could not beat. At Ohio Stadium, the Lions were crushed 28–9. This was all despite only allowing 326 yards and 14 offensive points. The Buckeyes recovered a fumble in the end zone and blocked a punt for a touchdown to get their other 14 points, changing a close game into a rout.[4]

Before Penn State could get to Michigan, they had some easier opponents coming up first. Minnesota also blocked a Penn State punt and returned it for a touchdown, but the Lions managed to win this game 27–17. The defense held the Golden Gophers to just 224 total yards.[5] The thrill-a-minute Purdue Boilermakers came to Happy Valley for Penn State's first home game in over a month. Defensive end Courtney Brown won Big Ten Defensive Player of the Week for his six tackles. Running back Eric McCoo came up with 163 yards in the 31–13 victory.[6]

The next two games would finish with 27–0 scores. First, it was Penn State winning by that margin over Illinois. The Nittany Lions had five sacks, allowing only 244 yards for the game. Kevin Thompson had the best game of his career, throwing for 269 yards on 19 completions. Receiver Chafie Fields led the team in receiving with 115 yards.[7] But the following week, Penn State fell by a 27–0 margin. Everything went wrong against Michigan, as the Lions put up a mere 200 offensive yards at the "Big House," while turning the ball over five times. They were shut out for the first time since 1987.[8]

The Lions rebounded with a home win over Northwestern. Brown came up with two sacks and six tackles for loss, as Penn State gave up just 21 yards rushing in the contest. Meanwhile, the PSU running game was on fire, rushing for 248 yards. The Lions defeated the Wildcats easily, 41–10.[9] Against Wisconsin, linebacker LaVar Arrington had

11 tackles, and McCoo rushed for 91 yards. Despite all that, the Lions gained only one field goal in a 24–3 loss at Camp Randall Stadium.[10]

But the Nittany Lions had a good ending to the regular season, crushing Michigan State 51–28. McCoo rushed for a Penn State freshman-record 206 yards. Kicker Travis Forney made five field goals, tying the school record, while the defense picked up three interceptions and seven sacks. That gave the Lions 47 sacks for the year, which also tied a school record.[11]

McCoo led the team in rushing with 822 yards. Fullback Mike Cerimele had the most rushing touchdowns with eight. Thompson threw for nearly 1,700 yards and six touchdowns. The biggest stars were on defense, where Brown had 23 tackles for loss and 11-and-a-half sacks, while Arrington recorded 17 tackles for loss and seven sacks.[12]

Penn State finished the season at 8–3, 5–3 in the Big Ten. While that was only good enough for fifth place, the Nittany Lions benefited from the creation of the Bowl Championship Series. The BCS took both Ohio State (Sugar) and Wisconsin (Rose),[13] moving up the other teams in the league one notch. While the Citrus Bowl took Michigan, the Outback Bowl passed up Purdue and went with Penn State as their choice to go up against Kentucky in the New Year's Day game.

1999 Outback Bowl

#22 Penn State (8–3) vs. Kentucky (7–4)
January 1, 1999, at Raymond James Stadium in Tampa, Florida

Unlike the last time Penn State played in Tampa, there were perfect weather conditions for the game, no rain at all. The Outback Bowl had previously been played at Tampa Stadium; that stadium was now abandoned, and the bowl as well as the NFL's Tampa Bay Buccaneers moved on to the new Raymond James Stadium. This was the first bowl to be played at the Bucs' new stadium, and due to Kentucky's proximity, there were a lot more Wildcats fans in Tampa than Penn Staters.

Quarterback Tim Couch was playing his final career game for the Wildcats. He would declare for the NFL draft after this game and be selected number-one overall by the Cleveland Browns. With his strong arm and good legs, he proved a challenge for the Penn State defense. Kentucky stated that their goal this season was to reach a New Year's Day bowl game; Couch had delivered on that promise. Now they hoped to win one on January 1 for the first time since 1952.[14] (By comparison, Penn State was playing its eighth consecutive New Year's Day bowl game.)

The Wildcats got the ball to start the game. Running back Anthony White ran for a first down, then receiver Quentin McCord got another. The teams traded offside and false start penalties; this game would be full of flags. Couch tried a screen to fullback Derek Homer, only to see him get blown up by linebackers LaVar Arrington and Brandon Short for a loss of five. Kentucky was forced to punt, and Lions linebacker Eric Sturdifen rushed in and blocked the kick, giving Penn State great field position.

However, the Nittany Lions proved unable to do anything with it. Running back Eric McCoo got three yards on a first-down carry, and that was it. Quarterback Kevin Thompson threw a pair of incompletions, including a long one to receiver Chafie Fields that he couldn't haul in. On fourth down, kicker Travis Forney tried a career-long 51-yard field goal, but it fell well short of the goal posts.

Defensive end Courtney Brown blew up Homer for a loss, and the Lions put Kentucky in a hole. They committed another false start penalty, so when Couch threw to tight end James Whalen for 13 yards, they were still short of the first down. On fourth-and-two, Kentucky head coach Hal Mumme chose to go for it. Couch ran a fake reverse in which he ended up handing the ball to receiver Craig Yeast, who picked up the first down. Two plays later, he hit receiver Lance Mickelsen for a 37-yard touchdown, and Kentucky led 7–0.

Penn State responded, though. Thompson threw to tight end Tony Stewart for a first down. McCoo then found a hole on the left side, and he burst for a 25-yard pickup. Two plays after that, Thompson threw to a wide-open Stewart who could walk into the end zone—but he dropped it. The Nittany Lions settled for a 43-yard Forney field goal to cut the deficit to four.

Defensive back Matt Joyner made a tackle of Yeast on the ensuing kickoff return, which likely saved a touchdown. So, Couch decided to get a touchdown the hard way. He threw to receiver Kevin Coleman to get within a yard of a first down, then followed with a pass to Homer for eight more. Mickelsen broke wide open, and Couch found him down at the 16. Couch then hit White for a walk-in touchdown, and the Wildcats were up by 11.

Penn State ended up punting, and punter Pat Pidgeon made a perfect kick that landed at the 6. On the first play of the drive, Couch dropped back to pass, and Brown sacked him in the end zone for a safety. That would have been a real game-changer for the Lions, but one of the defenders was called for being offside. The Wildcats then picked up a pair of first downs, as the first quarter came to a close.

To start out the second quarter, the Nittany Lions stopped White short on a third-down reception. Punter Jimmy Carter kicked the potato out of bounds at midfield for a mere 14-yard punt. The Lions lost six yards on the next two snaps, but Thompson made up for it. Receiver Joe Nastasi broke wide open, and Thompson found him for a 56-yard touchdown. Head coach Joe Paterno chose not to go for two here, so Forney kicked the extra point to pull within four.

Yeast returned the ensuing kickoff 67 yards to the Penn State 31. The Wildcats were set up to score, but defensive back Anthony King picked off a Couch pass. Fields then ran it on a reverse, and he picked up 29 yards. Fullback Aaron Harris added another nine yards, and Thompson threw to Fields for a first down. Nastasi got open deep again, and Thompson threw in his direction. This time, the Kentucky defender dragged Nastasi down to save the touchdown, but the officials missed it and didn't throw a flag. That led to a Penn State punt.

Defensive end Brad Scioli and linebacker Brandon Short sacked Couch to start the next drive. Couch then scrambled for a 30-yard pickup, making up the lost yardage and then some. He scrambled again later in the drive to get to the Penn State 35. But King made a tackle for a loss, and the Wildcats were forced into going for it on fourth-and-14. Couch's pass for Yeast fell incomplete, and Penn State took over on downs.

Thompson threw to Stewart for a first down into Kentucky territory, but then McCoo fumbled. Defensive back Ronnie Riley forced the fumble and recovered it himself. The Wildcats threatened again, only to see King ruin their chances yet again. This time he picked off a lob by Couch and returned it to the 48.

Now with great field position, Penn State had to take advantage. They started by drawing a pass interference penalty. Thompson then hit Stewart for a first down to the 22, and Harris followed with a run that picked up half the distance to the goal. The Nittany Lions couldn't punch it in, but they did get a 26-yard field goal by Forney. They went to the half trailing Kentucky, 14–13.

McCoo ran for a 20-yard pickup on his first carry of the second half. Thompson then hit Stewart on a seven-yard pass, but he injured his left wrist on the play. He had to go to the sideline, while backup Rashard Casey came in to replace him. Casey didn't throw a pass while he was in there, and the Lions ended up punting.

Brown picked up another sack of Couch, and the Wildcats were pushed back very deep in their own territory. Carter barely got away the kick, which Penn State got at the Kentucky 35. Head coach Joe Paterno wanted a safety on the play, as the Wildcats were called for holding, but it occurred out of the end zone. Paterno would have to settle for the great field position his team now had.

Thompson came back into the game, as the wrist injury was minor. He immediately threw to Stewart for six yards. Harris burst through the line for a 19-yard pickup down to the 10, and he carried the ball a couple of other times to get down to the 2. But on third down, he slipped and fell down in the backfield, losing yardage and forcing a field goal try. Forney banked his kick off the right upright and through for a 21-yard field goal, giving Penn State their first lead of the day, 16–14.

White and Couch each picked up big first downs on the ground, and Kentucky moved it into field goal range. Couch went for the end zone, and a penalty flag flew. It was for pass interference, but Penn State defensive coordinator Jerry Sandusky disagreed. He ran downfield to start yelling at the officials, who eventually changed the call to a "no foul" because the pass was uncatchable. The Wildcats settled for a 29-yard field goal attempt by kicker Seth Hanson, but Arrington blocked it to keep PSU in the lead.

McCoo ran for a first down to midfield, and Stewart caught one for another first down to the 37. On a third down, Thompson found McCoo wide open down at the 15, and the Lions got even more yardage tacked on when Kentucky was called for a late hit. While unable to get in the end zone, the Lions were able to get a 25-yard Forney field goal to go up 19–14 after three quarters.

The biggest play of the game perhaps was a fourth-and-one on Kentucky's side of the field. Mumme chose to go for it, but Arrington made the tackle shy of the line to gain. That gave Penn State the ball with great field position, and they too faced a fourth-and-short. The Lions converted, however, on a run by fullback Mike Cerimele. Two plays later, Fields took an end around and broke several tackles on his way to a 19-yard touchdown. The Lions now had a 12-point lead and all the momentum.

Now in desperation mode, the Wildcats went on a long drive, converting two fourth downs along the way. Once they got down inside the 10, Brown took over. He sacked Couch on consecutive plays. That forced Couch to have to throw a prayer on fourth down, which fell incomplete. The Lions could now run out almost all of the clock.

On the final play of the game, Couch completed his final collegiate pass, only to see the ball fumbled. King scooped it up and tried to return it for a touchdown. He came up one yard shy of ending this game with a 32–14 score. He was tackled at the 1, and the game was now officially over. The Nittany Lions had won their second Outback Bowl, by a final count of 26–14.

Brown was named MVP of the game for his outstanding defensive play. "Brown and Scioli are the unsung heroes of this team," Paterno said in a postgame interview on the field. "I think our defense adjusted to the pace; I think they played a great football game."

The Nittany Lions finished the season ranked #17 by the Associated Press; they'd start the next season with a much higher ranking.[15]

Box Score[16]:

1999 Outback Bowl	1st	2nd	3rd	4th	Final
Kentucky	14	0	0	0	14
Penn State	3	10	6	7	26

1st Quarter: UK—Mickelsen 36 pass from Couch (Hanson kick)
   PSU—Forney 43 FG
   UK—White 16 pass from Couch (Hanson kick)
2nd Quarter: PSU—Nastasi 56 pass from Thompson (Forney kick)
   PSU—Forney 26 FG
3rd Quarter: PSU—Forney 21 FG
   PSU—Forney 25 FG
4th Quarter: PSU—Fields 19 run (Forney kick)

1999 Season (9–3)

Penn State began the season ranked #3 in the Associated Press poll, up against #4 Arizona in their first game. The Nittany Lions raced to a 14-point lead in the first quarter, and they led 31–0 at halftime. Chafie Fields scored on a 37-yard reception as well as a 70-yard reverse in the first quarter. Running back Larry Johnson scored his first career touchdown on a screen pass that went 60 yards. Quarterback Kevin Thompson threw only eight passes, but they went for 135 yards, as Penn State beat Arizona 41–7.[1]

The Lions then poured on 70 points against Akron, scoring at least two touchdowns in every quarter. Thompson again only had to throw eight passes, which went for 188 yards and two touchdowns. Nine different players scored touchdowns for Penn State, the most since head coach Joe Paterno took over the team, as the Nittany Lions beat up Akron 70–24.[2]

Pitt was no Akron. They went toe-to-toe with the Lions till the end. Thompson threw a 51-yard pass to Eddie Drummond with less than two minutes to go with the game tied at 17. That set up a 24-yard field goal by kicker Travis Forney, giving Penn State a 20–17 lead with 80 seconds to play. Drummond then saved a touchdown with a tackle of returner Hank Poteat on the kickoff. The Panthers got into field goal range, only to have Lions linebacker LaVar Arrington swat away the game-tying 52-yard kick with four seconds left, preserving the three-point win.[3]

The Lions made their first trip of the season away from home, and this one was no easy one—at the Miami Orange Bowl against the Hurricanes. Penn State took a 10–0 lead in the first quarter, as Casey threw a 49-yard touchdown pass to Fields. The Hurricanes came back to take a 23–20 lead in the fourth quarter. Thompson then hit Fields on a 79-yard touchdown pass to give Penn State the 27–23 win. The 177 receiving yards by Fields ranked as the fourth-highest total in Nittany Lion history.[4]

Defensive back Bruce Branch returned a punt 90 yards for a touchdown against Indiana, as the Lions went on to beat the Hoosiers 45–24. Casey completed all but two of his 15 passes for 196 yards, with three total touchdowns.[5] In Iowa, Drummond opened the scoring with a 68-yard end-around run. Running back Eric McCoo ran for a 47-yard touchdown, part of his 130 rushing yards for the game. Fullback Aaron Harris added a touchdown run, as Penn State went on to win 31–7.[6]

It was Ohio State week, and ordinarily this would mean doom and gloom. But not so on this day at Beaver Stadium, as the Lions held the Buckeyes to a mere 143 total yards of offense. McCoo ran it 22 times for 211 yards, a career-high. It wasn't easy, as it never is against Ohio State, but the Lions held on for a 23–10 win.[7]

Quarterback Drew Brees proved a problem for the Penn State defense as they went to visit Purdue. He threw for 379 yards and two touchdowns, keeping the Boilermakers in it to the end. But Arrington scored on a two-yard fumble return, and defensive end Courtney Brown returned an interception 25 yards for a score, and the Lions pulled out a 31–25 win.[8]

After falling behind Illinois 7–0 after one quarter, the Lions stormed back, getting touchdown passes from each Thompson and Casey. In a bizarre move, Paterno deferred on the opening coin toss, then chose to take the wind to start the second half. But it worked, as the Fighting Illini struggled on offense in the third quarter. With the score at 17–7, Casey ripped off a show-stopping 34-yard touchdown run, as the Lions won 27–7.[9]

Everything was coming up sugary for the Nittany Lions. As in, the Sugar Bowl, where the Bowl Championship Series title game would be held. They were #2 in the Associated Press poll and at the same ranking in the BCS standings. Three more wins, and they'd almost certainly be headed to New Orleans, where their likely opponent would be Florida State.[10]

Against Minnesota, Thompson threw for 158 yards and a first-half touchdown. McCoo ran for 107 yards, and Cerimele scored on a first-quarter five-yard run. The Lions had the ball at the Minnesota 33 up by two with about two minutes to go, but the Gophers got a stop. After a 46-yard completion and then a miraculous fourth-and-16 conversion, Minnesota made it into field goal range. Kicker Dan Nystrom made a 32-yard field goal as the clock ran out to give Minnesota a 24–23 win, the first time Paterno had ever lost a game on a play that ended with triple zeroes.[11]

The old saying is "don't let the same team beat you twice." In this case, the Lions let Minnesota beat them twice by coming out flat against Michigan. The Wolverines hopped out to a 10–0 lead in the first quarter. Branch got the Lions back in it with a 79-yard punt return for a score, and Thompson later threw a 38-yard touchdown pass to Drummond. When defensive back Bhawoh Jue scored on a 46-yard pick-six, Penn State led by ten with nine-and-a-half minutes left. However, Michigan quarterback Tom Brady led a comeback, scoring on a five-yard run and throwing an 11-yard touchdown pass. The Lions had one last chance with the ball, but Thompson was strip-sacked, and Michigan held on for a 31–27 win.[12]

Everything had fallen apart for Penn State, and things only got worse at Michigan State. The Lions fell into a 28–7 hole at halftime, but Thompson rallied the team with his 185 passing yards and two touchdowns as well as a two-point conversion pass to McCoo. The Lions tied the game at 28, making the largest comeback to at least tie a game since 1994. But Michigan State T.J. Duckett ran for an 11-yard touchdown with two-and-a-half minutes left, and the Lions fell 35–28.[13]

The rotating quarterback strategy with Thompson and Casey worked for the first three quarters of the season. Thompson threw for over 1,900 yards and 13 touchdowns, while Casey added another 856 yards and six scoring throws. But ultimately the Big Ten schedule was just too hard for a team to win it while not having a starter set in stone. McCoo led the team with 739 rushing yards, scoring four times. Fields and Drummond led in receptions, each of them going over 650 receiving yards and both catching at least 35 balls and five touchdowns.[14]

This 1999 season had ended in disaster, but the Lions still finished in a tie for fourth place in the Big Ten at 5–3. The Bowl Championship Series again took two Big Ten teams (Wisconsin in the Rose and Michigan in the Orange), which moved Penn State up a spot in the bowl hierarchy. However, with the Citrus taking Michigan State, the next bowl up was the Outback. They didn't want the same team two straight years, so they passed up PSU and took Purdue.[15] The Nittany Lions were left to go to the Alamo Bowl, in its seventh year of existence. It would take place on December 28, so for the first time since 1990, Penn State would not play in a New Year's bowl.[16]

1999 Alamo Bowl

#13 Penn State (9–3) vs. #18 Texas A&M (8–3)
December 28, 1999, at the Alamodome in San Antonio, Texas

This was the final game of defensive coordinator Jerry Sandusky's career. He was retiring after having spent 32 years at Penn State.[17] It was also the final game for standout defensive players Courtney Brown and LaVar Arrington. Each of them figured to go in the first round of the NFL Draft; how high was still a mystery, but the Cleveland Browns were greatly considering Brown for their #1 pick.

Texas A&M was a strong opponent for Penn State; the Aggies won just two fewer games than Penn State in the nineties, going into this bowl. Texas A&M was still grieving at the loss of 12 people in a bonfire accident. For an emotional game against archrival Texas, over 86,000 fans came out, the largest-ever crowd in the state of Texas. The Aggies beat the Longhorns 20–16 on a late touchdown pass. They finished in a tie for second place in the Big 12 South at 5–3.[18]

The Aggies won the toss and deferred to the second half. Rashard Casey started at quarterback for Penn State because to a shoulder injury to Kevin Thompson. On his first pass of the game, he rolled out on a play-action pass and hit fullback Mike Cerimele for a 16-yard gain. He then ran for nine more yards, but the drive stalled and punter Pat Pidgeon kicked it away.

A&M quarterback Randy McCown was under heavy pressure from the very start. On first down, he was pressured by Arrington, and he threw up a bad pass that was intercepted by defensive back David Macklin. Running back Cordell Mitchell ran for 12 yards, setting up Penn State in field goal range. Kicker Travis Forney converted the 38-yard attempt, but A&M was called for roughing the kicker (Forney did a great acting job). This would only hurt Penn State. Head coach Joe Paterno decided to erase the points and take the first down. But they couldn't gain all that much, and Forney came back out to try a 30-yarder. This one he missed wide to the right.

Defensive end Justin Kurpeikis sacked McCown on second down, and A&M was in a third-and-long situation. McCown threw another interception, this one to defensive back Derek Fox. He returned it 34 yards for a touchdown. McCown had only thrown two passes so far, and both of them had been picked off.

Starting at their own 16, the Aggies put together a drive. Running back Ja'Mar Toombs ran for a first down to the 29, and McCown fired to receiver Matt Bumgardner for another two first downs. Running back D'Andre Hardeman picked up the next A&M first down. The Aggies then tried running an option, but Arrington made the tackle for a loss of five, ending the first quarter. McCown made up for it with a pass to receiver Chris Taylor for a first down. The drive was killed when the Aggies were called for a chop block. Kicker Shane Lechler tried a 44-yard field goal, but it sailed wide to the right.

Running back Eric McCoo ran for a first down on a third-down play, and Casey got another on a third down. On his run, he faked a handoff, juked a defender, then scampered to the marker. He followed that with a bomb to receiver Eddie Drummond, who came down with the catch and scored a 45-yard touchdown, putting PSU up 14-0.

The Aggies went three-and-out, giving Penn State the ball back. Casey slipped throwing a long pass on third down, and he was picked off by defensive back Brandon Jennings. It worked out like a short punt. The Aggies only got one first down on a run by Toombs before having to punt. Penn State got the ball back with little time left on the clock.

Receiver Kenny Wilson ran for nine yards, and McCoo ripped off a 27-yard run to the A&M 43. Now with less than a minute left, Paterno yelled for Casey to spike the ball. He did so, but that just left Penn State without a first-down play. After an incompletion and a failed reverse, they already had to punt. Pidgeon's punt went for a touchback, and that was the end of the first half.

The Aggies' first drive of the second half went pretty well for a while. Toombs was the do-everything man of the A&M offense, as he ran for 13-yard pickups twice and also caught a 12-yard pass. None of that would matter. Arrington hit McCown again as he tried to throw, and the pass was picked off by linebacker Ron Graham.

Penn State's next series wasn't notable for its result. McCoo did pick up a first down on a catch, and Casey also ran for another 11 yards. What was most notable, though, was the fact that running back Larry Johnson carried the ball for the first time, gaining three yards on the carry. His time would come, but for right now he was just making a cameo appearance.

Arrington made another sack, and A&M had to punt again. Receiver Chafie Fields took a handoff and ran for a first down, then Casey threw to tight end John Gilmore for a big gain. Gilmore fought off two tackles and picked up a first down at the A&M 26. Casey hit tight end Tony Stewart for 20 more yards, setting up first-and-goal at the 5. He then ran a bootleg and snuck into the right corner of the end zone for a four-yard touchdown. The fourth quarter had just begun, with Penn State holding a 21-point lead.

All Aggie hopes would end on the next kickoff return. Receiver Bethel Johnson fumbled on the return, having the ball punched out by defensive back Askari Adams. Shawn Mayer recovered the ball at the A&M 23. The Nittany Lions failed to get a first down, but they were already in field goal range. Forney kicked a 39-yard field goal to go up by 24.

The only thing left was to see if Penn State could get the shutout. The answer was a resounding "yes." Kurpekis picked up a sack, while Arrington hit McCown's arm again to force another bad pass that was intercepted by Fox. After an A&M fourth-down incompletion on a later drive with five minutes left, the Nittany Lions had finished off a 24-0 victory.

Casey was named the offensive MVP award, throwing for 146 yards and rushing for 27 more. He accounted for two touchdowns, one a long pass, the other a short run. Arrington was named defensive MVP, which was no surprise. He had forced multiple interceptions, picked up a slew of tackles, and completely disrupted the A&M offense, which barely broke 200 yards for the day.

Brown, a defensive end, wound up going first overall in the NFL Draft to the Cleveland Browns, while Arrington, a linebacker, went second to the Washington Redskins. They were the first pair of Penn State teammates to be drafted one-two overall. The Nittany Lions finished #11 in the final rankings, an impressive ranking for an Alamo Bowl champion.

Box Score[19]:

1999 Alamo Bowl	1st	2nd	3rd	4th	Final
Penn State	7	7	0	10	24
Texas A&M	0	0	0	0	0

1st Quarter: PSU—Fox 34 interception return (Forney kick)
2nd Quarter: PSU—Drummond 45 pass from Casey (Forney kick)
3rd Quarter: No Scoring
4th Quarter: PSU—Casey 4 run (Forney kick)
    PSU—Forney 39 FG

2002 Season (9–3)

Penn State started the season against Central Florida. Running back Larry Johnson ran for 92 yards and also caught a touchdown pass. Quarterback Zack Mills passed for 194 yards and two scores, including the one to Johnson. It was Johnson and Johnson and Johnson catching passes for Penn State: Larry (30 yards), Bryant (90), and Larry's brother Tony (49). The Lions went up 27–9 in the fourth quarter, before allowing a couple of garbage touchdowns for a final score of 27–24.[1]

Nebraska (#7) came into Beaver Stadium for the Lions' second game, and a record crowd of 110,753 fans watched as Penn State dominated the Cornhuskers. Larry Johnson ran for 123 yards on 19 carries, scoring a pair of touchdowns. Backup quarterback Michael Robinson got some playing time, and he ran for 56 yards and two touchdowns. Mills threw for 259 yards, which was nearly 200 more than Nebraska managed. The Lions won this one easily, 40–7.[2]

Next came Louisiana Tech, whose quarterback Luke McCown threw for 406 yards and two touchdowns. While that may sound great, he also threw three interceptions, as Penn State completely dominated the game. Johnson ran for 147 yards and two touchdowns, and Robinson tied an NCAA record by scoring touchdowns on three carries in a row. The Lions outrushed Tech by over 250 yards in the 49–17 victory.[3]

Iowa came into Happy Valley and jumped out to a 23–0 lead. Larry Johnson ran for a touchdown in the third quarter, but the extra point was blocked and returned for two points by Iowa. While it looked like the game was over, it was anything but. Mills fired four touchdown passes, including three in the fourth quarter, as the Lions stormed back from a 22-point fourth-quarter deficit to tie the game. In overtime, Iowa quarterback Brad Banks threw a six-yard touchdown pass, and the Lions couldn't match it. It was a heart-wrenching 42–35 loss for Penn State.[4]

The Lions bounced back against Wisconsin. Johnson ran for 111 yards and a touchdown, while Mills threw for 287 yards and scored on the ground in a 34–31 win. The next week, the Lions went back to overtime against Michigan. This time, the Lions had to settle for a short field goal by kicker Robbie Gould in the first OT. The Wolverines then scored a touchdown to send Penn State to their second loss in three weeks, this one by a 27–24 score.[5]

Penn State had no trouble with Northwestern, stomping them by a 49–0 margin. Johnson ran for a school-record 257 yards and two touchdowns, and all that came in just three quarters of play. Head coach Joe Paterno pulled him with the game out of reach; that decision will come into question later. Johnson started out the following game at Ohio Stadium with a five-yard touchdown run, but #4 Ohio State shut down the Penn State offense for the rest of the game and beat the Lions, 13–7.[6]

Johnson broke the school record for the second time in three games. After besting the previous mark by Curt Warner by just one yard, he beat this new record by another 22 yards against Illinois. He ran for 279 yards and an 84-yard touchdown, the longest Penn State run since 1968. Penn State got off to an 18–0 lead at halftime, then held on for an 18–7 win. The next week, Johnson broke the school all-purpose yards record with 188 rushing yards and 23 more through the air. Defensive end Michael Haynes picked up three sacks and forced two Virginia fumbles, as the Lions beat the Cavaliers, 35–14.[7]

The records really started falling against Indiana. Johnson ran for his third school record of the season, this time 327 yards, while scoring four touchdowns. He broke Lydell Mitchell's school-best 1,567 rushing yards in a season, with another game to play. The Lions scored at least ten points in all four quarters on their way to a 58–25 win.

Michigan State was Penn State's final opponent. On Senior Day, Johnson (a senior) played perhaps the greatest game of his career. He ran for 279 yards and four touchdowns—at halftime! That broke Bob Campbell's record for the most rushing yards in a half. The Lions were up 48–0 at halftime, so Paterno sat Johnson out for the second half. Again, there would be ramifications for this.

Johnson rushed for 2,015 yards and 20 touchdowns, while also catching 39 balls for 341 yards and another three touchdowns. He won the Doak Walker, the Maxwell, and the Walter Camp awards, the latter two for being the best player in the nation. All of Happy Valley was stunned when Johnson finished only third in the Heisman Trophy balloting. Perhaps if Johnson had been allowed to stay in those games of which he was pulled out, maybe he would have put up numbers that no voter could refuse. He could have possibly run for 400 yards on multiple occasions. But as it was, he finished behind USC quarterback Carson Palmer and Iowa quarterback Brad Banks, who would play each other in the Orange Bowl.[8]

Johnson's numbers were so far over the rest of the team, that it's hard to compare his teammates to his. Mills passed for 2,350 yards and 17 touchdowns, while only throwing nine interceptions. Robinson, the backup quarterback, was the team's second-leading rusher with 233 yards and six touchdowns. Bryant Johnson led the team in receiving with 48 catches for 917 yards. Tony Johnson was second in yards with 495 on 32 catches.[9]

Penn State finished fourth in the Big Ten, behind Ohio State, Iowa, and Michigan. Ohio State was ranked #2, so they were off to the Fiesta Bowl, which was the Bowl Championship Series title game. Iowa was right behind them, ranked #3. They got a BCS berth as well. But instead of going to the Rose Bowl as customary for a Big Ten team, they were selected by the Orange Bowl. The next domino to fall was Michigan. The Wolverines had been to the Citrus Bowl the year before, so the newly-renamed Capital One Bowl didn't want them to come back to Orlando. That sent Michigan to the Outback Bowl. Penn State moved up a spot in the hierarchy, getting their fourth trip to the Capital One/Citrus Bowl, where they would play Auburn.

2003 Capital One Bowl

#10 Penn State (9–3) vs. #19 Auburn (8–4)
January 1, 2003, at the Florida Citrus Bowl in Orlando, Florida

Having lost their three games by such small margins, the Nittany Lions were considered a better team than their record showed. Running back Larry Johnson had ripped up many a defense down the stretch, and the Lions figured to do the same to Auburn. However, the Tigers zeroed in on stopping Johnson, and when they did, the rest of the Penn State offense didn't respond.

On Auburn's first possession, Penn State defensive tackle Anthony Adams forced a fumble from quarterback Jason Campbell, and linebacker Derek Wake recovered at the Auburn 15. Quarterback Zack Mills took his first carry for ten yards, getting down inside the 5. Surprisingly, the Lions only went with one carry by Johnson in the next three plays, and they couldn't gain more than a yard. Kicker Robbie Gould made the 21-yard field goal, though, and Penn State took the early lead.

Adams sacked Campbell on the next drive to force a punt. Johnson was given the ball but once on Penn State's second possession, on which he slipped down for a loss. Penn State punted it back, and Auburn then went on a long drive. It would have never happened had it not been for a personal foul on Penn State on a third-down stop. Running back Ronnie Brown carried the ball on four of the next five plays, picking up a pair of first downs. But Wake blocked kicker Damon Duval's 24-yard field goal try, and the Lions remained ahead.

Mills took off on a 37-yard run, but Penn State ended up having to punt. The Lions got the ball back at their own 31, and Johnson had his first good run of the game to the 48. Auburn got called for a personal foul, then Mills passed to receiver Tony Johnson for 19 more yards. Penn State had their drive stalled thanks to two consecutive false start penalties, and Gould missed a 33-yard kick wide to the right.

After forcing a quick three-and-out, the Lions got good field position thanks to a fair catch interference call. Auburn then got called for a late hit, and Penn State moved further into field goal range. But on their final three plays of the drive, Johnson didn't touch the ball once. The Lions settled for a Gould 27-yard field goal. After defensive back Bryan Scott picked off Campbell, Penn State went to the locker room with a six-point lead.

The Lions offense continued to flounder in the second half. Johnson got the ball more on the first drive, but ultimately Penn State was forced to punt. Brown then took over the game, running the ball ten times on Auburn's next drive. The Tigers marched from their own 27 all the way down to the goal line, where Brown punched it in on fourth down. With Duval's extra point, Auburn took a 7–6 lead entering the fourth quarter.

Head coach Joe Paterno had seen enough of Mills, so he put backup Michael Robinson in at quarterback to try to find a spark. Robinson ran for a first down to the 37 on third down. He then found Tony Johnson for 34 yards down to the Auburn 36. He ran for another 20 yards, before Larry Johnson ran for nine yards. However, the Lions couldn't get that next yard, so they settled for a Gould 32-yard field goal to take a 9–7 lead.

The Lions forced an Auburn punt, but the Tigers managed to down the ball at the Penn State 1. Robinson then fumbled on a carry, but luckily center Joe Iorio recovered the ball. That at least allowed the Lions to get a punt away instead of turning it over inside the 10. From that distance, though, the Tigers were in easy position to take the lead. After one pass by Campbell, Brown ran the ball five times in a row. On his fifth run, he bounced off the right side for a 17-yard touchdown. Campbell couldn't connect with receiver Marcel Willis on the two-point play, but Auburn now had a 13–9 lead with 2:19 to play.

Paterno put Mills back into the game, but he failed to spark the offense. He threw two incompletions before throwing a bad one that was intercepted by defensive back Roderick Hood. The Tigers had the chance to run out the clock from there, so they gave the ball to Brown on four straight plays. Paterno used his timeouts, and the defense made a stop in order to get the ball back at their own 27 with 42 seconds left.

It was now or never for Mills and the Penn State offense. He started their last drive with a 15-yard run. He then threw two consecutive passes to receiver Matt Kranchick, who got out of bounds each time. What made those passes special was that they were the first two catches of Kranchick's career, and they came in such a tight spot! Mills threw incomplete on his next two passes, leaving Penn State only a few seconds left. He was under immense pressure on third down, so he just shoveled the ball to fullback Sean McHugh. While McHugh tried lateraling the ball in vain, there was nowhere to go, and time ran out on the Lions.

It was a terribly disappointing finish to Johnson's career. After having lit up so many teams down the stretch to winning the Maxwell, Johnson managed just 72 yards on 20 carries and no touchdowns. The Lions' two quarterbacks, Mills and Robinson, combined for more rushing yards (86) than him. Meanwhile, Brown rushed for 184 yards and two touchdowns. While Penn State only lost by four, it felt like they had been completely dominated.

Penn State finished this season 9–4 but with a ton of questions. They hadn't been to a bowl in three years, and as it would turn out, they wouldn't be in another bowl until three years later. A movement began within Happy Valley to call into question whether Paterno should still coach. In 2005, however, he proved that he still could.

Box score[10]:

2003 Capital One Bowl	1st	2nd	3rd	4th	Final
Penn State	3	3	0	3	9
Auburn	0	0	7	6	13

1st Quarter: PSU—Gould 21 FG
2nd Quarter: PSU—Gould 27 FG
3rd Quarter: AUB—Brown 1 run (Duval kick)
4th Quarter: PSU—Gould 32 FG
        AUB—Brown 17 run (pass failed)

2005 Season (10–1)

Penn State started the 2005 season with low expectations. The Nittany Lions were coming off two consecutive losing seasons and four in the last five years, without a single bowl victory in the 21st century. They started out this season at home against South Florida. Running back Tony Hunt rushed for 140 yards and a touchdown, while quarterback Michael Robinson threw for 90 yards and rushed for another 39, as Penn State went on to win 23–13.[1]

Against Cincinnati, Robinson had a big game, throwing for 220 yards and three touchdowns, while also rushing for 62 yards and another score. Three of his completions went for at least 40 yards, including a 45-yard touchdown pass to receiver Deon Butler in the fourth quarter. The final score of 42–24 was very misleading; both of Cincinnati's scores came in the final minute of the game with the game long decided.[2]

Next came Central Michigan, who didn't put up much of a fight. Robinson threw for 274 yards and three touchdowns, and he rushed two yards for the first touchdown of the game. Butler caught two long passes (54 and 24 yards) for touchdowns on his way to a 108-yard day. The Lions led by 23 points at halftime and went on to win 40–3.[3]

It was the Big Ten opener at Northwestern where the magic really began, the previous three games being warm-ups. Penn State fell into a 13–0 hole early, and they trailed 23–14 at the half. Penn State got the ball back trailing with two minutes to go from their own 20. On fourth-and-15, Robinson hit tight end Isaac Smolko on a 20-yard pass to keep the drive alive. Later, facing a third-and-six, he fired to Derrick Williams for a 36-yard touchdown with 51 seconds left to give Penn State a 34–29 win. It was Robinson's third straight three-touchdown game, as he threw for 271 yards.[4]

The Nittany Lions came back home to face #18 Minnesota. This one was no contest, as the Lions jumped out to a 20–0 lead and never looked back. They did most of their damage on the ground, with Hunt rushing for 114 yards and two third-quarter touchdowns, and Robinson adding another 112 rushing yards. Linebacker Paul Posluszny picked up nine tackles to earn Walter Camp National Defensive Player of the Week honors, as the Lions went on to a 44–14 victory.[5]

The next game was one of the most memorable in school history, a battle against #6 Ohio State in prime time. The Penn State student section all wore white, marking the first-ever "White Out" game in a tradition that lives on to this day. The game got great ratings for ESPN, with its 4.91 rating being the highest for an ESPN game in eight years. In the first half, Williams rushed for a 13-yard touchdown to put the Lions up 7–3. Defensive back Calvin Lowry then intercepted a pass and returned it 36 yards to the Ohio State 2. Robinson ran in a one-yard touchdown, and the Lions went up 14–3. In the fourth quarter, with Penn State hanging on to a 17–10 lead, defensive end Tamba Hali sacked quarterback Troy Smith and forced a fumble, which defensive tackle Scott Paxson recovered to seal the win. Penn State leaped to #8 in the Associated Press poll after this victory.[6]

The Lions then went to the Big House to take on Michigan. They trailed 10–3 going into the fourth quarter, before one of the most exciting periods of the entire college football season. Hunt ripped off a 61-yard run that set up a Robinson four-yard run to tie the game. Alan Zemaitis then stripped Michigan quarterback Chad Henne and took the ball back 35 yards to put Penn State in the lead. The extra point snap was bobbled, but kicker Kevin Kelly picked it up and ran it in for two points. However, Michigan matched the touchdown and two-pointer, then they made a 47-yard field goal with just under four minutes left. Robinson led the Nittany Lions on an 81-yard drive, converting a fourth down on a run and later scoring on a three-yard run. Penn State led 25–21 with 53 seconds to go. But Wolverines receiver Steve Breaston took the kick back to the Michigan 47, and Michigan moved down to the Penn State 10. Along the way, Michigan head coach Lloyd Carr argued to get two extra seconds put on the clock. Those two seconds proved enormous when the Wolverines got one last play with one second on the clock. Henne found receiver Mario Manningham for a ten-yard touchdown, and Michigan beat Penn State 27–25.[7]

After such a heartbreaking loss, Penn State may have been expected to have a letdown the next week in Illinois, but Robinson didn't let that happen. He threw four touchdown passes in the first quarter, then ran for two more in the second quarter to tie a school record by accounting for six total touchdowns in a game. And he didn't even play a full half! He came out with four minutes to go in the first half, as Penn State won, 63–10.[8]

The Nittany Lions came home to face Purdue. This time, the running game proved to be the difference, as they rolled up over 300 rushing yards on their way to a 33–15 win. Robinson threw for 213 yards and ran for 96 more along with a touchdown. Hunt led the team with 129 rushing yards. Kelly kicked four field goals, the first Penn State kicker to do so since Robbie Gould in 2002.[9]

The Penn State defense held Wisconsin to minus-11 rushing yards. They sacked Badgers quarterback John Stocco nine times, their most sacks since 1999. Meanwhile, Robinson threw for 238 yards and two touchdowns, while running for another 125. Hunt added another 151 rushing yards and two touchdowns, and the Lions beat Wisconsin, 35–14, to finish out their home schedule 7–0.[10]

To win the Big Ten, the Lions had to beat Michigan State on the road in the battle for the Land Grant Trophy. In the second quarter, defensive back Donnie Johnson blocked a Spartan punt, and running back Matt Hahn recovered it in the end zone for a touchdown. The Lions led 17–0 at halftime, but the Spartans battled back. Hunt then took over the game, ripping off two runs for 40 yards, before scoring from a yard away to seal the 31–22 victory.[11]

It was a record-setting season for the Penn State offense, and in particular for Robinson. He put up 2,882 yards of total offense, the most in a season in school history. He finished fifth in the Heisman Trophy voting and was voted as both Most Valuable Player and Offensive Player of the Year in the Big Ten.[12] His 27 touchdowns accounted for were the second-most in school annals, behind only Lydell Mitchell's 29 in 1971. He threw for over 2,000 yards, the eighth-most in school history, while becoming the first Penn State player to run and pass for 1,000 yards in his career. But beyond all that, he was an exemplary leader on and off the field. This all came after waiting his turn for three years, playing sporadically at all sorts of offensive positions. He was patient and humble, while also fierce and determined. It is easy to argue that no other player in Penn State history had more of an impact in one season than he did in 2005.[13]

He wasn't the only one who stood out for the Nittany Lions. Hali and Posluszny were both named to the Associated Press All-America first-team, and Zemaitis and offensive tackle Levi Brown were named to the second team. Posluszny won the Bednarik (best defensive player) and Butkus (best linebacker) awards. Hali was named Big Ten Defensive Lineman of the Year. Altogether, 13 players were named to the coaches' and media's all-Big Ten first and second teams or honorable mentions. Beside the players named to the All-America team and Robinson, also named were Lowry, defensive tackle Scott Paxson, Hunt, defensive tackle Jay Alford, Butler, defensive back Chris Harrell, defensive end Matthew Rice, and punter Jeremy Kapinos. In addition, head coach Joe Paterno was named Associated Press Coach of the Year.[14]

Hunt was Penn State's leading rusher with 1,047 yards, and his six rushing touchdowns ranked him second behind Robinson's 11. Butler led the team in receiving in all categories, with 36 catches for 678 yards and nine touchdowns. Posluszny racked up 60 tackles and 51 assists, with 11 tackles for loss and three of them sacks.[15]

It was a historic season for Big Ten champion Penn State, who won ten of 11 games and had a chance at the national championship game had either USC or Texas lost its conference championship game. Both teams won, though, and they went on to play a very memorable Rose Bowl. Penn State finished #3 and qualified for the Bowl Championship Series automatically. Since Penn State could not go to the Rose Bowl, since it was the title game, the Nittany Lions became an at-large team eligible for any of the other three BCS bowls. The Fiesta Bowl passed on Penn State to go with #6 Notre Dame instead.[16] The Orange Bowl then selected Penn State to go up against automatic qualifier, ACC champion Florida State. It would be a battle between FSU head coach Bobby Bowden (most Division I-A wins) and Paterno (second-most) in South Florida.[17]

2006 Orange Bowl

#3 Penn State (10–1) vs. #22 Florida State (8–4)
January 3, 2006, at Dolphins Stadium in Miami Gardens, Florida

While Penn State was one play from going undefeated in 2005, Florida State had a much bumpier ride to the BCS. They finished only 5–3 in the ACC, tied with Boston College for first place in the Atlantic Division. They lost their final three games of the season, two ACC games and one non-conference game against archrival Florida by a 34–7 margin. Florida State looked to be easy fodder for Coastal Division champion Virginia Tech, but the Seminoles pulled out a 27–22 victory in the ACC Championship Game to book their trip to the Orange Bowl.[18]

The story going into this bowl had everything to do with the two head coaches, Joe Paterno and Bobby Bowden. Not only were they the top two Division I-A winners, but they were both in their upper seventies and well past the usual age for retirement. Yet, neither wanted to talk about that subject. When pressed on the issue by ABC's Mike Tirico in a joint interview, Paterno jokingly suggested that Tirico should retire.[19] Both Bowden and Paterno had so much fire in them during this game that they seemed to be in the prime of their careers.

Upon winning the coin toss, Paterno chose to defer his option to the second half. Quarterback Drew Weatherford started for Florida State, with so much pressure on him due to the Seminoles' lack of a running game. He completed a third-down pass to receiver Willie Reid for 22 yards. Running back Leon Washington broke off a rare run for ten yards, but FSU was stymied after that. Penn State defensive tackle Jay Alford tackled Washington for a loss on a third-down screen pass, and the Seminoles were forced to punt.

The teams traded three-and-outs, and Penn State got the ball back at their own 15. Starting running back Tony Hunt was injured on the opening drive, so Austin Scott took his place for the remainder of the game. He ran for six yards on his first carry. Quarterback Michael Robinson threw a swing pass to receiver Justin King for a first down at the 29. He then went to a wide-open Ethan

FedEx Orange Bowl ticket, 2006. Author's collection.

Kilmer for 25 yards down into FSU territory. Scott then took over for the remainder of the drive. He carried the ball four times in five plays, with only a Robinson incompletion breaking up his string of great runs. He picked up gains of 12, 28, nine, and finally a two-yard touchdown to give the Lions a 7–0 lead.

Florida State went three-and-out, and Penn State took over at their own 24. Scott pounded up the middle for a gain of 12 to start the drive. Robinson then went long, but he had his pass picked off by defensive back Tony Carter, who returned it to the Penn State 47. The Seminoles couldn't score off the great field position, though, and the first quarter came to an end with the Nittany Lions up by seven.

Robinson picked up the first down on an option play at the 35, and Scott followed with a 13-yard run up the middle. Robinson pump faked and pulled the ball down, and he took off for nine yards. Running back Rodney Kinlaw then got the first down. Robinson threw his next pass to receiver Deon Butler, and the Nittany Lions had first down at the FSU 29. However, they only went backward from there, and Robinson got called for intentional grounding on third down. The Nittany Lions had to punt it away.

The teams exchanged three-and-outs, and Florida State started to get something going. Reid returned the punt 18 yards to the 35, and Weatherford followed with a 14-yard pass to receiver Chris Davis. He got another first down on a pass to receiver Fred Rouse, but his next pass was intercepted by defensive back Alan Zemaitis and returned to the Penn State 33.

Scott took a read option handoff for 11 yards to open up the next series. After that, though, tackle Levi Brown got called for a personal foul, and Robinson's third-down pass to King came up well short of the first down. Punter Jeremy Kapinos came on to kick it away, and Reid caught it and took it up the middle. This return would be even better than his last one; in fact, it would go longer than any other in the history of the Orange Bowl, an 86-yard touchdown. It was Reid's third punt return of the season, and this one tied the game at seven.

Penn State went three-and-out, and Kapinos's next punt only reached the Florida State 43. Weatherford threw a little flare pass to running back Lorenzo Booker, and within seconds, he was gone. Booker sprinted 57 yards down the right side of the field for a touchdown. The Seminoles now had a six-point lead, but only six; kicker Gary Cismesia missed the extra point wide to the left, a crucial miss.

Robinson completed a pass to receiver Jordan Norwood for 21 yards, which at least flipped field position. The Nittany Lions were forced to punt, and Kapinos put it down at the 3. The Seminoles had only a minute left on the clock, so they wanted to just run out the clock. Paterno still had all three of his timeouts in his holster. He used the first one after defensive tackle Scott Paxson hit fullback James Coleman for a two-yard loss to the 1. Paterno argued for a safety, but after review, the call stood with the ball just outside the goal line. Weatherford then ran two quarterback sneaks, with Paterno firing off both of his timeouts to stop the ball with 22 seconds left. Defensive back Calvin Lowry fair caught the punt at the FSU 40.

The Lions had very little time left, but they made it count. Robinson took a hit as he fired to Norwood, who caught the pass and got out of bounds at the 24. On his next play, he threw down the right sideline, where a leaping Kilmer went up and got the ball and came down with it in the end zone with just six seconds left. The play stood upon further review, and kicker Kevin Kelly made the extra point to give Penn State a 14–13 lead at the half.

The third quarter was all defense. The next seven possessions were all three-and-outs, four by Penn State's offense and three by Florida State. The Seminoles got the ball past midfield after a poor Kapinos punt which Reid returned to the Penn State 26. An illegal block in the back penalty cost Florida State some yards, but they quickly gained them back on an eight-yard pass to tight end Matt Root. Booker took a screen to the Penn State 33, but he was two yards shy of a first down. Bowden chose to go for it on fourth down. Weatherford tossed it to Booker, but Lowry hauled him down short of the first down.

Robinson got one first down on a pass to Kilmer before Penn State had to punt again. This was a much better kick by Kapinos, getting downed at the 6. The teams switched sides for the fourth quarter, then Florida State's offense started going backward. Booker ran it twice for little gain, and on third down, Weatherford dropped back into his own end zone. Paxson caught on to the fact that he was going to throw a screen to Booker, and as a result Weatherford had nowhere to go with the ball as Penn State defenders closed in. He threw it away, and he was called for intentional grounding in the end zone—a safety for Penn State.

King took back the free kick beyond the midfield stripe to set up Penn State with great field position. Robinson hit Norwood on a third-down pass for 21 yards to the Florida State 26. He hit Norwood for eight more yards, then he picked up a new set of down on an option keeper. On the next third down, Scott picked up the first down at the 5. The Nittany Lions were so close to a game-clinching touchdown, as there was no way the Florida State offense was scoring twice at this point. However, center E.J. Smith botched the snap, and Robinson never got it. Florida State defensive lineman Andre Fluellen fell on the loose ball, keeping the Seminoles in the game.

Weatherford then marched the Seminoles down the field for their first sustained drive of the game. He threw a screen to Washington for a first down at the 17. On third down, he rolled to his right, bought some time, then launched a 39-yard pass to Davis down the sideline. Penn State linebacker Paul Posluszny injured his leg two plays later and would have to be carted off. Weatherford continued the drive with a 13-yard pass to Reid. That all set up a 48-yard Cismesia field goal which hooked to the left but barely went inside the upright. The game was tied at 16 as the clock struck midnight on the East Coast.

The Seminoles got called for roughing the passer to start the next drive. Linebacker Lawrence Timmons sacked Robinson on a second down, and Penn State was backed up deep. But Robinson made up for it, finding tight end Isaac Smolko for a first down at the Florida State 49. He followed by firing to a wide-open Norwood down at the 11. All the Nittany Lions needed to do now was run down the clock and kick a short field goal. They did the first part of that quite well, with Florida State running out of timeouts, and Robinson setting up the ball in the middle of the field with 35 seconds left. Kelly came on to try a 29-yard field goal to win the Orange Bowl. He didn't get quite the best hold from Jason Ganter, and he pushed the kick to the left. This game was headed to overtime.

Robinson called heads on the coin toss, and he was right. The Nittany Lions got to go on defense to start overtime. Florida State's offense gained a first down after a nine-yard pass to Reid and a short run by Coleman, but then they got called for holding. Weatherford launched two long passes that fell incomplete, and the Seminoles were forced to try a 44-yard field goal. This one Cismesia missed to the right, and now Penn State could win with a mere field goal.

Paterno got a bit too conservative in this situation. Yes, a pick-six or something similar would lose the game, but Kelly needed some help to get closer for his field goal. Scott ran on first down and Robinson ran two quarterback draws, super-safe plays that didn't gain much yardage at all. Kelly came back on to try a 38-yard winner. He missed this one too wide to the left, and the game was headed to a second overtime.

The teams switched end zones and the order of play for the second OT. Robinson fired to Norwood for six yards, then two plays later he hit Kilmer on a pass down to the 1. Scott could not punch it in on a first-down run, so the Nittany Lions ran the triple option. Robinson pitched the ball to Scott on the left side for a one-yard touchdown run, and Kelly made the extra point to put Penn State up 23–16.

It didn't take Florida State long to answer. Weatherford fired to Reid for 11 yards, then he hit receiver Greg Carr for 13 more down to the 1. He tried a quarterback sneak on first down, but that failed. So, on second down, he handed off to fullback B.J. Dean, who scored. Cismesia made the extra point, and the game was again tied, at 23-all.

Florida State started this overtime period, on which their offense couldn't get anything going. Weatherford scrambled for four yards, then he threw too low for his receiver and the ball hit the ground. On third down, his receiver slipped, and his pass went incomplete. Cismesia came back on for a 38-yard field goal, but he missed the kick off the right upright.

For a third time, Penn State could win the game with only a field goal. Robinson's final pass as a Nittany Lion was a swing to King, who got about nine yards on the play. His final run with the Lions was a third-down rush where he got the first down at the 13. After

Scott picked up one more yard, Paterno sent on Kelly to win it. This time, Kelly nailed the 29-yard field goal, and Penn State had won the longest Orange Bowl of all time, 26–23.

Robinson threw for 253 yards and a touchdown, while also running for 21 yards. Scott, who took Hunt's place after his early injury, rushed for 110 yards on 26 carries and two touchdowns. Norwood and Kilmer each had six catches, and King had five. Norwood gained the most yards with 110, and Kilmer had the touchdown catch at the end of the first half. The Nittany Lions were snubbed for the MVP award; the Orange Bowl committee gave it to Reid instead.[20]

The joyous Nittany Lions passed out oranges as Paterno accepted the trophy. "It's almost past my bedtime!" Paterno joked, referring to the 1 a.m. East Coast finishing time. "We got it, and I'm taking it."[21] Robinson had been hit on nearly every pass he threw in the second half, but he didn't mind. "It was all worth it," he said. "We finished it right."[22] And the Nittany Lions finished with their highest ranking since 1994, ending up #3 in both polls with an 11–1 record.

Box score[23]:

2006 Orange Bowl	1st	2nd	3rd	4th	1st OT	2nd OT	3rd OT	Final
Penn State	7	7	0	2	0	7	3	26
Florida State	0	13	0	3	0	7	0	23

1st Quarter: PSU—Scott 2 run (Kelly kick)

2nd Quarter: FSU—Reid 87 punt return (Cismesia kick)

    FSU—Booker 57 pass from Weatherford (kick missed)

    PSU—Kilmer 25 pass from Robinson (Kelly kick)

3rd Quarter: No Scoring

4th Quarter: PSU—Safety

    FSU—Cismesia 48 FG

1st Overtime: No Scoring

2nd Overtime: PSU—Scott 2 run (Kelly kick)

    FSU—Dean 1 run (Cismesia kick)

3rd Overtime: PSU—Kelly 29 FG

2006 Season (8–4)

Penn State started their 2006 season in a rainstorm at home against Akron. Quarterback Anthony Morelli, taking the reins from the now-graduated Michael Robinson, threw three touchdown passes on his way to a 206-yard day. Receivers Deon Butler and Jordan Norwood hauled in scoring catches in the first half, as the Nittany Lions jumped out to a 17–3 lead at halftime and won 34–16.[1]

The Lions went to South Bend for their first game against Notre Dame since 1992. This one got out of hand, with the Fighting Irish going up 27–0 not even 31 minutes into the game. By the time Penn State finally reached the end zone, they were down 41–3. The Lions scored two garbage touchdowns to pull within 41–17 as the final gun sounded.[2]

Penn State had been scheduled to host Louisiana Tech in Week 3, but they backed out, and the Lions were forced to schedule Division I-AA opponent Youngstown State.[3] Running back Tony Hunt rushed for 143 yards and a second-quarter touchdown, as the Lions went up 20–0 at halftime and never looked back. Backup quarterback Daryll Clark got his first career touchdown on an 18-yard run in garbage time, as the Lions cleaned up a 37–3 victory.[4]

#1 Ohio State was next on the schedule, with this year's game at Ohio Stadium. The Lions surprised everyone by taking a 3–0 lead into the half, and only trailing 7–3 entering the final quarter. Then Morelli threw two pick-sixes, turning a 14–6 nail-biter into a 28–6 romp. Hunt was a bright spot for Penn State, as he rushed for 135 yards in the loss.[5]

Kicker Kevin Kelly made three field goals in the first half against Northwestern, giving Penn State an early nine-point lead. Hunt then took over the game from there, rushing for 137 yards and three touchdowns. Morelli had a good bounce-back performance, throwing for 288 yards, as Penn State won 33–7.[6]

Morelli threw for 281 more yards at Minnesota, two of his passes going for touchdowns. Hunt had another big day with 159 scrimmage yards and three touchdowns scored. The Golden Gophers rallied to tie the game in the fourth quarter, sending this one into overtime. Minnesota then scored a 25-yard touchdown, but they missed the extra point. Hunt then pounded it in from two yards away, and Kelly won the game with his extra point.[7]

Over 110,000 fans came to Beaver Stadium to watch Penn State take on Michigan. It was a revenge game; nearly all Penn State fans were bitter over the two seconds that had been added to the clock the previous season to help Michigan win the game. However, the Wolverines just completely shut down the Penn State running game. Hunt ran for a mere 33 yards, and the Lions actually ended up with minus-14 rushing yards, the least in Paterno's career. The Lions were lucky to only lose by a 17–10 margin.[8]

It was the Penn State defense that stepped up to beat Illinois. They picked up six sacks, held Illinois to two-for-14 on third down, and forced four turnovers. Linebacker Paul Posluszny sacked Illinois quarterback Juice Williams and forced a fumble, which defensive back Tony Davis returned six yards for a score. Linebacker Dan Connor sacked Williams in the end zone for a safety, and Penn State defensive back Anthony Scirrotto returned an onside kick 29 yards for a touchdown to seal the 26–12 victory.[9] At Purdue, Hunt ran for 142 yards, while the defense shut down the Boilermakers, allowing less than 250 yards, picking off two passes, recovering a fumble, and picking up three sacks. The Lions recorded their first shutout since the 1999 Alamo Bowl in a 12–0 triumph.[10]

The next game at Wisconsin was known only for its bizarre incidents. First, at the end of the first half, Wisconsin head coach Bret Bielema took advantage of a new rule in college football which essentially made it possible to intentionally jump offside in order to waste time. Paterno was furious over it, but in the second half, he'd have an even tougher time. Tight end Andrew Quarless made a catch near the sideline and ended up running right into Paterno. The collision broke Paterno's left leg and tore ligaments in his knee. At that point, no Penn Stater cared that the team lost to the Badgers 13–3; the only concern was Paterno's health.[11]

Still recovering from surgery, Paterno missed the Temple game, the first time he wasn't at a game since 1977, and the first time he missed a home game since 1949. The team played an inspired game in honor of him, shutting down the Temple offense so much that the Owls never crossed the midfield stripe. They held the Owls to two first downs, 16 rushing yards, and 74 yards overall, while forcing three turnovers. Hunt had a career-high 192 yards from scrimmage, scoring four touchdowns in a 47–0 victory.[12]

In the season finale at home, Penn State had the chance to clinch a spot in a New Year's Day bowl in the battle for the Land Grant Trophy against Michigan State. The Lions lost four fumbles in the first half, but Hunt rushed for 130 yards, and Quarless caught four passes for 87 yards. The Lions came back to beat Sparty, 17–13.[13]

Hunt was the star of the Penn State offense, rushing for 1,228 yards and 11 touchdowns, while also catching 26 passes for 252 yards and three more scores. Butler led the team in receiving with 45 catches for 564 yards. Receiver Derrick Williams caught 37 passes for 413 yards while also averaging 11.8 yards per punt return. As for Morelli, he threw for 2,227 yards and ten touchdowns, in a solid if unspectacular season.[14]

The Nittany Lion got five players on the Associated Press All-America Team. Connor made the second team, while defensive tackle Jay Alford, offensive tackle Levi Brown, and punter Jeremy Kapinos made the third team. But the star of the team was first-team All-American Paul Posluszny. He won the Bednarik Trophy for best defensive player in the nation. He finished as a finalist for the Butkus and Lombardi awards, while being named on every national All-America team as either first-team or second-team. In addition, he was a great student off the field, and he was named an Academic All-American and Scholar-Athlete of the Year. He was the heart and soul of the Nittany Lions, taking over the role that Michael Robinson filled a year before.[15]

The three Big Ten teams Penn State lost to were all at the top of the conference. Ohio State finished undefeated and earned a berth in the Tostitos BCS National Championship Game. Michigan lost only once, to Ohio State, and they were invited to the Rose Bowl. Wisconsin got a berth in the Capital One (Citrus) Bowl as the top Big Ten team outside the BCS. Penn State was in fourth place in the Big Ten, so they got a trip to the other New

Year's Day bowl with a Big Ten tie-in, the Outback Bowl. It would be the Nittany Lions' third trip to Tampa.[16]

2007 Outback Bowl

Penn State (8–4) vs. #17 Tennessee (9–3)
January 1, 2007, at Raymond James Stadium in Tampa, Florida

The Nittany Lions had a chance to earn some respect by going up against a SEC team. The Big Ten was winless in bowl games for the 2006–07 season coming into the Outback Bowl, where the Lions would take on Tennessee. The Volunteers finished in second place in the SEC Eastern Division, with losses to eventual national champion Florida as well as LSU and Arkansas. Quarterback Eric Ainge threw for over 2,700 yards and 19 touchdowns during the regular season.[17]

With injured head coach Joe Paterno watching from the booth, Penn State got the ball to start the game. Quarterback Anthony Morelli went down the right sideline for receiver Deon Butler to pick up a first down to begin the game. Running back Tony Hunt took the first of his 31 carries for eight yards. Butler got another first down on a good pass, and Hunt took a screen down to the 27. Short of the first down, the Nittany Lions settled for a 45-yard field goal attempt. Kicker Kevin Kelly missed the kick wide left, and the game remained scoreless.

Tennessee went three-and-out, giving the ball right back to Penn State. Defensive back A.J. Wallace came in on offense and ran the ball up the middle to the 34. After a holding call, Hunt burst up the middle to pick up 12 yards. Tennessee then jumped offside, setting up third-and-short. However, Morelli's third down pass was knocked down by defensive back Demetrice Morley. Punter Jeremy Kapinos came on and kicked the ball down to the 26.

Ainge threw to receiver Jayson Swain for two first downs, including a big gain where Swain evaded a tackle on his way down to the Penn State 35. Facing a third-and-two a bit later, Tennessee head coach Phillip Fulmer called timeout to talk it over. Ainge was unable to complete his third-down pass, so out came kicker James Wilhoit. He made the 44-yard field goal, and the Volunteers had a 3–0 lead after one quarter.

Hunt pounded the ball on three straight carries, getting a first down. Morelli then fired to receiver Jordan Norwood for a first down past midfield. The Lions were stopped after that, but Kapinos pinned the Vols down at their own 3. Tennessee got a pair of first downs before the ball came loose on a handoff to Swain, and defensive end Tim Shaw recovered for Penn State. Morelli hit receiver Derrick Williams for a first down, getting the Nittany Lions into chip shot range. Kelly made this field goal from 34 yards, tying the game at three.

Running back Arian Foster picked up a couple of first downs before the Volunteers were again forced to punt. Penn State took over inside their own 10. On second down, Hunt broke through a huge hole and fought through tacklers for a gain of 24. He took his next carry for ten yards, then Morelli threw a screen to fullback Matt Hahn for another first down. Two plays later, Morelli gunned it down the right sideline for Butler, who hauled it in for a 31-yard gain down to the 2. Hunt couldn't punch it in, but Morelli followed with a play action pass to tight end Andrew Quarless in the left side of the end zone. The three-yard touchdown pass gave Penn State a 10–3 lead.

Shaw came up with his seventh sack of the season early in Tennessee's next possession. However, Ainge bounced back, throwing to tight end Brad Cottom for a first down. Two plays later, running back LaMarcus Coker took a draw and found an opening down the left sideline. Forty-two yards later, he was in the end zone, and the Volunteers tied the game at ten.

With little time left in the half, Morelli handed to Hunt twice, and he got a first down, and the Lions decided to call a timeout. After a roughing the passer call, Penn State had the ball near midfield. Morelli then hit Norwood for another first down, and he barely missed Butler down the sideline for a big gain. Kelly had a 54-yard field goal attempt, but he missed wide to the left, and the game remained tied at halftime.

Tennessee got a pair of first downs on passes from Ainge to receiver Robert Meachem and Swain. However, Meachem got called for offensive pass interference on a long pass which he ended up dropping. The penalty resulted in a third-and-28 a couple plays later, which the Vols couldn't convert. Punter Britton Colquitt put the ball down at the 7.

The Nittany Lions managed just one first down, on a pass to Williams, before being forced to punt again. Defensive back Anthony Scirrotto then came up with a big play, intercepting an Ainge pass. The Nittany Lions were set up to score, only to have an offensive pass interference call of their own. Williams couldn't come down with a foot in bounds on a third-down catch, and the Lions had to punt. The third quarter came to an end with the score tied at ten.

The Penn State defense stepped up and forced another Tennessee punt. Hunt ran the ball twice for nine yards, then Morelli launched a bomb to receiver Terrell Golden. It was only the sixth catch of the year for Golden, and it got Penn State a first down at the Tennessee 36. Morelli then hit Quarless on what looked to be a first down, but the play was overturned on replay and ruled incomplete. Kelly ended up forced into trying a 50-yard field goal, and this one way blocked by Morley.

On the second play of the next series, Ainge fired to tight end Chris Brown, who broke wide open and ran it 53 yards down into the red zone. If not for a tackle by Scirrotto, he may have gone for a touchdown. That proved huge, as on the very next play, linebacker Dan Connor knocked the ball out of Foster's hands. Defensive back Tony Davis scooped it up and ran 87 yards for a touchdown. What should have been a seven-point lead for Tennessee had turned into a seven-point lead for Penn State.

The Nittany Lions forced a quick three-and-out, then Hunt took over the game. He took seven consecutive carries, gaining three first downs and moving the ball all the way down inside the 5. Along the way, he went over 100 yards for the eighth time this season. Surprisingly, the Lions gave the ball to fullback BranDon Snow on third-and-goal from the 1, and he was stymied. Hunt didn't get his chance to score, but Kelly kicked a 22-yard field goal to make it 20–10 with only three-and-a-half minutes to go.

Tennessee now needed to score twice in that little amount of time, and they hadn't scored all half. Ainge hit Coker for a gain of 20 to start the next drive. However, on the next play, linebacker Sean Lee came up with a sack. Tennessee called timeout, before a pair of incompletions sandwiching an offside call on Penn State. On fourth-and-15 after a delay of game, Ainge threw a prayer. Defensive back Justin King got underneath it, and he was ready to pick the pass off, when Scirrotto came in out of nowhere to swat the ball away. King didn't get his pick, but the Lions got a ton of field position. In the end, it didn't matter, because Hunt ran for another first down, sealing the ten-point victory.

Hunt was named Outback Bowl MVP for his 31 carries for 158 yards.[18] He completely dominated the game in the fourth quarter, when the Nittany Lions kept pounding away with him and the Volunteers were powerless to stop him. "We take pride in our endurance," Hunt said after the game. "They knew we were coming; they couldn't match up with us."[19] Paterno earned his 22nd bowl victory from the booth, and Penn State finished the season ranked #24 in the Associated Press poll.[20]

Box score[21]:

2007 Outback Bowl	1st	2nd	3rd	4th	Final
Tennessee	3	7	0	0	10
Penn State	0	10	0	10	20

1st Quarter: TENN—Wilhoit 44 FG
2nd Quarter PSU—Kelly 34 FG
    PSU—Quarless 3 pass from Morelli (Kelly kick)
    TENN—Coker 42 run (Wilhoit kick)
3rd Quarter: No Scoring
4th Quarter: PSU—Davis 87 fumble return (Kelly kick)
    PSU—Kelly 22 FG

2007 Season (8–4)

The Nittany Lions opened up the season against Sun Belt foe Florida International with a 59–0 win. Quarterback Anthony Morelli threw for 231 yards in the first half, setting a new school record for yards in a first half. The defense forced five turnovers, while also blocking a field goal and a punt. They allowed FIU only 114 total yards, the third-fewest a Joe Paterno-coached team had ever allowed. Linebacker Sean Lee forced a fumble and came up with a sack to be named Big Ten Defensive Player of the Week.[1]

Week 2 was revenge week against Notre Dame. After having been embarrassed in South Bend a year ago, the Nittany Lions made up for it by crushing the Fighting Irish 31–10. The defense held ND to just 144 yards of offense. Receiver Derrick Williams returned a punt 78 yards for a touchdown, and running back Austin Scott ran for two scores in the second half.[2]

Against Buffalo, running back Rodney Kinlaw ran for 129 yards, for the first 100-yard game of his career. Morelli threw four touchdown passes, becoming only the 11th Penn State quarterback to accomplish that in a single game. Tight end Andrew Quarless caught two of those touchdowns, as Penn State won 45–24.[3]

There was no team Penn State fans wanted to beat more than Michigan. They celebrated in the bowels of Beaver Stadium when the then-ranked #5 Wolverines lost to Division I-AA school Appalachian State in the season opener. This surely would be the year the Lions would get by Michigan, right? Wrong. The Wolverines squeezed the life out of the clock, holding the ball for nearly 35 minutes and running 26 more plays than Penn State. It was another heart-wrenching loss to Michigan, this one by a 14–9 score.[4]

The Nittany Lions allowed Michigan to beat them twice. After having put so much effort into trying to finally beat the Wolverines, they suffered a hangover the next week at Illinois and lost 27–20. Despite a career-high 298 passing yards, Morelli threw three interceptions in the red zone.[5] The Lions finally got their first conference victory with a 27–7 stomping of Iowa at Beaver Stadium. Morelli threw for 233 yards and a score, while Kinlaw rushed for a career-best 168 yards. Freshman running back Evan Royster showed his first flashes of greatness, rushing for 86 yards on only 16 carries.[6]

The Lions then put together their best game in two years. They crushed #19 Wisconsin 38–7, their first win by at least 30 points over a ranked opponent since 2002. Morelli threw for 216 yards and a touchdown. The defense completely dominated, holding the potent Wisconsin running game to just 87 yards. The victory moved Penn State back into the top 25.[7]

Penn State went to Bloomington and defeated Indiana for the 11th straight time. The victory made the Nittany Lions 6–2 and bowl eligible, but it didn't come easy.

Indiana hung around, only to turn the ball over four times in the second half to the fierce Penn State defense. Norwood caught eight passes for 65 yards and a touchdown, as the Lions pulled out a 36–31 victory.[8] Up next was a battle with #1 Ohio State at home. The second-largest crowd in Beaver Stadium history saw the Nittany Lions get whipped 37–17.[9]

In the home finale, the Lions pulled out a 26–19 win over Purdue. Morelli went over 2,000 passing yards for the season with a 210-yard performance, throwing a five-yard touchdown pass to Williams. For Williams, it was a career day, scoring two touchdowns and putting up a career-high 151 all-purpose yards. Royster continued to come on strong at the end of the season, as shown here by his 126 yards and one touchdown.[10]

Penn State fans whited out Lincoln Financial Field, home of the Temple Owls, out-numbering Temple fans by a wide margin. The football team then whited out the Owls, giving up zero points and just four rushing yards. Kinlaw tied his career-best day with 168 yards, as Penn State went on to a 31–0 win.[11] The season ended in East Lansing, where Penn State's dreams of a third consecutive New Year's bowl fell flat. Morelli broke the school record for completions in a season with 219, and Kinlaw ran for 125 yards and two touchdowns, but the Spartans scored two late touchdowns to beat the Lions by a 35–31 margin.[12]

Morelli finished with over 2,500 yards passing and 18 touchdowns, while Kinlaw ended up with 1,186 yards for the season and ten touchdowns. The Lions finished the season in a share of fifth place at 4–4 in the Big Ten, trailing three teams they lost to as well as Wisconsin.[13] #1 Ohio State was headed to the Allstate BCS National Championship Game in New Orleans, while the Rose Bowl selected #13 Illinois to replace the Buckeyes as Pac-10 champion USC's opponent. Michigan and Wisconsin were awarded the presti-gious New Year's slots in Orlando (Capital One/Citrus) and Tampa (Outback), respec-tively. The Lions were left in the lurch for lower-tier bowls, and the Valero Alamo Bowl picked them up to play against unranked Texas A&M.[14]

2007 Alamo Bowl

Penn State (8–4) vs. Texas A&M (7–5)
December 29, 2007, at the Alamodome in San Antonio, Texas

As disappointed as Penn State was to be playing in the Alamo Bowl, Texas A&M had an even more frustrating season. They started out 5–1, before losing four of five games to lead to the firing of head coach Dennis Franchione. The Aggies won their season finale against archrival Texas to send Franchione out on a high note, but they too were headed to a bowl far below what they had hoped for. Defensive coordinator Gary Darnell would coach the Aggies in the Alamo Bowl, with former Green Bay Packers head coach Mike Sherman waiting in the wings to take over.[15]

Penn State won the toss and chose to defer. Texas A&M went three-and-out to start the game, but punter Jordan Brantly changed field position with a 60-yard punt. Quarter-back Anthony Morelli came out to lead the Nittany Lions from their own 13. He threw his first pass to receiver Deon Butler, who got a first down at the 30. Running back Rodney Kinlaw burst for a 13-yard gain, then receiver Derrick Williams took a handoff for eight more. Kinlaw got another first down, and Morelli threw to Williams for nine more. Fac-ing fourth-and-one a few plays later, Morelli used a quarterback sneak to pick up the first down. Kinlaw picked up another seven yards, before the Penn State drive came to an end. Kicker Kevin Kelly continued his poor performance in bowl games, missing a kick for the third straight bowl, this one a 47-yarder wide to the right.

The Aggies offense then caught fire. Quarterback Stephen McGee scrambled for 18 yards, then threw to tight end Martellus Bennett for 24 more. He ran the option next, pitching to running back Jorvorski Lane for nine more. Fullback Chris Alexander picked up the next first down, before taking the ball down to the 1. Running back Mike Goodson then took it in on a pitch and kicker Richie Bean made the PAT, giving A&M a 7–0 lead.

On the ensuing kickoff, defensive back A.J. Wallace fumbled for Penn State, with A&M defensive back Kenny Brown knocking the ball out of his hands and coming up with the football. It took Goodson just one play to score, starting left before cutting back to his right for a 16-yard touchdown run. In the blink of an eye, A&M led 14–0.

The teams traded punts, and Penn State took over at their own 35 for their third possession. On this one, Kinlaw did a lot of the heavy lifting, running for two first downs and pickups of 16 and seven. Facing fourth down from the A&M 30, head coach Joe Paterno chose to go for it. Morelli threw a lob pass down the left sideline for Butler, who caught it for a 30-yard touchdown. Replays were inconclusive as to whether Butler trapped the ball, so the call on the field stood, and Kelly made the extra point to cut the deficit to seven.

Linebacker Tyrell Sales came up with a sack of McGee on a second-down play. McGee then threw a short one to Goodson, and defensive end Maurice Evans knocked the ball out of his hands. Wallace made amends for his fumble on the kickoff by recovering this loose ball. Paterno then put in backup quarterback Daryll Clark, who took the snap and burst right up the middle for an 11-yard touchdown. Just as quickly as A&M had gone up 14, the game was now tied.

The next three drives (two by A&M, one by Penn State) were three-and-outs. The Nittany Lions got the ball back at their own 14, and A&M got called for pass interference on the first play. Morelli hit Williams at the 35, before Clark came back in and burst up the middle for a first down to the 45. Morelli took the next snap, throwing a pass that was batted by an Aggie, tipped by guard Rich Ohrnberger, and caught by center A.Q. Shipley for a four-yard gain. Kinlaw got the next first down for Penn State. Morelli completed a third-down pass to receiver Terrell Golden, getting into the red zone. Clark came back in again, running down the left sideline for a first down at the 7. That set up a 25-yard field goal by Kelly, giving the Lions a 17–14 lead at the half.

Kinlaw got a 15-yard gain on the first play of the second half, but Penn State was soon forced to punt. The teams then traded interceptions on long throws. Wallace intercepted a deep ball by McGee, only for Morelli to return the favor with a pick to defensive back Stephen Hodge. The Aggies went on a long drive, with Alexander picking up a first down, and Bennett getting another one on a fourth-and-one catch. McGee fired to receiver Earvin Taylor for fourteen yards, getting the Aggies down to the 25. Kicker Matt Szymanski made a 38-yard field goal, tying the game at 17.

Kinlaw was injured early on during the next Penn State drive. Without him, the Penn State offense found other ways to move the ball. Morelli hit Williams for 21 yards, then he fired to Butler at the midfield stripe. Clark came back in to take a handoff and plow for a first down. Freshman running back Evan Royster came into the game, and he proved why he would be a fixture in the Penn State offense for years to come. He first gained four yards, before bursting right up the middle for a 38-yard touchdown run. The Lions led 24–17 after three quarters.

A&M's next drive went nowhere, and they punted. Morelli and the offense went three-and-out, but punter Jeremy Boone pinned the Aggies down at their own 1. Again Texas A&M went on a long drive. McGee hit receiver E.J. Shankle for fourteen yards, then he found Bennett for sixteen, both passes coming on third down. After a pass to Lane for seven yards, McGee ran it up the middle for a first down at the PSU 40. He ran for another seven before throwing to Alexander for a first down. Goodson took the ball down to the 10, but the Aggies soon faced a fourth-and-one. On a curious play call, McGee ran the option, but before he could pitch, he ended up slipping and falling down. This turnover on downs killed the Aggies' hopes.

Penn State would punt, and A&M got one last chance. Again, though, a fourth-down call made little sense. This time, after Goodson got a couple of first downs, the Aggies got called for holding and forced into a second-and-long. McGee threw two incompletions, setting up fourth-and-long with just over two minutes to play. Trailing by seven, there was no doubt about it; the Aggies had to go for it, even if the probability of converting it was small. Instead, Darnell sent out the punting unit, and Brantly kicked it for a touchback. Morelli spent his final five snaps as a Nittany Lion handing off to Royster, who picked up a first down and ran out the clock to give Penn State a 24–17 victory.

It was Penn State's running game that was the big difference. They ran for over 100 yards more than the Aggies, with Offensive MVP Kinlaw picking up 143, Royster gaining 65, and Clark another 50. Morelli's final game as a Lion was much like the two years preceding it; good, but not great. He completed just under his passes for 143 yards, with one touchdown and one interception. Linebacker Sean Lee was named Defensive MVP. The Nittany Lions finished at 9–4 for the season, giving Paterno a victory in his 500th game as head coach.

Box Score[16]:

2007 Alamo Bowl	1st	2nd	3rd	4th	Final
Penn State	0	17	7	0	24
Texas A&M	14	0	3	0	17

1st Quarter: A&M—Goodson 1 run (Bean kick)
   A&M—Goodson 16 run (Szymanski kick)
2nd Quarter: PSU—Butler 30 pass from Morelli (Kelly kick)
   PSU—Clark 11 run (Kelly kick)
   PSU—Kelly 25 FG
3rd Quarter: A&M—Szymanski 38 FG
   PSU—Royster 38 run (Kelly kick)
4th Quarter: No Scoring

2008 Season (11–1)

Daryll Clark took over as starting quarterback in 2008, with Evan Royster at starting running back. The two had shown such great potential in the Alamo Bowl victory over Texas A&M, and now they got their chance to shine. And did they ever! Royster ran for 64 yards and three touchdowns in the season opener against Coastal Carolina, which Penn State won 66–10. The Nittany Lions led 38–7 at the half on their way to head coach Joe Paterno's 373rd victory, tying him with Bobby Bowden for the most Division I-A wins ever.[1]

The Beavers of Oregon State came to Beaver Stadium only to find themselves overwhelmed by the potent Penn State offense. Clark threw two touchdown passes and ran for another, totaling over 275 yards of offense. The Nittany Lions cruised to a 45–14 win over the final Pac-10 team they had never faced, earning them a boost to a #17 ranking.[2]

The offense continued to cruise at Syracuse, putting up 38 points in the first half in another easy victory, 55–13. Clark threw a 55-yard touchdown pass to receiver Jordan Norwood in the first quarter, along with a 17-yarder to receiver Deon Butler. Royster went over 100 yards again, as the Nittany Lions racked up 560 yards of offense.[3]

Against Temple, the Nittany Lions scored 31 points in the second quarter, on their way to a 45–3 win. Clark put up over 200 total yards and three touchdowns. Freshman running back Stephfon Green rushed for 132 yards and a touchdown, and Royster also scored on a 32-yard run. The Owls' field goal made it three total points scored in the last three years against Penn State.[4]

The Big Ten schedule began against Illinois. Derrick Williams took over the game, putting up nearly 250 all-purpose yards, including a 94-yard kickoff return for a score, a 21-yard touchdown catch, and a five-yard scoring run. He was the first player under Paterno to score in those three ways in a single game, while he had the most all-purpose yards since Larry Johnson in 2002. Clark completed a 17-yard touchdown pass to tight end Andrew Quarless in the fourth quarter to put away a 38–24 victory.[5] At Purdue, running back Evan Royster ended up with almost 200 yards of total offense, as Penn State clinched a bowl bid with a 20–6 win.[6]

A mere six wins and a bowl bid wasn't what Penn State was after. They were after the Big Ten title. And what better way to make a statement in the conference than to go to Wisconsin and completely blow out the Badgers! Clark threw for 244 yards and a touchdown, while running for two more touchdowns, as the Nittany Lions crushed Wisconsin 48–7.[7]

Penn State fans had waited three years for this day. It was finally time to get revenge on Michigan for the "two extra seconds" loss in 2005. With over 110,000 fans in attendance, the Lions fell behind 17–7, and it looked like the Wolverines might continue the curse. But Royster ran for 174 yards and a 44-yard touchdown, while Clark threw for 171 yards and accounted for three touchdowns. Defensive tackle Jared Odrick made a sack for a safety, while linebacker Nate Stupar blocked a punt to set up a field goal, and Penn State ended the Michigan hex with a resounding 46–17 victory.[8]

The 8–0 Nittany Lions jumped to #3 in the rankings going into their game at Ohio State. They hadn't beaten a top-ten team on the road since 1999. In this one, they trailed 6–3 entering the fourth quarter, and Clark had to come out of the game due to a concussion. Ohio State had the ball with eleven minutes to play and looked to chew up more time, but PSU defensive back Mark Rubin knocked the ball out of quarterback Terrelle Pryor's grip, which linebacker Navorro Bowman recovered. Pat Devlin then led the Lions on a 38-yard drive, sneaking in from the 1 to give the Lions a 10–6 lead. Later, kicker Kevin Kelly added another field goal, in his 29th straight game with a field goal. Defensive back Lydell Sargeant then intercepted a desperation pass by Pryor to clinch the 13–6 win.[9]

Now at 9–0, the Lions remained #3 in the rankings, and all the discussion involved whether they'd be able to get into the top two in order to play for the national title. That all became a moot point when they fell to Iowa, 24–23. It was the worst offensive day of the year for the Lions, as they failed to reach 300 yards. Despite that, they had a 23–14 lead in the fourth quarter, before allowing two late Iowa drives. Kicker Daniel Murray made a 31-yard field goal with one second left to end the unbeaten season.[10]

Despite the loss, Penn State was still in great position to win the Big Ten. They struggled for a half against Indiana, but Clark went on to throw for 240 yards and two touchdowns, and the Lions pulled away for a 34–7 win. The Lions now had the chance to clinch the Big Ten title against Michigan State.[11] Clark had the game of his career against the Spartans, throwing for four touchdowns and 341 yards, the sixth-most in school history, while Norwood and Butler both went over 120 yards receiving. By the fourth quarter, players were passing out roses in celebration. With their 49–18 victory, the Nittany Lions won the Big Ten for the second time in four years, and this time, they were going to the Rose Bowl.[12]

But should they have gone to the BCS title game? After all, they only lost one game, by one point, to an awfully good Iowa team which finished 8–4 and was headed to the Outback Bowl. Meanwhile, their victories came over 10–2 Ohio State (Fiesta), 9–3 Michigan State (Capital One/Citrus), 7–5 Wisconsin (Champs Sports), and 8–4 Oregon State (Sun). Somehow, despite all those good victories, the Nittany Lions were ranked only #6. Perhaps Penn State would have made the FedEx BCS National Championship Game if someone had given a great postgame speech after their one loss, like Tim Tebow did to the media after Florida's loss to Ole Miss. Tebow's Gators rose like a meteor in the media rankings after his famous speech, and they went on to beat Oklahoma for the national title.[13]

National championship or not, this was still a historic season for the Nittany Lions. Clark finished second in the voting for the Big Ten's Most Valuable Player award, while being named a semifinalist for the prestigious Maxwell Award. He threw for 2,319 yards and rushed for another 265, responsible for 26 touchdowns.[14] No fewer than 19 Nittany Lions made first-team, second-team, or honorable mention All-Big Ten media honors, including Royster, who rushed for over 1,200 yards.[15] Center A.Q. Shipley won the Rimington Trophy, and defensive end Aaron Maybin was a finalist for the Bednarik Award.[16]

The Nittany Lions certainly looked like they'd be playing Oregon State in the Rose

Bowl Game presented by Citi, in a rematch of their Week 2 contest. The Beavers led the Pac-10 until their final game, the Civil War against Oregon. After getting blown out 65–38, they dropped to the Sun Bowl. Instead, 11–1 USC earned their fourth consecutive berth in the Rose Bowl. The one-loss Big Ten champions against the one-loss Pac-10 champions. It was a matchup made in heaven—but it should have been played in Miami as the FedEx BCS National Championship Game. Both the Nittany Lions and the Trojans deserved better.

2009 Rose Bowl

#6 Penn State (11–1) vs. #5 USC (11–1)
January 1, 2009, at the Rose Bowl in Pasadena, California

Rose Queen Courtney Chou Lee finished her cruise down Colorado Boulevard, with Tournament of Roses Grand Marshal Cloris Leachman wrapping up her journey down the parade route.[17] The pregame festivities were over, and now it was time for the Rose Bowl game. Happy Valley had come out in full force to Pasadena, holding their own against the Trojan fans for whom this was practically a home game. After Leachman tossed the coin and the SC logo came up, the Nittany Lions prepared to receive the opening kickoff (USC deferred).

Both teams struggled on offense coming out of the gate. Each of them went three-and-out and punted the ball away. On Penn State's second drive, running back Evan Royster ripped off a 15-yard gain to start things off. He ran the ball three more times but got stuffed on third down. The Trojans took the ball back at their own 14 after a PSU punt.

Running back C.J. Gable picked up USC's first new set of downs of the game on a run to the 31. Running back Joe McKnight added another first down two plays later. The Nittany Lions thought they had a turnover, when quarterback Mark Sanchez went down for a sack and lost the ball. However, the only reason they got the sack in the first place was because they were offside. USC took advantage, with McKnight running for another first down, before Sanchez hit tight end Anthony McCoy for nine more yards. Running back Stafon Johnson broke off a 13-yard run, then Sanchez threw down the middle to receiver Damian Williams for a 27-yard touchdown to put SC up seven.

Penn State came right back downfield and answered. Quarterback Daryll Clark threw to receiver Brett Brackett for seven yards, and receiver Derrick Williams got the first down on an option pitch. Clark then hit Williams at the 46 for another first down. Receiver Deon Butler caught a long ball and got down to the 10, only to see it called back for an illegal shift. That was okay, though, because Clark got most of those yards back on a screen to running back Stephfon Green and a subsequent slant to Butler. After a timeout, Clark plowed up the middle on a quarterback draw, and the game was tied at seven after one quarter.

The second quarter was all USC. Sanchez threw to receiver Patrick Turner for 26 yards, then he hit McCoy down at the 13. McKnight took the ball down to the 6 on a dump-off pass before having to come out due to a toe injury. After he was taken out, Sanchez ran a quarterback draw of his own, and he scored to make it 14–7.

The Trojans weren't the only ones suffering running back injuries. Royster had apparently injured his knee on the last drive, and like McKnight, he'd miss the rest of the game. Green was now pressed into a heavy-duty role. On Penn State's next series, he ran it three times but failed to pick up a first down. Punter Jeremy Boone pinned USC down at their 17.

Sanchez threw a quick pass to Williams, and PSU defensive back Anthony Scirrotto got called for a late hit. After a holding call on USC, Sanchez fired down the left sideline to Williams for 34 more yards. The Trojans couldn't get another first down, but they did get a 30-yard field goal from kicker David Buehler to go up by ten.

Penn State went three-and-out again, and here came the Trojans again. Sanchez hit Williams for another first down, and Penn State jumped offside on the next play. On a rare good play for the Nittany defense, linebacker Navorro Bowman picked up a sack of Sanchez. However, Sanchez came right back with a 16-yard pass to Williams. He'd find Williams for still another first down, then he'd go to receiver Ronald Johnson for a 19-yard touchdown. The Trojans now led by 17.

Trying to score right before the half, Clark threw a screen to Green, who burst for a huge gain. However, defensive back Taylor Mays knocked the ball out of his hands, and fellow defensive back Cary Harris was there to recover it. This led to another USC touchdown, helped out by a personal foul facemask penalty on the Lions. Sanchez threw a screen to Gable, who went 20 yards for a score, and the Trojans led by a 31–7 margin at the half.

Head coach Joe Paterno couldn't like what he was seeing, as he sat up in the press box. He was left by his lonesome when all the assistant coaches went down to the locker room at halftime. Whatever they said may have worked at first. Defensive end Josh Gaines forced a fumble, which defensive back Tony Davis recovered. Clark hit Williams for a first down, and the Lions had the ball in Trojan territory. However, on fourth-and-seven, Clark's pass to receiver Jordan Norwood fell short of the first down.

The Lions forced a punt and got the ball back at their own 20. Running back Brandon Beachum ran for a first down, and Clark hit Butler for a first down at the 40. Next, the Trojans got called for a personal foul, and Penn State had the ball in the red zone as the third quarter expired. Clark then survived a fumble that was ruled by instant replay to have occurred after he was down. With a second chance, he rolled to his left, then fired to Williams for a two-yard touchdown. This is where Penn State should have gone for two, and they likely would have if Paterno was on the sideline. Instead, defensive coordinator Tom Bradley called for an extra point, which made it a 31–14 game.

If there was any chance that the Trojans would blow the lead, they made sure to put those fears to rest. Sanchez threw to Williams and Turner for first downs, getting past midfield. Ronald Johnson then broke super wide-open, with no one even close to him. Sanchez easily found him for a 45-yard touchdown, and USC's lead was back up to 24.

With the clock running down, Penn State needed no less than three touchdowns and three two-point conversions. However, Bradley would again make a curious call. Clark threw to Butler for 35 yards, and Green burst up the middle for a first down at the 15. But on fourth-and-three, Bradley chose not to go for it, and to instead send kicker Kevin Kelly on for a 25-yard field goal. He made the kick, cutting the deficit to 21, but that just wasn't going to cut it.

After a USC three-and-out, Penn State again moved it down the field. Williams picked up a first down on a reverse to the USC 38, and Clark followed by throwing to tight end Andrew Quarless for another first down. Two plays later, he hit Norwood for a first down at the 11. Green took it down to the 4, and after a false start, Clark fired to Norwood in the end zone for a nine-yard touchdown. The Nittany Lions had pulled within 14.

The Lions forced another quick punt, and they got their last real chance to make a comeback with three minutes to go. However, Clark got hit as he passed it downfield for Quarless. The tight end slipped down, causing the pass to be intercepted by defensive back Will Harris. That enabled the Trojans to run the clock all the way down to 45 seconds.

There was still a bit of drama to go. Long snapper Cooper Stephenson hiked the ball over punter Greg Woidneck's head, and Penn State got the ball way back at the USC 14. Was a miracle still possible? The answer was no, as Butler caught Clark's second-down pass but failed to get out of bounds. After a spike, only seven seconds remained. Clark then was intercepted by Cary Harris in the right corner of the end zone. The Nittany Lions had come up short, 38–24.[18]

Clark had a great day, throwing for 273 yards and two touchdowns. Both of his interceptions were desperation passes, so he couldn't be faulted for either one. Butler led in receiving with 97 yards, while Green was the leading rusher with 57 yards. The big numbers were on the other side: Sanchez had lit up the PSU defense for 413 yards and four touchdowns.

There are so many "what ifs" about this game. What if Penn State had gone for two down 31–13? Do they then eschew the ensuing field goal, and possibly get another two points? Would Clark's desperation interception on the final play instead have been a pass to possibly tie the game with a 38–30 score? It is true that USC dominated, but not by nearly as much as the announcers thought. Penn State finished the season with a #8 ranking and an 11–2 record; the bitter taste of roses marred what had been the sweetest smelling of seasons.

Box score[19]:

2009 Rose Bowl	1st	2nd	3rd	4th	Final
Penn State	7	0	0	17	24
USC	7	24	0	7	38

1st Quarter: USC—Da. Williams 27 pass from Sanchez (Buehler kick)
   PSU—Clark 9 run (Kelly kick)
2nd Quarter: USC—Sanchez 6 run (Buehler kick)
   USC—Buehler 30 FG
   USC—R. Johnson 19 pass from Sanchez (Buehler kick)
   USC—Gable 20 pass from Sanchez (Buehler kick)
3rd Quarter: No Scoring
4th Quarter: PSU—De. Williams 2 pass from Clark (Kelly kick)
   USC—R. Johnson 45 pass from Sanchez (Buehler kick)
   PSU—Kelly 25 FG
   PSU—Norwood 9 pass from Clark (Kelly kick)

2009 Season (10–2)

Quarterback Daryll Clark and running back Evan Royster were back for the 2009 season, but most of the rest of the offense was either new or inexperienced. In the season opener against Akron, it didn't show, though. Clark threw for a career-high 353 yards and three touchdowns, to receivers Chaz Powell, Derek Moye, and Graham Zug. Royster ran for 61 yards and a touchdown, as the Nittany Lions got off to a 31–0 halftime lead before going on cruise control for a 31–7 win.[1]

Linebacker Sean Lee made 13 tackles against Syracuse, in another solid if unspectacular Penn State win. The Lions scored a touchdown in each of the four quarters, as they defeated the Orange 28–7. Clark passed for 240 yards and three touchdowns.[2] Next up against Temple, the Nittany Lions got off to a fast start in the first half. This time, Clark threw two first-half touchdown passes in leading Penn State to a 21–3 halftime lead. Royster finally got going on the ground, rushing for 134 yards and a first-half touchdown in a 31–6 victory.[3]

Iowa came into Happy Valley having spoiled the Lions' last undefeated season, and they'd do it again. The game started out so promising, with Clark throwing a 79-yard bomb to Powell not even two minutes into the game. However, punter Jeremy Boone had a punt blocked and returned for a touchdown in the fourth quarter, and the Hawkeyes pulled away for a 21–10 win.[4]

The Lions bounced back with a 35–17 win in Illinois. They only led 7–3 at halftime, but they outgained the Illini by 200 yards in the third quarter. Running back Stephfon Green and Royster each went over 100 rushing yards and scored a touchdown, becoming the first Penn State duo of running backs to do so in a Big Ten game. Clark added another 83 rushing yards and two scoring runs.[5]

The Lions got a breather on the schedule, with Eastern Illinois serving up as fodder. Clark threw for 234 yards and three second-quarter touchdowns, while also running for a touchdown. Royster ran for 94 first-half yards, then sat out the second half with the Lions up by 38. Linebacker Navorro Bowman returned a fumble 91 yards for the longest such return in Penn State history, and PSU waltzed to a 52–3 victory.[6] Minnesota next came to Happy Valley only to come away with nary a point. Penn State allowed just 138 yards of offense, while holding the ball for nearly 42 minutes, its best time-of-possession since 1991, as they won 20–0.[7]

But the goal was a BCS bowl, not just any bowl, and standing in the way was Michigan. The Lions picked up their first win at the Big House since 1996. With Clark putting up 230 yards and four touchdowns, the Lions claimed their biggest victory yet with a 35–10 triumph.[8] At Evanston, the Lions trailed Northwestern 13–10 at halftime, but they went on to shut out the Wildcats for the rest of the game. Clark had another great performance, completing 22 of his 31 attempts for 274 yards and accounting for two scores. Royster ran for another 118 yards and a touchdown. The Lions won 34–13 to improve to 8–1 and set up a gigantic matchup with Ohio State in Happy Valley.[9]

The Nittany Lions hung with the Buckeyes for a half, with Clark rushing for a first-half touchdown. At the break, they trailed just 10–7. But Ohio State quarterback Terrelle Pryor, who had been recruited heavily by Joe Paterno, threw two second-half touchdowns. The Buckeyes held Penn State to just over 200 yards of offense. The Lions' 24–7 loss eliminated them from Big Ten title contention and dropped them behind both OSU and Iowa.[10]

Perhaps suffering from a hangover from their loss to the Buckeyes, the Nittany Lions fell into a 10–0 first-quarter hole to Indiana. Clark led the Lions back into a tie with a 13-yard touchdown pass to Royster. Then Bowman made the play of the game, picking off a pass and going 73 yards to the house for the longest interception return for PSU since 2005, as the Lions won 31–20.[11]

In his final regular-season game as a Nittany Lion, Clark saved his best for last. He passed for 310 yards and four touchdowns against Michigan State, as the Lions blew open a 7–7 game at halftime to win by 28. Quarless caught two of Clark's scoring passes and put up 62 yards, while Zug caught the other two and racked up 99 yards. Royster ran for 114 yards, and the Lions finished another ten-win regular season with a 42–14 win in East Lansing.[12]

Clark had another spectacular season, setting Penn State passing records with 2,787 yards and 23 touchdowns. Being responsible for 30 touchdowns, he now held two of the top three such totals in a season (he had 29 in 2008).[13] He shared the Big Ten Most Valuable Player award with Michigan defensive end Brandon Graham.[14]

Royster moved into eighth place in Penn State history with 2,853 rushing yards. Like Clark, he was named to the coaches' All-Big Ten first-team, along with Bowman, defensive tackle Jared Odrick, tackle Dennis Landolt, and center Stefen Wisniewski.[15] He rushed for over 1,100 yards and six touchdowns during the 2009 season, while adding another 187 yards receiving. He was fifth in receiving for the Lions, behind Moye (732 yards), Zug (549), Quarless (448), and Powell (355).[16]

Penn State finished 10–2 and #11 in the Associated Press poll. They ended up at 6–2 in the Big Ten, behind first-place Ohio State (7–1) and tied with Iowa (6–2) but losing the head-to-head tiebreaker.[17] The Lions were ranked #13 in the final Bowl Championship Series rankings, making them eligible for an at-large spot after Ohio State got the automatic Rose Bowl bid. However, mainly due to the fact that Iowa beat them, the Lions were passed over for the BCS in favor of the Hawkeyes, who got a bid in the Orange Bowl.[18] Only two teams per conference were eligible for the BCS, which meant that the Lions were headed to the Capital One Bowl, formerly (and later) known as the Citrus Bowl. It was the top bowl for any non–BCS Big Ten team, and it offered a big-time matchup against SEC power Louisiana State.[19]

2010 Capital One Bowl

#11 Penn State (10–2) vs. #13 LSU (9–3)
January 1, 2010, at the Florida Citrus Bowl in Orlando, Florida

The Citrus Bowl field was an utter mess. The Champs Sports Bowl and several high school championship games had been played on it in the previous few days, making the field conditions even worse than those of the 1996 Outback Bowl. LSU head coach Les Miles had his players change their cleats before the game, but the mud made it hard for centers to even snap the ball.

Because of the poor conditions, the offenses were quite limited. The first six drives of the game ended in punts. As quarterback Daryll Clark began his fourth drive of the first half, he fired to receiver Graham Zug for 21 yards on a third-and-long. He then went down the left sideline for a wide-open Derek Moye, who caught it for a 37-yard touchdown. The Nittany Lions led 7–0 after one quarter.

LSU brought a short kickoff back into Penn State territory. Quarterback Jordan Jefferson threw to receiver Brandon LaFell for a big gain down to the 10. The Lions defense then held strong, stopping the Tigers for two straight losses. LSU was forced to try a field goal, and kicker Josh Jasper made the 25-yard field goal to make it 7–3.

After the teams exchanged punts, Penn State started at their own 45. Fullback Joe Suhey plowed ahead for a gain of five, and Clark hit tight end Andrew Quarless for a first down at the LSU 29. On a third down, Clark threw to Moye, who at first had the first down before being pushed back behind the line. The officials incorrectly ruled him short, before changing the call on a replay. Running back Stephfon Green then took it down to the 10, where the drive stalled. Kicker Collin Wagner made a 26-yard field goal to extend the lead to 10–3.

The offenses continued their stalemate, with a punt by each team, and Jefferson throwing an interception to defensive back A.J. Wallace shortly before the half. Running back Evan Royster ran for a first down to the 6, and Suhey further took it down to the 1. The Nittany Lions ran down the clock to give LSU no time, but they couldn't get it in the end zone. Wagner made an 18-yard field goal to put Penn State up 13–3 at the half.

LSU started the second half at the 48 after a good return by Trindon Holliday. Jefferson fired his next two passes to LaFell, picking up a first down. However, that's where their drive ended, and they punted it down to the 2. The Lions then started playing musical chairs with their running backs. Royster and Green kept exchanging carries, and the plan was working. They got a couple of first downs, along with Clark throwing to Moye for a first down. Eventually, the drive stalled past midfield, and Boone kicked it for a touchback.

Early in the next drive, linebacker Navorro Bowman knocked the ball out of running back Steven Ridley's hands, and Sean Lee picked it up at the LSU 20. Clark then passed to receiver Chaz Powell to get a first-and-goal. The Lions got it as far as the 3 before having to settle for a Wagner 20-yard field goal to go up 16–3.

A 13-point lead is the most dangerous lead in football, and this game proved exactly why. After returning the kickoff past midfield, the LSU offense made a quick strike. Jefferson completed two passes to Terrence Tolliver, moving down to inside the Penn State 25. He then found LaFell in the middle of the field for a 24-yard touchdown to cut the deficit to six at the end of three quarters.

The Lions went three-and-out, and Holliday returned the ensuing punt 39 yards to midfield. Only a tackle by Boone saved a touchdown. The Tigers scored anyway, with Holliday running for ten yards, and Jefferson hitting Tolliver for 39 yards down to the 1. Ridley took a pitch in for a touchdown, and Jasper's extra point gave LSU a 17–16 lead.

On the next drive, the officials had an amusing dilemma when they forgot what down it was, and they had to go to instant replay to just to realize that it was third down and not fourth down. The Lions had to punt anyway, and LSU took over at their own

17. Jefferson avoided a couple of near-interceptions on this possession, before having to punt. Penn State took over this ultimate drive at their own 31.

The drive started with LSU getting called for pass interference. Clark then hit receiver Curtis Drake for a first down past midfield. Royster ran it twice, getting close to a first down, which Zug picked up on a catch. Clark then went back to Zug for 18 more yards. On the next third down, Green ran it for a first down inside the 10. The Lions then ran the ball three times, before turning the game over to Wagner. He had to make a 21-yard field goal from a wide angle on the right side of the field in the horrible field conditions. His kick made it just inside the right upright, and Penn State took a two-point lead with less than a minute to go.

Holliday again made a good return, taking the kick back to the 41. Jefferson scrambled for a first down, before throwing a short pass to LaFell to the Penn State 46. Since he was tackled in bounds, the clock kept running, and LSU got called for a personal foul when they tried pulling Penn State players off the pile. After an incompletion and a failed lateral play, the game was over, and the Nittany Lions had won, 19–17.

In his final game as a Nittany Lion, Clark completed just over half his passes for 216 yards and a touchdown, while also rushing for 20 yards. He was named MVP of the game. "I'm trying to get people to understand how good he is," head coach Joe Paterno said, referring to Clark's draft status.[20] The Lions finished the season ranked #9 in the Associated Press poll with a spectacular 11–2 record.

Box score[21]:

2010 Capital One Bowl	1st	2nd	3rd	4th	Final
LSU	0	3	7	7	17
Penn State	7	6	3	3	19

1st Quarter: PSU—Moye 37 pass from Clark (Wagner kick)
2nd Quarter: LSU—Jasper 25 FG
   PSU—Wagner 26 FG
   PSU—Wagner 18 FG
3rd Quarter: PSU—Wagner 20 FG
   LSU—LaFell 24 pass from Jefferson (Jasper kick)
4th Quarter: LSU—Ridley 1 run (Jasper kick)
   PSU—Wagner 21 FG

2010 Season (7–5)

Rob Bolden kicked off the 2010 season with the greatest performance by a freshman quarterback in Penn State history. He completed 20 of 29 passes for 239 yards and two touchdowns, as the Lions beat Youngstown State, 44–14. Receiver Brett Brackett caught eight passes for 98 yards. It was head coach Joe Paterno's 38th win in 45 opening-day games.[1]

The Nittany Lions headed to Alabama, where they were blown off the field. It was their first game against the Crimson Tide since 1990, and this time the Lions managed just a single field goal in a 24–3 loss. But the team bounced back with a 24–0 win over Kent State. Running back Evan Royster went over 3,000 yards for his career in the win.[2]

Kicker Collin Wagner tied the Penn State record for most field goals in a game with five of them against Temple. Because the Lions weren't scoring touchdowns, this one stayed close till the end. Eventually, the Lions pulled away to win 22–13. But the smoke-and-mirrors offense would only work so long. Both Iowa and Illinois crushed Penn State on back-to-back weeks. The Lions fell 24–3 in Iowa and 33–13 at home to the Illini.[3]

The Lions then turned things around against Minnesota. Bolden completed his first nine passes of the game against Minnesota, before coming out with an injury. Matt McGloin entered the game and fired a 42-yard pass to receiver Derek Moye. The Lions beat the Golden Gophers, 33–21. That led into a pair of historic weeks in Penn State football.[4]

Royster ran for 150 yards on 29 carries against Michigan, breaking Curt Warner's mark for most career rushing yards at Penn State. McGloin started for the first time, throwing for 250 yards and a touchdown. The Lions beat the Wolverines, 41–31. The next week, Penn State fell into a 21-point hole against Northwestern. They then outscored the Wildcats 28–0 in the second half, while putting up a season-most 528 yards, to deliver Paterno his 400th career victory, 35–21.[5]

The Lions got a real reality check against Ohio State. After getting off to a 14–3 half-time lead in Columbus, the Lions collapsed in the second half. The Buckeyes went on to beat them 38–14. Penn State clinched a winning season with a 41–24 win over Indiana, in which McGloin set a career-high with 315 passing yards and two touchdowns.[6]

The season ended in Happy Valley against Sparty, where the Lions tried to overcome a huge fourth-quarter deficit in the freezing cold. Most of the suffering fans cleared out of Beaver Stadium with the Lions trailing 28–10. McGloin, who threw for 312 yards, rallied the Lions to within six. A late onside kick was unsuccessful, though, and Michigan State won, 28–22.[7]

Bolden and McGloin finished in almost a dead heat in passing yards. Bolden had

1,360 yards; McGloin had 1,337. The big difference was in the touchdown-to-interception ratio. McGloin threw 13 touchdowns as opposed to four picks. Bolden, on the other hand, had only five touchdown passes, and seven interceptions.[8]

Royster ran for 916 yards in his senior season for the Nittany Lions. He scored six touchdowns, while going into the record books as the leading ground-gainer in Penn State history. Moye caught 48 passes for 806 yards and seven touchdowns to lead the team in all categories. Brackett also had a fine year, catching 37 balls for 497 yards and five scores.[9]

Michigan State, Ohio State, and Wisconsin all shared the Big Ten championship with 11–1 overall records. Wisconsin and Ohio State got the Bowl Championship Series nods, with the Badgers headed to the Rose Bowl and Ohio State off to the Sugar Bowl. Michigan State got the best non–BCS bowl for the Big Ten, going to the Capital One (formerly Citrus) Bowl. That left the Outback, Gator, and TicketCity Bowls for the 7–5 Big Ten teams, including Penn State. The Nittany Lions were selected to the Outback Bowl to go up against Florida; it would be their fourth trip to Tampa.

2011 Outback Bowl

Penn State (7–5) vs. Florida (7–5)
January 1, 2011, at Raymond James Stadium in Tampa, Florida

Florida won the toss and chose to defer to the second half. The Lions went three-and-out, and Gators head coach Urban Meyer's choice seemed to have been justified. But Meyer, coaching his last game for Florida, could not have envisioned quarterback John Brantler throwing an interception to defensive back D'Anton Lynn on the very first play. Penn State took over with good field position.

Quarterback Matt McGloin passed to running back Evan Royster coming out of the backfield, and he picked up a first down to the 34. He then fired passes for first downs to receivers Justin Brown and Graham Zug. Two plays later, he found receiver Derek Moye in the back of the end zone for an apparent touchdown. Not so, the officials said; Moye stepped out of bounds before catching the pass. So, after a five-yard penalty, McGloin went back to Moye on a fade pattern down the left sideline. Moye hauled it in for the touchdown, and Penn State had the early 7–0 lead.

Although Penn State forced a three-and-out, McGloin threw an interception to defensive back Ahmad Black. He returned it deep into Penn State territory at the 14. The Gators got it down to about the 2, where quarterback/tight end Trey Burton took a snap. He fumbled, however, and Lynn recovered the loose ball in the end zone for a touchback.

The Lions punted, and Meyer inserted Jordan Reed at quarterback. Reed filled the Tim Tebow role for the Gators, and he moved the ball right down the field. He hit receiver Frankie Hammond for eight yards and Burton for 18 more. The drive stalled after a bad snap, which went right past Reed. He fell on it for a loss of 19. Gators punter Chas Henry pinned the Lions down at the 1 as the second quarter began.

Facing third down from around his own 5, McGloin threw another poor pass. This one was intercepted by defensive back Cody Riggs. It took Florida just two plays to take advantage. After a pass to running back Chris Rainey that picked up nothing, the Gators gave the ball to receiver Omarius Hines, who ran it 16 yards down the sideline for a tying touchdown.

Neither offense did much on their next possession. Penn State got one first down on their next drive on an eight-yard run by Royster, but they were soon forced to punt again. Solomon Patton rushed in and blocked the kick, which defensive end Lerentee McCray picked up and returned 27 yards for a touchdown. The Gators now had a 14–7 lead.

The Lions answered quickly, though. Royster ran for eight yards, and running back Joe Suhey pounded ahead for a first down. McGloin then went to receiver Brett Bracket for a first down. On the next snap, McGloin went for the deep ball, which Moye caught for an apparent touchdown. Again, though, he'd have it taken away, this time on replay when it was revealed that his knee went down inches from the goal line. That was okay, though, because running back Michael Zordich pounded it in on the next play to tie it at 14.

The Nittany defense forced a quick punt, and the kick went only 14 yards out of bounds at the Florida 37. McGloin was under heavy pressure on first down, but he spun away from defenders and flipped the ball to Royster. The speedy back took it for a gain of 30. The Lions couldn't punch it in after getting to the 3, which they'd regret later. Kicker Collin Wagner made a 20-yard field goal, and Penn State led 17–14 at the half.

On the first play of the third quarter, Rainey took off up the middle for a 51-yard run. The Gators didn't gain much else, though, and they punted. Penn State went three-and-out, and back came in Reed to play the Tebow game. He threw to Hines for 21 yards, then ran it twice right up the gut for sixteen yards combined. All that set up Henry for a 30-yard field goal, which tied the game at 17.

McGloin threw what should have been a third interception to defensive back Janoris Jenkins, but Jenkins dropped the ball. Penn State punted, and Florida took over at the 27. The Gators couldn't do anything with the ball, but on fourth down, Meyer decided to fake the punt. The Lions easily tackled Henry short of the marker, and they took over deep in Gator territory. McGloin threw to receiver Devon Smith for 18 yards, then he ran the ball in himself for a two-yard touchdown to give Penn State a 24–17 lead.

Patton returned the ensuing kickoff 48 yards into Penn State territory at the 44. The Gators got one first down on a pass from Brantley to receiver Deonte Thompson. Reed took over, but he fumbled a snap on third down and had to jump on top of the loose ball for a loss. Henry tried a 47-yard field goal, and his kick was perfect. The third quarter came to a close with Penn State still up by four.

McGloin threw his third interception of the game on the next drive. This one was picked off by linebacker Brandon Hicks, who returned it to the 24. Rainey ran for eight, before the Gators faced fourth-and-short. Meyer left the offense out there, and Reed hit Burton for a first down. The Lions stopped Florida on another third down, but this one got overturned thanks to an illegal hit and a personal foul call. Running back Mike Gillis-lee got the ball in short range, and he punched it in to give the Gators a 27–24 lead.

The next kickoff was quite confusing. The Lions got called for an illegal block in the back, but what made it interesting was that running back Silas Redd fumbled the kickoff. When announcing the penalty, the referee also stated that a Penn State player recovered the ball. But both announcers, Mike Tirico and Jon Gruden, somehow missed that call. Tirico and Gruden chirped at the officials to call for an instant replay, because they saw the fumble. Of course, since Penn State recovered the fumble, it didn't matter whether Redd was down or not.

All that didn't mean much anyway. The Nittany Lions were forced to punt, and Rainey returned the punt to the PSU 15, only to have it called back on an illegal block penalty. Reed then led the Gators across midfield and into field goal range. He carried the ball six times on the next drive, which ended with a Henry 20-yard field goal.

Down by six, the Lions needed to get something going, but they ended up punting on the next drive. The Gators now tried to eat up some clock. Paterno carefully used all three timeouts on Florida's possession, which consisted solely of Reed runs. After forcing a punt, Penn State got the ball back one last time at their own 21.

McGloin started the fateful drive with a pass to Moye for a first down to the 39. Royster ripped off a 23-yard run on the next third down, and Penn State had it at the Florida 32. Royster's final run as a Penn Stater came on the next play, as a six-yard run. McGloin threw incomplete, and the clock showed 1:11. On the next play, McGloin was picked off by Black, who returned it 80 yards for the clinching score. McGloin would have one last desperation pass picked off by Jenkins, giving him five interceptions for the day, a Penn State bowl record. It was a crushing 37–24 loss for the Lions.

Royster closed out his Penn State career with 98 yards on 20 carries, plus 51 receiving yards on four catches. Moye led the way in receiving with five catches for 79 yards and a touchdown. For McGloin, it was a really rough day. Not only did he have the five interceptions, but he only completed 17 of 41 passes for 211 yards.

No one knew it at the time, but this would be the final bowl game Paterno coached in his illustrious career. He saw the Gators pick apart the Penn State passing game. The Lions actually outgained the Gators by over 70 yards, but the turnovers did them in. It was a tough final loss for Paterno. However, the worst was yet to come.

Box score[10]:

2011 Outback Bowl	1st	2nd	3rd	4th	Final
Penn State	7	10	7	0	24
Florida	0	14	6	17	37

1st Quarter: PSU—Moye 5 pass from McGloin (Wagner kick)
2nd Quarter: FLA—Hines 16 run (Henry kick)
   FLA—McCray 27 blocked punt return (Henry kick)
   PSU—Zordich 1 run (Wagner kick)
   PSU—Wagner 20 FG
3rd Quarter: FLA—Henry 30 FG
   PSU—McGloin 2 run (Wagner kick)
   FLA—Henry 47 FG
4th Quarter: FLA—Gillislee 1 run (Henry kick)
   FLA—Henry 20 FG
   FLA—Black 80 interception return (Henry kick)

2011 Season (9–3)

The most turbulent season in Penn State history became with the calm of a victory over Indiana State. Defensive back Chaz Powell returned the opening kickoff of the new season 95 yards for a touchdown. Running back Silas Redd led the team with 104 rushing yards and two touchdowns. Head coach Joe Paterno won his 39th and final season opener in his career.[1]

Alabama came to Beaver Stadium for the first time since 1989, ranked #3 in the nation. There was no contest in this one. Penn State turned it over three times, while Alabama didn't do so once in a 27–11 defeat of the Lions.[2] Penn State then went to Philadelphia to take on Temple. Linebacker Michael Mauti picked off a pass at the Owls 44 to set up running back Michael Zordich for the game-winning touchdown. The Lions came away with a too-close-for-comfort 14–10 win.[3]

The Lions had a passing explosion against Eastern Michigan, winning 34–6. Rob Bolden and Matt McGloin both spent time at quarterback, with McGloin throwing for 220 yards and three touchdowns, and Bolden passing for another 115 yards and a score.[4] Against Indiana, McGloin found receiver Derek Moye for a 74-yard touchdown pass, and kicker Anthony Fera made three short field goals in a 16–10 win.[5]

In the fourth quarter against Iowa, linebacker Gerald Hodges came up with a strip-sack which fellow linebacker Nate Stupar recovered, setting up McGloin's two-yard touchdown pass to tight end Kevin Haplea. The Lions kept the Hawkeyes out of the end zone, winning 13–3.[6] Then Redd ran for 131 yards and a touchdown against Purdue, as the Lions survived another close shave. Running back Curtis Dukes ran for an early touchdown, and Stupar intercepted a late pass to help clinch the 23–18 victory.[7]

The Lions then took a trip to Illinois to take on Northwestern. Redd rushed for 164 yards and a touchdown, and McGloin passed for just under 200 yards and two touchdowns. The defense then shut down Northwestern in the second half, and Redd's 19-yard touchdown run sealed a 34–24 victory.[8] In a snowy game against Illinois at Happy Valley, Penn State and its opponent combined for zero points for the first time since 1984. Redd ran for 137 yards and a touchdown, and Illinois missed a last-second field goal to give Penn State a 10–7 win.[9]

Everything was coming up roses (as in Rose Bowl) for Penn State. Paterno had just passed Eddie Robinson for the most wins for any Division I coach ever with 409. Ranked at #12, the Lions were at 8–1, the only loss coming to Alabama. They were 5–0 in the Big Ten, the only undefeated team remaining, and they were in first place in the Leaders Division. This was turning into a dream season.

Then, over the bye week, the scandal hit, and the season turned into a nightmare.

Everything changed in a matter of two weeks, as former defensive coordinator Jerry Sandusky was accused of child molestation, and the media put all the blame on Paterno. Under heavy pressure from everyone from Bristol, Connecticut to Harrisburg, Pennsylvania, the Penn State Board of Trustees decided to fire Paterno on November 9, 2011, ending a 46-year run for him as head coach.

Defensive coordinator Tom Bradley took over as head coach. In his first game, the Lions lost 17–14 to Nebraska in the season finale at Beaver Stadium. McGloin threw for 193 yards in the loss, while Green rushed for 71 yards and both of Penn State's touchdowns.[10] The Nittany Lions had won at Ohio State just once since 1978, but this year they somehow did in the worst of circumstances. They won 20–14, giving themselves a chance to win the Big Ten Leaders Division in their season finale at Wisconsin.[11] But that wasn't happening, as Wisconsin quarterback Russell Wilson threw for two touchdowns in leading the 45–7 blowout. There would be no Big Ten Championship Game for the Lions.[12]

Despite the team's struggles on offense, Redd rushed for over 1,200 yards and seven touchdowns. McGloin threw for 1,571 yards and eight touchdowns, while Bolden also threw for 548 and a touchdown as the Lions somewhat rotated quarterbacks this season. Moye led the team with 40 grabs for over 650 yards, scoring three times. Fera made 14 of his 17 field goal attempts and converted all 18 of his extra point tries.[13]

With the media circling around Happy Valley like vultures, there was total chaos for the Lions those last three weeks, making it hard to believe that they even won one game and nearly won another. No bowl wanted to invite Penn State, whose players were being punished for something that had nothing to do with them. In the end, the Nittany Lions were invited to the TicketCity Bowl, a game that came into existence once the Cotton Bowl Classic moved out of the Cotton Bowl stadium. Dallas wanted to still have a bowl game, so they created the TicketCity Bowl to take place at the old stadium. Penn State's opponent would be Houston, a strong team from Conference USA.

2012 TicketCity Bowl

#22 Penn State (9–3) vs. #19 Houston (12–1)
January 2, 2012, at the Cotton Bowl in Dallas, Texas

Both teams were coming off devastating losses in their final game which kept them from going to a Bowl Championship Series game. Both teams were without a permanent head coach. Both teams were ranked in the top 25. But only one of these teams had an NFL-caliber quarterback, and unfortunately for the Nittany Lions, he was wearing red and white.

Interim head coach Tom Bradley was coaching his final game for Penn State before Bill O'Brien would take over the team in the offseason. The football program was an absolute mess, and you could not fault the players for being distracted. There was a non-stop media circus following the university. Joe Paterno was diagnosed with cancer with little time left to live, but his son Jay was still an assistant coach on the roster. This game may have been the lowest point in Penn State history.

Penn State won the toss, and Bradley chose to defer. Big mistake. Houston's quarterback was Case Keenum, and he directed a high-flying offense that could march 80 yards in a minute. The Cougars lost in the Conference USA title game to Southern Mississippi, costing them a berth in the BCS. That was their only loss of the year. Keenum proved exactly why his team had won all those games, as he quickly brought the Cougars down the field. He fired two long passes to receiver Patrick Edwards, both on third downs. The first one went for 39, while the second one was a 40-yard touchdown pass. It was Edwards's 19th touchdown of the season, putting the Cougars up 7–0.

Quarterback Rob Bolden had a really rough start to this game. He and the Penn State offense went three-and-out on their first possession. The Cougars took over with great field position and moved into range for a field goal. While Keenum's third-down pass to receiver Tyron Carrier came up short of the first down, kicker Matt Hogan made a 35-yard field goal to extend the lead to ten.

Bolden ran for ten yards on a third-down play, but since running back Silas Redd had been hit for a loss, it wasn't enough for a first down. Punter/kicker Anthony Fera booted the ball away for a touchback. Here came the Cougars, flying down the field again. Keenum found Edwards for a 26-yard gain, then he hit receiver Justin Johnson for an eight-yard touchdown. The Nittany Lions ended the first quarter without a first down or a completed pass, and they trailed 17–0.

Once the second quarter began, the Lions finally got some life. Running back Stephfon Green ran for eight yards, then picked up the first down. Bolden was sacked, but he came back with a long pass downfield for receiver Devon Smith for 43 yards down to the 20. Redd and Green split carries on the next four plays, with Green taking a direct snap and scampering through the middle of the line for a six-yard touchdown. The Lions were finally on the board, down 17–7.

Their good fortunes would be short-lived. Later in the second quarter, Keenum launched one downfield for Edwards, who was left so wide open that it couldn't even be possible in a video game. Edwards simply walked in for a 75-yard touchdown. It was now 24–7, and this one was getting out of reach for Penn State.

The Lions went three-and-out, and the Cougars called two timeouts to get the ball back. Keenum then moved the ball into field goal range, passing to running back Charles Sims for nine yards, and hitting Johnson down at the Penn State 35. Houston tried to tack on three right before the half, but Hogan's 50-yard attempt went wide to the right.

A promising drive for Penn State went awry when Bolden threw an interception to defensive back Nick Saenz. The Nittany Lion defense made a stop, but their offense hardly held the ball. Bolden ran for one first down, and that was it. Fera punted again, and Houston took over at their own 33. Keenum fired to receiver Ronnie Williams for 17 yards, then Sims sprinted up the middle for a first down at the 28. That set up a 38-yard Hogan field goal, and Houston went up by 20.

Bolden fumbled, but the Nittany Lions fell on it for a loss of ten. On third-and-long, Bolden made up for all of it, launching one downfield for receiver Justin Brown. He was just as open as Edwards was earlier, and he went 69 yards for a touchdown. The Lions still had hope, only down two touchdowns.

Keenum put the game away on the next drive, though. He threw to running back Michael Hayes for 11 yards, then he fired to Johnson for 18 more. Hayes then made an athletic run where he almost hit the ground, but he managed to regain his balance and make it all the way down to the Penn State 20. Keenum gunned it to Williams to get down to the 10, and the third quarter came to a close. When the next quarter began, Hogan made a 22-yard field goal to extend the lead to 16.

Penn State's last-ditch comeback effort came up short. Bolden threw an interception to linebacker Phillip Steward on one possession, and on the next one, his pass fell incomplete on fourth-and-14. This nightmare of a season was finally over, as the Nittany Lions fell to the Cougars by a final count of 30–14.

Keenum had a field day against the Penn State defense, completing 45 passes for 532 yards and three touchdowns. Meanwhile, the Penn State offense fired blanks. Bolden completed only seven passes, and his total would have been under 100 yards if not for the one 69-yard bomb. Green had a good game, rushing for 65 yards and a touchdown while also catching two passes. Ultimately, though, this was a game and a season that Penn Staters would just rather forget.

Box Score[14]:

2012 TicketCity Bowl	*1st*	*2nd*	*3rd*	*4th*	*Final*
Houston	17	7	3	3	30
Penn State	0	7	7	0	14

1st Quarter: HOU—Edwards 40 pass from Keenum (Hogan kick)
   HOU—Hogan 35 FG
   HOU—Johnson 8 pass from Keenum (Hogan kick)
2nd Quarter: PSU—Green 6 run (Fera kick)
   HOU—Edwards 75 pass from Keenum (Hogan kick)
3rd Quarter: HOU—Hogan 38 FG
   PSU—Brown 69 pass from Bolden (Fera kick)
4th Quarter: HOU—Hogan 22 FG

2014 Season (6–6)

After the sanctions had been lifted from the Penn State program, the football team was immediately allowed to go to bowls again. But thanks to the reduction of scholarships and many transfers brought on by the penalties, becoming bowl eligible was not all that easy. New head coach James Franklin had his work cut out for him.

Penn State began the season in Ireland. They took on Central Florida at Croke Park in Dublin. They leaped out to a 20–10 lead on the Knights thanks to a 79-yard touchdown pass from quarterback Christian Hackenberg to receiver Geno Lewis. Hackenberg threw for 454 yards as he set up Sam Ficken to convert a 36-yard field goal on the game's final play to give Penn State a 26–24 win.[1] The next week against Akron, tight end Jesse James caught two touchdown passes from Hackenberg, who threw for 319 yards to set the school record for the most passing yards in back-to-back games. Penn State defeated the Zips 21–3.[2]

Rutgers entered the Big Ten in 2014, and in their first-ever conference game, they got off to a 10–0 halftime lead at home against Penn State. But the Nittany Lion defense picked off five passes of quarterback Gary Nova, in an ugly 13–10 comeback win.[3] The offense went back to its bombastic ways against Massachusetts. Belton ran for 76 yards and two second-quarter touchdowns, while fellow running back Zach Zwinak added another two touchdowns in the same quarter, and the final margin ended up 48–7.[4]

But then the offense suffered a power outage. Against Northwestern, the Lion offense could muster only two field goals for the Homecoming crowd in a 29–6 loss.[5] At the Big House, Penn State took a 13–7 lead on a ten-yard pass from Hackenberg to Hamilton, but then they gave up three straight field goals and a late safety to lose 18–13.[6]

Up against #13 Ohio State, Penn State fell into a 17–0 hole at halftime, and it seemed likely that the Buckeyes were going to win in a rout. But defensive tackle Anthony Zettel scored on a 40-yard pick-six, and Hackenberg threw a 24-yard touchdown pass to receiver Saeed Blacknall, making it 17–14. Ficken tied the game with a 31-yard field goal with just nine seconds to play. The game went into overtime, where Belton scored first to give Penn State a 24–17 lead. They just couldn't stop the Ohio State rushing attack, as quarterback J.T. Barrett scored on two runs. The first was from five yards out in the first overtime, and the second came from four yards out in the second OT. The game ended when Hackenberg was sacked on fourth down from the 20 in the second extra period, and Penn State lost a heart-wrencher, 31–24.[7]

If that wasn't bad enough, Maryland then came into Beaver Stadium to rip out the Lions' hearts again. Kicker Brad Craddock put through a 43-yard field goal to beat the Lions 20–19.[8] In Bloomington, Penn State finally put an end to the four-game losing streak by shutting down the Indiana offense. The Hoosiers passed for just 68 yards on the PSU defense, and they didn't score a single offensive point. The Nittany Lions came out with a 13–7 victory.[9]

All that was between the Lions and their first bowl under James Franklin was Temple. Akeel Lynch had a great game running the ball against the Owls, carrying the ball 18 times for 130 yards and a 38-yard touchdown. The Lions beat Temple 30–13 for that magic sixth victory, ensuring them a spot in the postseason.[10]

But which game would it be? If the Lions wanted a better bowl, they'd have to win their last two against Illinois and Michigan State. Instead, they couldn't beat either team. Against Illinois, Hackenberg had the Lions ahead on an 18-yard touchdown pass to receiver Chris Godwin and a 47-yard scoring run by Lynch. But Illini kicker David Reisner made two fourth-quarter field goals, including one with eight seconds left, as Illinois beat Penn State, 16–14.[11] Michigan State was ranked #10 coming into Beaver Stadium, and they returned the opening kickoff for a touchdown on their way to a 34–10 rout of Penn State. That left the Lions at 6–6, and a putrid 3–4 at Beaver Stadium.

Penn State got an invite to the New Era Pinstripe Bowl at Yankee Stadium in the Bronx against ACC opponent Boston College. The Eagles got a signature win over the USC Trojans, but otherwise plodded along in their 7–5 season much like the Lions did. It wasn't Pasadena, it wasn't Miami, it wasn't even Orlando. But it was a bowl, and at this point, Penn State fans would take any positives they could get.

2014 Pinstripe Bowl

Penn State (6–6) vs. Boston College (7–5)
December 27, 2014, at Yankee Stadium in Bronx, New York

Penn State won the opening coin toss and chose to receive. The drive started out well, with running back Bill Belton getting past the 30, and quarterback Christian Hackenberg throwing to receiver DaeSean Hamilton for a first down. Belton came out of the backfield and hauled in a catch for seven yards, then running back Akeel Lynch took off on an eight-yard run for another first down. Hackenberg went play action, and he found tight end Kyle Carter for still another first down at the Boston College 39. But a snap infraction call set back the Lions, and they ended up punting it away.

Boston College went three-and-out, and Penn State took back over at their own 32. Hackenberg threw to receiver Saeed Blacknall for a first down at the 50. Carter then hauled in his second catch, which set up a first down when the Eagles jumped offside. This time it was an illegal formation penalty that stalled the Penn State drive. They ended up punting again, and punter Daniel Pasquariello's kick went for a touchback.

Running back Jon Hilliman broke off a 44-yard run, and the Eagles got into Penn State territory. They'd go for it on a fourth-and-five, but quarterback Tyler Murphy's pass fell incomplete, and Penn State took over. Facing third-and-long, Hackenberg threw a bomb down the sideline, and receiver Chris Godwin caught it! He was gone, 72 yards for a touchdown, and Penn State had the early 7–0 lead.

Head coach James Franklin then went with a surprise onside kick, but it didn't work. The ball was ruled to be out of bounds, and BC took over in great field position. Two plays later, Hilliman took off on a 49-yard touchdown run. At the end of the first quarter, Penn State and Boston College were knotted up at seven points apiece.

On his next drive, Hackenberg fumbled away a snap, and the Eagles recovered it. They got into Penn State territory, before having to punt it back. That began a procession of punts that lasted throughout the rest of the second quarter. Altogether there were six straight punts in the quarter, and not a whole lot of offense, as the teams went to the locker rooms tied at seven.

Boston College got things going to start the second half. After a kickoff return to the 40, Murphy took the ball into Penn State territory. Hilliman picked up another seven yards, and running back Marcus Outlow ran for a first down. Outlow carried the ball three more times, then Murphy threw a play action pass to receiver Shakim Phillips for a first down. Three plays later, Murphy went back to Phillips, who was open in the end zone. He hauled it in for a 19-yard touchdown, and the Eagles took a seven-point lead.

Lynch started the Lions out on a good drive, running for a first down, and catching an eight-yard pass. Hackenberg found receiver Geno Lewis for 12 yards, then he rolled out and hit Godwin for a first down. He went back to Lewis, getting 11 more, and the Nittany Lions were close to field goal range. But Hackenberg again fumbled away a snap, and the Eagles recovered it. Only four plays later, Murphy took off on a 40-yard touchdown run, and the Eagles led 21–7.

Franklin got the Penn State offense into an up-tempo mode, and Hackenberg ran it well. He threw to Lewis, who got a good gain down to the BC 30, and a personal foul facemask penalty added 15 more. He then scrambled for four yards, and Lynch got several more. With time running out in the third quarter, Hackenberg rushed his team to the line, and he threw a slant that was tipped right to Lewis. He brought it in for a seven-yard touchdown, and Penn State cut the deficit to seven as the quarter ended.

The next three possessions all ended in punts, two by BC and one by PSU. On the Eagles' second of those drives, Lions defensive back Jordan Lucas came up with a sack, and defensive tackle Anthony Zettel came up with a big open-field tackle to stop Outlow shy of a first down. Penn State took over at their own 45 after a wobbly kick by punter Alex Howell.

Hackenberg fired two nine-yard passes, which went to Godwin and Lewis. Lynch then took off on a long run down the left sideline to the 1. It looked like he crossed the goal line, but the officials ruled him short. On the next play, Lynch couldn't pound it in, and the Lions were called for unsportsmanlike conduct. That suddenly made it second-and-goal from the 16, a much harder proposition. But it wasn't too hard for Hackenberg, who fired into the middle of the end zone to Hamilton for a touchdown. The Lions had tied it at 21.

Boston College took over at their own 28. Murphy threw to Phillips for 13 yards, then he ran a fake option play for a 26-yard gain. Hilliman ran the ball a couple of times, and Penn State defensive back Adrian Amos got called for a personal foul for hitting him too late. The Nittany Lions were forced to call two timeouts on the next two runs, as the Eagles wanted to bleed the clock. On third down, Murphy tried keeping it and going for the end zone, but defensive back Marcus Allen tackled him at the 3-yard line, saving a touchdown. The Eagles settled for a 20-yard field goal by kicker Mike Knoll, and they led by three with just about two minutes to play.

Hackenberg had to have the drive of his life now. Starting at his own 23, he threw to Hamilton for seven yards. He then hit tight end Jesse James for seven more and a first down, getting out of bounds. He passed to Lynch for a short gain, and the clock ticked under 90 seconds. He then fired to Godwin down the left sideline for a first down to the

BC 35. Two plays later, he scrambled to get into field goal range at the 28. After a failed third down attempt, Franklin called timeout with 25 seconds left. On came kicker Sam Ficken, a second-team Big Ten choice. He nailed the 45-yard field goal, and for only the second time in Penn State bowl history, the Lions would play in overtime.

The Eagles called tails, but the coin came up heads, and the Nittany Lions chose to play on defense to start the overtime period. It took the Eagles just three plays to score. Murphy hit receiver David Dudeck on a 21-yard pass. It was Dudeck's first catch of the game, and it was a big one—a touchdown that put his team ahead 30–24. But Knoll missed the extra point wide right! Now Penn State could win it with a touchdown and an extra point.

Facing third-and-15 early in the series, Hackenberg found James for 16 yards and a first down at the 14. Lynch got brought down for a loss, but Hackenberg got those yards back on a pass to Lewis at the 10. He then fired toward the left corner of the end zone, where Carter hauled it in for the tying touchdown. Ficken came on, nailed the extra point, and for the first time since 2010, the Nittany Lions had won a bowl game!

Hackenberg was named player of the game for setting Penn State bowl records with 371 passing yards while completing 34 of his 50 attempts. He threw for four touchdowns, all of them to different receivers. Godwin had the biggest game, catching seven passes for 140 yards and a score. Lynch was the only threat on the ground for Penn State in this game, rushing for 75 yards (the rest of the team netted just seven more yards).

Franklin gave all the credit for the win to the seniors who had stuck with the program through its darkest days and lowest moments. "Those seniors will be remembered forever," he said. "Every win that we get next season and moving forward is on their backs, and we're forever indebted to those guys."[12] There would be a lot of those wins to come!

Box Score[13]:

2014 Pinstripe Bowl	1st	2nd	3rd	4th	OT	Final
Boston College	7	0	14	3	6	30
Penn State	7	0	7	10	7	31

1st Quarter: PSU—Godwin 72 pass from Hackenberg (Ficken kick)
   BC—Hilliman 49 run (Knoll kick)
2nd Quarter: No Scoring
3rd Quarter: BC—Phillips 19 pass from Murphy (Knoll kick)
   BC—Murphy 40 run (Knoll kick)
   PSU—Lewis 7 pass from Hackenberg (Ficken kick)
4th Quarter: PSU—Hamilton 16 pass from Hackenberg (Ficken kick)
   BC—Knoll 20 FG
   PSU—Ficken 45 FG
Overtime: BC—Dudeck 21 pass from Murphy (kick missed)
   PSU—Carter 10 pass from Hackenberg (Ficken kick)

2015 Season (7–5)

The Penn State football program was still in a stage of rebuilding entering 2015. The Pinstripe Bowl victory had masked the fact that there was a long way to go before they'd be competitive again. That'd be proven by the result of their first game of the season, in Philadelphia. They went up 10–0 on Temple on a 42-yard touchdown run by running back Akeel Lynch. After that, though, everything fell apart. Quarterback Christian Hackenberg threw a key interception that aided in the Temple comeback, and the Nittany Lions never scored again in a 27–10 loss.[1]

They'd manage to beat Buffalo, although even that wasn't easy. They led by only three points in the third quarter, before running back Saquon Barkley took over the game. He rushed for 115 yards on just 12 attempts, and he scored a nine-yard touchdown to help seal the victory. The Nittany Lions came out of their home opener with a 27–14 victory that was too close for comfort.[2]

The Lions needed a weak opponent to ease them into the Big Ten schedule, and they got that in the form of Rutgers. Barkley ran for 195 yards and two touchdowns, as the Lions took a 21–0 lead at halftime. It was Barkley's best game of the season, but he wasn't alone. Lynch ran for 120 yards on just ten carries, and the Nittany Lions cruised to a 28–3 win.[3]

Their next two games were easy on paper, but not easy on the field. First, they played San Diego State at home. The Aztecs had a 14–13 lead in the first half, before fumbling away their chances. Two fumbles led to two touchdown passes by Hackenberg, and defensive tackle Austin Johnson scooped up a fumble and took it back 71 yards for a touchdown to seal a 37–24 win.[4]

Next up was Army. Their triple-option offense always creates bizarre statistics, so you could throw out the fact that Penn State allowed just one pass completion—because Army threw the ball just one time! The Nittany Lions recovered three fumbles, and that proved to be just enough, as they won 20–14.[5] Back into the Big Ten schedule, Hackenberg threw for 262 yards and two touchdowns while rushing for another two touchdowns against Indiana, going over 7,000 passing yards for his career. The Lions won 29–7 to cap off a 5–0 home record to start the season.[6]

Unfortunately, the Lions couldn't play them all in Happy Valley. They went to their house of horrors, Ohio Stadium, and the results were predictable. Ohio State rolled to a 38–10 victory. Despite that, Barkley had a great game, rushing for 194 yards, including one 56-yard run. The Lions were as close as 14 points in the fourth quarter before Ohio State put it away.[7]

The next game was held at a neutral site: Baltimore, for a meeting with the Maryland

Terrapins. Hackenberg only completed 13 passes in the game, but it was more than enough. He got 315 yards and three touchdowns on those 13 completions, breaking the school records for completions and passing yards, as Penn State won 31–30.[8]

The Lions got their first shutout in the Big Ten since 2009 and largest Big Ten win since 2008 with a 39–0 victory over Illinois. The defense allowed only 167 yards of offense and recorded four sacks. Hackenberg threw for 266 yards and two touchdowns, while also catching a 14-yard touchdown pass from running back Nick Scott. Barkley ended up with 142 all-purpose yards in the win.[9]

If the season had stopped there, it would have been considered a success for the most part. But they still had three Big Ten games left to play, and they lost all three. First came a two-point loss to Northwestern, which they nearly won. Barkley scored two touchdowns to lead the Lions back from a 13–0 deficit, and defensive end Carl Nassib set a school record with 15-and-a-half sacks on the season. Wildcats kicker Jack Mitchell made a 35-yard field goal with nine seconds to go, though, handing the Lions a 23–21 loss.[10]

Next came perennial season-spoiler Michigan. This ended up as Penn State's only home loss of the year. The mighty Wolverines prevailed, 28–16.[11] The Nittany Lions ended their season on the road, where they had zero victories on the season (their one win outside Happy Valley came at a neutral site). Hackenberg threw two touchdown but that was the only positive from this game. The Lions fell by a whopping 55–16 score, and that sparkling 7–2 start had turned into a 7–5 finish.[12]

Hackenberg ended his Penn State career with a 2,346-yard, 16-touchdown season, setting team career records in passing yards (8,457) and touchdowns (48). His top receiver was sophomore Chris Godwin, who caught 63 passes for just shy of 1,000 yards and five touchdowns. Barkley, a freshman, was the team's leading rusher with just over 1,000 yards and seven touchdowns. It had taken him little time to prove his stardom.[13]

Penn State finished in fourth place in the Big Ten East Division with a 4–4 record. East Division champion Michigan State defeated Iowa in the Big Ten Championship Game to earn a trip to Texas for the Cotton Bowl, a national semifinal game for the College Football Playoff. Iowa and Ohio State were selected to New Year's Six bowls in the Rose and Fiesta Bowls, respectively. The top two non–NY6 spots got filled by Michigan and Northwestern in the Citrus and Outback Bowls, respectively. Wisconsin got a berth in the Holiday Bowl, which ranked third in the Big Ten non–NY6 bowl hierarchy. The Nittany Lions were selected by the TaxSlayer Bowl, formerly known as the Gator Bowl, for a January bowl date. While there used to be prestige associated with both the Gator Bowl and the New Year's date, those honors had been watered down in recent years. In any case, the Lions would face Georgia, a 9–3 team from the Southeastern Conference, in the teams' first postseason meeting since the 1983 Sugar Bowl national championship game.[14]

2016 TaxSlayer Bowl

Penn State (7–5) vs. Georgia (9–3)
January 2, 2016, at EverBank Field in Jacksonville, Florida

The bowl formerly (and later) known as the Gator Bowl had NASCAR racer Dale Earnhardt, Jr., drive his car out on to the field as part of the pregame festivities. Once the game had begun, the Nittany Lions would be racing from behind for nearly the entire game. Things started out okay, with quarterback Christian Hackenberg throwing to receiver Chris Godwin for 18 yards on the first third down of the game. He then hit receiver Geno Lewis for 20 more. Receiver DaeSean Hamilton got in on the action, catching one for a first down. But on the next third down, Hackenberg had his pass go of the hands of running back Saquon Barkley and right into the arms of Georgia defensive back Dominick Sanders for an interception. That set up a 44-yard field goal by kicker Marshall Morgan that went off the right upright and through, giving Georgia a 3–0 lead.

Each team punted on its next three drives in what proved to be an offensive stalemate. The Nittany Lions got the ball back at their own 11, where Hackenberg tried scrambling for a first down. On the play, he injured his shoulder. He stayed in the game, throwing to Godwin for 19 yards. Later, on third down, he found Godwin for a 51-yard gain. The Lions got a 34-yard field goal by kicker Tyler Davis out of it, tying the game at three, but the bigger story was Hackenberg's health.

Georgia struck quickly on their next drive. Receiver Isaiah McKenzie took a handoff for a 26-yard gain, getting across the midfield stripe. Two plays later, receiver Terry Godwin took a snap out of the Wildcat formation. He launched a pass deep downfield for running back Keith Marshall, who hauled it in for a 44-yard touchdown. The Bulldogs now had a 10–3 lead.

Into the game stepped backup quarterback Trace McSorley. His story was just beginning; when he first came in, he was limited to runs and short passes. On his first two drives, the Lions failed to get a first down. Head coach James Franklin even tried a fake punt to get the offense going, but it was snuffed out. The Bulldogs used some rushes by running back Sony Michel to get down into the red zone, where Lambert fired to Terry Godwin for a 17-yard touchdown. Morgan had gotten injured earlier, so kicker Patrick Beless took over on extra points. The Bulldogs led 17–3 at the half.

Franklin took the training wheels off McSorley for the second half, with Hackenberg gone for the game and his Penn State career over. The Lions couldn't get a first down on their first drive of the second half, however, and McKenzie returned punter Daniel Pasquariello's kick 37 yards to the Penn State 21. The Nittany defense held strong, though. With Morgan out of the game, punter Collin Barber tried his first career field goal. He missed his 48-yard kick wide left, keeping the margin at 14.

McSorley completed a pass to Chris Godwin to get across the midfield stripe and a first down. Facing fourth down shortly afterward, Franklin chose to go for it, and McSorley tried a shovel pass to Barkley. It fell incomplete, and Georgia took over in great field position. Several plays later, Michel ripped off a 21-yard touchdown run where he fought off several defenders, and the Bulldogs opened up a 24–3 lead.

But that was when the McSorley magic began. He threw to Godwin for 21 yards, getting to midfield. He then carried for six, before Barkley broke off a 29-yard run. The Lions would be forced into a fourth-and-12 as the fourth quarter began. They had to go for it being down by 21, and McSorley fired a perfect pass to the right corner of the end zone to Lewis for a 17-yard touchdown. Penn State still had life, down by 14.

The Lions forced punts on both of Georgia's next two possessions. They got the ball back at their own 42, where Barkley ripped off a 20-yard run. Facing fourth-and-eight a bit later, McSorley again found Lewis, completing one for a first down to the 20. Two plays later, he fired to the end zone, where Hamilton made a spectacular catch for a 20-yard touchdown, cutting the deficit to seven.

The Bulldogs put the ball in the hands of Marshall and Michel, who pounded away to get down to near the Penn State 25. With under two minutes to go, the Lions forced a fourth-and-two. With their kicker injured, Georgia decided to go for it. Marshall couldn't make it, getting stuffed, and the Nittany Lions took over with no timeouts, down by seven.

Penn State again faced a fourth down, and again McSorley converted it, finding Hamilton for a first down at the 42. He threw to Barkley for five yards, and the clock ran down under 30 seconds. With yet another fourth down to go, McSorley ran for the first down to the Georgia 39. He spiked the ball with eight seconds to go, leaving time for one Hail Mary. He put it up high, but the Bulldogs batted it away. The valiant Penn State comeback had come up just short, in a 24–17 loss.

McSorley threw for 142 yards and two touchdowns while playing only slightly more than a half. The Hackenberg era was over, and the McSorley era had begun. Yes, the Lions had lost the TaxSlayer Bowl, but they had a new star at quarterback. Over the next three years, McSorley would lead the Nittany Lions to one of the most successful three-year runs in school history.

Box Score[15]:

2016 TaxSlayer Bowl	1st	2nd	3rd	4th	Final
Penn State	0	3	0	14	17
Georgia	3	14	7	0	24

1st Quarter: UGA—Morgan 44 FG
2nd Quarter: PSU—Davis 34 FG
    UGA—Marshall 44 pass from T. Godwin (Morgan kick)
    UGA—T. Godwin 17 pass from Lambert (Beless kick)
3rd Quarter: UGA—Michel 21 run (Beless kick)
4th Quarter: PSU—Lewis 17 pass from McSorley (Davis kick)
    PSU—Hamilton 20 pass from McSorley (Davis kick)

2016 Season (11–2)

The 2016 season was the season where Penn State came "back." The Nittany Lions started with a 33–13 win over Kent State. Quarterback Trace McSorley, now firmly entrenched as the starter, threw for 209 yards and two touchdowns, to receiver DaeSean Hamilton and tight end Mike Gesicki. The Lions blew open a 16–13 game in the third quarter when defensive back Amani Oruwariye took back an interception 30 yards for a touchdown.[1]

The Penn State–Pitt series was back for the first time since 2000, and this one proved to be a thriller. Running back Saquon Barkley ran for five touchdowns, the first Penn State player to put up 30 points in a single game since Ki-Jana Carter in 1994. However, even with McSorley throwing for 332 yards, the Lions weren't able to come all the way back from a 21-point deficit, as they fell 42–39.[2]

Receiver Chris Godwin racked up 111 receiving yards against Temple, who hung tight with the Lions for much of the game. Barkley ran for a 55-yard touchdown with seven minutes to go to clinch a 34–27 win. But the season looked completely lost in Ann Arbor, as all three starting linebackers were injured, and the Lions were crushed 49–10 by Michigan.[3]

The season turned around against Minnesota. With the Golden Gophers up by three late in the fourth quarter, McSorley led a 53-yard drive to set up a 40-yard field goal by kicker Tyler Davis to tie the game on the fourth quarter's final play. The Lions won the toss and chose to play defense. After yielding a field goal, Barkley ran 25 yards on the only overtime play for PSU, scoring the winning touchdown in a 29–26 triumph.[4]

The Lions cruised to an easy victory over Maryland. They put up 524 yards of offense, their most in three years. McSorley ran for 81 yards and a touchdown, while Barkley rushed for 202 yards and a score. Both numbers were career highs. McSorley also threw a pair of touchdown passes, one of them being a 70-yard bomb to receiver DeAndre Thompkins. The Lions won 38–14 to set up a huge showdown with Ohio State.[5]

The Buckeyes came in ranked #2 in the nation. But there was something to these "White Out" games. This time, the Buckeyes took a 14-point lead into the fourth quarter, before the Nittany Lions roared back. McSorley ran for a touchdown and Davis kicked a field goal, making it a four-point game. The Buckeyes went for a field goal to try to put away the win. Defensive back Grant Haley blocked the kick, which his teammate Marcus Allen returned 60 yards for a touchdown with four minutes to go. The Lions then stopped Ohio State to put away a 24–21 win.[6]

Purdue played Penn State tight for a half, with the score tied at 17 when the teams went to their locker rooms. The Lions came back out and outscored the Boilermakers by a 45–7 margin. Barkley set a new career high with 207 rushing yards, while also gaining

70 yards through the air. He was the first Penn State running back to rush for 200 yards twice in the same season since 2002, as the Lions won 62–24.[7]

Barkley went over 200 all-purpose yards again the next week, when Penn State beat Iowa 41–14. The Lions put up 599 yards of offense, their most in any game since 1995. Indiana proved to be a tougher challenge, as the Lions fell behind by ten in the third quarter. McSorley then led the team back with 332 passing yards and three total touchdowns. The Hoosiers managed to hold Barkley to just 58 yards, but he still scored two fourth-quarter touchdowns in Penn State's 45–31 win. Rutgers proved to be a pushover, totaling 87 yards and five first downs, as the Lions beat them 39–0. Davis kicked four field goals, and running back Mark Allen caught a 27-yard touchdown pass.[8]

Now the Nittany Lions could reach the Big Ten Championship Game, but only with help. They needed Ohio State to beat Michigan early on Saturday. Ohio State won "The Game," and the Lions could now get into the title game with a win over Michigan State. They did just that, with McSorley throwing for 376 yards and four touchdowns. The Spartans led 12–10 at the half, but as was a common theme this season, Penn State stampeded them in the second half on their way to a 45–12 triumph.[9]

It was off to Indianapolis to face Wisconsin in the Big Ten title game. This time, the Nittany Lions fell into a 28–7 hole. But as usual, they stormed back to victory. Hamilton caught eight passes for 118 yards, while receiver Saeed Blacknall put up six catches for 155 yards and a couple of scores. McSorley threw for 384 yards and four touchdowns, both Big Ten Championship Game records. Barkley scored the go-ahead touchdown on an 18-yard reception in the fourth quarter, and the Lions won it, 38–31.[10]

Penn State was Big Ten champion for the first time since 2008. Unlike 2005 and 2008, this time the Nittany Lions were sole champions of the conference, having been tied for first place those two years by Buckeye teams that they defeated. Barkley was named Big Ten Offensive Player of the Year by rushing for over 1,300 yards and 16 touchdowns. Receiver Chris Godwin caught 50 passes for nine touchdowns, with Gesicki right behind him with 47 catches. McSorley threw 25 touchdown passes as opposed to just five interceptions.[11] This offense was by far the best since 2008's "Spread HD" offense.

But there would be no trip to the College Football Playoff for the Nittany Lions. They finished #5 in the final CFP rankings, behind #1 Alabama, #2 Clemson, #3 Ohio State, and #4 Washington.

Rose Bowl tickets, 2017. Author's collection.

The Buckeye selection was a real sticking point with Penn State fans, since the Lions had beaten them. Alas, the blowout loss to Michigan was too much for PSU to overcome in the rankings. Of note, the Buckeyes were shut out in the CFP Semifinal at the Fiesta Bowl; Penn State would score many more points than zero in the Rose Bowl. That game, the Granddaddy of Them All, was the Lions' destination as Big Ten champions.

2017 Rose Bowl

#5 Penn State (11–2) vs. #9 USC (9–3)
January 2, 2017, at the Rose Bowl in Pasadena, California

For the third time in their four Rose Bowl appearances, the Nittany Lions were going up against the University of Southern California. This time, USC hadn't won the Pacific-12 Conference, or even the Pac-12 South Division. But since Washington was selected to the College Football Playoff, USC was the highest remaining Pac-12 team, so they got the Rose Bowl berth. They also came into the bowl on fire; Penn State had won nine in a row, and the Trojans had won eight straight.

After Rose Parade Grand Marshal Janet Evans tossed the coin, the Nittany Lions won the toss and chose to receive. It was a disastrous decision. Running back Miles Sanders misjudged the opening kickoff and let it bounce; he fell on it at his own 3. Quarterback Trace McSorley and receiver DeAndre Thompkins had a bit of confusion on the first play; Thompkins broke off his pattern too soon, and McSorley's pass ended up being intercepted by defensive back Iman Marshall. Fortunately for the Lions, their defense forced a three-and-out, and USC kicker Matt Boermeester missed a 51-yard field goal.

Running back Saquon Barkley took both of his first two carries for first downs, and the Lions reached the USC 43. But Thompkins and McSorley again were not on the same page, and McSorley's pass was too early. Thompkins had it go off his hands into the arms

Penn State band performing before 2017 Rose Bowl. Author's collection.

of defensive back Adoree' Jackson. It took USC just five plays to take advantage, as quarterback Sam Darnold found receiver JuJu Smith-Schuster for a first down inside the 30, and receiver Deontay Burnett for a 26-yard touchdown over the middle.

McSorley continued to struggle to start the game. He threw two incompletions, and Penn State punted. USC moved the ball easily again, with Smith-Schuster catching an eight-yard pass, and Darnold finding receiver Darreus Rogers for a first down. Running back Justin Davis hauled in a pass for 14 yards, and Jackson came in on offense to run the ball down to the 4. The USC drive ended there, but Boermeester made a 22-yard field goal to go up by ten.

After an incompletion and a punt on the next drive, McSorley was 0-for-5. Meanwhile, the Trojans were moving the ball again. Running back Ronald Jones ran for a first down, and Darnold found tight end Daniel Imatorbhebhe for another new set of downs. USC then ran a flea flicker, with Darnold completing to receiver Jalen Greene for a first down to the 26. Three incompletions later, Boermeester made a 43-yard field goal to give USC a 13–0 lead at the end of one quarter.

McSorley completed a pass on the final play of the first quarter to snap his streak of incompletions. He then converted a third down as the second quarter began on a pass to receiver Chris Godwin. Barkley was tackled for a loss of five, but then McSorley rolled out and found Godwin for a first down at the USC 45. Barkley hauled in a pass for 17 more yards, and running back Andre Robinson ran for four more. Barkley then took a handoff up the middle and went 24 yards to put Penn State on the board.

The Lions kicked it short, and USC got the ball to start at their 42. Darnold immediately went over the middle for Burnett, who got a first down at the 28. Davis took a carry, broke a tackle, and he ran it down inside the 5. Darnold then threw a pass to Burnett in the flat, and he went for a three-yard touchdown. While the officials originally called pass interference on USC for a pick, they overturned it after seeing on replay that Burnett caught the pass behind the line of scrimmage. Penn State fans didn't like it, but it was the right call, and it put USC up 20–7.

It took just four plays for the Lions to answer. McSorley went long downfield for Godwin, who hauled it in for a first down at the USC 41. Barkley ran for ten more yards on his next carry. Two plays later, McSorley went deep down the right sideline for Godwin, who got a foot down inside the right sideline of the end zone. Replays were inconclusive, making this play stand for a 30-yard touchdown.

Back and forth the teams went. Darnold threw to Rogers for a first down at the 39, then he went long for Smith-Schuster to get to the 26. A few plays later, Darnold hit Rogers down the left sideline to make it 27–14. But the Lions answered. McSorley fired to Godwin for three first downs on the ensuing drive, then finished the drive with a pass to tight end Mike Gesicki in the right side of the end zone to cut the USC lead back to six.

Unfortunately for the Lions, USC had a minute to go, which was too much time. Darnold threw to Rogers for a first down at the 40, then he scrambled to the Penn State 43 for another new set of downs. After going to Burnett to get to about the 31, the Trojans had time for a field goal try. Boermeester missed this one barely to the right, though, and Penn State went to the half only down by a touchdown. "We hate first halves," PSU head coach James Franklin said going into the locker room.[12]

But the Lions loved third quarters. After forcing the first USC punt of the game, the Lions took over at their own 21. Barkley took a handoff that was designed to go up the middle. He bounced it outside, then cut back to the left. Breaking a tackle, he broke into the clear, and soon he was off for a 79-yard touchdown. With kicker Tyler Davis's extra point, the Lions took their first lead of the game.

Penn State got called for pass interference once on the next drive, before they forced another punt. They got the ball back at their own 28. This time McSorley launched one down the left sideline, and Godwin hauled it in for a 72-yard touchdown. If that wasn't enough, linebacker Brandon Bell intercepted a tipped pass on USC's next possession. He returned it to the 3. McSorley ran it in on the next play for Penn State's fourth touchdown in their last four offensive plays. The Nittany Lions held a 15-point lead, and it looked like this one was going to get out of reach.

Unfortunately for PSU fans, Darnold was the quarterback on the other sideline. He was just too good. He completed a pass to Rogers for a first down at the 48, then he threw a screen to running back Aca'cedric Ware for another fresh set of downs at the Penn State 32. Jones picked up a first down on the ground, and Davis ran for another nine yards. Darnold then found Smith-Schuster in the end zone for a touchdown. The Trojans went for two in a most unique formation, with most of their players lined up near the left side-line. Darnold took the snap and rolled right, on what appeared to be a designed run. He then stopped and threw back to tight end Taylor McNamara for the two points.

But Penn State wasn't done scoring in the third quarter. Barkley took a pass to the 38, then the Lions got two first downs on personal foul flags. The first came on a McSorley run, where defensive back Chris Hawkins hit him late. The second one was on an incom-pletion, where linebacker Cameron Smith was called for targeting and ejected from the game. Barkley followed that with a run for a first down to the 7. He then hauled in a touchdown pass in the right side of the end zone, and Penn State led 49–35 going into the final quarter.

When USC punted on their next possession, this game looked to be over. The Penn State offense had seven touchdowns on their last seven drives, and it looked like they couldn't be stopped. But for some reason, whether it was conservative play-calling, better focus by the Trojans, or simply lack of execution, the Lions ended up not scoring a single point in the fourth quarter. That wasn't going to do it against Darnold.

The Lions nearly got a turnover on a third-down play when Darnold threw a pass right into coverage. However, it was deflected to Smith-Schuster, who picked up a first down. Burnett caught one for 20 more yards, and Jones ran off right tackle for seven more. After Jones moved the chains on a run, Darnold threw down the right sideline for Smith-Schuster. He was initially ruled out of bounds, but replays showed that he got a foot in bounds at the 3. After being awarded the play, USC scored on a three-yard run by Jones.

The teams traded punts, and Penn State got the ball back at their own 25 needing one first down to seal a victory. On third-and-four with just over two minutes to play, Franklin called for a run by Barkley, but USC was ready for it. The Trojans tackled him for a huge loss, and Penn State had to punt again. Darnold then took under a minute to go 80 yards. He threw to Smith-Schuster and Imatorbhebhe for first downs, before Penn State got called for pass interference on two plays in a row. Darnold then went over the middle to Burnett for his Rose Bowl record-setting fifth touchdown pass, and the Trojans tied it at 49.

With a minute to go in the fourth quarter, the Lions went from ultra-conservative to super-aggressive. McSorley twice threw deep downfield into coverage, and both times USC defensive back Leon McQuay got his hands on the ball. The first time he dropped

USC band performing before 2017 Rose Bowl. Author's collection.

it, but the second time he picked it off in front of Godwin. He then returned it to the Penn State 30. After a USC run to set up a field goal, Penn State fans hoped that the kick with five seconds left would be a repeat of the Ohio State kick—a block and a return for a touchdown. It was not to be. Boermeester made the 46-yard attempt, and the Lions lost a heartbreaker, 52–49.

It was a record-setting day on both sides, as the two teams set the record for the most points in a Rose Bowl. While that record was broken the following year, it remains the record for the most points in a regulation game. McSorley was responsible for five touchdowns, tying a Rose Bowl record along with Darnold. He threw for 254 yards and four scores, though he also threw three interceptions. Barkley ran for 194 yards and two scores while also catching five passes for 55 yards and a touchdown. Godwin lit it up with nine catches for 187 yards and a pair of scores. It was a truly electric game.

The Nittany Lions had nothing to be ashamed of in losing this Rose Bowl. They finished the season ranked #7 in the Associated Press poll at 11–3. They had gone from oblivion to the Granddaddy of Them All in just a few short years. Plus, McSorley and Barkley were only sophomores. They were coming back for another run at a New Year's Six bowl game.

Box score[13]:

2017 Rose Bowl	1st	2nd	3rd	4th	Final
USC	13	14	8	17	52
Penn State	0	21	28	0	49

1st Quarter: USC—Burnett 26 pass from Darnold (Boermeester kick)
    USC—Boermeester 22 FG
    USC—Boermeester 44 FG
2nd Quarter: PSU—Barkley 24 run (Davis kick)
    USC—Burnett 3 pass from Darnold (Boermeester kick)

PSU—Godwin 30 pass from McSorley (Davis kick)

USC—Rogers 3 pass from Darnold (Boermeester kick)

PSU—Gesicki 11 pass from McSorley (Davis kick)

3rd Quarter: PSU—Barkley 79 run (Davis kick)

PSU—Godwin 72 pass from McSorley (Davis kick)

PSU—McSorley 3 run (Davis kick)

USC—Smith-Schuster 13 pass from Darnold (McNamara pass from Darnold)

PSU—Barkley 7 pass from McSorley (Davis kick)

4th Quarter: USC—Jones 3 run (Boermeester kick)

USC—Burnett 27 pass from Darnold (Boermeester kick)

USC—Boermeester 46 FG

2017 Season (10–2)

Coming off their Big Ten championship, there were high hopes for the Nittany Lions in 2017. The first game of the season gave no reason to doubt those. The Lions beat Akron 52–0, with running back Saquon Barkley rushing for 172 yards and two touchdowns. Quarterback Trace McSorley passed for 280 yards and two touchdowns to tight end Mike Gesicki.[1]

Nearly 110,000 fans came out to Beaver Stadium for the Nittany Lions' revenge meeting with Pitt. Barkley put up 183 all-purpose yards, while McSorley threw two touchdown passes to Gesicki in the first quarter. In the second half, McSorley found Barkley for a 46-yard touchdown. Pitt pulled back within 14 in the fourth quarter, but defensive back Marcus Allen forced a safety to set up a 24-yard field goal by kicker Tyler Davis that put away a 33–14 victory.[2]

Next came Georgia State, who provided little resistance in a 56–0 blowout. Barkley caught the longest pass by a Penn Stater in Beaver Stadium history, an 85-yarder for a touchdown. McSorley threw for a school-record 258 first-half yards, going for three touchdowns. Eight different players scored Penn State's eight touchdowns.[3]

The next game came down to the wire. Iowa took a 19–15 lead with 1:42 to go, and it looked like the unbeaten season was over. But McSorley took over at his own 20 and led a 12-play, 80-yard march. Twice the Lions faced fourth down, and twice they converted. The first one was an eight-yard pass to Barkley on fourth-and-two, and the second came with four seconds left from the 7. McSorley fired a pass to receiver Juwan Johnson in the back of the end zone for six points, and the Nittany Lions won 21–19 as time expired.[4]

The Lions had easy assignments the next two weeks, starting with Indiana. Barkley began the game by returning the kickoff 98 yards for a touchdown, his first career return score. He later threw a 16-yard touchdown pass to DaeSean Hamilton, who had three touchdown catches on 122 receiving yards. The Lions led 28–0 at the end of the fourth quarter, making the 45–14 win a breeze.[5] Barkley scored two touchdowns against Northwestern, who managed to keep the Lions offense in check. However, the Nittany defense didn't allow a score until under two minutes to go in the game, with Penn State already up 31–0. The 31–7 win made Penn State 6–0 headed into their big game with Michigan.[6]

The Lions got sweet revenge against the Wolverines in front of the most fans in Beaver Stadium history (110,823). Although Michigan hung around for a half, ultimately the duo of McSorley and Barkley was too much. Barkley put up 161 scrimmage yards and scored three touchdowns, including a 69-yard run. McSorley totaled 358 yards of offense and four touchdowns, three of them coming on the ground. The Nittany Lions didn't let up until the very end, winning this game 42–13 and moving to 7–0 going into an even bigger game against Ohio State.[7]

It was #2 Penn State against #6 Ohio State at the Horseshoe for likely the Big Ten East title, not to mention a possible College Football Playoff berth. Barkley returned the opening kickoff 97 yards for a touchdown, then scored on a 36-yard run as the Lions took a 21–3 second-quarter lead. McSorley threw for two touchdowns and ran for another, as Penn State led by 15 at the end of the third quarter. But very much like the Rose Bowl, the Lions folded in the fourth quarter. The Buckeyes got three touchdowns in the final stanza to beat Penn State 39–38 and ruin the Lions' undefeated season.[8]

Now ranked #7, the Nittany Lions were clearly better than the #24 Michigan State Spartans, but two things beat them: Ohio State and the weather. The Lions suffered a hangover from the Ohio State loss, never asserting their dominance against Sparty. Halfway through the second quarter, bad thunderstorms caused a weather delay of over three hours. Michigan State hung around long enough to tie the game in the fourth quarter and then beat the Lions 27–24 on a last-second, 34-yard field goal.[9]

The Lions fell behind Rutgers 6–0 early, but they dominated after that. Barkley only ran for 35 yards, but he scored two touchdowns. He also set the school record for most career all-purpose yards, as Penn State won 35–6.[10] The next week, Nebraska and Penn State combined for 100 points in their meeting at Beaver Stadium, but the score was deceiving. The Nittany Lions led 42–10 at halftime, as they racked up over 600 yards of offense, their most since 1995. McSorley threw for 325 yards and three touchdowns, while Barkley ran for 158 yards and three scores. The Lions called off the dogs with a 56–31 lead, at which point the Cornhuskers scored a couple of garbage touchdowns in the final seconds to make the final score 56–44.[11]

The season ended at Maryland, with Penn State setting a record for their biggest margin of victory in their Big Ten history. They beat the Terrapins by 63 points, clinching the victory by halftime with a 31–0 lead. Backup quarterback Tommy Stevens got a lot of playing time, running for 113 yards and scoring three touchdowns. Barkley and Gesicki also got into the end zone twice in a 66–3 victory.[12]

McSorley threw for 3,228 yards on 252 completions in 2017, third-most in team history. His completion percentage of .653 was the second-highest in school history behind only Kerry Collins in 1994. Barkley, the Big Ten Offensive Player of the Year, put up the second-most all-purpose yards in Penn State annals with 2,154, trailing only Larry Johnson's near-Heisman year of 2002. He had the most all-purpose yards in a game (358 vs. Iowa) and in his career (5,363) in school history. The tandem of McSorley and Barkley was clearly one of the greatest to ever play in Happy Valley together.[13]

Slotted at #9 in the College Football Playoff rankings, the Nittany Lions were guaranteed a berth into one of the New Year's Six bowls. The only question was which it would be. It couldn't be the Rose or the Sugar, as those were the playoff bowls. It likely wouldn't be the Peach, either, since one spot belonged to the best Group of Five team (UCF). Penn State fans were expecting to be headed to Arlington, Texas for the Goodyear Cotton Bowl, but they got a surprise when the Lions were instead invited to the PlayStation Fiesta Bowl in Arizona. The Lions would go up against the Washington Huskies, the team who nudged them out for the final spot in the CFP the year before and promptly got embarrassed by Alabama in the Chick-fil-A Peach Bowl. It would be the Lions' seventh visit to the Fiesta Bowl and the first since the bowl moved into the climate-controlled setting of University of Phoenix Stadium.[14]

2017 Fiesta Bowl

#9 Penn State (10–2) vs. #12 Washington (10–2)
December 30, 2017, at University of Phoenix Stadium in Glendale, Arizona

Running back Saquon Barkley could have skipped this bowl game, as several other top draft prospects had in recent years. Instead, he chose to play, and he made an immediate impact on the offense. On the initial third down of the game, he took a catch behind the line to gain and found a way to pick up the first down. After an eight-yard run by quarterback Trace McSorley, Barkley pounded right up the middle for 13 yards. McSorley threw to receiver Juwan Johnson for five yards, though a pass to backup quarterback Tommy Stevens didn't advance the ball. On third-and-eight, McSorley launched one toward the goal line for receiver DaeSean Hamilton. He hauled it in for a 48-yard touchdown, and Penn State took the early 7–0 lead.

The Lions forced a quick three-and-out. McSorley converted another third down with a pass over the middle to tight end Mike Gesicki at the Washington 45. He then went long for the end zone, but defensive back Byron Murphy picked it off and got one foot in bounds. The Nittany defense went back out and stopped the Huskies on three plays, including a sack by defensive tackle Tyrell Chavis. Penn State got the ball back at their own 36.

McSorley ran for a first down and slid feet first, hoping to avoid a hit. He got nailed anyway, and for some inexplicable reason, the officials chose not to throw a flag. McSorley shook it off, throwing to Hamilton for a first down to the Washington 40. He then hit receiver Saeed Blacknall for a first down, before Barkley picked up eight more off left tackle. A pair of passes to Gesicki got the Lions down to the 2, where Barkley pushed in for a touchdown and a 14–0 lead after one quarter.

Washington answered nicely, using a trick play. Quarterback Jake Browning set up the double pass by throwing the ball backward to receiver Andre Baccellia. He then launched one downfield to tight end Will Dissly for a gain of 52. Browning found running back Myles Gaskin for a first down at the 1, then he kept the ball himself for a touchdown to cut the Nittany lead to seven.

McSorley converted another third down to start the next drive, this one a pass to Gesicki for a first down into Washington territory to the 46. He hit Johnson for 11 more yards, then lofted one long for receiver DeAndre Thompkins. He caught it for 34 yards, setting up running back Miles Sanders for a one-yard plunge up the middle. The Lions were back out in front by 14.

Washington got the ball near midfield on a 26-yard pass from Browning to receiver Dante Pettis. They'd face a fourth-and-four shortly afterward, and instead of going for it from beyond midfield, Washington head coach Chris Petersen had Browning perform a quick kick. That pinned the Lions back inside their own 10, but who cares about field position when you've got Barkley? He took a handoff down the left sideline 92 yards for the longest run in both Fiesta Bowl history and Penn State bowl history. He jumped as he crossed the goal line, far out in front from any Washington defender. The Nittany Lions now had a 28–7 advantage.

Penn State forced another punt thanks to a sack by defensive tackle Kevin Givens. They could have ended the game for all intents and purposes had they scored on the next drive. Instead, though, McSorley tried a pitch to Sanders which resulted in a fumble. Defensive lineman Shane Bowman recovered for Washington at the Penn State 33. Six plays later, Gaskin took a snap from the Wildcat formation for a 13-yard touchdown, and the Penn State lead was just 14 at the half.

Washington started the second half with a long drive, starting at their own 20. Browning threw eight passes on the drive as the Huskies marched it down the field. One of his passes in Penn State territory was caught by a Nittany Lion, or rather, *the* Nittany Lion, the mascot. He recovered from that "interception" to throw a 28-yard touchdown pass to receiver Aaron Fuller, and suddenly the Huskies were back within a touchdown.

Starting at his 30, McSorley got back that touchdown. He ran for 26 yards on a second-down carry, and he found Johnson on a third down for a fresh set of downs at the Washington 30. Barkley ran for five yards, and McSorley got another one, before the big play. This time McSorley went over the top to Hamilton, and he hauled it in for his second touchdown of the day. The Lions led 35–21 going into the final quarter.

Defensive end Shareef Miller sacked Browning to end Washington's next possession. The Lions could have put the final nail in the coffin on their next drive. McSorley got them into position to do so, throwing to Gesicki, Hamilton, and Johnson for a first down each. On a fourth-and-six, McSorley hit Barkley on the left sideline, and he hurdled to get the first down. However, with the ball squarely in the red zone, McSorley had a pass batted in the air and intercepted by defensive back Austin Joyner. Washington was still breathing.

The teams exchanged punts, and Washington took over at their own 21. After a sack by defensive end Yetur Gross-Matos, the Huskies looked to be out of luck. However, on third down, Gaskin burst through the line up the middle and into the secondary. He could not be caught, as he went 69 yards for a touchdown. Kicker Tristan Vizcaino made the extra point barely inside the left upright to cut the Penn State advantage back down to seven.

It was time for the four-minute offense, and Penn State ran it to perfection, moving the chains on third downs. McSorley hit Johnson on a third down for a new set of downs at the 40. Barkley ran for the next Penn State first down on third down, and McSorley converted yet another third down with a pass to Hamilton. The Huskies were exhausted of timeouts, and probably exhausted on the field as well. With 38 seconds left, PSU finally failed on a third down, as Barkley came up just short of the line to gain on his final carry at Penn State. Head coach James Franklin sent out the offense to pick up that one yard to win the game, but a false start changed his plans. He then sent out kicker Tyler Davis for a 45-yard field goal, but it missed wide to the right. Washington would have one last chance with 34 seconds to go.

The Penn State defense confused Browning, as he threw three incompletions and the clock trickled down to 15 seconds. On fourth-and-ten, Washington ran the old hook-and-lateral. Fuller caught the pass and lateraled to Pettis, who had some room down the right sideline. But instead of stepping out of bounds near the Penn State 35 with five seconds to go, he decided to lateral again. This one was intercepted by linebacker Brandon Smith, and the game was over.

McSorley was named Offensive Player of the Game for his performance, as he passed for 342 yards and two touchdowns, completing 32 out of 41 attempts. He also ran for 60 yards on 12 carries. Defensive back Marcus Allen recorded seven tackles and was named Defensive Player of the Game. Barkley didn't get a trophy, but he had rushed for 137 yards and two touchdowns while catching seven passes for another 38 yards. His legacy in Nittany Lion lore was set in stone.[15]

The Lions finished the season #8, moving up above Peach Bowl loser Auburn and Cotton Bowl loser USC. They conceded a spot to UCF, who won the Peach Bowl to finish undefeated and claimed to be the real national champions instead of Alabama. There were too many times to count that Penn State could have claimed a national title, such as in 1968, 1969, 1973, and 1994; Penn State's national title count should be set as six. Regardless of who the national champion was, this was one very special Penn State team, which finished 11–2.

Box score[16]:

2017 Fiesta Bowl	*1st*	*2nd*	*3rd*	*4th*	*Final*
Washington	0	14	7	7	28
Penn State	14	14	7	0	35

1st Quarter: PSU—Hamilton 48 pass from McSorley (Davis kick)
    PSU—Barkley 2 run (Davis kick)
2nd Quarter: WASH—Browning 1 run (Vizcaino kick)
    PSU—Sanders 1 run (Vizcaino kick)
    PSU—Barkley 92 run (Davis kick)
    WASH—Gaskin 13 run (Vizcaino kick)
3rd Quarter: WASH—Fuller 28 pass from Browning (Vizcaino kick)
    PSU—Hamilton 24 pass from McSorley (Davis kick)
4th Quarter: WASH—Gaskin 69 run (Vizcaino kick)

2018 Season (9–3)

Coming off two straight New Year's Six appearances, hopes were high for the Nittany Lions entering 2018, even with Saquon Barkley having gone pro. But the entire season almost went up in flames in Week 1 against Appalachian State. The Lions trailed 38–31 with less than two minutes to go. That was when quarterback Trace McSorley drove his team 52 yards, finishing the drive with a 15-yard touchdown pass to receiver K.J. Hamler to tie the game. In overtime, running back Miles Sanders ran four times for 25 yards and a touchdown, and defensive back Amani Oruwariye picked off a pass to clinch a 45–38 victory.[1]

The Lions went to Heinz Field next, where they washed out Pitt in a rainstorm, 51–6. Sanders had his first 100-yard rushing game, as the Lions ripped off 44 unanswered points in beating Pitt by the most points since 1968. They'd repeat the blowout process against Kent State. McSorley totaled 283 yards and five touchdowns passing and rushing combined. In the fourth quarter of the 63–10 win, backup quarterback Sean Clifford threw a 95-yard touchdown pass to receiver Daniel George, the longest play from scrimmage in Penn State history.[2]

In a Friday night special, Penn State crushed Illinois 63–24. The Lions actually blew a 21–7 lead, falling behind 24–21 in the third quarter. But Sanders rushed for 200 yards and three touchdowns, as the Lions scored 42 unanswered points to put away the win. McSorley completed 12 of his 19 passes for 160 yards and three touchdowns, as Penn State went over 50 points for an unprecedented third straight week.[3]

But the season fell on hard times the next two weeks. McSorley totaled 461 yards of offense at home against Ohio State, throwing for 286 yards and rushing for another 175. It was not enough, though. Ohio State came back from a 12-point deficit to beat the Lions, 27–26. A week later, Michigan State came into Beaver Stadium and defeated Penn State by a 21–17 margin. The Lions had a three-point lead with 90 seconds to go, but Sparty drove 76 yards for the winning score.[4]

McSorley went over 10,000 career yards of offense against Indiana, as he threw for 220 yards and rushed for another 107. Running back Johnathan Thomas returned a kickoff 94 yards to set up a touchdown, as the Lions defeated the Hoosiers 33–28. Iowa proved to be another challenge, staying within a touchdown as well. Lions defensive back Nick Scott picked off a pass late in the game to preserve a 30–24 victory.[5]

But things got ugly in the Big House. Michigan absolutely dominated Penn State in every facet of the game. They limited the Lions to just 186 yards on offense and stole the ball away three times. Meanwhile, the Wolverines put up six touchdowns. Only a late touchdown run by backup quarterback Tommy Stevens allowed the Lions to avoid a shutout, in a 42–7 loss.[6]

The defense had a point to prove down the stretch, to let everyone know that the Michigan game was a fluke. The Lions allowed a mere 20 points in the final three games combined. Wisconsin hadn't been held to ten points since 2016, but that's all they got, as Penn State beat them 22–10. Rutgers was a feisty opponent, bogging down the Nittany offense, but the Lions eventually got enough to pull out a 20–7 win. Finally, Maryland was a pushover, as McSorley broke the Penn State career completion record with his 703rd in a 38–3 triumph.[7]

This season was all about McSorley. While his numbers were actually down from the last two years, he didn't have Barkley in the backfield as an option this year. He still threw for 2,284 yards and 16 touchdowns, setting numerous career records, too many to list. He also ran for 723 yards and 11 scores. Sanders did a great job stepping into Barkley's shoes, rushing for 1,223 yards and nine touchdowns. Hamler led the team in receiving with 41 catches for 713 yards. He had five touchdown receptions, two shy of tight end Pat Freiermuth.[8]

The Nittany Lions finished one spot in the College Football Playoff rankings away from a New Year's Six bowl. They finished #12 in the CFP rankings (#13 in the Associated Press poll), just behind Florida and LSU. Those two teams got Peach and Fiesta Bowl invites, respectively. While Penn State finished ahead of #15 Texas, the Longhorns got an automatic bid to the Sugar Bowl as the top-ranked Big 12 team not in the College Football Playoff. That meant that the Lions got the top bowl for Big Ten teams outside the NY6. They were headed to Orlando to play in the VRBO Citrus Bowl against #14 Kentucky.

2019 Citrus Bowl

#13 Penn State (9–3) vs. #16 Kentucky (9–3)
January 1, 2019, at Camping World Stadium in Orlando, Florida

This was quarterback Trace McSorley's final game as a Nittany Lion, and it went much like his first bowl appearance. In that one, he came off the bench to replace Christian Hackenberg, who was injured in the TaxSlayer Bowl. McSorley nearly led his team back to win. Here, in this one, he'd get injured himself, but he'd come back in and lead another late comeback.

The Lions started the game by going three-and-out. Head coach James Franklin ran a fake punt, but it backfired badly, as the upback was tackled short of the first down marker. Kentucky got one first down on a run by running back Benny Snell. After that, the Lions made a stop, so kicker Miles Butler came on and kicked a 28-yard field goal to put the Wildcats up 3–0.

McSorley quickly led the Lions back for a kick of their own. He completed a long pass over the middle to receiver DeAndre Thompkins, setting up Penn State in field goal range. Top NFL prospect defensive end Josh Allen sacked him on a third down, forcing kicker Jake Pinegar to try a 40-yard kick. He missed it wide right, and Penn State remained at zero.

The teams traded three-and-outs. Penn State's was more devastating, however, because of what happened after it. They had to punt from their own end zone, and receiver Lynn Bowden returned it 58 yards for a Kentucky touchdown. With Butler's extra point, the Wildcats led by a 10–0 score at the end of one quarter.

McSorley started his team's next drive with a nine-yard run. He followed that with a sprint to midfield for a first down. Running back Miles Sanders ran for eight more yards. McSorley then fired to receiver K.J. Hamler, who made defenders miss on a catch-and-run down to the 1. The drive finished with McSorley throwing a one-yard touchdown pass to tight end Nick Bowers to pull Penn State within three.

Defensive end Shareef Miller picked up a sack of Kentucky quarterback Terry Wilson, and the Lions got the ball back after a punt at their own 49. McSorley took the first snap forward for a 16-yard gain, then running back Ricky Slade picked up another first down inside the 25. Another sack ended this drive, though, and Pinegar's field goal attempt was blocked. The Nittany Lions went to the half trailing, 10–7.

Snell broke off a big run to start the half, going from his own 35 to the Penn State 33. Wilson found Bowden for a first down, with a personal foul giving Kentucky more yards. He ran it himself to get down to the 2, then Snell took it in off the left side for a touchdown. The Wildcats took a 17–7 lead with that score.

The bigger problem for Penn State right now was the health of McSorley. He didn't come back into the game on the next possession; instead, backup Sean Clifford came in. Sanders ran for one first down before the Lions had to punt; Clifford threw only one pass, which fell incomplete. Once Kentucky got the ball back, another pass to Bowden coupled with a personal foul flag got the Wildcats deep in Penn State territory. Butler made another 28-yard field goal, and Kentucky now led 20–7.

McSorley talked to his parents on the sideline, presumably to let them know that he was going back into the game, injured or not. He went long on his first pass back in the game, but defensive back Lonnie Johnson picked it off and returned it to the 35. Wilson then hit Bowden on a 57-yard catch-and-run, setting up a 12-yard touchdown run by Snell that put Kentucky up by 20 at the end of three quarters.

But McSorley wasn't about to let this one get away. He threw to receiver Justin Shorter for a first down, before running for a fresh set of downs himself. He then hit Thompkins for a 24-yard gain down to the 3. After Slade got the ball down within a yard of the end zone, McSorley plowed up the middle for a touchdown to cut the deficit to 13.

The Penn State defense forced a quick three-and-out, and back came the Lions down the field. McSorley completed a third-and-18 pass to receiver Jahan Dotson for 24 yards to the Kentucky 44. He followed that with a pass for a first down to tight end Pat Freiermuth. Two plays later, he went back to Freiermuth, who crossed the right pylon for a touchdown to pull the Lions within six.

The Nittany comeback continued when the defense forced another three-and-out. McSorley hit Freiermuth for a first down at the 30, and Sanders bounced off left side for another first down. McSorley got the Lions as far as the 15, before they faced a fourth-and-medium with four minutes to play. Every Penn State fan in the world called for Franklin to go for it, but instead he sent on Pinegar for a 32-yard field goal to cut the deficit to three.

Unfortunately, there was nothing that could be done about Snell. He carried the ball on a whopping eight plays in a row, picking up two first downs. He piled up a total of 144 yards for the game, while setting the Kentucky record for most career rushing yards. The Lions got the ball back with one second left at their own 17, where they failed on a hook-and-lateral. McSorley had given all he had and come up short, 27–24.

It was a remarkable performance by McSorley, who threw for 246 yards and two touchdowns while carrying the ball 75 yards for a score, all while nursing an injury. The trouble was, he didn't get much help on the ground; Sanders ran for only 51 yards on 13 carries. Running back Journey Brown carried the ball once for four yards; that seemed insignificant, but he'd blow everyone away next bowl season.

Penn State finished the season with a 9–4 record, ranked #17 in the nation. They had hoped to win at least ten games three years in a row for the first time since the eighties, but they came up just a whisker short. McSorley would be drafted late by the Baltimore Ravens; the quarterback who relieved him in this bowl, Clifford, would become the new starter in 2019.

Box score[9]:

2019 Citrus Bowl	1st	2nd	3rd	4th	Final
Kentucky	10	0	17	0	27
Penn State	0	7	0	17	24

1st Quarter: UK—Butler 28 FG
    UK—Bowden 58 punt return (Butler kick)
2nd Quarter: PSU—Bowers 1 pass from McSorley (Pinegar kick)
3rd Quarter: UK—Snell 2 run (Butler kick)
    UK—Butler 28 FG
    UK—Snell 12 run (Butler kick)
4th Quarter: PSU—McSorley 1 run (Pinegar kick)
    PSU—Freiermuth 18 pass from McSorley (Pinegar kick)
    PSU—Pinegar 32 FG

2019 Season (10–2)

The great Trace McSorley graduated after the 2018 season, drafted in the sixth round of the 2019 season by the Baltimore Ravens.[1] Now that McSorley was gone to the NFL, and Tommy Stevens having transferred to Mississippi State,[2] it was up to Sean Clifford to step into McSorley's huge shoes. Penn State opened the season at home against Idaho, in what proved to be no more than an exhibition game. Unlike the previous year, when they nearly lost to Appalachian State, the Nittany Lions cruised to a 79–7 victory. The Lions had 673 yards of offense, the third-most in school history, as well as 35 first downs, the most in 14 years. The Lions led 44–0 at halftime and 58–0 after three quarters. Running back Devyn Ford ran for an 81-yard touchdown, in PSU's largest margin of victory (72) since 1991 against Cincinnati.[3]

The next week, it was another game that seemed like it would be a walkthrough—at home against Buffalo. Defensive back John Reid picked off a pass and returned it 36 yards for a touchdown and the Nittany Lions would go on to score four touchdowns in the third quarter, in a 45–13 win. Clifford became the 16th Penn State quarterback to throw four touchdown passes in a game.[4]

It was time for the 100th meeting all time between Penn State and Pitt. In the first quarter, running back Journey Brown ripped off an 85-yard run, for the second-longest non-scoring run in team history, setting up a Ford one-yard scoring run. Nittany Lions kicker Jordan Stout made a school-record 57-yard field goal on the final play of the first half to tie the game at ten. Running back Noah Cain ran for a 13-yard touchdown in the third quarter, giving Penn State a seven-point lead. Penn State survived a missed 19-yard field goal and a Hail Mary to pull out a 17–10 victory, their third straight over Pitt.[5]

Much was made of the Friday night Big Ten season-opener in Maryland, with Maryland fans determined to have their team make a statement, and Penn State fans determined to "white out" Maryland's stadium. In the end, the game proved to be no contest. Clifford threw for 398 yards on 26 completions, both personal highs, and he only played three quarters. The Lions outgained the Terrapins by nearly 500 yards, while piling up triple the number of first downs as their opponents in a 59–0 win.[6]

The Lions piled up ten sacks against Purdue in their Homecoming game, as they raced to a 21–0 first-quarter lead. Clifford threw for three touchdowns on 264 passing yards, and he also ran for a touchdown. The PSU defense stopped Purdue for minus-19 yards, marking the best performance against the run in their Big Ten history, as they won 35–7.[7]

In Iowa City, the Lions faced a tough battle against the Hawkeyes. Iowa held Penn State to just 117 passing yards, but the Nittany Lions made up for it with their ground game. Cain ran for 102 yards and a touchdown, and he also helped the Lions run out the clock in the fourth quarter with his team holding on to a tenuous 17–12 lead.[8]

It was time for the annual White Out game, this one against Michigan. Clifford threw two first-half touchdown passes to Freiermuth and Hamler and also ran for a two-yard touchdown, as Penn State took a 21–0 lead midway through the second quarter. Michigan came back to pull within seven, but a pass breakup by defensive back Lamont Wade with two minutes to play saved the Lions and sealed the 28–21 victory.[9]

Freiermuth had a huge game at Michigan State, catching three touchdowns from 16, 19, and six yards out. Clifford added a 27-yard touchdown pass to Hamler, as the Nittany Lions took a 28–0 lead early in the third quarter. Defensive end Shaka Toney blocked a 46-yard field goal attempt in the first half, and receiver Dan Chisena fell on top of a muffed punt deep in Michigan State territory to set up Freiermuth's third touchdown catch. That was all Penn State needed, as they cruised to a 28–7 victory.[10]

At 8–0, Penn State was ranked #4 in the College Football Playoff rankings. While going undefeated probably would have meant a CFP berth anyway, the #4 ranking confirmed it. Going into Minneapolis, the Lions were five wins away from the playoffs. But it was not meant to be, as they lost a heartbreaker to Minnesota, 31–26. Brown ran for a 45-yard touchdown in the first quarter, but Minnesota's offense put up two touchdowns in the first quarter to go ahead 14–10. Penn State fell into a 24–10 hole in the second quarter, but they battled back. Clifford threw a ten-yard touchdown pass to tight end Nick Bowers, and Brown ran for another touchdown, as Penn State pulled within five points with less than four minutes to go. Penn State made it all the way to the Minnesota 11 with two minutes to go, but Clifford threw an interception in the end zone, sealing the Lions' fate.

Would the Lions suffer a hangover against Indiana? They'd have some problems on defense, but the offense was still in good form. Clifford threw a 12-yard touchdown to Bowers, while running for a 38-yard touchdown, as Penn State took a 17–14 lead after the first quarter. Brown added a 35-yard touchdown in the third quarter, part of his 100 rushing yards. Late in the game, on fourth down, Clifford ran for a one-yard touchdown to give his team a ten-point lead. It would prove to be just enough; Indiana scored late, but Penn State held on to win 34–27.[11]

This set up a showdown in Columbus with Ohio State, a game few people gave the Nittany Lions any chance at winning. It looked like they were right, as Penn State fell into a 21–0 hole early in the third quarter. Worse, Clifford went down with a leg injury.[12] But Levis proved to be more than adequate in relief. He led the Lions on three scoring drives in the third quarter, one finishing with an 18-yard touchdown by Brown. Penn State ended up losing 28–17, but because they gave OSU such a good fight, they only dropped two spots in the polls from #8 to #10.[13]

In the season finale against Rutgers, the Lions were expected to completely dominate, but it didn't turn out that way. Penn State's lead was only seven points early in the fourth quarter. But Brown ran for a trio of touchdowns, two of them coming in the second half, as Penn State finished their regular season with a 27–6 win.[14]

Clifford threw for over 2,500 yards, completing nearly 60 percent of his passes, and throwing 22 touchdowns as opposed to just six interceptions.[15] He threw for four touchdowns in two games, with three touchdowns in three others. He ranked second in the Big Ten with 263.2 offensive yards per game.[16] Linebacker Micah Parsons was named as the best in the Big Ten at his position, after making 95 tackles throughout the season.

Other defensive players making the all-Big Ten team included defensive end Yetur Gross-Matos (first-team), defensive end Shaka Toney (second-team), and defensive back Tariq Castro-Fields (third-team).[17]

Leading the rushing offense was Brown, who ran for 688 yards and ten touchdowns. Cain was second on the team with 351 yards and six touchdowns. In the air, Hamler proved to be the biggest threat, catching 54 passes for eight touchdowns. Freiermuth added another 41 catches for seven touchdowns, while Dotson caught 24 more for four scores.[18]

Penn State finished with their ten-win season in their last four seasons, with appearances in New Year's Six bowls all three of those years. They ended up #10 in the final CFP rankings, which got them into the final at-large spot in the New Year's Six. Now they were headed to the Goodyear Cotton Bowl Classic against #17 Memphis, who won the American Athletic Conference and was the highest-rated Group of Five champion. For the first time ever, the Nittany Lions and Tigers would meet in a gridiron contest.[19]

2019 Cotton Bowl Classic

#10 Penn State (10–2) vs. #17 Memphis (11–1)
December 28, 2019, at AT&T Stadium in Arlington, Texas

Memphis won the coin toss and deferred their choice to the second half. Receiving the opening kickoff, running back Journey Brown took back a short kick to the 27. The Penn State offense came out trying to throw the ball, a strategy that would change as the game would go on. On their first possession, quarterback Sean Clifford threw two incompletions in a three-and-out, and the Nittany Lions punted it away. Punter Blake Gillikin got away a 57-yard kick.

The Tigers offense came out throwing. Quarterback Brady White hit receiver Damonte Coxie on a 39-yard pass on his team's second play. He also completed passes to running back Kenneth Gainwell and receiver Antonio Gibson, as the Tigers moved into field goal range. Running back Patrick Taylor, Jr., ran for a 15-yard gain, putting Memphis inside the 20. But PSU's All-American linebacker Micah Parsons burst through the line and hit receiver Calvin Austin III for a big loss. That forced the Tigers to settle for a 48-yard field goal by kicker Riley Patterson to go up 3–0.

Penn State would respond with a three-play drive that went 75 yards. Clifford fired to receiver Jahan Dotson for 12 yards along the left sideline. He then passed downfield for receiver K.J. Hamler, who broke wide open for a 31-yard pickup. Brown took the next handoff, and he simply ran right over several Memphis defenders in a showstopping run. He went 32 yards to the end zone, and Penn State took a 7–3 lead.

Defensive back John Reid knocked down a pass, setting up a third-and-long for Memphis. White went deep down the middle, and he completed the pass to receiver Kedarian Jones for a 56-yard gain to the PSU 17. Three plays later, Taylor pounded it in for a touchdown, and Memphis went ahead by a 10–7 margin.

The Nittany Lions offense was still in a pass-first mode, and it wasn't working. Clifford was sacked on consecutive plays by defensive tackle Jonathan Wilson and defensive end Bryce Huff. The Lions were forced to punt. Memphis then drove down into Penn State territory again, with a 13-yard pass to Austin and a couple of runs for first downs by Gainwell. The Tigers took a 37-yard field goal to go ahead by six points at the end of the first quarter.

Head coach James Franklin and the coaching staff changed their offensive strategy as the second quarter began. Clifford had been sacked again by linebacker Xavier Cullens to end their last drive, but the Penn State defense forced a short punt that only reached the Memphis 45. PSU was now going to ditch the pass-heavy attack and instead ground-and-pound. That didn't mean they'd totally stop passing; Clifford completed a pair of passes to Dotson and Hamler for first downs on their next drive. But both Brown and Clifford ran the ball twice on the drive, and the Lions reached the Memphis 1. Running back Noah Cain then pounded in a one-yard touchdown run, and the Lions went ahead 14–13.

Parsons picked up a sack and forced a fumble on Memphis's next drive. The Tigers recovered, and they survived an interception by PSU defensive back Jaquan Brisker when defensive end Jayson Oweh was ruled to be offside on the play. Defensive end Yetur Gross-Matos made up for it, picking up a sack on the next play. Backed up deep in their own territory, Memphis's punt only reached their own 32-yard line.

Clifford suffered another sack on first down, but he then gained it all back on a 16-yard run off a read option play. He followed with a pass to the left side to tight end Pat Freiermuth, who gave a hard stiff-arm as he pounded his way down inside the 5. Running back Devyn Ford then scampered up the middle for a touchdown, and the Lions led by eight.

The Memphis offense went nowhere on the next possession, picking up just one first down before having to punt. Penn State took over at their own 44-yard line, and it'd take the Lions just one play to score. Brown took a handoff, burst up the middle, and outran everyone all the way to the end zone for a 56-yard touchdown, putting Penn State up by 15.

Memphis struck back quickly, with White throwing to Coxie for a 41-yard gain. That set up a two-yard touchdown run by Gainwell, and the Tigers made it an eight-point game. But the Penn State offense kept humming, this time using running back Ricky Slade as their main weapon. He took off on the first play after the kickoff for a 44-yard gain. He'd run for another first down, while Clifford would also take it himself for a first down. The drive ended with Clifford throwing to his left to Dotson, who dived in for a touchdown, and Penn State's 15-point lead was restored.

The Tigers managed to get downfield quickly, with White completing six passes to get down to the Penn State 26-yard line with just a few seconds left in the half. Patterson hit a 44-yard field goal, cutting the Nittany Lions' lead to 35–23 at the half. The 58 combined points in the first half were an all-time Cotton Bowl record.

Penn State kicked off to start the second half, and Memphis built off the momentum they had gained. White threw passes to Coxie and Gainwell to get to the Penn State 26. Jones then took a reverse and threw a pass to White, who was stopped just shy of the goal line. White then scored on a quarterback sneak, and Memphis pulled within five.

Clifford threw an interception to linebacker Austin Hall, and it looked like Memphis might go ahead. Lions defensive tackle PJ Mustipher sacked White for a nine-yard loss, though, stopping the Tigers from getting a first down. They settled for a 51-yard field goal by Patterson, which was the longest field goal in Cotton Bowl history. Penn State's lead was down to two.

Brown took off on a good run into Tigers territory at the 45. Memphis defensive tackle Morris Joseph then sacked Clifford and forced a fumble, but the Lions managed to get it back. Cain ran the ball twice up the middle for first downs, getting down to the 17.

A pair of holding penalties on Penn State prevented them from getting the ball into the end zone, but kicker Jake Pinegar hit a 45-yard field goal, and the Nittany Lions took a 38–33 lead.

Memphis got the ball back downfield into Penn State territory, and they got a 41-yard field goal by Patterson to cut the Penn State lead back down to just two points. They gained even more momentum on the Lions' next drive. Brown had ripped off a 44-yard run down to the Memphis 30, but then the Lions soon faced a fourth-and-one. The Tigers defense stopped Brown on the play, and they took over, with everything going their way.

That was when Parsons stepped in and turned the game on its head. He burst through the Memphis offensive line on a blitz, nailing White and knocking the ball out. Defensive back Garrett Taylor caught the loose ball and returned it for a touchdown. Parsons's game-breaking play put the Nittany Lions up 45–36 at the end of the third quarter.

Memphis wasn't going away. They got back into field goal range with a 24-yard pass from White to Gibson. However, the bend-but-don't-break Penn State defense yet again refused to allow them into the end zone. The Tigers settled for a 42-yard field goal by Patterson, his sixth successful kick of the day, and Penn State's lead was down to six. Patterson's six field goals were the most ever in any bowl all-time.

But Franklin knew exactly what to do in this situation: ground-and-pound. While Clifford completed a couple of passes to Daniel George, the next drive belonged to Cain. He just kept on pounding the ball over and over again. He ran the ball seven times on the drive, including the final six plays in a row. Memphis just couldn't stop him. On his final run, he went one yard for a touchdown, putting Penn State up 12. Clifford then threw a two-point conversion pass over the middle to Freiermuth, and the Nittany Lions took a 53–39 lead.

The Penn State defense would finish off this victory with a few good plays. Defensive tackle Robert Windsor picked up a sack, then defensive back Marquis Wilson picked off a White pass as the Memphis offense was threatening to score. Finally, Oweh sacked White to finish out the 14-point victory for the Nittany Lions.

It was the highest-scoring Cotton Bowl ever, with 92 combined points scored. Parsons was an obvious choice for the most outstanding defensive player thanks to his game-breaking ability and for forcing the game-sealing touchdown. Brown was named offensive MVP, as he ran for 202 yards, the most by any Penn State running back in a bowl game all-time. He had two of the seven longest runs in Penn State bowl history just in this one game. Franklin had his second New Year's Six bowl victory in three seasons, and PSU would finish #9 in the final polls at 11–2, their third 11-win season in the last four years. "We've done some good things in the last six years," he said, "but the best is ahead of us."[20]

Box Score[21]:

2019 Cotton Bowl	1st	2nd	3rd	4th	Final
Memphis	13	10	13	3	39
Penn State	7	28	10	8	53

1st Quarter: MEM—Patterson 48 FG
    PSU—Brown 32 run (Pinegar kick)
    MEM—P. Taylor Jr. 3 run (Patterson kick)
    MEM—Patterson 37 FG
2nd Quarter: PSU—Cain 1 run (Pinegar kick)
    PSU—Ford 2 run (Pinegar kick)

PSU—Brown 56 run (Pinegar kick)
MEM—Gainwell 2 run (Patterson kick)
PSU—Dotson 4 pass from Clifford (Pinegar kick)
MEM—Patterson 44 FG
3rd Quarter: MEM—White 1 run (Patterson kick)
MEM—Patterson 51 FG
PSU—Pinegar 45 FG
MEM—Patterson 41 FG
PSU—G. Taylor 15 interception return (Pinegar kick)
4th Quarter: MEM—Patterson 42 FG
PSU—Cain 1 run (Freiermuth pass from Clifford)

Lists

Now that you know the stories of every single one of Penn State's 50 bowl teams, it's time to have a little fun. Before closing out the book, I want to stir debate by ranking the top Penn State teams and players. The only criterion for ranking is that the player or team must have appeared in a bowl game; other than that, it is all completely subjective. A team with a loss in a bowl may have a better ranking than some with wins in bowls. It's all in fun, and hopefully you will make your own lists to compare with mine.

Lists:

- Top 25 Teams
- Top 15 Running Backs
- Top 15 Quarterbacks
- Top 10 Receivers
- Top 10 Defensive Players
- Top 10 Most Exciting Bowl Games

Top 25 Teams

#1: 1986 (12–0, Fiesta Bowl champions, national champions)

The 1986 team is the greatest because of what a titanic opponent they had to defeat to win the national title—a Miami Hurricanes team littered with future NFL stars. They are the only undefeated "official" national champions in Penn State history, although that's only because the pollsters have robbed many other teams of their glory. Their defense was so good that it turned the Miami offense into goo at the Fiesta Bowl. Heisman Trophy-winning quarterback Vinny Testaverde was harassed into throwing five interceptions—two to linebacker Shane Conlan, two to linebacker Pete Giftopoulos. On the way to the Fiesta Bowl, running back D.J. Dozier led the way, and quarterback John Shaffer played just enough mistake-free to win. If the 1982 team had finished undefeated, they'd get the #1 spot; but as it is, only the 1986 team finished without a loss and at #1 in the polls, so they get the top spot on this list.

#2: 1982 (11–1, Sugar Bowl champions, national champions)

Led by quarterback Todd Blackledge and running back Curt Warner, the 1982 team was an absolute powerhouse, going through one of the most brutal schedules in school history and managing to get to #2 in the nation by the end of the regular season. The only knock on the 1982 team is their loss to Alabama during the regular season, but they made up for it by beating another SEC team, Georgia, in the Sugar Bowl. This team had playmakers at every position, and they were the ones to finally break through and get head coach Joe Paterno that long-awaited first national championship.

#3: 1994 (12–0, ROSE BOWL CHAMPIONS, BIG TEN CHAMPIONS)

This team was probably the greatest team in college football history not to be recognized as national champions. They were an absolute powerhouse, destroying teams along the way, scoring 63 points on Ohio State, just running roughshod over opponents. They had a future Super Bowl quarterback in Kerry Collins, a #1-overall pick in running back Ki-Jana Carter, and a great defense to boot. I have not researched the Nebraska team that stole away their rightful crown, but I have a hard time believing anyone could have defeated this team. It is a true tragedy that this team never got the chance to play for the national title on the field.

#4: 2005 (11–1, ORANGE BOWL CHAMPIONS, BIG TEN CHAMPIONS)

My favorite Penn State team of all time was the 2005 team. Granted, I didn't start following college football in full until 2002, so all those teams of the eighties and nineties were off-limits. But I've never enjoyed a team like I did this one, through all the ups and downs, though admittedly there weren't too many downs. Quarterback Michael Robinson is my all-time favorite Penn State player, because of his guidance throughout this season. He may not have had the big numbers, but outside of Blackledge, no one before him ever could compare to him in leadership skills. If not for two seconds at Michigan, this team would have gone down as the 1994 team: undefeated, yet uncrowned.

#5: 1973 (12–0, ORANGE BOWL CHAMPIONS)

This was the first 12–0 team in school history. John Cappelletti won the Heisman Trophy, the only one ever at Penn State, by putting up ridiculous numbers on the ground. Tom Shuman was a really good quarterback for his time, throwing only five interceptions all year. The fact that this team finished only #5 in the final Associated Press poll rankings tells you exactly how bunk they really are. In today's world, they wouldn't have even gotten a College Football Playoff spot! Yet they won the Orange Bowl convincingly, and they proved that they deserved much more recognition than they received.

#6: 1947 (9–0–1, TIE IN COTTON BOWL)

If the Lions could have only come down with a catch in the end zone at the end of the Cotton Bowl, they would have finished with a perfect record. As it was, they tied a powerful Southern Methodist team and still ended up undefeated. But what makes this team great is not just their victories, it was their resilience through the hardest kind of adversity. They were told to leave their two black players at home; instead, they came out with the message of "We are Penn State" and refused to go without them. They then stayed far out of town, not allowed to stay in Dallas because no hotel would accept their black players. After staying at a military base, they came out and played a great game in the Cotton Bowl. They were a different kind of champion, but in no way inferior to the teams ahead of them on this list.

#7: 1969 (11–0, Orange Bowl champions)

This team wiped out Missouri in the Orange Bowl, intercepting the Mizzou quarterbacks too many times to count, in an absolutely fantastic defensive effort. The only reason they didn't win the national championship was because of President Richard Nixon. He ranked Texas #1, and the media blindly agreed with him. Knowing what we know now about Nixon, perhaps he shouldn't have been given the job of naming national champions.

#8: 1968 (11–0, Orange Bowl champions)

The year before, Penn State also went 11–0, won the Orange Bowl, and finished #2 in the nation. The only reason I rank this team a notch lower is because of the margin of victory in the Orange Bowl. The 1969 team took a 10–0 lead early in the bowl and never were in danger despite only winning by seven. The 1968 team, however, would have lost the game had Kansas not had 12 men on the field. That penalty gave them a reprieve and let them try a second two-point conversion, which they made. That's not to say anything bad about this team, though, which was Paterno's first undefeated squad.

#9: 2008 (11–2, Big Ten champions, lost in Rose Bowl)

I still maintain that the 11–1 regular season that Penn State had should have been enough to get them into the BCS National Championship Game in South Florida. They beat Ohio State at the Horseshoe, they curb-stomped Michigan and Oregon State, and their one loss was by one point with one second left to a good Iowa team. Instead, Tim Tebow gave an inspiring speech after a loss, and the sheeple in the media lapped it up and voted Florida into the title game against Oklahoma. The Lions had a letdown in the Rose Bowl, which had been reckoned meaningless by the BCS. That doesn't take away from how great quarterback Daryll Clark and this team was.

#10: 1978 (11–1, lost in Sugar Bowl)

This should have been Paterno's first national champions, as they came into the Sugar Bowl undefeated and ranked #1 in the nation. Sadly, after a goal-line stand by Alabama, the Nittany Lions came up seven points short. Some Penn State fans claim that running back Mike Guman actually scored on that fourth-down play and was given a bad spot. In any case, there's no taking away from the greatness of this team, despite its one close loss.

#11: 1985 (11–1, lost in Orange Bowl)

Penn State's other runner-up team was in 1985, when the Lions came into the Orange Bowl undefeated and ranked #1 in the nation. Quarterback John Shaffer had the worst game of his career, but even then the Lions weren't dead. Backup Matt Knizner led them back, and if kicker Massimo Manca doesn't miss a chip-shot field goal, they may have still came back to win. They finished ranked third after the 25–10 loss to Oklahoma, but they were well in position to win the following year.

#12: 2017 (11–2, Fiesta Bowl champions)

It's very hard to discern between head coach James Franklin's four excellent teams of the last four seasons. I give the nod to the 2017 team because they won their bowl game, they blew out Pitt and Michigan, and both of their losses were excruciatingly close. True, they didn't win the Big Ten, but a play here and a play there, and they're undefeated and playing for the national title. Their win over a great Washington team in the Fiesta Bowl proved exactly what they were made of.

#13: 2016 (11–3, Big Ten champions, lost in Rose Bowl)

This is probably everyone's favorite team of the last four seasons, but I had to rank it below the 2017 team thanks to that loss to Michigan. They were blown out by the Wolverines, and that 2017 team was never blown out. That doesn't take away from the fact that they came back to beat Ohio State, and that they again recovered from a deficit to win the Big Ten Championship Game over Wisconsin. While they let a lead slip away in the Rose Bowl, this still was one of the great teams in school history.

#14: 1981 (10–2, Fiesta Bowl champions)

Sports Reference ranks this team #2 in Penn State history using its Simple Rating System, behind only the 1994 team.[1] Ranked as high as #1 during the season, these Lions ended up third after their win in the Fiesta Bowl over USC and Heisman-winning running back Marcus Allen. They are largely snubbed in fans' memories, but they led the groundwork for the national title the year later.

#15: 2019 (11–2, Cotton Bowl champions)

It's easy to rank a team when they're the most recent one you've seen. Obviously, the 2019 team wasn't on the level of most of the top teams ahead of them. But for this team's rushing effort in the Cotton Bowl to be the largest production in the 50 bowl games in school history, it obviously says something about exactly how good this offense was. Penn State fans may have been disappointed about this team, but in reality, they were highly successful.

#16: 1996 (11–2, Fiesta Bowl champions)

This Nittany Lion team walloped Texas in the Fiesta Bowl, beating them by three touchdowns and showing their dominance in the second half. They got as high as #3 in the nation during the regular season, before settling it at #7 after the bowls.[2] This was also the only Penn State team to reach a Bowl Alliance game (Fiesta, Orange, Sugar) in the three years of its existence.

#17: 1991 (11–2, Fiesta Bowl champions)

Quarterback Tony Sacca led this team, which had a giant second half in the Fiesta Bowl, as they crushed Tennessee. They ended up ranked #3 in the nation after the season, ranked behind only the co-national champions Miami and Washington. This was a sneaky good team that deserved a lot more credit than they got.

#18: 2018 (9–4, lost in Citrus Bowl)

Despite the fact that most Penn State fans were disappointed in the 2018 team, they still pulled off some feats worth noting. They defeated Pitt by a 51–6 margin. They came back from a seven-point deficit against Appalachian State with less than two minutes to go, to win in overtime. They had Ohio State beat, until they let a late lead slip away again. And they fought tooth-and-nail against Kentucky with their quarterback Trace McSorley injured, eventually succumbing by only a field goal. They were much better than their record showed.

#19: 2009 (11–2, Capital One Bowl champions)

I honestly think this team would get more credit if the name of the bowl had not been the "Capital One" but instead the "Citrus." It's the same bowl, but one of them sounds like it's in the same category as the Dollar General or the PapaJohns.com. The other sounds like a bowl that's been around for over half a century. No matter what their bowl was named, they were a great team.

#20: 1977 (11–1, Fiesta Bowl champions)

It's hard to believe that this team was only one game from going unbeaten. They may not be remembered that well, but they had quite the team. The offense put up 42 points in the Fiesta Bowl against Arizona State, in the first of many, many happy trips for Penn State to the desert. They also laid the groundwork for a team that nearly won it all the next year.

#21: 1980 (10–2, Fiesta Bowl champions)

When you beat Ohio State in a bowl game, no matter which one it is, it's an accomplishment. Of course, if you're even *playing* Ohio State in a bowl game, then it has to be a good bowl game, and that it was for Penn State in the Fiesta. Since PSU and OSU can no longer meet in a bowl game, unless it's the College Football Playoff, the Nittany Lions have bragging rights for life when it comes to head-to-head in bowls.

#22: 1971 (11–1, Cotton Bowl champions)

This team finished the job the 1969 team started. While the 1969 team never got the opportunity to win the national title over Texas on the field, this team went down to Dallas and beat the Longhorns to prove that they deserved that title. Oh, and they only lost one game all year, which probably means they are underrated, even by me.

#23: 1993 (10–2, Citrus Bowl champions)

This team is important to Penn State history simply because it was the first season in the Big Ten for Penn State. It took only one year for teams to take notice and realize that Penn State was here to stay. A Citrus Bowl victory over Tennessee later, the Nittany Lions were in position to go for all the Roses the following year.

#24: 2002 (9–4, lost in Capital One Bowl)

Running back Larry Johnson deserved to win the Heisman, and it shouldn't have even been a close vote. Yet again, though, the Nittany Lions were jobbed by the media. Sure, the Lions lost the Capital One Bowl to a good Auburn team, but all four of their losses were by one possession, including two in overtime. They were a play here and a play there from the BCS.

#25: 1967 (8–2–3, tie in Gator Bowl)

Paterno took the blame after the bowl game, in which he chose to go for it on fourth-and-short deep in his own territory. The Nittany Lions failed, then Florida State roared back to tie the game. That doesn't take away from the fact that this was a very solid team, and that the Gator Bowl was higher in prestige back in the sixties.

Top 15 Quarterbacks

#1: Trace McSorley (2015–2018, bowls started in: Rose, Fiesta, Citrus)

McSorley owns all the major records in Penn State history, and for good reason. There simply was no other quarterback like him in all the years of Nittany Lion football. He passed for just shy of 10,000 yards in his Penn State career, with 107 total touchdowns. He was one of the most beloved quarterbacks in program history, having set many team records, including most passing yards in a season (3,614 in 2016), most 200-yard passing games in a career (28), most touchdown passes in a season (29 in 2016) and a career (70), longest pass (95 yards in 2018), most completions in a season (284 in 2017) and a career (720), and the most rushing yards by a Penn State quarterback in a career with nearly 1,700 yards.[3] There may be other quarterbacks who break his records, but there was absolutely no one who could break McSorley's spirit.[4]

#2: Todd Blackledge (1980–1982, Fiesta, Fiesta, Sugar)

If it wasn't for Blackledge, we may be talking about Jeff Hostetler's reign at quarterback at Penn State in the early eighties. But Blackledge beat him out, and then he later beat Hoss straight up when Penn State played West Virginia. Blackledge overcame some interception problems early in his career; he threw eight more interceptions than touchdowns his first two years. In his senior year, however, he passed for 22 touchdowns as opposed to just 14 interceptions, and of course won the national title. The fact that Blackledge didn't pan out in the NFL doesn't ruin his legacy; in fact, it only enhances it, because he proved to be the right guy at the right time for Penn State. He was a champion on the field, and now he is a champion in the booth, as one of the best color analysts in the game.[5]

#3: Kerry Collins (1991–1994, Citrus, Rose)

The first two years of Collins's career, he was a mere backup, but once he won the job, he became one of the greatest passers in Penn State history. He would have won the Heisman if not for his own running back Ki-Jana Carter being so good (and Carter could say the same about him). Collins threw for nearly 2,700 yards and 21 touchdowns his senior year, leading the greatest offense in school history to an undefeated season. He deserves to be called "national champion Kerry Collins," but unfortunately, the media jobbed him there too. Collins went on to start in Super Bowl XXXV for the New York Giants.[6]

#4: Michael Robinson (2002–2005, Orange)

Robinson started his career as a Kordell Stewart–type "Slash" player. He got significant time in the Capital One Bowl his freshman year, trying to spark a dormant Penn

State offense that couldn't reach the end zone. Three years later, Robinson went from being "Slash" to Superman. He was Mr. Everything for the Nittany Lions, the ultimate leader, the guy got behind. Totaling over 3,000 yards of offense his senior year didn't hurt, either.[7] Robinson was also humble; unlike Tim Tebow, when the scouts told him he'd be better fit in the NFL as a fullback, he gladly changed positions. As a result, he has a Super Bowl ring on his finger, while Tebow is flailing at outside pitches in the minor leagues of baseball.

#5: Daryll Clark (2006–2009, Rose, Capital One)

Clark had to wait for his chance. My friend and I always thought it was weird that, in the video game NCAA Football 07, the backup quarterback #17 had a higher overall rating than the starting quarterback #14. In 2008 and 2009, Clark showed why. He threw for over 5,500 yards and 43 touchdowns in the "Spread HD" offense.[8] He is one of only four quarterbacks than can call themselves Big Ten champions at Penn State.

#6: Chuck Fusina (1975–1978, Gator, Fiesta, Sugar)

Fusina finished second in the Heisman Trophy voting in 1978, as he led Penn State to the national championship game against Alabama. Yet Fusina was even better the year before, throwing for more yards and having a better touchdown-to-interception ratio. Fusina proved to be exactly what the Nittany Lions needed in an era where they slowly transitioned from "run-run-run" to passing much more often. His completion percentage for his career was nearly 56 percent, an outstanding number in the seventies. If not for one goal-line stand, he may have been Penn State's first national champion quarterback.[9]

#7: Wally Richardson (1992, 1994–1996, Outback, Fiesta)

Richardson's two years as a starter came in 1995 and 1996, when he had a pair of outstanding bowl performances. He lit it up in the Outback Bowl, then helped his team steamroll over Texas in the Fiesta Bowl. Richardson threw touchdowns-to-interceptions at a 3:1 ratio in 1995, and he threw for over 4,400 yards in his Penn State career.[10]

#8: Tony Sacca (1988–1991, Holiday, Blockbuster, Fiesta)

Sacca took over full-time by the 1989 Holiday Bowl, but it was his 1991 season that blew everyone away. He completed nearly 58 percent of his passes and threw four times more touchdowns than interceptions. He led the team to a come-from-behind victory over Tennessee in the Fiesta Bowl, ending up with nearly 6,000 passing yards as a Penn Stater.[11]

#9: Tom Shuman (1972–1974, Orange, Cotton)

How many quarterbacks can say that they started in both the Orange and Cotton Bowls? Shuman completed 51.5 percent of his passes and threw for 28 touchdowns as opposed to just 12 interceptions in his career.[12] His team also won both of those bowls that he started in. He may be largely forgotten, but he was a heck of a quarterback.

#10: Chuck Burkhart (1967–1969, Orange, Orange)

Burkhart's meager stats obviously do not tell the whole story. A quarterback in the sixties wasn't supposed to be terribly accurate or a gunslinger who lit up the scoreboard.

What he was supposed to be was a field general who kept the offense going, whether it would be from a pass, handoff, or lateral. Burkhart did all three well, and even with a 1:9 touchdown-to-interception ratio his senior year, he led the Lions to back-to-back Orange Bowl wins and undefeated seasons.[13]

#11: Christian Hackenberg (2013–2015, Pinstripe, TaxSlayer)

Hackenberg will always deserve credit for taking over at quarterback under the worst of circumstances. I don't put a lot of stock in his numbers as opposed to the guys before him, because of the era he played in, and because neither of his bowl-eligible teams were all that spectacular. Even so, Hackenberg and his nearly 8,500 yards should always be remembered as the bridge to greatness.[14]

#12: Sean Clifford (2018–2019, Cotton)

I have never understood why some Penn State fans have a problem with Clifford. Is it because he took over for McSorley? He's put up comparable numbers to McSorley through the air, throwing for over 2,600 yards and 23 touchdowns in his first year as a starter.[15] He managed to get a "rebuilding" team into the New Year's Six. I truly believe the best is yet to come for Clifford.

#13: Galen Hall (1959–1961, Gator)

There is nothing about Hall's numbers that stick out, but the biggest impact he made was by stepping in as backup quarterback in the 1959 Liberty Bowl and leading his team to victory. His total numbers through three years (over 1,600 yards and 15 touchdowns) don't tell the whole story.[16] Hall became the offensive coordinator for the Lions many years later.

#14: Anthony Morelli (2004–2007, Outback, Alamo)

Morelli was the biggest disappointment in Penn State history. He was a highly sought-after recruit, but he never led the Lions to the promised land. That doesn't mean he was a bad quarterback; he completed 30 touchdowns as opposed to 18 interceptions in his two starting years.[17] Penn State fans just wish that he had gotten the team to the Rose Bowl, given all the hype surrounding him. Of note, Penn State went undefeated in bowls while he was on the team.

#15: John Shaffer (1983–1986, Orange, Fiesta)

This is the most controversial pick on this list. If I was only going by winning, then Shaffer would be #1. However, the 1985 and 1986 Nittany Lions won in spite of Shaffer, rather than because of him. Over the course of his career, he threw for 24 interceptions as opposed to just 18 touchdowns. He never reached ten touchdown passes in a season, and he threw for only 1,510 yards in his best year.[18] Regardless of all that, Shaffer only lost one game as a starter, the 1986 Orange Bowl. And he is one of only two quarterbacks that can "officially" call themselves national champions at Penn State.

Top 15 Running Backs

#1: Curt Warner (1979–1982, bowls played in: Liberty, Fiesta, Fiesta, Sugar)

If you look at Warner's statistics (just over 1,000 rushing yards in a season twice, just under 3,400 for his career, 30 total touchdowns), they don't blow you away. But Warner was so dynamic, so elusive, and so clutch at coming up with a big play when the team needed it the most. He was the main guy during one of the greatest periods in Penn State history, when they went to three major bowls in a row. His records may all be broken, but he has that national championship, making him the best of the best.[19]

#2: Ki-Jana Carter (1992–1994, Blockbuster, Citrus, Rose)

Carter scored 23 touchdowns in Penn State's undefeated season of 1994, rushing for over 1,500 yards.[20] His entire career could be summed up in one play: his very first carry of the Rose Bowl, when he burst right through the line to go 83 yards for a touchdown. He also had the honor of going #1 in the draft, and while his NFL career never panned out, it doesn't diminish his great collegiate career. Would Carter be #1 if Penn State had been ranked #1 in 1994? Possibly.

#3: John Cappelletti (1972–1973, Sugar, Orange)

Cappelletti only played for Penn State for two years, yet left a lasting impact that went beyond football. He played for his younger brother Joey, who later died of leukemia. His Heisman Trophy speech was one of the most touching in the history of the award. He rushed for over 1,500 yards and 17 touchdowns his senior year, winning Penn State's only Heisman, and leading the Nittany Lions to an undefeated season.[21] Had he played longer, he may be #1.

#4: Larry Johnson (1999–2002, Alamo, Capital One)

The only running back in Penn State history to rush for over 2,000 yards in a season, Johnson's career was a bit of an enigma. His first three years, he played sporadically, totaling under 900 rushing yards. Then he burst out of a cannon in 2002, scoring 20 touchdowns and rewriting the Penn State record book.[22] He deserved the Heisman for certain, but yet again the media snubbed a Penn Stater. It will be hard for any back to ever top Johnson's senior season.

#5: Saquon Barkley (2015–2017, TaxSlayer, Rose, Fiesta)

It's hard to understand just how important Barkley was to the turnaround to the Penn State program. He and McSorley were tied at the hip, the two players who helped transform Penn State from mediocre back into being a national powerhouse again. He rushed for over 1,000 yards in all three of his seasons at Penn State, totaled nearly 1,200 receiving yards, and scored 53 touchdowns.[23] He might have deserved a Heisman Trophy as well. Penn State fans will forever be thankful to Barkley for coming to Happy Valley.

#6: D.J. Dozier (1983–1986, Aloha, Orange, Fiesta)

Dozier was the starter for Penn State's second national championship team, and he scored the game-winning touchdown in the Fiesta Bowl. Quite simply, without him, the

Nittany Lions would never have beaten Miami or even been in position to play them. Dozier's career is unique in that his largest yard output came in his freshman year, not his senior year. He scored 29 touchdowns in his career, picking up the tough yards.[24]

#7: FRANCO HARRIS (1969–1971, ORANGE, COTTON)

I'll admit, Harris gets this spot more based on what he did once he left Penn State than for his three-year career as a Nittany Lion. He rushed for just over 2,000 yards over three years, scoring 25 touchdowns.[25] Once he left Penn State, he became a Pro Football Hall of Famer with the Pittsburgh Steelers. He is also such a class act off the field that he deserves this high ranking. Statistics do not tell the whole story.

#8: LYDELL MITCHELL (1969–1971, ORANGE, COTTON)

Mitchell ran for over 1,500 yards and scored 29 touchdowns his senior year at Penn State. I feel bad for not ranking him higher, but it's just that Penn State has had so many fine running backs in their history. In his three seasons, Mitchell totaled over 3,400 yards from scrimmage, winning two major bowls in the process.[26]

#9: WALLY TRIPLETT (1946–1948, COTTON)

Triplett faced extreme discrimination because he was black. Miami refused to play against Penn State because they wouldn't face a black player, and the city of Dallas forced him to stay far outside city limits if he wanted to play in the Cotton Bowl. Despite all that, he caught a touchdown pass in the Classic to become the first black player to score in that bowl. And without his catch, Penn State doesn't come out of there with a tie and an unbeaten season. Triplett will never be forgotten, even over 70 years later.

#10: CURTIS ENIS (1995–1997, OUTBACK, FIESTA)

Unfortunately, Enis is most remembered for committing the unpardonable sin of accepting a free suit coat before the 1998 Citrus Bowl. He wasn't allowed to play, which is a shame, because he had rushed for over 1,300 yards and 19 touchdowns that season. Enis's huge performance in the 1997 Fiesta Bowl along with his 3,700 career scrimmage yards make him one of the finest backs in Penn State history, suit coat or no suit coat.[27]

#11: EVAN ROYSTER (2007–2010, ALAMO, ROSE, CAPITAL ONE, OUTBACK)

The all-time leading rusher in Penn State history, Royster got to that spot slowly but surely. He burst on to the scene in the 2007 Alamo Bowl, and from there he became the most consistent running back in Penn State history. He went over 1,000 yards in all of his final three seasons, with his best year coming in the 2008 Big Ten championship season when he rushed for over 1,200 yards and scored 12 touchdowns.[28]

#12: BLAIR THOMAS (1985–1989, ORANGE, FIESTA, HOLIDAY)

Thomas was plagued with injury problems, unable to play in the Citrus Bowl following the 1987 season due to a knee ailment. Nevertheless, he ran for over 1,400 yards and 11 touchdowns that season, and he bounced back two years later (after taking a year off) to rush for over 1,300 yards. He helped the Lions win the 1986 national championship, then ended up with a fantastic Holiday Bowl to end his Penn State career.[29]

#13: MATT SUHEY (1976–1979, GATOR, FIESTA, SUGAR, LIBERTY)

Suhey was remarkably consistent over his four years at Penn State. He never rushed for 1,000 yards or ten touchdowns in a season, but every season he managed to rush for at least 450 yards and five touchdowns.[30] He of course went on to an outstanding career with the Chicago Bears after his four grind-it-out years at PSU were over.

#14: TONY HUNT (2003–2006, CAPITAL ONE, ORANGE, OUTBACK)

Hunt was injured on Penn State's first series in the 2006 Orange Bowl, forcing him to miss the rest of the triple-overtime game after having rushed for over 1,000 yards in the 2005 season. He bounced back in 2006 to rush for nearly 1,400 yards and 11 scores, and making a statement in the Outback Bowl with a huge performance. He ended up with over 4,100 yards from scrimmage in his career.[31]

#15: JOURNEY BROWN (2018–2019, CITRUS, COTTON)

This is a book about bowl games, right? Then it's impossible to leave off the list the player who rushed for more yards in a single bowl game than any other in school history. It's not like Brown didn't have great numbers his 2019 season, either. He rushed for 890 yards and 12 touchdowns. The most important 202 of those came in the Cotton Bowl, where he blew away the Memphis defense on his way to becoming the first-ever 200-yard rusher at PSU in a bowl game.[32]

Top 10 Receivers

#1: BOBBY ENGRAM (1991–1995, BOWLS PLAYED IN: CITRUS, ROSE, OUTBACK)

Engram went over 850 yards all three of his starting seasons at Penn State, with a pair of 1,000-yard seasons in his junior and senior years. He ended up with over 3,000 receiving yards and 31 touchdowns, and he was a key cog in the juggernaut that was the 1994 offense. He was also a pretty good punt returner; in 1993 he returned 33 punts for over 400 yards.[33]

#2: O.J. McDUFFIE (1988–1992, HOLIDAY, FIESTA, BLOCKBUSTER)

McDuffie caught 63 passes for nearly 1,000 yards and nine touchdowns in his final season, which ended in an appearance in the Bowl Coalition's Blockbuster Bowl. He ended up with just shy of 2,000 receiving yards for his career, scoring 20 times, including three punt returns for touchdowns and a rushing touchdown.[34]

#3: DaeSEAN HAMILTON (2014–2017, PINSTRIPE, TAXSLAYER, ROSE, FIESTA)

In an unusual case, Hamilton's highest output came in his blockbuster freshman season, one in which he caught 82 passes for just south of 900 yards. He ended up as Penn State's all-time leading receiver, catching over 200 passes for 2,842 yards and 18 touchdowns. That included two touchdowns in his final game, the 2017 Fiesta Bowl.[35]

#4: GREGG GARRITY (1980–1982, FIESTA, FIESTA, SUGAR)

Garrity is best known for his game-winning touchdown catch in the 1983 Sugar Bowl against Georgia. He was featured on the cover of *Sports Illustrated* after that win.[36] While his numbers weren't huge, he was highly important to that national championship team, and he went on to a fine career with the Philadelphia Eagles.

#5: JIMMY CEFALO (1974–1977, COTTON, SUGAR, GATOR, FIESTA)

Cefalo is better known for his post–Penn State career, going on to a successful career with the Miami Dolphins, and then joining the NBC announcing booth (including the broadcast of the 1987 Fiesta Bowl). He was remarkably versatile in Penn State's augmented Wing-T offense, especially his freshman year, when he ran for 328 yards and put up 144 receiving yards. By the end of his career, he was a great pass catcher, hauling in 28 for over 500 yards.[37]

#6: CHRIS GODWIN (2014–2016, PINSTRIPE, TAXSLAYER, ROSE)

Godwin will forever be remembered for the huge game he had in Pasadena, nearly leading the Nittany Lions to a victory over USC. He totaled nearly 2,100 yards his sophomore and junior seasons.[38] He went on to the NFL early, skipping his senior season, and getting drafted by the Tampa Bay Buccaneers.

#7: DEON BUTLER (2005–2008, ORANGE, OUTBACK, ALAMO, ROSE)

It's hard to find a receiver who was more consistent than Butler. He went over 600 receiving yards and 35 receptions in all four seasons of his career, with his lowest output being 37 catches and his highest being 48. Similarly, his lowest receiving total was 633 and his highest was 810. He caught 22 touchdown passes, the most coming in his freshman year when he caught nine.[39]

#8: DAVID DANIELS (1988–1990, HOLIDAY, BLOCKBUSTER)

While Daniels is forgotten about because his teams never played in major bowls, he was a remarkably productive receiver. He caught nearly 70 passes in his career, with over 1,300 total yards of offense and nine touchdowns. The best game of his career had to be the Blockbuster Bowl, when he went over 150 receiving yards.[40]

#9: JOE JUREVICIUS (1994–1997, ROSE, OUTBACK, FIESTA)

Jurevicius never got a chance to play in the Citrus Bowl his senior year, because his grades weren't up to the standard that head coach Joe Paterno set. Nevertheless, who can forget him breaking out in the Rose Bowl after a season in which he had just one catch for nine yards? His best season came in 1996, when he caught 41 passes for 869 yards. He had ten touchdowns his senior year, before he failed to make the grades.[41]

#10: JORDAN NORWOOD (2005–2008, ORANGE, OUTBACK, ALAMO, ROSE)

Like Butler, Norwood was an incredibly consistent receiver over his four years at Penn State. He never went under 400 or over 650 receiving yards. His highest reception total was 45 and his lowest was 32.[42] While Butler and Norwood were overshadowed by Derrick Williams, the top recruit in their class, the two of them outperformed him on the field.

Top 10 Defensive Players

#1: SHANE CONLAN, LB (1983–1986, ALOHA, ORANGE, FIESTA)

Conlan came up with two clutch interceptions in the 1987 Fiesta Bowl and was one of the biggest reasons why Penn State won that game. He was a consensus All-American during the 1986 season, and he went on to be drafted eighth overall by the Buffalo Bills.[43] In 2014, the Big Ten Network named him part of the "Mount Rushmore of Penn State Football."[44]

#2: PAUL POSLUSZNY, LB (2003–2006, ORANGE, OUTBACK)

One of the most heartbreaking moments was when Posluszny was carted off the Dolphins Stadium field at the Orange Bowl, unable to help his team in a brutal defensive battle. He had recorded 116 tackles during the course of the season but could only watch as the game went to triple overtime. He came back as a senior and recorded 116 tackles again, as one of the most beloved linebackers in school history.[45]

#3: LAVAR ARRINGTON, LB (1998–1999, OUTBACK, ALAMO)

Arrington may have been number one had he played longer as a Lion. He went to the NFL early and was drafted second overall. He managed to finish ninth in the Heisman voting in 1999 despite being a defensive player on a team that was far out of the national picture.[46]

#4: DENNIS ONKOTZ, LB (1967–1969, GATOR, ORANGE, ORANGE)

Onkotz was named All-American in back-to-back seasons as the Lions won multiple Orange Bowls. He intercepted 11 passes during his career, still the most of any linebacker at Penn State. He is considered responsible for helping Penn State get the nickname of "Linebacker U."[47]

#5: JACK HAM, LB (1968–1970, ORANGE, ORANGE)

Ham was another one of the Big Ten Network's "Mount Rushmore," alongside Conlan, Arrington, and John Cappelletti.[48] He won back-to-back Orange Bowls, piled up over 250 tackles, and blocked a school-record three punts in 1968.[49] He then went on to a Pro Football Hall of Famer career with the Pittsburgh Steelers.

#6: COURTNEY BROWN, DE (1996–1999, CITRUS, OUTBACK, ALAMO)

Well known as one of the many draft busts of the Cleveland Browns, this linebacker had a fantastic senior year and was named an All-American. He won Big Ten Defensive

Player of the Year and Defensive Lineman of the Year as well.[50] It is truly puzzling why this outstanding player never made it in the NFL.

#7: Sean Lee, LB (2006–2009, Outback, Alamo, Capital One)

Lee piled up 138 tackles during the 2007 season, ranking him first in the entire NCAA. While he missed 2008 with a knee injury, he bounced back for a great year in 2009, making 86 tackles. All told he made over 300 tackles before heading to the NFL, where he became a star for the team with the star on their helmet, the Dallas Cowboys.[51]

#8: Navorro Bowman, LB (2007–2009, Alamo, Rose, Capital One)

In Lee's absence in 2008, Bowman made it look like Lee was still playing. He made 106 tackles, becoming the new main guy in the Penn State linebacking corps. When Lee came back in 2009, Bowman teamed with him to become one of the most fearsome linebacking crews in the country. He ended up with 215 career tackles and three interceptions.[52]

#9: Tamba Hali, DE (2002–2005, Orange)

Hali broke out during the magical 2005 season, recording 11 sacks, 17 tackles for loss, and 65 total tackles. He was a big reason why that 2005 team was as good as it was. Like Lee (Cowboys) and Bowman (49ers), Hali went on to a successful career in the NFL (Chiefs).[53]

#10: Pete Giftopoulos, LB (1984–1987, Orange, Fiesta, Citrus)

How could I leave off the player who made the most famous play in Penn State history? Giftopoulos's second interception of Vinny Testaverde won the Fiesta Bowl and the national championship. Not bad for a guy who started out his Penn State career as a tight end.[54]

Top 10 Most Exciting Bowl Games

#1: 1987 Fiesta (Penn State 14, Miami 10)

There's no arguing this one. The 1987 Fiesta Bowl was one of the top five college football games of all time. The only game I can think of that was hyped as heavily and proceeded to live up to that hype was the 2006 Rose Bowl between Texas and USC. But while that game had no defense, this game had stellar defense, and just as good of an ending. More people watched this game live than any other college football game in history. Penn State won the classic matchup of "good vs. evil," and it's still (technically) their most recent national championship.

#2: 2006 Orange (Penn State 26, Florida State 23, 3OT)

Triple overtime! It doesn't get much better than that. It makes one wonder what would have happened in the 1948 Cotton and 1967 Gator Bowls if the college game had overtime then. Like the 1987 Fiesta Bowl, this one was a defensive struggle. It had everything; last-minute drives, a safety, missed kicks galore, and two coaching legends. This Orange Bowl still remains my favorite Penn State memory.

#3: 2017 Rose (USC 52, Penn State 49)

Now *this* would be my favorite Penn State memory had the Nittany Lions won. I was at this Rose Bowl game, hoping and praying that the Lions could hold on to a two-touchdown lead in the final minutes. I knew they needed more points; at one point I said to myself, "52 points will win this game." That was long before the USC comeback, and I saw it coming the whole way. Even though the Lions lost, they gained a ton of respect for playing such a fine offensive game against a national power like USC.

#4: 1983 Sugar (Penn State 27, Georgia 23)

The Nittany Lions' first national championship was also a really exciting game. Quarterback Todd Blackledge had the game of his life, and the defense held Georgia running back Herschel Walker in check. This game had a bizarre ending; the clock hit triple zeroes as a Penn State punt crossed the goal line. That play took off just enough time to deliver Penn State their first national championship.

#5: 1979 Sugar (Alabama 14, Penn State 7)

This one came down to a goal-line stand, where running back Mike Guman came up just shy of the end zone. It was yet another classic defensive struggle, and the Lions were in it to the very end. Who knows whether head coach Joe Paterno would have gone for two had the Lions punched it in on that fourth down, but they came up just short.

#6: 1969 Orange (Penn State 15, Kansas 14)

Perhaps we know the answer to whether Penn State would have gone for two in that game, because ten years earlier, Paterno *did* go for it against Kansas after a late touchdown. The Nittany Lions were stopped but given a reprieve when the Jayhawks were caught with too many men on the field. They made the second two-pointer, winning the Orange Bowl by one point.

#7: 1948 Cotton (Penn State 13, Southern Methodist 13)

SMU took a 13–0 lead on the Nittany Lions, who stormed back to tie the game. The Lions missed an extra point, and they couldn't convert on a last-second pass to the end zone that would have won the game. Running back Wally Triplett broke the color barrier in the Cotton Bowl and caught the tying touchdown pass; he just missed catching the Hail Mary at the end.

#8: 1967 Gator (Penn State 17, Florida State 17)

Unlike the previous game, this tie ended on a sour note for Penn State. Paterno went for it on fourth-and-one and failed, and the Seminoles came all the way back from down 17–0 to tie the game. As much as Paterno was criticized for that decision, he would have impressed all the analytic guys of today's world by being bold enough to go for it.

#9: 2010 CAPITAL ONE (PENN STATE 19, LSU 17)

I have often said that the most dangerous lead in football is a 13-point lead. It seems comfortable enough that you can sit on it and let the clock run out. But as soon as you give up that one touchdown, the opposing team gets momentum, then scores again to take the lead. That very scenario happened in this game; fortunately, quarterback Daryll Clark led a drive and set up kicker Collin Wagner for the winning field goal.

#10: 2017 FIESTA (PENN STATE 35, WASHINGTON 28)

The Nittany Lion offense was on fire in this one, as quarterback Trace McSorley set records for being the most total yards by a Penn Stater in a bowl game. The Lions led by as much as 21 before having to hold on in a heart-stopping finish. The Huskies pulled off a perfect hook-and-lateral, but they made one lateral too many, and Penn State recovered the fumble. Running back Saquon Barkley, who ripped off a 92-yard touchdown run, went out with a bang.

Conclusion

I hope you have enjoyed this intimate look into Penn State's 50 bowl games. Half a hundred is quite the number, and even more so when your goal is to cover all of them and even watch most of them. I have fully enjoyed getting to go back and watch all eras of Penn State football, including silent black-and-white film of the 1948 Cotton Bowl. While the first 50 bowls have been exciting, my hope is that there are many more bowls to come.

My final thoughts are on "We are Penn State," as a Penn State alumnus myself. We are the first ones to attempt to play in Miami against the Hurricanes with black players. We are the first ones to defy the Cotton Bowl and choose not to leave our black players at home. We are the ones to choose to stay at a military base in order to allow our black players somewhere to stay, since no hotel would let them in. We are the team with the first black players in a Cotton Bowl and eventually the first black player to be drafted into the NFL. We are trailblazers in the field of racial justice. We are going to continue to fight until racial inequality is no more. If there is anything today's America needs to hear, it is "We are Penn State."

Appendix A

Bowl Scores[1]

Bowl	Season	Date	Winner	Score	Loser	Score
Rose	1922	01/01/1923	USC	14	Penn State	3
Cotton	1947	01/01/1948	Penn State	13**	Southern Methodist	13**
Liberty	1959	12/19/1959	Penn State	7	Alabama	0
Liberty	1960	12/17/1960	Penn State	41	Oregon	12
Gator	1961	12/30/1961	Penn State	30	Georgia Tech	15
Gator	1962	12/29/1962	Florida	17	Penn State	7
Gator	1967	12/30/1967	Penn State	17**	Florida State	17**
Orange	1968	01/01/1969	Penn State	15	Kansas	14
Orange	1969	01/01/1970	Penn State	10	Missouri	3
Cotton	1971	01/01/1972	Penn State	30	Texas	6
Sugar	1972	12/31/1972	Oklahoma	14	Penn State	0
Orange	1973	01/01/1974	Penn State	16	LSU	9
Cotton	1974	01/01/1975	Penn State	41	Baylor	20
Sugar	1975	12/31/1975	Alabama	13	Penn State	6
Gator	1976	12/27/1976	Notre Dame	20	Penn State	9
Fiesta	1977	12/25/1977	Penn State	42	Arizona State	30
Sugar (NC)	1978	01/01/1979	Alabama	14	Penn State	7
Liberty	1979	12/22/1979	Penn State	9	Tulane	6
Fiesta	1980	12/26/1980	Penn State	31	Ohio State	19
Fiesta	1981	01/01/1982	Penn State	26	USC	10
Sugar (NC)	1982	01/01/1983	Penn State	27	Georgia	23
Aloha	1983	12/26/1983	Penn State	13	Washington	10
Orange (NC)	1985	01/01/1986	Oklahoma	25	Penn State	10
Fiesta (NC)	1986	01/02/1987	Penn State	14	Miami (FL)	10
Citrus	1987	01/01/1988	Clemson	35	Penn State	10
Holiday	1989	12/29/1989	Penn State	50	BYU	39
Blockbuster	1990	12/28/1990	Florida State	24	Penn State	17
Fiesta	1991	01/1/1992	Penn State	42	Tennessee	17
Blockbuster	1992	01/01/1993	Stanford	24	Penn State	3
Citrus	1993	01/01/1994	Penn State	31	Tennessee	13
Rose	1994	01/01/1995	Penn State	38	Oregon	20
Outback	1995	01/01/1996	Penn State	43	Auburn	14
Fiesta	1996	01/01/1997	Penn State	38	Texas	15

Appendix A

Bowl	Season	Date	Winner	Score	Loser	Score
Citrus	1997	01/01/1998	Florida	21	Penn State	6
Outback	1998	01/01/1999	Penn State	26	Kentucky	14
Alamo	1999	12/28/1999	Penn State	24	Texas A&M	0
Capital One	2002	01/01/2003	Auburn	13	Penn State	9
Orange	2005	01/03/2006	Penn State	26***	Florida State	23
Outback	2006	01/01/2007	Penn State	20	Tennessee	10
Alamo	2007	12/29/2007	Penn State	24	Texas A&M	17
Rose	2008	01/01/2009	USC	38	Penn State	24
Capital One	2009	01/01/2010	Penn State	19	LSU	17
Outback	2010	01/01/2011	Florida	37	Penn State	24
TicketCity	2011	01/02/2012	Houston	30	Penn State	14
Pinstripe	2014	12/27/2014	Penn State	31*	Boston College	30
TaxSlayer	2015	01/02/2016	Georgia	24	Penn State	17
Rose	2016	01/02/2017	USC	52	Penn State	49
Fiesta	2017	12/30/2017	Penn State	35	Washington	28
Citrus	2018	01/01/2019	Kentucky	27	Penn State	24
Cotton	2019	12/28/2019	Penn State	53	Memphis	39

*single overtime; **tie; ***triple overtime
(NC) denotes national championship game
Citrus and Capital One are same bowl; Gator and TaxSlayer are same bowl

Appendix B

Major Bowl Records

National Championship Games	
Record: 2–2	
1979 Sugar (L)	1983 Sugar (W)
1986 Orange (L)	1987 Fiesta (W)

Bowl Championship Series Games (1998–2013)	
Record: 1–1	
2006 Orange (W)	2009 Rose (L)

New Year's Six Games (2014–2019)	
Record: 2–1	
2017 Rose (L)	2017 Fiesta (W)
2019 Cotton (W)	

Rose Bowl		Sugar Bowl	
Record: 1–3		*Record: 1–3*	
1923 (L)	1995 (W)	1972 (L)	1975 (L)
2009 (L)	2017 (L)	1979 (L)	1983 (W)

Orange Bowl		Cotton Bowl	
Record: 4–1		*Record: 3–0–1*	
1969 (W)	1970 (W)	1948 (T)	1972 (W)
1974 (W)	1986 (L)	1975 (W)	2019 (W)
2006 (W)			

Fiesta Bowl		Citrus Bowl	
Record: 7–0		*Record: 2–4*	
1977 (W)	1980 (W)	1988 (L)	1994 (W)
1982 (W)	1987 (W)	1998 (L)	2003 (L)
1992 (W)	1997 (W)	2010 (W)	2019 (L)
2017 (W)			

Gator Bowl		Outback Bowl	
Record: 1–3–1		*Record: 3–1*	
1961 (W)	1962 (L)	1996 (W)	1999 (W)
1967 (T)	1976 (L)	2007 (W)	2011 (L)
2015 (L)			

Most Common Opponents			
Opponent	*Games*	*Record vs.*	*Bowls*
USC	4	1–3	Rose (3x), Fiesta
Alabama	3	1–2	Liberty, Sugar (2x)
Florida State	3	1–1–1	Gator, Blockbuster, Orange
Florida	3	0–3	Gator, Citrus, Outback
Tennessee	3	3–0	Fiesta, Citrus, Outback

Appendix C

Individual Records[1]

	Rushing Yards, Single Game		
	Player	*Yards*	*Bowl*
1.	Journey Brown	202	2019 Cotton
2.	Saquon Barkley	194	2017 Rose
3.	Blair Thomas	186	1989 Holiday
4.	Tony Hunt	158	2007 Outback
5.	Ki-Jana Carter	156	1995 Rose
6.	Curt Warner	155	1980 Fiesta
7.	Lydell Mitchell	146	1972 Cotton
8.	Curt Warner	145	1982 Fiesta
9.	Rodney Kinlaw	143	2007 Alamo
10.	Saquon Barkley	137	2017 Fiesta
11.	Charlie Pittman	124	1967 Gator
12.	Stephen Pitts	118	1996 Outback
13.	Curt Warner	117	1983 Sugar
14.	Tom Donchez	116	1975 Cotton
15.	Matt Suhey	112	1979 Liberty
16.	Steve Geise	111	1977 Fiesta
17.	Austin Scott	110	2006 Orange
18.	Bob Torrey	107	1977 Fiesta
19.	Eric McCoo	105	1999 Outback
20.	D.J. Dozier	102	1987 Fiesta
21.	Bob Campbell	101	1969 Orange

	Rushing Touchdowns, Single Game		
	Player	*TD*	*Bowl*
1.	Ki-Jana Carter	3	1995 Rose
2.	Dick Hoak	2	1960 Liberty
2.	Matt Suhey	2	1977 Fiesta
2.	Curt Warner	2	1982 Fiesta
2.	Curt Warner	2	1983 Sugar
2.	Leroy Thompson	2	1989 Holiday
2.	Ki-Jana Carter	2	1994 Citrus
2.	Curtis Enis	2	1997 Fiesta
2.	Austin Scott	2	2006 Orange
2.	Saquon Barkley	2	2017 Rose
2.	Saquon Barkley	2	2017 Fiesta
2.	Journey Brown	2	2019 Cotton
2.	Noah Cain	2	2019 Cotton

	Rushing Attempts, Single Game		
	Player	*Att.*	*Bowl*
1.	Blair Thomas	35	1989 Holiday
2.	Tony Hunt	31	2007 Outback
3.	Lydell Mitchell	27	1972 Cotton
4.	John Cappelletti	26	1974 Orange
4.	Steve Geise	26	1977 Fiesta
4.	Curt Warner	26	1982 Fiesta
4.	Austin Scott	26	2006 Orange

	Rushing Average (Min. 10 Attempts)		
	Player	*Avg.*	*Bowl*
1.	Journey Brown	12.6	2019 Cotton
2.	Curt Warner	8.6	1980 Fiesta
3.	Stephen Pitts	7.9	1996 Outback
4.	Saquon Barkley	7.8	2017 Rose
5.	Booker Moore	7.6	1980 Fiesta
5.	Saquon Barkley	7.6	2017 Fiesta
7.	Ki-Jana Carter	7.4	1995 Rose

Rushing Attempts, Single Game			
	Player	*Att.*	*Bowl*
8.	Saquon Barkley	25	2017 Rose
8.	Tom Donchez	25	1975 Cotton
8.	Frank Rogel	25	1948 Cotton

Rushing Average (Min. 10 Attempts)			
	Player	*Avg.*	*Bowl*
8.	Brian Milne	6.8	1996 Outback
8.	Rodney Kinlaw	6.8	2007 Alamo
10.	Zack Mills	6.2	2003 Capital One

Longest Run			
	Player	*Yds*	*Bowl*
1.	Saquon Barkley	92	2017 Fiesta
2.	Chafie Fields	84	1997 Fiesta
3.	Ki-Jana Carter	83	1995 Rose
4.	Saquon Barkley	79	2017 Rose
5.	Curt Warner	64	1980 Fiesta
6.	Journey Brown	56	2019 Cotton
7.	Journey Brown	44	2019 Cotton
8.	Stephen Pitts	43	1996 Outback
9.	Evan Royster	38	2007 Alamo
10.	Booker Moore	37	1980 Fiesta

Passing Yardage, Single Game			
	Player	*Yds*	*Bowl*
1.	Christian Hackenberg	371	2014 Pinstripe
2.	Trace McSorley	342	2017 Fiesta
3.	Daryll Clark	273	2009 Rose
4.	Trace McSorley	254	2017 Rose
5.	Michael Robinson	253	2006 Orange
6.	Trace McSorley	246	2019 Citrus
7.	Todd Blackledge	228	1983 Sugar
8.	Tom Shuman	226	1975 Cotton
9.	Wally Richardson	217	1996 Outback
10.	Daryll Clark	216	2010 Capital One
11.	Matt McGloin	211	2011 Outback
12.	Tony Sacca	206	1989 Holiday
13.	Kerry Collins	200	1995 Rose
14.	Anthony Morelli	197	2007 Outback
15.	Tony Sacca	194	1990 Blockbuster
16.	Chuck Burkhart	187	1970 Orange
16.	Kevin Thompson	187	1999 Outback
18.	Galen Hall	175	1961 Gator
18.	Todd Blackledge	175	1982 Fiesta
20.	Chuck Fusina	163	1979 Sugar

	Touchdown Passes, Single Game		
	Player	*TD*	*Bowl*
1.	Tony Sacca	4	1992 Fiesta
1.	Wally Richardson	4	1996 Outback
1.	Christian Hackenberg	4	2014 Pinstripe
1.	Trace McSorley	4	2017 Rose
5.	Galen Hall	3	1961 Gator
6.	Tom Sherman	2	1967 Gator
6.	Tony Sacca	2	1989 Holiday
6.	Daryll Clark	2	2009 Rose
6.	Trace McSorley	2	2016 TaxSlayer
6.	Trace McSorley	2	2017 Fiesta
6.	Trace McSorley	2	2019 Citrus

	Completions, Single Game		
	Player	*Comp.*	*Bowl*
1.	Christian Hackenberg	34	2014 Pinstripe
2.	Trace McSorley	32	2017 Fiesta
3.	Michael Robinson	21	2006 Orange
3.	Daryll Clark	21	2009 Rose
5.	Kerry Collins	19	1995 Rose
6.	Daryll Clark	18	2010 Capital One
6.	Trace McSorley	18	2017 Rose
8.	Matt McGloin	17	2011 Outback
8.	Trace McSorley	17	2019 Citrus
10.	Chuck Fusina	15	1979 Sugar
10.	Kerry Collins	15	1993 Blockbuster
10.	Anthony Morelli	15	2007 Alamo

	Pass Attempts, Single Game		
	Player	*Att.*	*Bowl*
1.	Christian Hackenberg	50	2014 Pinstripe
2.	Matt McGloin	41	2011 Outback
2.	Trace McSorley	41	2017 Fiesta
4.	Michael Robinson	39	2006 Orange
5.	Daryll Clark	36	2009 Rose
6.	Daryll Clark	35	2010 Capital One
7.	Doug Strang	34	1983 Aloha
8.	Chuck Fusina	33	1975 Sugar
8.	Trace McSorley	33	2019 Citrus
10.	Mike McQueary	32	1998 Citrus

Completion % (Min. 10 Att.)			
	Player	*%*	*Bowl*
1.	Trace McSorley	78.0	2017 Fiesta
2.	Matt Knizner	72.7	1986 Orange
3.	Christian Hackenberg	68.0	2014 Pinstripe
4.	Kerry Collins	63.3	1995 Rose
5.	Kerry Collins	62.5	1994 Citrus
6.	Trace McSorley	62.0	2017 Rose
7.	Wally Richardson	60.0	1997 Fiesta
8.	Matt Knizner	59.1	1988 Citrus
9.	Daryll Clark	58.3	2009 Rose
10.	Todd Blackledge	56.5	1983 Sugar

Longest Completion (All TDs)				
	QB	*Receiver*	*Yds*	*Bowl*
1.	Tom Shuman	Chuck Herd	72	1974 Orange
1.	Christian Hackenberg	Chris Godwin	72	2014 Pinstripe
1.	Trace McSorley	Chris Godwin	72	2017 Rose
4.	Rob Bolden	Justin Brown	69	2012 TicketCity
5.	John Hufnagel	Scott Skarzynski	65	1972 Cotton
6.	Tony Sacca	David Daniels	56	1990 Blockbuster
6.	Kevin Thompson	Joe Nastasi	56	1999 Outback
8.	Todd Blackledge	Gregg Garrity	52	1982 Fiesta
8.	Tony Sacca	David Daniels	52	1989 Holiday
10.	Tom Shuman	Jimmy Cefalo	49	1975 Cotton

Interceptions Thrown, Single Game			
	Player	*INT*	*Bowl*
1.	Matt McGloin	5	2011 Outback
2.	Chuck Fusina	4	1979 Sugar
3.	Harry Wilson	3	1923 Rose
3.	John Shaffer	3	1986 Orange
3.	Mike McQueary	3	1998 Citrus
3.	Rob Bolden	3	2012 TicketCity
3.	Trace McSorley	3	2017 Rose

Receiving Yards, Single Game			
	Player	*Yds*	*Bowl*
1.	Chris Godwin	187	2017 Rose
2.	David Daniels	154	1990 Blockbuster
3.	Chris Godwin	140	2014 Pinstripe
4.	Chris Godwin	133	2016 TaxSlayer
5.	Gregg Garrity	116	1983 Sugar
6.	Bobby Engram	113	1983 Sugar
7.	O.J. McDuffie	111	1993 Blockbuster

Receiving Yards, Single Game

	Player	Yds	Bowl
8.	Jordan Norwood	110	2006 Orange
8.	DaeSean Hamilton	110	2017 Fiesta
10.	Bobby Engram	107	1994 Citrus
11.	Jimmy Cefalo	102	1975 Cotton
12.	Terry Smith	100	1990 Blockbuster
13.	Deon Butler	97	2009 Rose
14.	Andrew Quarless	88	2010 Capital One
15.	Geno Lewis	82	2014 Pinstripe
16.	Lydell Mitchell	81	1970 Orange
16.	Scott Skarzynski	81	1972 Cotton
18.	Ethan Kilmer	79	2006 Orange
18.	Derek Moye	79	2011 Outback
20.	O.J. McDuffie	78	1992 Fiesta

Receptions, Single Game

	Player	Rec.	Bowl
1.	Chris Godwin	9	2017 Rose
2.	Andrew Quarless	8	2010 Capital One
3.	David Daniels	7	1990 Blockbuster
3.	Bobby Engram	7	1994 Citrus
3.	Tony Stewart	7	1999 Outback
3.	Chris Godwin	7	2014 Pinstripe
3.	DaeSean Hamilton	7	2014 Pinstripe
3.	Geno Lewis	7	2014 Pinstripe
3.	Saquon Barkley	7	2017 Fiesta
10.	Ted Kwalick	6	1969 Orange
10.	Dean DiMidio	6	1986 Orange
10.	O.J. McDuffie	6	1993 Blockbuster
10.	Jordan Norwood	6	2006 Orange
10.	Chris Godwin	6	2016 TaxSlayer
10.	Juwan Johnson	6	2017 Fiesta
10.	Mike Gesicki	6	2017 Fiesta

Yards Per Reception (Min. 3 Rec.)

	Player	Avg.	Bowl
1.	Jimmy Cefalo	34.0	1975 Cotton
2.	Gregg Garrity	29.0	1983 Sugar
3.	Bobby Engram	28.3	1996 Outback
4.	Deon Butler	24.3	2007 Outback
5.	Deon Butler	24.2	2009 Rose
6.	Chris Godwin	22.2	2016 TaxSlayer
7.	David Daniels	22.0	1990 Blockbuster
8.	Chris Godwin	20.8	2017 Rose
9.	Michael Timpson	20.3	1988 Citrus

	Touchdown Receptions, Single Game		
	Player	*TD*	*Bowl*
1.	Bobby Engram	2	1996 Outback
1.	Chris Godwin	2	2017 Rose
1.	DaeSean Hamilton	2	2017 Fiesta

	Total Offense, Single Game		
	Player	*Yds*	*Bowl*
1.	Trace McSorley	402	2017 Fiesta
2.	Christian Hackenberg	371	2014 Pinstripe
3.	Trace McSorley	321	2019 Citrus
4.	Daryll Clark	290	2009 Rose
5.	Michael Robinson	274	2006 Orange
6.	Trace McSorley	267	2017 Rose
7.	Tom Shuman	240	1975 Cotton
8.	Daryll Clark	236	2010 Capital One
9.	Blair Thomas	232	1989 Holiday
10.	Tony Sacca	222	1990 Blockbuster

	Touchdowns Responsible For, Single Game		
	Player	*TD*	*Bowl*
1.	Trace McSorley	5	2017 Rose
2.	Tony Sacca	4	1992 Fiesta
2.	Wally Richardson	4	1996 Outback
2.	Christian Hackenberg	4	2014 Pinstripe
5.	Dick Hoak	3	1960 Liberty
5.	Galen Hall	3	1961 Gator
5.	Ki-Jana Carter	3	1995 Rose
5.	Daryll Clark	3	2009 Rose
5.	Trace McSorley	3	2019 Citrus

	Points Scored, Single Game						
	Player	*TD*	*FG*	*PAT*	*2-PT*	*Pts*	*Bowl*
1.	Curtis Enis	3	0	0	1	20	1997 Fiesta
2.	Ki-Jana Carter	3	0	0	0	18	1995 Rose
2.	Saquon Barkley	3	0	0	0	18	2017 Rose
4.	Travis Forney	0	4	2	0	14	1999 Outback
5.	Brett Conway	0	3	4	0	13	1996 Outback
5.	Collin Wagner	0	4	1	0	13	2010 Capital One

Extra Points, Single Game

	Player	PAT	Bowl
1.	Tyler Davis	7	2017 Rose
2.	Craig Fayak	6	1992 Fiesta
2.	Jake Pinegar	6	2019 Cotton
4.	George Reihner	5	1975 Cotton
4.	Tyler Davis	5	2017 Fiesta
6.	Henry Oppermann	4	1960 Liberty
6.	Herb Mendhart	4	1980 Fiesta
6.	Craig Fayak	4	1994 Citrus
6.	Brett Conway	4	1995 Rose
6.	Brett Conway	4	1996 Outback
6.	Sam Ficken	4	2014 Pinstripe

Field Goals, Single Game

	Player	FG	Att.	Bowl
1.	Travis Forney	4	5	1999 Outback
1.	Collin Wagner	4	4	2010 Capital One
3.	Alberto Vitiello	3	3	1972 Cotton
3.	Herb Mendhart	3	4	1979 Liberty
3.	Ray Tarasi	3	3	1983 Aloha
3.	Brett Conway	3	4	1996 Outback
3.	Robbie Gould	3	4	2003 Capital One

Longest Field Goal

	Player	Yds	Bowl
1.	Ray Tarasi	51	1989 Holiday
2.	Nick Gancitano	49	1983 Aloha
3.	Nick Gancitano	45	1983 Sugar
3.	Sam Ficken	45	2014 Pinstripe
3.	Jake Pinegar	45	2019 Cotton
6.	Chris Bahr	44	1974 Orange
7.	Brett Conway	43	1995 Rose
7.	Travis Forney	43	1999 Outback
9.	Chris Bahr	42	1975 Sugar
9.	Travis Forney	42	1998 Citrus
11.	Travis Forney	39	1999 Alamo

Longest Punt

	Player	Yds	Bowl
1.	Blake Gillikin	71	2019 Citrus
2.	Bob Campbell	68	1967 Gator
3.	Ralph Giacomarro	63	1982 Fiesta
4.	Pete Liske	62	1961 Gator
4.	Ralph Giacomarro	62	1983 Sugar
4.	George Reynolds	62	1983 Aloha
7.	Scott Fitzkee	59	1977 Fiesta

Punt Average (Min. 3 Punts)

	Player	Avg.	Bowl
1.	Jeremy Boone	51.4	2007 Alamo
2.	Blake Gillikin	51.2	2019 Citrus
3.	Chris Clauss	51.0	1988 Citrus
4.	Ralph Giacomarro	50.8	1982 Fiesta
4.	Blake Gillikin	50.8	2017 Rose

Punt Average (Min. 3 Punts)

	Player	Avg.	Bowl
6.	Chris Bahr	48.5	1975 Sugar
7.	Doug Helkowski	47.9	1992 Fiesta

Interceptions, Single Game

	Player	INT	Bowl
1.	Tim Montgomery	2	1967 Gator
1.	George Landis	2	1970 Orange
1.	Dennis Onkotz	2	1970 Orange
1.	Neal Smith	2	1970 Orange
1.	Mark Robinson	2	1983 Sugar
1.	Shane Conlan	2	1987 Fiesta
1.	Pete Giftopoulos	2	1987 Fiesta
1.	Sherrod Rainge	2	1989 Holiday
1.	Reggie Givens	2	1992 Fiesta
1.	Chuck Penzenik	2	1995 Rose
1.	Kim Herring	2	1996 Outback
1.	Anthony King	2	1999 Outback
1.	Derek Fox	2	1999 Alamo

Tackles, Single Game

	Player	Tkl	Bowl
1.	Matt Millen	18	1977 Fiesta
2.	Lance Mehl	17	1979 Sugar
3.	Kurt Allerman	16	1976 Gator
4.	Keith Goganious	15	1992 Fiesta
5.	Gary Gray	14	1972 Cotton
5.	Ron Coder	14	1975 Sugar
5.	Randy Sidler	14	1976 Gator
5.	Tom DePaso	14	1977 Fiesta
5.	Scott Radecic	14	1983 Sugar
5.	Carmen Masciantonio	14	1983 Aloha
5.	LaVar Arrington	14	1999 Alamo
5.	Sean Lee	14	2007 Alamo
5.	Micah Parsons	14	2019 Citrus
5.	Micah Parsons	14	2019 Cotton

Tackles for Loss, Single Game

	Player	TFL	Bowl
1.	NaVorro Bowman	5.0	2009 Rose
2.	Courtney Brown	4.0	1999 Outback
2.	Justin Kurpeikis	4.0	1999 Alamo
4.	Devon Still	3.5	2011 Outback
5.	Bruce Clark	3.0	1977 Fiesta
5.	Frank Case	3.0	1980 Fiesta
5.	Gene Gladys	3.0	1980 Fiesta
5.	Leo Wisniewski	3.0	1982 Fiesta
5.	Trey Bauer	3.0	1988 Citrus
5.	Todd Atkins	3.0	1995 Rose
5.	Courtney Brown	3.0	1999 Alamo
5.	Micah Parsons	3.0	2019 Cotton

Sacks, Single Game

	Player	Sacks	Bowl
1.	Todd Burger	2.0	1989 Holiday
1.	Todd Atkins	2.0	1995 Rose
1.	Phil Yeboah-Kodie	2.0	1995 Rose
1.	Terry Killens	2.0	1996 Outback
1.	Courtney Brown	2.0	1999 Outback
1.	Brad Scioli	2.0	1999 Outback
1.	Justin Kurpeikis	2.0	1999 Alamo
1.	Kevin Givens	2.0	2019 Citrus
1.	Micah Parsons	2.0	2019 Cotton
10.	Jay Alford	1.5	2006 Orange

Kickoff Returns, Single Game

	Player	Ret	Bowl
1.	Leroy Thompson	6	1988 Citrus
2.	O.J. McDuffie	5	1989 Holiday
3.	Chaz Powell	4	2010 Citrus
3.	Silas Redd	4	2011 Outback
3.	Miles Sanders	4	2017 Fiesta

Kick Return Yardage, Single Game

	Player	Yds	Bowl
1.	O.J. McDuffie	128	1989 Holiday
2.	Leroy Thompson	127	1988 Citrus
3.	Ambrose Fletcher	85	1995 Rose
4.	Kenny Watson	81	1997 Fiesta
5.	Chaz Powell	78	2010 Citrus
6.	Silas Redd	74	2011 Outback

Kick Return Avg. (Min. 3 Returns)			
	Player	*Avg.*	*Bowl*
1.	O.J. McDuffie	25.6	1989 Holiday
2.	Curt Warner	23.0	1980 Fiesta
2.	Brandon Polk	23.0	2016 TaxSlayer
4.	Eddie Drummond	21.3	1999 Outback
5.	Leroy Thompson	21.2	1988 Citrus
6.	Jim Coates	20.3	1986 Orange

Longest Kickoff Return			
	Player	*Yds*	*Bowl*
1.	Kenny Watson	81	1997 Fiesta
2.	Ambrose Fletcher	72	1995 Rose
3.	Joe Jackson	50	1975 Cotton
4.	O.J. McDuffie	46	1989 Holiday
5.	D.J. Dozier	42	1983 Aloha
5.	Shelly Hammonds	42	1992 Fiesta

Punt Returns, Single Game			
	Player	*Ret*	*Bowl*
1.	Kevin Baugh	5	1983 Sugar
2.	Rich Mauti	3	1975 Sugar
2.	Jim Coates	3	1986 Orange
2.	Jim Coates	3	1987 Fiesta
2.	Bobby Engram	3	1994 Citrus
2.	Mike Archie	3	1996 Outback
2.	Justin Brown	3	2010 Citrus
2.	DeAndre Thompkins	3	2017 Fiesta

Punt Return Yardage, Single Game			
	Player	*Yds*	*Bowl*
1.	Kevin Baugh	106	1983 Sugar
2.	O.J. McDuffie	71	1992 Fiesta
3.	Jimmy Cefalo	67	1977 Fiesta
4.	Gary Hayman	61	1974 Orange
5.	Terry Smith	53	1990 Blockbuster
6.	Kenny Watson	52	1998 Citrus

Punt Return Avg. (Min. 3 Returns)			
	Player	*Avg.*	*Bowl*
1.	Kevin Baugh	21.2	1983 Sugar
2.	Gary Hayman	20.3	1974 Orange
3.	O.J. McDuffie	17.8	1992 Fiesta
4.	Bobby Engram	14.0	1994 Citrus
5.	Mike Archie	10.0	1996 Outback

Longest Punt Return			
	Player	*Yds*	*Bowl*
1.	Jimmy Cefalo	67	1977 Fiesta
2.	Kenny Watson	52	1998 Citrus
3.	Terry Smith	42	1990 Blockbuster
4.	O.J. McDuffie	39	1992 Fiesta
5.	Gary Hayman	36	1974 Orange

Career TD Receptions			
	Player	*TD*	*Bowls w/TD*
1.	DaeSean Hamilton	4	3
2.	Bobby Engram	3	2
2.	Chris Godwin	3	2
4.	Roger Kochman	2	2
4.	Gregg Garrity	2	2
4.	David Daniels	2	2
4.	Terry Smith	2	2
4.	Derek Moye	2	2
4.	Geno Lewis	2	2

Appendix D

Team Bowl Records[1]

Most Points Scored	53	2019 Cotton
Fewest Points Allowed	0	1959 Liberty, 1999 Alamo
Most Combined Points	101	2017 Rose
Fewest Combined Points	7	1959 Liberty
Most 1st Qtr Points	14	1977 Fiesta, 2017 Fiesta
Most 2nd Qtr Points	28	2019 Cotton
Most 3rd Qtr Points	28	2017 Rose
Most 4th Qtr Points	24	1975 Cotton
Most 1st Half Points	35	2019 Cotton
Most 2nd Half Points	38	1975 Cotton, 1989 Holiday
First Downs	26	1989 Holiday
Most Combined 1st Downs	61	1989 Holiday
Rushing Yards	396	2019 Cotton
Combined Rushing Yards	486	1996 Outback
Rushing Average	7.5	1996 Fiesta, 2019 Cotton
Passing Yards	371	2014 Pinstripe
Combined Passing Yards	791	1989 Holiday
Completions	34	2014 Pinstripe
Pass Attempts	50	2014 Pinstripe
Touchdown Passes	4	1992 Fiesta, 1996 Outback,
		2014 Pinstripe, 2017 Rose
Interceptions Thrown	5	2011 Outback
Total Offense	545	2017 Fiesta
Combined Offense	1,115	1989 Holiday
Total Plays	87	1960 Liberty, 2006 Orange
Fumbles Lost	4	1959 Liberty, 1972 Sugar
Turnovers	5	1962 Gator, 1972 Sugar,
		1986 Orange, 2011 Outback
Penalties	12	1977 Fiesta
Penalty Yardage	126	1977 Fiesta

Punts	12	1923 Rose, 1970 Orange
Fewest Punts	2	1975 Cotton, 1989 Holiday
Largest Comeback Win	14	2007 Alamo, 2014 Pinstripe
Fewest Points Scored	0	1972 Sugar
Fewest Points in a Win	7	1959 Liberty
Most Points in a Loss	49	2017 Rose
Field Goals	4	1999 Outback, 2010 Capital One

Appendix E

Passing Statistics[1]

Player	Pos.	Comp	Att	Comp %	Yds	TD	INT	Rating	Bowl Games*
Trace McSorley	QB	81	130	62.31%	984	10	6	142.0	TS16, R17, F17, CIT19
Tony Sacca	QB	33	73	45.21%	550	7	3	131.9	H89, B90, F92
Todd Blackledge	QB	32	69	46.38%	520	2	2	113.4	F80, F82, S83
Christian Hackenberg	QB	42	64	65.63%	510	4	1	150.1	P14, TS16
Kerry Collins	QB	46	84	54.76%	507	2	3	106.2	F92, B93, CIT94, R95
Daryll Clark	QB	39	71	54.93%	489	3	2	121.1	OU07, ALM07, R09, CAP10
Tom Shuman	QB	16	37	43.24%	383	2	1	142.6	S72, OR74, COT75
Chuck Fusina	QB	38	86	44.19%	364	3	6	77.3	G76, F77, S79
Chuck Burkhart	QB	23	49	46.94%	341	1	3	99.9	OR69, OR70
Anthony Morelli	QB	29	56	51.79%	340	2	1	111.0	OR06, OU07, ALM07
Wally Richardson	QB	26	52	50%	323	5	2	126.2	B93, R95, OU96, F97
Michael Robinson	QB	23	42	54.76%	284	1	1	114.7	CAP03, OR06
John Hufnagel	QB	19	43	44.19%	284	1	2	98.0	COT72, S72
Galen Hall	QB	17	35	48.57%	240	4	0	143.9	L59, L60, G61
Matt Knizner	QB	21	33	63.64%	238	1	3	116.0	OR86, F87, CIT88
Matt McGloin	QB	17	41	41.46%	211	1	5	68.4	CAP10, OU11, TC12
Kevin Thompson	QB	14	27	51.85%	187	1	0	122.3	F97, CIT98, OU99, ALM99
Rashard Casey	QB	8	16	50%	146	1	1	134.8	CIT98, OU99, ALM99
Rob Bolden	QB	7	26	26.92%	137	1	3	60.8	TC12
Sean Clifford	QB	11	22	50%	133	1	1	106.7	CIT19, COT19
John Shaffer	QB	15	38	39.47%	127	0	4	46.5	ALO83, OR86, F87
Doug Strang	QB	14	34	41.18%	118	0	1	64.4	S83, ALO83
Mike McQueary	QB	11	36	30.56%	96	0	4	30.7	OU96, F97, CIT98
Elwood Petchel	QB	7	15	46.67%	91	1	0	119.6	CIT48
Tom Bill	QB	3	7	42.86%	84	1	1	162.2	CIT88, H89, B90
Tom Sherman	QB	6	19	31.58%	69	2	2	75.8	G67
Zack Mills	QB	8	24	33.33%	67	0	1	48.5	CAP03
Dick Hoak	RB	3	5	60%	67	1	0	238.6	L59, L60
Pete Liske	QB	5	18	27.78%	58	0	1	43.7	G61, G62
John Andress	QB	8	14	57.14%	57	0	1	77.1	S75, G76
Frank Rocco	QB	5	10	50%	56	0	2	57.0	L79, F80
Darin Roberts	QB	1	1	100%	46	0	0	486.4	F87, CIT88
Joel Coles	RB	1	1	100%	39	0	0	427.6	L79, F80, S83

Player	Pos.	Comp	Att	Comp %	Yds	TD	INT	Rating	Bowl Games*
Richie Lucas	QB	1	4	25%	23	0	0	73.3	L59
Terry Smith	WR	1	1	100%	9	0	0	175.6	H89, B90, F92
Harry Wilson	RB	2	2	100%	5	0	0	121.0	R23
Jon Lang	QB	1	1	100%	5	0	0	142.0	L60
Mike Archie	RB	1	2	50%	2	0	0	58.4	B93, CIT94, R95, OU96
Mike Palm	QB	3	9	33.33%	1	0	3	3.3	R23
Ron Coates	QB	0	2	0%	0	0	0	0.0	G62
John Sacca	QB	0	2	0%	0	0	0	0.0	B93
Don Jonas	RB	0	1	0%	0	0	0	0.0	L60, G61
Don Caum	QB	0	1	0%	0	0	1	-200.0	G61, G62
Steve Joachim	QB	0	1	0%	0	0	0	0.0	COT72
D.J. Dozier	RB	0	1	0%	0	0	0	0.0	ALO83, OR86, F87
Bill Belton	RB	0	1	0%	0	0	0	0.0	TC12, P14

Bowl games as member of team; player may not have thrown a pass in all listed bowls

ALO—Aloha, ALM—Alamo, B—Blockbuster, CAP—Capital One, CIT—Citrus, COT—Cotton, F—Fiesta, G—Gator, H—Holiday, L—Liberty, OR—Orange, OU—Outback, P—Pinstripe, S—Sugar, TC—TicketCity, TS—TaxSlayer

Appendix F

Rushing Statistics[1]

Player	Pos.	Att	Yds	TD	Avg	Bowl Games*
Curt Warner	RB	76	474	5	6.2	L79, F80, F82, S83
Saquon Barkley	RB	60	400	4	6.7	TS16, R17, F17
Matt Suhey	RB	51	276	2	5.4	G76, F77, S79, L79
Charlie Pittman	RB	54	265	0	4.9	G67, OR69, OR70
Evan Royster	RB	52	262	1	5.0	ALM07, R09, CAP10, OU11
Ki-Jana Carter	RB	43	256	2	6.0	B93, CIT94, R95
Journey Brown	RB	17	206	2	12.1	CIT19, COT19
Steve Geise	RB	46	193	1	4.2	S75, G76, F77
Blair Thomas	RB	36	183	1	5.1	OR86, F87, CIT88, H89
Trace McSorley	QB	44	179	2	4.1	TS16, R17, F17, CIT19
Bob Torrey	RB	23	177	0	7.7	G76, F77, S79
D.J. Dozier	RB	47	175	2	3.7	ALO83, OR86, F87
Tony Hunt	RB	31	158	0	5.1	OR06, OU07
Leroy Thompson	RB	28	156	2	5.6	CIT88, H89, B90
Stephfon Green	RB	32	155	1	4.8	R09, CAP10, OU11, TC12
Eric McCoo	RB	27	148	0	5.5	OU99, ALM99
Lydell Mitchell	RB	32	147	1	4.6	OR70, COT72
Chafie Fields	WR	4	144	1	36.0	F97, CIT98, OU99, ALM 99
Rodney Kinlaw	RB	23	143	0	6.2	OR06, OU07, ALM07
Jon Williams	RB	39	136	1	3.5	F80, F82, S83, ALO83
Mike Archie	RB	23	136	0	5.9	B93, CIT94, R95, OU96
Booker Moore	RB	32	131	1	4.1	F77, S79, L79, F80
Brian Milne	RB	24	131	1	5.5	CIT94, R95, OU96
Stephen Pitts	RB	16	122	0	7.6	B93, CIT94, R95, OU96
Curtis Enis	RB	28	119	3	4.3	R95, OU96
Austin Scott	RB	26	110	0	4.2	OR06, ALM07
Chris Eberly	RB	22	106	0	4.8	OU96, F97, CIT98, OU99
Larry Johnson	RB	26	102	0	3.9	ALM99, CAP03
Bob Campbell	RB	18	101	1	5.6	G67, OR69
Roger Kochman	RB	19	98	0	5.2	L59, G61, G62
Richie Anderson	RB	30	97	1	3.2	H89, F92, B93
Fran Rogel	RB	25	95	0	3.8	CTN48
Franco Harris	RB	28	93	0	3.3	OR70, COT72

Player	Pos.	Att	Yds	TD	Avg	Bowl Games*
Noah Cain	RB	15	92	2	6.1	COT19
Dick Hoak	RB	16	91	2	5.7	L59, L60
Mike Meade	RB	16	90	0	5.6	S79, L79, F80, F82
Daryll Clark	QB	24	87	2	3.6	OU07, ALM07, R09, CAP10
Ricky Slade	RB	9	85	0	9.4	CIT19, COT19
Akeel Lynch	RB	18	79	0	4.4	P14, TS16
Neil Hutton	RB	12	79	0	6.6	COT75, G76, F77
Jimmy Cefalo	WR	20	78	1	3.9	COT75, S75, G76, F77
Sam Sobczak	RB	17	78	0	4.6	L59, L60
Cordell Mitchell	RB	14	71	0	5.1	F97, CIT98, OU99, ALM 99
Aaron Harris	RB	17	67	1	3.9	F97, CIT98, OU99, ALM 99
Silas Redd	RB	22	66	0	3.0	OU11, TC12
Miles Sanders	RB	19	66	1	3.5	R17, F17, CIT19
Jim Kerr	RB	17	63	0	3.7	L59, L60
Al Gursky	RB	19	60	1	3.2	L60, G61, G62
Joel Coles	RB	9	59	0	6.6	S79, L79, F80, F82, S83
Zack Mills	QB	9	56	0	6.2	CAP03
Harry Wilson	RB	20	55	0	2.8	R23
Richie Lucas	QB	9	54	0	6.0	L59
Dick Pae	RB	15	52	0	3.5	L59, L60
Galen Hall	QB	12	52	0	4.3	L59, L60, G61
Bob Nagle	RB	17	51	0	3.0	COT72, S72, OR74
Michael Robinson	QB	2	51	0	25.5	CAP03, OR06
John Cappelletti	RB	26	50	1	1.9	S72, OR74
Dave Hayes	RB	19	50	0	2.6	L60, G61, G62
Tim Manoa	RB	13	50	1	3.8	ALO83, OR86, F87
Pat Botula	RB	13	50	0	3.8	L59
Gary Brown	RB	14	46	0	3.3	CIT88, H89, B90
Bill Belton	RB	9	46	0	5.1	TC12, P14
Brian O'Neal	RB	16	44	0	2.8	H89, B90, B93, CIT94
Don Jonas	RB	13	40	1	3.1	L60, G61
Bobby Engram	RB	2	40	0	20.0	F92, CIT94, R95, OU96
Duane Taylor	RB	13	39	0	3.0	OR74, COT75, S75, F77
Buddy Torris	RB	14	38	1	2.7	L60, G61, G62
Steve Smith	RB	13	36	0	2.8	ALO83, OR86, F87
Tom Donchez	RB	12	36	0	3.0	COT72, S72, OR74
Derrick Williams	WR	10	34	0	3.4	OR06, OU07, ALM07, R09
Mike Guman	RB	14	31	0	2.2	G76, F77, S79, L79
Anthony Cleary	RB	5	31	1	6.2	F97, CIT98
Tom Cherry	RB	13	28	0	2.2	G67, OR69
Rashard Casey	QB	7	27	0	3.9	CIT98, OU99, ALM99
Mike Palm	QB	16	25	0	1.6	R23
K.J. Hamler	WR	3	25	0	8.3	CIT19, COT19
Sean Clifford	QB	14	24	0	1.7	CIT19, COT19
Kenny Watson	RB	8	24	0	3.0	F97, CIT98, ALM99

Appendix F

Player	Pos.	Att	Yds	TD	Avg	Bowl Games*
Tom Sherman	QB	6	24	0	4.0	G67
John Andress	QB	5	22	0	4.4	S75, G76
Mike Cerimele	RB	5	21	0	4.2	CIT98, OU99, ALM99
Michael Timpson	WR	1	21	0	21.0	OR86, F87, CIT88
Tom Shuman	QB	10	18	1	1.8	S72, OR74, COT75
Walt Addie	RB	7	18	0	2.6	S72, OR74, COT75
Don Abbey	RB	5	18	0	3.6	G67, OR69, OR70
Devon Smith	WR	4	18	0	4.5	CAP10, OU11, TC12
Scott Fitzkee	WR	1	18	0	18.0	S75, G76, F77, S79
Rob Bolden	QB	6	16	0	2.7	OU11, TC12
Harold Powell	RB	4	16	0	4.0	G61, G62
Sam Gash	RB	7	15	0	2.1	CIT88, B90, F92
J.T. Morris	RB	3	15	0	5.0	F92, B93
Skeeter Nichols	RB	6	13	0	2.2	F80, F82, S83, ALO83
Terry Smith	WR	1	13	0	13.0	H89, B90, F92
Dan Lucyk	RB	7	12	0	1.7	G67
Jeff Hostetler	QB	1	12	0	12.0	L79, F80
Frank Rocco	QB	8	11	0	1.4	L79, F80, F82
Woody Petchel	RB	7	11	0	1.6	OR74, COT75, S75
Jon Witman	RB	4	11	1	2.8	CIT94, R95, OU96
Gary Hayman	RB	4	11	0	2.8	S72, OR74
Jason Sload	RB	4	11	0	2.8	R95, OU96, F97
Joe Suhey	RB	4	11	0	2.8	R09, CAP10, OU11, TC12
A.J. Wallace	DB	1	11	0	11.0	OU07, ALM07, R09, CAP10
Brandon Polk	WR	3	10	0	3.3	TS16, R17, F17, CIT19
R.J. Luke	RB	3	10	0	3.3	OU99, ALM99
Dick Barvinchak	WR	1	10	0	10.0	OR74, COT75, S75
Gerald Smith	WR	1	10	0	10.0	CAP03
Shelly Hammonds	RB	1	10	0	10.0	B90, F92, B93, CIT94
Kenny Jackson	WR	3	9	0	3.0	F80, F82, S83, ALO83
Omar Easy	RB	3	9	0	3.0	OU99, ALM99
Kenn Andrews	RB	1	9	0	9.0	COT72, S72
Roger Grimes	RB	3	8	0	2.7	G67
Brandon Beachum	RB	1	8	0	8.0	R09, CAP10, TC12
Barney Wentz	RB	4	7	0	1.8	R23
Gerry Collins	RB	4	7	0	1.8	H89, B90, F92
Tom Barr	RB	2	7	0	3.5	L79, F80, F82, S83
Ted Kwalick	WR	1	7	0	7.0	G67, OR69
Jordan Norwood	WR	1	7	0	7.0	OR06, OU07, ALM07, R09
John Greene	RB	4	6	0	1.5	CIT88
Ed Caye	RB	3	6	1	2.0	L59, L60
Squeak Hufford	RB	2	6	0	3.0	R23
Anthony Morelli	QB	2	6	0	3.0	OR06, OU07, ALM07
Michael Zordich	RB	3	5	1	1.7	CAP10, OU11, TC12
David Clark	RB	2	5	0	2.5	OR86, F87

Player	Pos.	Att	Yds	TD	Avg	Bowl Games*
Tom Bill	QB	2	5	0	2.5	CIT88, H89, B90
Freddy Flock	RB	1	5	0	5.0	R23
Matt Hahn	RB	1	5	0	5.0	OR06, OU07, ALM07
Christian Hackenberg	QB	9	4	0	0.4	P14, TS16
Dan Lawlor	RB	2	4	0	2.0	OR06, OU07, ALM07, R09
Ed Stuckrath	RB	1	4	0	4.0	G62
Larry Suhey	RB	1	4	0	4.0	COT75, S75, G76
Brian Moser	RB	1	4	0	4.0	B90, F92, B93
Nick Scott	RB	1	4	0	4.0	TS16, R17, F17, CIT19
Andre Robinson	RB	1	4	0	4.0	TS16, R17, F17
Mark Allen	RB	1	4	0	4.0	TS16, R17, F17, CIT19
John Hufnagel	QB	14	3	1	0.2	COT72, S72
Matt McGloin	QB	2	3	1	1.5	CAP10, OU11, TC12
Rich Mauti	RB	2	3	0	1.5	COT75, S75, G76
Ray Roundtree	WR	1	3	0	3.0	OR86, F87, CIT88
Mike Alexander	WR	1	3	0	3.0	OR86, CIT88
Jeff Nixon	RB	1	3	0	3.0	F97
O.J. McDuffie	WR	6	2	0	0.3	H89, B90, F92, B93
Devyn Ford	RB	2	2	1	1.0	COT19
Chuck Herd	WR	1	2	0	2.0	COT72, S72, OR74
Bob Kline	RB	1	2	0	2.0	L60, G61
Tony Wayne	RB	1	2	0	2.0	L59, L60, G61
Bill Emerson	RB	1	2	0	2.0	F82, S83, ALO83
Paul Jefferson	RB	1	2	0	2.0	CAP03
BranDon Snow	RB	2	1	0	0.5	OR06, OU07
Bernie Sabol	RB	1	1	0	1.0	G61
Steve Stilley	RB	1	1	0	1.0	COT72, S72
Tom Donovan	WR	1	0	0	0.0	S75, G76, S79, L79
Joel Ramich	RB	1	0	0	0.0	OR69, OR70
Evan Schwan	RB	1	0	0	0.0	P14, TS16, R17
Johnathan Thomas	RB	1	0	0	0.0	TS16, F17, CIT19
Craig Fayak	K	1	0	0	0.0	B90, F92, B93, CIT94
Saeed Blacknall	WR	1	-1	0	-1.0	P14, TS16, R17, F17
Frank Hershey	RB	1	-1	0	-1.0	G62
Doug Ostrosky	QB	1	-1	0	-1.0	OU96
Justin King	DB	1	-1	0	-1.0	OR06, OU07, ALM07
Tony Sacca	QB	14	-2	0	-0.1	H89, B90, F92
Wally Richardson	QB	2	-2	0	-1.0	B93, R95, OU96, F97
Curtis Drake	WR	1	-3	0	-3.0	CAP10, TC12
Kerry Collins	QB	2	-4	0	-2.0	F92, B93, CIT94, R95
Pete Liske	QB	4	-7	1	-1.8	G61, G62
Matt Knizner	QB	3	-7	0	-2.3	OR86, F87, CIT88
Doug Strang	QB	10	-8	0	-0.8	F82, S83, ALO83
Mike McQueary	QB	7	-14	0	-2.0	OU96, F97, CIT98
John Shaffer	QB	9	-39	1	-4.3	ALO83, OR86, F87

Player	Pos.	Att	Yds	TD	Avg	Bowl Games*
Todd Blackledge	QB	18	-45	1	-2.5	F80, F82, S83
Chuck Burkhart	QB	15	-71	1	-4.7	G67, OR69, OR70
Chuck Fusina	QB	11	-89	0	-8.1	G76, F77, S79

Bowl games as member of team; player may not have rushed in all bowls

ALO—Aloha, ALM—Alamo, B—Blockbuster, CAP—Capital One, CIT—Citrus, COT—Cotton, F—Fiesta, G—Gator, H—Holiday, L—Liberty, OR—Orange, OU—Outback, P—Pinstripe, S—Sugar, TC—TicketCity, TS—TaxSlayer

Appendix G

Receiving Statistics[1]

Player	Pos.	Rec	Yds	TD	Avg	Bowl Games*
Chris Godwin	WR	22	460	3	20.9	P14, TS16, R17
DaeSean Hamilton	WR	17	232	2	13.6	P14, TS16, R17, F17
Saquon Barkley	RB	17	106	1	6.2	TS16, R17, F17
Bobby Engram	WR	16	272	3	17.0	F92, CIT94, R95, OU96
Jimmy Cefalo	WR	13	219	1	16.8	COT75, S75, G76, F77
Jordan Norwood	WR	13	177	1	13.6	OR06, OU07, ALM07, R09
Deon Butler	WR	12	242	1	20.2	OR06, OU07, ALM07, R09
O.J. McDuffie	WR	12	225	1	18.8	H89, B90, F92, B93
Andrew Quarless	TE	12	117	1	9.8	OU07, ALM07, R09, CAP10
Derrick Williams	WR	12	100	1	8.3	OR06, OU07, ALM07, R09
Geno Lewis	WR	10	135	2	13.5	P14, TS16
Dean DiMidio	TE	10	85	0	8.5	S83, ALO83, OR86
David Daniels	WR	9	218	2	24.2	H89, B90
Tony Stewart	TE	9	98	0	10.9	CIT98, OU99, ALM99
Derek Moye	WR	8	132	2	16.5	R09, CAP10, OU11, TC12
DeAndre Thompkins	WR	8	122	0	15.3	TS16, R17, F17, CIT19
Ted Kwalick	WR	8	99	1	12.4	G67, OR69
Brad Scovill	TE	8	97	0	12.1	S79, L79, F80
Freddie Scott	WR	8	77	0	9.6	CIT94, R95, OU96
Stephfon Green	RB	8	74	0	9.3	R09, CAP10, OU11, TC12
D.J. Dozier	RB	8	34	0	4.3	ALO83, OR86, F87
Terry Smith	WR	7	129	2	18.4	H89, B90, F92
Mike Gesicki	TE	7	73	1	10.4	P14, TS16, R17, F17
Mike Guman	RB	7	69	0	9.9	G76, F77, S79, L79
Mike Archie	RB	7	48	0	6.9	B93, CIT94, R95, OU96
Ethan Kilmer	TE	6	79	1	13.2	OR06
Juwan Johnson	WR	6	66	0	11.0	TS16, R17, F17, CIT19
Cuncho Brown	TE	6	57	0	9.5	F97, CIT98, OU99
Troy Drayton	TE	6	56	0	9.3	F92, B93
Leroy Thompson	RB	6	48	0	8.0	CIT88, H89, B90
Curt Warner	RB	6	33	0	5.5	L79, F80, F82, S83
Jon Williams	RB	6	33	0	5.5	F80, F82, S83, ALO83
Gregg Garrity	WR	5	168	2	33.6	F80, F82, S83

Player	Pos.	Rec	Yds	TD	Avg	Bowl Games*
Joe Jurevicius	WR	5	118	0	23.6	R95, OU96, F97
Kenny Jackson	WR	5	90	0	18.0	F80, F82, S83, ALO83
Mike McCloskey	TE	5	82	0	16.4	L79, F80, F82, S83
Lydell Mitchell	RB	5	81	1	16.2	OR70, COT72
Kevin Baugh	WR	5	78	0	15.6	F80, F82, S83, ALO83
Harold Powell	RB	5	76	1	15.2	G61, G62
Graham Zug	WR	5	66	0	13.2	ALM07, R09, CAP10, OU11
Dave Robinson	WR	5	58	0	11.6	L60, G61, G62
Tom Donchez	RB	5	51	0	10.2	COT72, OR74, COT75
Brett Brackett	WR	5	49	0	9.8	ALM07, R09, CAP10, OU11
Justin King	DB	5	27	0	5.4	OR06, OU07, ALM07
Bob Torrey	RB	5	10	1	2.0	G76, F77, S79
Joe Nastasi	WR	4	96	1	24.0	OU96, F97, CIT98, OU99
Michael Timpson	WR	4	81	0	20.3	OR86, F87, CIT88
Pat Freiermuth	TE	4	77	1	19.3	CIT19, COT19
Jim Scott	WR	4	69	0	17.3	COT72, S72, OR74
Scott Fitzkee	WR	4	62	1	15.5	S75, G76, F77, S79
Eric Hamilton	WR	4	62	0	15.5	F82, OR86, F87
Evan Royster	RB	4	51	0	12.8	ALM07, R09, CAP10, OU11
Jahan Dotson	WR	4	50	1	12.5	CIT19, COT19
Henry Oppermann	WR	4	49	0	12.3	L59, L60
Eric McCoo	RB	4	45	0	11.3	OU99, ALM99
Brian Siverling	TE	4	43	0	10.8	ALO83, OR86, F87
Kyle Brady	TE	4	35	2	8.8	F92, B93, CIT94, R95
Kyle Carter	TE	4	33	1	8.3	P14, TS16
Mickey Shuler	TE	4	28	0	7.0	S75, G76, F77
Charlie Pittman	RB	4	22	0	5.5	G67, OR69, OR70
KJ Hamler	WR	3	87	0	29.0	CIT19, COT19
Justin Brown	WR	3	82	1	27.3	CAP10, OU11, TC12
Dan Natale	TE	3	74	0	24.7	S72, OR74, COT75
Terrell Golden	WR	3	67	0	22.3	OR06, OU07, ALM07
Tom Donovan	WR	3	64	0	21.3	S75, F77, S79, L79
Roger Kochman	RB	3	54	2	18.0	L59, G61, G62
Bob Parsons	TE	3	48	0	16.0	OR70, COT72
Greg Edmonds	WR	3	46	0	15.3	OR69, OR70
Saeed Blacknall	WR	3	42	0	14.0	P14, TS16, R17, F17
Dick Anderson	WR	3	40	0	13.3	G61, G62
Dave Bland	WR	3	39	0	13.0	S72, OR74
Gary Hayman	WR	3	35	0	11.7	S72, OR74
Nick Bowers	TE	3	32	1	10.7	TS16, F17, CIT19, COT19
Chris Eberly	RB	3	27	0	9.0	OU96, F97, CIT98, OU99
Jesse James	TE	3	27	0	9.0	P14
Tisen Thomas	WR	3	24	0	8.0	H89, B90, F92, B93
Matt Suhey	RB	3	19	1	6.3	G76, F77, S79, L79

Player	Pos.	Rec	Yds	TD	Avg	Bowl Games*
Bill Belton	RB	3	14	0	4.7	TC12, P14
Brian Milne	RB	3	13	0	4.3	CIT94, R95, OU96
Akeel Lynch	RB	3	12	0	4.0	P14, TS16
Miles Sanders	RB	3	11	0	3.7	R17, F17, CIT19
Harry Wilson	RB	3	1	0	0.3	R23
Tommy Stevens	QB	3	-1	0	-0.3	TS16, R17, F17, CIT19
Scott Skarzynski	WR	2	81	1	40.5	COT72, S72
Bob Campbell	RB	2	55	0	27.5	G67
Tony Johnson	WR	2	54	0	27.0	CAP03
Devon Smith	WR	2	49	0	24.5	CAP10, OU11, TC12
Blair Thomas	RB	2	46	0	23.0	O86, F87, CIT88, H89
Mike Alexander	WR	2	43	1	21.5	OR86, CIT88
Vyto Kab	TE	2	43	0	21.5	S79, F80, F82
Bob Bassett	WR	2	28	0	14.0	F77, S79
Ken Andrews	RB	2	25	0	12.5	COT72, S72
Jack Curry	WR	2	22	1	11.0	G67
Dan Lucyk	RB	2	22	0	11.0	G67
Tim Manoa	RB	2	21	0	10.5	ALO83, OR86, F87
Keith Olsommer	TE	2	21	0	10.5	CIT94, R95, OU96, F97
Isaac Smolko	TE	2	21	0	10.5	OR06
Steve Smith	RB	2	20	0	10.0	ALO83, OR86, F87
Brian O'Neal	RB	2	19	0	9.5	H89, B90, B93, CIT94
Richie Anderson	RB	2	17	0	8.5	H89, F92, B93
Justin Shorter	WR	2	17	0	8.5	CIT19, COT19
Curtis Enis	RB	2	15	1	7.5	OU96, F97
Kenny Watson	WR	2	15	0	7.5	F97, CIT98, ALM99
Matt Kranchick	TE	2	15	0	7.5	CAP03
Daniel George	WR	2	15	0	7.5	CIT19, COT19
Gary Brown	RB	2	14	0	7.0	CIT88, H89, B90
Woody Petchel	RB	2	13	0	6.5	OR74, COT75, S75
Chafie Fields	WR	2	11	0	5.5	F97, CIT98, OU99, ALM99
Steve Geise	RB	2	10	0	5.0	S75, G76, F77
Tony Hunt	RB	2	10	0	5.0	OR06, OU07
Chip LaBarca	WR	2	8	1	4.0	B90, F92, B93, CIT94
Larry Johnson	RB	2	8	0	4.0	ALM99, CAP03
Michael Robinson	QB	2	7	0	3.5	CAP03, OR06
Journey Brown	RB	2	7	0	3.5	CIT19, COT19
Mike Palm	QB	2	5	0	2.5	R23
Aaron Harris	RB	2	5	0	2.5	F97, CIT98, OU99, ALM99
Brandon Polk	WR	2	5	0	2.5	TS16, R17, F17, CIT19
Rodney Kinlaw	RB	2	4	0	2.0	OR06, OU07, ALM07
Walt Addie	RB	2	3	0	1.5	S72, OR74, COT75
Chuck Herd	WR	1	72	1	72.0	COT72, S72, OR74
Paul Johnson	RB	1	56	0	56.0	G67, OR70

Player	Pos.	Rec	Yds	TD	Avg	Bowl Games*
Eddie Drummond	WR	1	45	0	45.0	OU99, ALM99
John Cappelletti	RB	1	40	0	40.0	S72, OR74
Larry Cooney**	RB	1	38	1	38.0	COT48
John Gilmore	TE	1	34	0	34.0	OU99, ALM99
Dick Pae	RB	1	33	1	33.0	L59, L60
Bob Mrosko	TE	1	25	0	25.0	F87, CIT88
John Bozick	WR	1	23	0	23.0	L59, L60
Rich Mauti	WR	1	21	0	21.0	COT75, S75, G76
Bud Yost	WR	1	18	0	18.0	G62
Matt Hahn	RB	1	18	0	18.0	OR06, OU07, ALM07
Mike Cerimele	RB	1	16	0	16.0	CIT98, OU99, ALM99
Silas Redd	RB	1	16	0	16.0	OU11, TC12
Jim Kerr	RB	1	14	0	14.0	L59, L60
Darrell Giles	WR	1	14	0	14.0	ALO83, OR86, F87
Al Gursky	RB	1	13	1	13.0	L60, G61, G62
David Jakob	TE	1	12	0	12.0	H89, B90
Curtis Drake	WR	1	12	0	12.0	CAP10, TC12
Kevin Haplea	TE	1	12	0	12.0	OU11, TC12
Jim Schwab	WR	1	11	0	11.0	G61
Brian Moser	RB	1	11	0	11.0	B90, F92, B93
Chaz Powell	WR	1	11	0	11.0	R09, CAP10, OU11, TC12
Sam Gash	RB	1	10	1	10.0	CIT88, B90, F92
Dick Barvinchak	WR	1	10	0	10.0	OR74, COT75, S75
Cordell Mitchell	RB	1	9	0	9.0	F97, CIT98, OU99, ALM99
Titcus Pettigrew	WR	1	9	0	9.0	CIT98, OU99
Sean McHugh	RB	1	8	0	8.0	CAP03
Gary Debes	WR	1	7	0	7.0	COT72
Kirk Bowman	TE	1	7	0	7.0	S83, ALO83
Paul Pomfret	TE	1	7	0	7.0	F87, CIT88
Michael Zordich	RB	1	7	0	7.0	CAP10, OU11, TC12
Wally Triplett**	RB	1	6	1	6.0	COT48
Franco Harris	RB	1	6	0	6.0	OR70, COT72
Ryan Grube	TE	1	6	0	6.0	B93
Casey Williams	TE	1	6	0	6.0	CAP03
Cliff Davis	DE	1	5	0	5.0	L60, G61
Paul Suhey	RB	1	5	0	5.0	S75
Irv Pankey	TE	1	5	0	5.0	S79
Sean Barowski	RB	1	5	0	5.0	F87, CIT88
Stephen Pitts	RB	1	4	1	4.0	B93, CIT94, R95, OU96
Bob Stephenson	TE	1	4	0	4.0	R95, OU96, F97, CIT98
A.Q. Shipley	C	1	4	0	4.0	OR06, OU07, ALM07, R09
Ki-Jana Carter	RB	1	2	0	2.0	B93, CIT94, R95
Kerry Collins	QB	1	2	0	2.0	F92, B93, CIT94, R95
Chris Campbell	WR	1	2	0	2.0	R95, OU96, F97

Player	Pos.	Rec	Yds	TD	Avg	Bowl Games*
Tom Cherry	RB	1	1	0	1.0	G67, OR69
Joe Suhey	RB	1	1	0	1.0	R09, CAP10, OU11, TC12
Booker Moore	RB	1	0	0	0.0	F77, S79, L79, F80
Mark Allen	RB	1	-8	0	-8.0	TS16, R17, F17, CIT19

Bowl games as member of team; player may not have caught pass in all bowls

**1948 Cotton Bowl statistics are incomplete*

ALO—Aloha, ALM—Alamo, B—Blockbuster, CAP—Capital One, CIT—Citrus, COT—Cotton, F—Fiesta, G—Gator, H—Holiday, L—Liberty, OR—Orange, OU—Outback, P—Pinstripe, S—Sugar, TC—TicketCity, TS—TaxSlayer

Chapter Notes

Introduction

1. Louis Prato. "Was It 1881 or 1887?" In *The Penn State Football Encyclopedia*, 27–30. Champaign: Sports Publishing, 1998.

1922 Season

1. Louis Prato. "In & Out of the Big Time with Bezdek." In *The Penn State Football Encyclopedia*, 116. Champaign: Sports Publishing, 1998.
2. *Ibid.*, 117.
3. *Ibid.*, 115–18.
4. *Ibid.*, 600.
5. *Ibid.*, 118.
6. *Ibid.*, 119.
7. *Ibid.*, 119–20.
8. Maxwell Stiles. *The Rose Bowl: A Complete Action and Pictorial Story of Rose Bowl Football*, 39. Los Angeles: Sportsmaster Publications, 1945.
9. *Ibid.*
10. *Ibid.*, 40.
11. Richard J. Shmelter. *The USC Trojans Football Encyclopedia*, 20. Jefferson, NC: McFarland, 2014.
12. Stiles, 40.
13. *Ibid.*, 40–41.
14. *Ibid.*, 41.
15. *Ibid.*
16. *Ibid.*, 42.
17. *Ibid.*
18. Louis Prato. "In & Out of the Big Time with Bezdek." In *The Penn State Football Encyclopedia*, 121. Champaign: Sports Publishing, 1998.
19. Stiles, 42.

1947 Season

1. Louis Prato. "The One and Only 'Hig.'" In *The Penn State Football Encyclopedia*, 192. Champaign: Sports Publishing, 1998.
2. *Ibid.*
3. *Ibid.*
4. *Ibid.*
5. *Ibid.*, 193.
6. *Ibid.*
7. *Ibid.*

8. *Ibid.*, 194.
9. *Ibid.*
10. *Ibid.*, 195.
11. *2019 Penn State Cotton Bowl Media Guide*, 8. 2019.
12. Louis Prato. "The One and Only 'Hig.'" In *The Penn State Football Encyclopedia*, 195–97. Champaign: Sports Publishing, 1998.
13. *2019 Penn State Cotton Bowl Media Guide*, 8. 2019.
14. Prato, 643.

1959 Season

1. Louis Prato. "Rip and his Protégé." In *The Penn State Football Encyclopedia*, 232. Champaign: Sports Publishing, 1998.
2. *Ibid.*
3. *Ibid.*
4. *Ibid.*, 232–33.
5. *Ibid.*, 233.
6. *Ibid.*
7. *Ibid.*
8. *Ibid.*, 233–34.
9. *Ibid.*, 234.
10. *Ibid.*
11. *Ibid.*, 228.
12. *Ibid.*, 232.
13. *Ibid.*, 234–35.
14. Louis Prato. "Rip and his Protégé." In *The Penn State Football Encyclopedia*, 235–36. Champaign: Sports Publishing, 1998.
15. *Ibid.*, 643.

1960 Season

1. Louis Prato. "Rip and his Protégé." In *The Penn State Football Encyclopedia*, 236–37. Champaign: Sports Publishing, 1998.
2. *Ibid.*, 237.
3. *Ibid.*
4. *Ibid.*, 237–38.
5. *Ibid.*, 238.
6. *Ibid.*
7. *Ibid.*
8. *Ibid.*

9. *Ibid.*, 240.

10. *Ibid.*, 238–39.

11. Louis Prato. "Rip and his Protégé." In *The Penn State Football Encyclopedia*, 239–40. Champaign: Sports Publishing, 1998.

12. *Ibid.*, 643.

1961 Season

1. Louis Prato. "Rip and his Protégé." In *The Penn State Football Encyclopedia*, 240. Champaign: Sports Publishing, 1998.

2. *Ibid.*, 240–41.

3. *Ibid.*, 241.

4. *Ibid.*

5. *Ibid.*, 241–42.

6. *Ibid.*, 242.

7. *Ibid.*

8. *Ibid.*

9. *Ibid.*, 242–43.

10. Rusty Cowan. *17th Annual Gator Bowl Program.* 1961.

11. Prato, 243.

12. Louis Prato. "Rip and his Protégé." In *The Penn State Football Encyclopedia*, 243–44. Champaign: Sports Publishing, 1998.

13. *Ibid.*, 643–44.

1962 Season

1. Louis Prato. "Rip and his Protégé." In *The Penn State Football Encyclopedia*, 244. Champaign: Sports Publishing, 1998.

2. *Ibid.*, 244–45.

3. *Ibid.*

4. *Ibid.*

5. *Ibid.*, 245–46.

6. *Ibid.*, 246.

7. *Ibid.*

8. *Ibid.*

9. *Ibid.*, 247.

10. *Ibid.*

11. *Ibid.*, 247–48.

12. *Ibid.*, 644.

1967 Season

1. Louis Prato. "The Grand Experiment." In *The Penn State Football Encyclopedia*, 264–65. Champaign: Sports Publishing, 1998.

2. *Ibid.*, 265.

3. *Ibid.*, 266.

4. *Ibid.*

5. *Ibid.*

6. *Ibid.*

7. *Ibid.*, 266–67.

8. *Ibid.*, 267–68.

9. Frank Bilovsky. *23rd Annual Gator Bowl Game Program.* 1967.

10. Prato, 268.

11. *Ibid.*

12. Bilovsky.

13. Louis Prato. "The Grand Experiment." In *The Penn State Football Encyclopedia*, 268–69. Champaign: Sports Publishing, 1998.

14. *Ibid.*, 644.

1968 Season

1. Louis Prato. "The Grand Experiment." In *The Penn State Football Encyclopedia*, 270. Champaign: Sports Publishing, 1998.

2. *Ibid.*

3. *Ibid.*, 270–71.

4. *Ibid.*, 271.

5. *Ibid.*, 272.

6. *Ibid.*, 272–73.

7. *Ibid.*, 273.

8. John Crittenden. *35th Annual Orange Bowl Classic Program.* 1968.

9. Prato, 272–73.

10. *Ibid.*, 274–75.

11. *Ibid.*, 644.

12. *Ibid.*, 275.

13. *Ibid.*, 644.

1969 Season

1. Louis Prato. "The Grand Experiment." In *The Penn State Football Encyclopedia*, 276. Champaign: Sports Publishing, 1998.

2. *Ibid.*, 276–77.

3. *Ibid.*, 277.

4. *Ibid.*, 277–78.

5. *Ibid.*, 279.

6. *Ibid.*, 279–80.

7. Everett A. Clay and Jack Houghteling. *Thirty-Sixth Annual Orange Bowl Classic Press-Radio-TV Brochure and Record Book.* 1969.

8. Prato, 280.

9. Prato, 279.

10. Louis Prato. *The Penn State Football Encyclopedia*, 644–45. Champaign: Sports Publishing, 1998.

11. *Ibid.*

1971 Season

1. Louis Prato. "The Grand Experiment." In *The Penn State Football Encyclopedia*, 285. Champaign: Sports Publishing, 1998.

2. *Ibid.*, 286.

3. *Ibid.*, 286–87.

4. *Ibid.*, 287–88.

5. *Ibid.*, 288.

6. *Ibid.*, 288–89.

7. *Ibid.*, 289.

8. *Ibid.*

9. *Ibid.*, 290.

10. *Ibid.*, 645.

11. *Ibid.*, 290.

12. *Ibid.*, 645.

1972 Season

1. Louis Prato. "The Grand Experiment." *The Penn State Football Encyclopedia*, 292. Champaign: Sports Publishing, 1998.
2. *Ibid.*, 292–93.
3. *Ibid.*, 293.
4. *Ibid.*, 293–94.
5. *Ibid.*, 294.
6. *Ibid.*
7. Bill Heufelder. "Penn State 1972." In *39th Annual Sugar Bowl Program*, 22–23. 1972.
8. Prato, 294.
9. *Ibid*, 294–95.
10. *Ibid.*, 645.

1973 Season

1. John Morris. *Penn State 1974 Orange Bowl Press Guide*, 19. 1973.
2. *Ibid.*, 19–20.
3. *Ibid.*, 20–21.
4. *Ibid.*, 21–22.
5. *Ibid.*, 22.
6. *Ibid.*, 23.
7. *Ibid.*, 24.
8. *Ibid.*, 25.
9. *Ibid.*, 6.
10. Louis Prato. "The Grand Experiment." In *The Penn State Football Encyclopedia*, 298–300. Champaign: Sports Publishing, 1998.
11. Louis Prato. *The Penn State Football Encyclopedia*, 645. Champaign: Sports Publishing, 1998.

1974 Season

1. John M. Morris and David L. Baker. *Penn State 1975 Cotton Bowl Press Guide*, 23. 1974.
2. *Ibid.*
3. *Ibid.*, 24.
4. *Ibid.*, 25.
5. *Ibid.*, 25–26.
6. *Ibid.*, 26–27.
7. *Ibid.*, 27–28.
8. *Ibid.*, 29.
9. Louis Prato. "The Grand Experiment." In *The Penn State Football Encyclopedia*, 304. *Champaign*: Sports Publishing, 1998.
10. Louis Prato. *The Penn State Football Encyclopedia*, 645. *Champaign*: Sports Publishing, 1998.

1975 Season

1. John Morris. *Penn State 1975 Sugar Bowl Press Guide*, 27. 1975.
2. *Ibid.*, 27–28.
3. *Ibid.*, 28–29.
4. *Ibid.*, 29–30.
5. *Ibid.*, 30–31.
6. *Ibid.*, 31–32.
7. *Ibid.*, 33–34.

8. Louis Prato. "The Grand Experiment." In *The Penn State Football Encyclopedia*, 309. Champaign: Sports Publishing, 1998.
9. *Ibid.*, 310.
10. *Ibid.*, 646.

1976 Season

1. John Morris. "1976 Season in Review." In *Penn State 1976 Gator Bowl Press Guide*, 26. 1976.
2. *Ibid.*, 26–28.
3. *Ibid.*, 28–30.
4. *Ibid.*, 30–31.
5. *Ibid.*, 31–32.
6. *Ibid.*, 33.
7. *Ibid.*, 17–18.
8. *Ibid.*, 11–17.
9. Louis Prato. "The Grand Experiment." In *The Penn State Football Encyclopedia*, 313–14. Champaign: Sports Publishing, 1998.
10. Louis Prato. *The Penn State Football Encyclopedia*, 646. Champaign: Sports Publishing, 1998.

1977 Season

1. Rex Naylor, Jr. *The Forgotten Seasons*, 12. (self-pub., Naylor Publishing, 2018).
2. John Morris. *Penn State Football 1977 Fiesta Bowl Press Guide*, 28. 1977.
3. *Ibid.*, 28–29.
4. *Ibid.*, 29–30.
5. *Ibid.*, 30–31.
6. *Ibid.*, 31–32.
7. *Ibid.*, 32.
8. *Ibid.*, 33.
9. *Ibid.*, 34.
10. *Ibid.*, 34–35.
11. *Ibid.*, 35–36.
12. *Ibid.*, 36–37.
13. *Ibid.*, 19.
14. Naylor Jr., 107–09.
15. *Ibid.*, 110.
16. *Ibid.*, 111.
17. 17 Louis Prato. *The Penn State Football Encyclopedia*, 646. Champaign: Sports Publishing, 1998.

1978 Season

1. Rex Naylor Jr.. *The Forgotten Seasons*, 138. (self-pub., Naylor Publishing, 2018).
2. Ron Bracken. *45th Annual Sugar Bowl Program*, 48. 1978.
3. Naylor Jr., 140–41.
4. Bracken, 48.
5. Naylor Jr., 152–54.
6. Bracken, 48.
7. Naylor Jr., 161.
8. *Ibid.*, 164–65.
9. *Ibid.*, 177.
10. *Ibid.*, 180.
11. *Ibid.*, 198–200.

12. *Ibid.*, 205–07.
13. *Ibid.*, 224–27.
14. *Ibid.*, 240–43.
15. Bracken, 49.
16. Naylor Jr., 234–36.
17. Louis Prato. *The Penn State Football Encyclopedia*, 646. Champaign: Sports Publishing, 1998.

1979 Season

1. Dave Baker. *1979 Liberty Bowl Press Guide*, 32. 1979.
2. *Ibid.*, 33.
3. *Ibid.*, 34.
4. *Ibid.*, 35.
5. *Ibid.*, 36.
6. *Ibid.*, 37.
7. *Ibid.*, 38.
8. *Ibid.*, 39.
9. *Ibid.*, 40.
10. *Ibid.*, 41.
11. *Ibid.*, 42.
12. *Ibid.*, 27–28.
13. Louis Prato. "The Grand Experiment." *The Penn State Football Encyclopedia*, 330. Champaign: Sports Publishing, 1998.
14. Louis Prato. *The Penn State Football Encyclopedia,* 647. Champaign: Sports Publishing, 1998.

1980 Season

1. Dave Baker. *1980 Penn State Fiesta Bowl Media Guide,* 37. 1980.
2. *Ibid.*, 38.
3. *Ibid.*, 39.
4. *Ibid.*, 40.
5. *Ibid.*, 41.
6. *Ibid.*, 42.
7. *Ibid.*, 43.
8. *Ibid.*, 44.
9. *Ibid.*, 45.
10. *Ibid.*, 46.
11. *Ibid.*, 47.
12. *Ibid.*, 32.
13. *Ibid.*, 32–33.
14. John Junker. "Lions Assemble Puzzle for Fiesta Berth." *1980 Fiesta Bowl Magazine,* 5–6. Phoenix Magazine Publishing, 1980.
15. Louis Prato. *The Penn State Football Encyclopedia,* 647. Champaign: Sports Publishing, 1998.
16. *Ibid.*, 647.

1981 Season

1. Dave Baker and Dick Sapara. *1982 Fiesta Bowl Guide,* 11. 1981.
2. *Ibid.*
3. *Ibid.*, 12.
4. *Ibid.*
5. *Ibid.*, 13.
6. *Ibid.*

7. *Ibid.*, 14.
8. *Ibid.*
9. *Ibid.*, 15.
10. *Ibid.*
11. *Ibid.*, 16.
12. *Ibid.*, 17–18.
13. Karen Churchard. "Happy New Year!" *1982 Fiesta Bowl Magazine,* 2. 1981.
14. Dave Baker and Dick Sapara. *1982 Fiesta Bowl Guide,* 4–5. 1981.
15. Louis Prato. *The Penn State Football Encyclopedia,* 647. Champaign: Sports Publishing, 1998.

1982 Season

1. Dave Baker. *1986 Orange Bowl Media Guide,* 55. 1985.
2. Baker. *1983 Sugar Bowl Guide,* 39. 1982.
3. *Ibid.*
4. *Ibid.*, 40.
5. Bill Contz. *When the Lions Roared: Joe Paterno and One of College Football's Greatest Teams,* 77. Chicago: Triumph Books, 2017.
6. Baker, 40.
7. *Ibid.*, 41.
8. *Ibid.*
9. *Ibid.*, 42.
10. *Ibid.*
11. Contz, 103.
12. Baker, 43.
13. *Ibid.*, 44.
14. *Ibid.*, 29.
15. *Ibid.*, 45–47.
16. Contz, 110.
17. "Sugar Bowl Classic." ABC, 1983.
18. *Ibid.*
19. John Papanek. "But How 'Bout Them Lions?" *Sports Illustrated,* January 10, 1983, 20.
20. Louis Prato. *The Penn State Football Encyclopedia,* 647. Champaign: Sports Publishing, Inc, 1998.

1983 Season

1. Dick Fishback. "Fight to Honolulu." In *Aloha Bowl Football Magazine,* 60. Tongg Publishing, 1983.
2. *Ibid.*
3. *Ibid.*, 60–64.
4. *Ibid.*, 64.
5. *Ibid.*
6. *Ibid.*
7. Louis Prato. "The National Champions." In *The Penn State Football Encyclopedia,* 352–53. Champaign: Sports Publishing, 1998.
8. Fishback, 64.
9. *Ibid.*
10. *Ibid.*, 64–76.
11. *Ibid.*, 76.
12. *Ibid.*
13. *Ibid.*
14. *Ibid.*, 28.
15. *Ibid.*

16. *Ibid.*, pp. 18–22.

17. Louis Prato. "The National Champions." In *The Penn State Football Encyclopedia,* 359. Champaign: Sports Publishing, 1998.

18. *Ibid.*, 648.

1985 Season

1. Ralph M. Grady. "The Lions' 11–0 Road to Miami." In *The 52nd Orange Bowl Classic Program,* 123. San Francisco: Touchdown Publications, 1986.

2. Dave Baker. *1986 Orange Bowl Media Guide,* 61. 1985.

3. Grady, 123.

4. *Ibid.*

5. Baker, 62.

6. Grady, 124.

7. Baker, 63.

8. *Ibid.*, 64.

9. Grady, 124.

10. *Ibid.*

11. Baker, 65.

12. Grady, 124.

13. Baker, 66.

14. Grady, 124.

15. Baker, 67.

16. *Ibid.*, 68.

17. Grady, 124.

18. *Ibid.*

19. *Ibid.*

20. Baker, 70.

21. *Ibid.*, 72–73.

22. Jim Sarni. "Showdown for No. 1." In *The 52nd Orange Bowl Classic Program,* 5–8. San Francisco: Touchdown Publications, 1985.

23. Louis Prato. *The Penn State Football Encyclopedia.* Champaign: Sports Publishing, Inc. p. 648. 1998.

1986 Season

1. Peggy Kearney and Patrick Moreira. "The Nittany Lions' Road to the Sunkist Fiesta Bowl." In *16th Annual Sunkist Fiesta Bowl Official Magazine,* 101. San Francisco: Touchdown Publications, 1986.

2. *Penn State Sunkist Fiesta Bowl Media Guide.* "Game Statistics—1986 Season." p. 34. 1986.

3. Kearney, 101.

4. *Ibid.*

5. *Ibid.*, 101–02.

6. *Penn State Sunkist Fiesta Bowl Media Guide,* 34.

7. Kearney, 102.

8. *Ibid.*

9. *Ibid.*

10. *Ibid.*

11. *Ibid.*

12. *Ibid.*

13. *Ibid.*

14. *Penn State Sunkist Fiesta Bowl Media Guide,* 30–32.

15. M.G. Missanelli. *The Perfect Season: How Penn State Came to Stop a Hurricane and Win a National Championship,* 12–13. University Park: Pennsylvania State University Press, 2007.

16. *Ibid.*

17. M.G. Missanelli. *The Perfect Season: How Penn State Came to Stop a Hurricane and Win a National Championship,* 63. University Park: Pennsylvania State University Press, 2007.

18. Louis Prato. *The Penn State Football Encyclopedia,* 648. Champaign: Sports Publishing, 1998.

1987 Season

1. Louis Prato. "'JoePa' & The Big Ten." In *The Penn State Football Encyclopedia*, 376. Champaign: Sports Publishing, 1998.

2. *Ibid.*

3. *Ibid.*

4. *Ibid.*, 376–77.

5. *Ibid.*, 377.

6. *Ibid.*

7. *Ibid.*

8. *Ibid.*, 377–78.

9. Kevin Fritz. "1987 Game by Game Highlights." In *The Official Florida Citrus Bowl Pre Bowl Guide to Orlando, Sports Holiday, Football Classic Program,* 45. Winter Park, FL: Special Editions Publishing, 1987.

10. Prato, 378.

11. *Ibid.*

12. *Ibid.*, 378–79.

13. Fritz, p. 40.

14. *Ibid.*, 24.

15. Louis Prato. "'JoePa' & The Big Ten." In *The Penn State Football Encyclopedia*, 379. Champaign: Sports Publishing, 1998.

16. *Ibid.*, 648.

1989 Season

1. Bob Boyles and Paul Guido. *The USA Today College Football Encyclopedia,* 485. New York: Skyhorse Publishing, 2008.

2. Budd L. Thalman. *Sea World Holiday Bowl Penn State 1989 Post-Season Media Guide,* 61. 1989.

3. Boyles and Guido, 486. 2008.

4. Thalman, 62.

5. *Ibid.*, 63.

6. *Ibid.*, 64.

7. *Ibid.*, 65.

8. *Ibid.*, 66.

9. Boyles and Guido, 489.

10. Thalman, 67.

11. *Ibid.*, 68.

12. *Ibid.*, 69.

13. *Ibid.*, 70.

14. *Ibid.*, 71.

15. *Ibid.*, 12.

16. *Ibid.*, 18.

17. *Ibid.*, 8.

18. ESPN. "Sea World Holiday Bowl." 1989.

19. Bob Boyles and Paul Guido. *The USA Today*

College Football Encyclopedia, 494. New York: Sky-horse Publishing, 2008.

20. Louis Prato. *The Penn State Football Encyclopedia,* 648–49. Champaign: Sports Publishing, 1998.

1990 Season

1. Louis Prato. "'JoePa' & The Big Ten." In *The Penn State Football Encyclopedia,* 391. Champaign: Sports Publishing, 1998.

2. Kyle French. "Nittany Lion Season in Review." In *Blockbuster Bowl Souvenir Program,* 46. Delray Beach, FL: Labelle & French, 1990.

3. Prato, 392.

4. French, 46.

5. Prato.

6. French, 47.

7. Prato, 392.

8. French.

9. Prato.

10. Prato.

11. French, 47–48.

12. Prato, 392–93.

13. French, 48–49.

14. Prato, 393.

15. French, 49.

16. Prato, 393–94.

17. *Ibid.,* 394.

18. French, 50.

19. Prato, 394–95.

20. French, 51.

21. Prato, 615–19.

22. *Ibid.,* 393–95.

23. Gary Ferman. "New Kid on the Block: How the Blockbuster Bowl Came to Be." In *Blockbuster Bowl Souvenir Program,* 6–11. Delray Beach, flFlorida: Labelle & French Publishing, 1990.

24. *Ibid.*

25. Prato, 395.

26. *Ibid.*

27. *Ibid.,* 649.

1991 Season

1. Budd L. Thalman. *Fiesta Bowl 1992 Media Guide,* 45. 1991.

2. *Ibid.,* 46.

3. *Ibid.,* 47.

4. *Ibid.,* 48.

5. *Ibid.,* 49.

6. *Ibid.,* 50.

7. *Ibid.,* 51.

8. *Ibid.,* 52.

9. *Ibid.,* 53.

10. *Ibid.,* 54.

11. *Ibid.,* 55.

12. *Ibid.,* 56.

13. Arlys Warfield. "Penn State's Road to the Fiesta." In *1992 Fiesta Bowl Game Official Souvenir Magazine,* 72. 1991.

14. Thalman, 2.

15. *Ibid.,* 39–40.

16. Louis Prato. "'JoePa' & The Big Ten." In *The Penn State Football Encyclopedia,* 399–400. Champaign: Sports Publishing, 1998.

17. Thalman, 1.

18. *Ibid.,* 401.

19. *Ibid.,* 649.

1992 Season

1. Budd L. Thalman. *1993 Blockbuster Bowl Media Guide,* 44. 1992.

2. *Ibid.,* 45.

3. *Ibid.,* 46.

4. *Ibid.,* 47.

5. *Ibid.,* 48.

6. *Ibid.,* 49.

7. *Ibid.,* 50.

8. *Ibid.,* 51.

9. *Ibid.,* 52.

10. Kip Richael. *Welcome to the Big Ten,* 15–18. Champaign: Sagamore Publishing, 1994.

11. Louis Prato. *The Penn State Football Encyclopedia,* 649. Champaign: Sports Publishing, 1998.

1993 Season

1. Jeff Nelson. *Florida Citrus Bowl 1994 Media Guide,* 10. 1993.

2. *Ibid.,* 53.

3. *Ibid.,* 54.

4. *Ibid.,* 55.

5. *Ibid.,* 56.

6. *Ibid.,* 57.

7. *Ibid.,* 58.

8. *Ibid.,* 59.

9. *Ibid.,* 60.

10. *Ibid.,* 61.

11. *Ibid.,* 62.

12. *Ibid.,* 63.

13. *Ibid.,* 40–41.

14. *Ibid.,* 1–3.

15. Louis Prato. "'JoePa' & The Big Ten." In *The Penn State Football Encyclopedia,* 415. Champaign: Sports Publishing, 1998.

16. *Ibid.,* 650.

1994 Season

1. Jeff Nelson. *1995 Rose Bowl Media Guide,* 57. 1994.

2. *Ibid.,* 58.

3. *Ibid.,* 59.

4. *Ibid.,* 60.

5. *Ibid.,* 61.

6. *Ibid.,* 62.

7. *Ibid.,* 63.

8. *Ibid.,* 64.

9. *Ibid.,* 65.

10. *Ibid.,* 66.

11. *Ibid.,* 67.

12. *Ibid.,* 12–13.

13. Tim Layden. "Roses with Thorns." In *Sports Illustrated Presents: That Perfect Season*, 72–85. 1995.

14. Tim Layden. "Small Change." In *Sports Illustrated*. December 26, 1994. https://vault.si.com/vault/1994/12/26/small-change-going-to-a-football-bowl-game-unless-its-one-of-the-biggies-makes-little-financial-sense-for-most-schools.

15. "Head Coach Joe Paterno." In *81st Rose Bowl Game Program*, 108–110. 1994.

16. *Rose Bowl Game*. ABC, 1995.

17. Tex Noel and Brener Zwikel. *2009 Rose Bowl Game Historical Reference Media Guide*, 94. 2008.

18. ABC.

19. *Ibid.*

20. Noel and Zwikel, 94.

1995 Season

1. Jeff Nelson. *1996 Outback Bowl Media Guide*, 50. 1995.

2. *Ibid.*, 51.

3. *Ibid.*, 52.

4. *Ibid.*, 53.

5. *Ibid.*, 54.

6. *Ibid.*, 55.

7. *Ibid.*, 56.

8. *Ibid.*, 57.

9. *Ibid.*, 58.

10. *Ibid.*, 59.

11. *Ibid.*, 60.

12. *Ibid.*, 19.

13. *1996 Outback Bowl*. ESPN, 1996.

14. Louis Prato. "All-Time Records." In *The Penn State Football Encyclopedia*, 639. Champaign: Sports Publishing, 1998.

15. *Ibid.*, 650.

1996 Season

1. Jeff Nelson. *1997 Penn State Fiesta Bowl Media Guide*, 56. 1996.

2. *Ibid.*, 57.

3. *Ibid.*, 58.

4. *Ibid.*, 59.

5. *Ibid.*, 60.

6. *Ibid.*, 61.

7. *Ibid.*, 62.

8. *Ibid.*, 63.

9. *Ibid.*, 64.

10. *Ibid.*, 65.

11. *Ibid.*, 66.

12. *Ibid.*, 67.

13. *Ibid.*, 43–46.

14. Ivan Maisel. "Who Will Be King of the Hill." In *TV Guide*, 16. December 28, 1996.

15. *Ibid.*, 1, 41, 54, 67.

16. Arlys Warfield. "Texas' Road to the Fiesta Bowl." In *Tostitos Fiesta Bowl XXVI Official Souvenir Magazine*, 84–85. 1997.

17. Louis Prato. "'JoePa' & The Big Ten." In *The Penn State Football Encyclopedia*, 437. Champaign: Sports Publishing, 1998.

18. *Ibid.*, 650.

1997 Season

1. Arlys Warfield. "Penn State's Road to the CompUSA Florida Citrus Bowl." *1998 CompUSA Florida Citrus Bowl Official Souvenir Magazine*, 67. 1997.

2. *Ibid.*

3. *Ibid.*

4. *Ibid.*

5. *Ibid.*, 68.

6. *Ibid.*

7. *Ibid.*

8. *Ibid.*

9. *Ibid.*

10. *Ibid.*, 17.

11. Louis Prato. "'JoePa' & The Big Ten." In *The Penn State Football Encyclopedia*, 441–42. Champaign: Sports Publishing, 1998.

12. Louis Prato. *The Penn State Football Encyclopedia*, 651. Champaign: Sports Publishing, 1998.

1998 Season

1. Rich Scarcella. "Penn State's Road to Tampa Bay." *1999 Outback Bowl Game Program*, 26. 1998.

2. *Ibid.*

3. *Ibid.*

4. *Ibid.*

5. *Ibid.*

6. *Ibid.*, 26–27.

7. *Ibid.*, 27.

8. *Ibid.*

9. *Ibid.*

10. *Ibid.*

11. *Ibid.*

12. *Ibid.*

13. *Bowl Championship Series 2013–2014 Media Guide*, 126. 2013.

14. Brad Sutton. "University of Kentucky Wildcats." In *1999 Outback Bowl Game Program*, 47. 1998.

15. Bob Boyles and Paul Guido. *The USA Today College Football Encyclopedia*, 616. New York: Skyhorse Publishing, 2008.

16. "NCAA Football—Kentucky vs. Penn State," *USA Today*, Accessed August 18, 2020, https://usatoday30.usatoday.com/sports/scores99/99001/99001308.htm.

1999 Season

1. Jeff Nelson. "1999 Game Reviews." *Penn State Nittany Lions 1999 Alamo Bowl Media Guide*, 57. 1999.

2. *Ibid.*, 58.

3. *Ibid.*, 59.

4. *Ibid.*, 60.

5. *Ibid.*, 61.

6. *Ibid.*, 62.

7. *Ibid.*, 63.

8. *Ibid.*, 64.

9. *Ibid.*, 65.

10. Bob Boyles and Paul Guido. *The USA Today College Football Encyclopedia,* 624. New York: Skyhorse Publishing, 2008.

11. Jeff Nelson. "1999 Game Reviews." In *Penn State Nittany Lions 1999 Alamo Bowl Media Guide,* 66. 1999.

12. *Ibid.*, 67.

13. *Ibid.*, 68.

14. *Ibid.*, 42–43.

15. Boyles and Guido, 628.

16. Nelson, 69.

17. Steve Downey, Steve Kirkwoods, and Peter Sullivan. "Tradition Rich." In *1999 Sylvania Alamo Bowl Program,* 11. 1999.

18. *Ibid.*, 37.

19. "1999 Game Recap," Alamo Bowl, accessed August 18, 2020, https://www.alamobowl.com/wp-content/uploads/2014/11/1999-GAME-RECAP.pdf.

2002 Season

1. Jeff Nelson. *2003 Capital One Bowl Media Guide,* 52. 2002.

2. *Ibid.*, 53.

3. *Ibid.*, 54.

4. *Ibid.*, 55.

5. *Ibid.*, 56–57.

6. *Ibid.*, 58–59.

7. *Ibid.*, 60–61.

8. *Ibid.*, 21–23.

9. *Ibid.*, 37–38.

10. "Penn State vs. Auburn—Game Summary—January 1, 2003." ESPN, January 1, 2003, https://www.sports-reference.com/cfb/boxscores/2003-01-01-auburn.html.

2005 Season

1. Jeff Nelson. *2006 Penn State FedEx Orange Bowl Media Guide,* 56. 2005.

2. *Ibid.*, 57.

3. *Ibid.*, 58.

4. *Ibid.*, 59.

5. *Ibid.*, 60.

6. *Ibid.*, 61.

7. *Ibid.*, 62.

8. *Ibid.*, 63.

9. *Ibid.*, 64.

10. *Ibid.*, 65.

11. *Ibid.*, 66.

12. *Ibid.*, 30.

13. *Ibid.*, 53.

14. *Ibid.*, 52.

15. *The 72nd Annual FedEx Orange Bowl Media Guide,* 22. 2005.

16. *Bowl Championship Series 2013–2014 Media Guide,* 133. 2013.

17. Nelson, 1.

18. *The 72nd Annual FedEx Orange Bowl Media Guide,* 16. 2005.

19. *ABC Sports Presents the 2006 FedEx Orange Bowl.* American Broadcasting Companies, 2006, DVD.

20. Orange Bowl Committee. *Orange Bowl Committee: Celebrating 75 Years,* 228. 2009.

21. *ABC Sports Presents the 2006 FedEx Orange Bowl.* American Broadcasting Companies, 2006, DVD.

22. *Ibid.*

23. "Penn State vs. Florida State—Game Summary—January 3, 2006—ESPN," ESPN, Accessed August 18, 2020, https://www.espn.com/college-football/game?gameId=260030052.

2006 Season

1. Jeff Nelson, *2007 Outback Bowl Media Guide,* 55. 2006.

2. *Ibid.*, 56.

3. Jeff Nelson. "Youngstown State joins Penn State's 2006 football schedule." Penn State News, December 9, 2005, https://news.psu.edu/story/206651/2005/12/09/youngstown-state-joins-penn-states-2006-football-schedule.

4. Jeff Nelson, *2007 Outback Bowl Media Guide,* 57.

5. *Ibid.*, 58.

6. *Ibid.*, 59.

7. *Ibid.*, 60.

8. *Ibid.*, 61.

9. *Ibid.*, 62.

10. *Ibid.*, 63.

11. *Ibid.*, 64.

12. *Ibid.*, 65.

13. *Ibid.*, 66.

14. *Ibid.*, 38–39.

15. *Ibid.*, 51.

16. *Ibid.*, 5.

17. Tom Satkowiak. "2006 Tennessee Football Season Review." In *2007 Outback Bowl Souvenir Magazine,* 52–60. 2006.

18. Michael Schulze. *The 2011 Official Outback Bowl Souvenir Magazine.* 2011.

19. *2007 Outback Bowl.* ESPN, 2007.

20. Bob Boyles and Paul Guido. *The USA Today College Football Encyclopedia,* 746. New York: Skyhorse Publishing, 2008.

21. "Tennessee vs. Penn State—Game Summary—January 1, 2007—ESPN," ESPN, Accessed August 18, 2020, https://www.espn.com/college-football/game?gameId=270010213.

2007 Season

1. Rick Hill. *Valero Alamo Bowl 2007 Football Media Guide,* 37. 2007.

2. *Ibid.*

3. *Ibid.*

4. *Ibid.*

5. *Ibid.*

6. *Ibid.*
7. *Ibid.*, 38.
8. *Ibid.*
9. *Ibid.*
10. *Ibid.*
11. *Ibid.*
12. *Ibid.*
13. *Ibid.*, 28.
14. *Ibid.*, 15.
15. Mainstream Media International. *2007 Valero Alamo Bowl Game Program,* 26–37. 2007.
16. "2007 Game Recap," Alamo Bowl, Accessed August 18, 2020, https://www.alamobowl.com/wp-content/uploads/2014/11/2007-GAME-RECAP.pdf.

2008 Season

1. Jeff Nelson. *2009 Rose Bowl Media Guide,* 57. 2008.
2. *Ibid.*, 58.
3. *Ibid.*, 59.
4. *Ibid.*, 60.
5. *Ibid.*, 61.
6. *Ibid.*, 62.
7. *Ibid.*, 63.
8. *Ibid.*, 64.
9. *Ibid.*, 65.
10. *Ibid.*, 66.
11. *Ibid.*, 67.
12. *Ibid.*, 68.
13. *Ibid.*, 37–55.
14. *Ibid.*, 18.
15. *Ibid.*, 29.
16. *Ibid.*, 53.
17. Julia Sheridan. *2009 Rose Bowl Game Presented by Citi Official Souvenir Magazine,* 40–45. 2008.
18. *2009 Rose Bowl Game Presented by Citi.* Genius Entertainment, 2009, DVD.
19. "Penn State vs. USC—Game Summary—January 1, 2009—ESPN," ESPN, January 1, 2009, https://www.espn.com/college-football/game?gameId=290010030.

2009 Season

1. Jeff Nelson. *2010 Capital One Bowl Media Guide,* 57. 2009.
2. *Ibid.*, 58.
3. *Ibid.*, 59.
4. *Ibid.*, 60.
5. *Ibid.*, 61.
6. *Ibid.*, 62.
7. *Ibid.*, 63.
8. *Ibid.*, 64.
9. *Ibid.*, 65.
10. *Ibid.*, 66.
11. *Ibid.*, 67.
12. *Ibid.*, 68.
13. *Ibid.*, 54.
14. *Ibid.*, 7.

15. *Ibid.*, 53–54.
16. *Ibid.*, 39.
17. *Ibid.*, 55.
18. *Bowl Championship Series 2013–2014 Media Guide,* 137. 2013.
19. Nelson, 37.
20. *Capital One Bowl,* ESPN, 2010.
21. "Capital One Bowl—Penn State vs LSU Box Score—January 1, 2010," Sports Reference, accessed August 18, 2020, https://www.sports-reference.com/cfb/boxscores/2010-01-01-louisiana-state.html.

2010 Season

1. Michael Schulze. "Penn State Road to Tampa." In *The Official Outback Bowl Souvenir Magazine,* 119. 2010.
2. *Ibid.*
3. *Ibid.*, 120.
4. *Ibid.*, 122.
5. *Ibid.*
6. *Ibid.*, 124.
7. *Ibid.*
8. *Ibid.*, 133.
9. *Ibid.*
10. "Outback Bowl—Penn State vs Florida Box Score, January 1, 2011," Sports Reference, Accessed August 18, 2020, https://www.sports-reference.com/cfb/boxscores/2011-01-01-florida.html.

2011 Season

1. "Penn State Pounces on Indiana State, 41–7." Penn State Athletics, September 3, 2011, https://gopsusports.com/news/2011/9/3/Penn_State_Pounces_on_Indiana_State_41_7.aspx.
2. "Nittany Lions Downed by No. 3 Alabama." Penn State Athletics, September 10, 2011, https://gopsusports.com/news/2011/9/10/Nittany_Lions_Downed_by_No_3_Alabama.aspx.
3. "Nittany Lions Nab Comeback Win Against Temple, 14–10." Penn State Athletics, September 17, 2011, https://gopsusports.com/news/2011/9/17/Nittany_Lions_Nab_Comeback_Win_Against_Temple_14_10.aspx.
4. "Penn State Belts Eastern Michigan," Penn State Athletics, September 24, 2011, https://gopsusports.com/news/2011/9/24/Penn_State_Belts_Eastern_Michigan_34_6.aspx.
5. "Penn State Wins Big Ten Leaders Division Opener," Penn State Athletics, October 1, 2011, https://gopsusports.com/news/2011/10/1/Penn_State_Wins_Big_Ten_Leaders_Division_Opener.aspx.
6. "Nittany Lions Stifle Iowa 13–3 To Win Second Straight Big Ten Game," Penn State Athletics, October 8, 2011, https://gopsusports.com/news/2011/10/8/Nittany_Lions_Stifle_Iowa_13_3_To_Win_Second_Straight_Big_Ten_Game.aspx.
7. "Redd, Defense Lead No. 25 Nittany Lions Past Purdue, 23–18," Penn State Athletics, October 15, 2011, https://gopsusports.com/news/2011/10/15/

Redd_Defense_Lead_No_25_Nittany_Lions_Past_
Purdue_23_18.aspx.

8. "No. 21 Nittany Lions Win at Northwestern To Remain Unbeaten in Big Ten," Penn State Athletics, accessed October 22, 2011. https://gopsusports.com/news/2011/10/22/No_21_Nittany_Lions_Win_at_Northwestern_To_Remain_Unbeaten_in_Big_Ten.aspx.

9. "Late Touchdown Leads No. 19 Penn State Past Illinois, 10–7," Penn State Athletics, October 29, 2011, https://gopsusports.com/news/2011/10/29/Late_Touchdown_Leads_No_19_Penn_State_Past_Illinois_10_7.aspx.

10. "No. 12 Penn State Falls to No. 19 Nebraska, 17–14," Penn State Athletics, November 12, 2011 https://gopsusports.com/news/2011/11/12/No_12_Penn_State_Falls_to_No_19_Nebraska_17_14.aspx.

11. "No. 21 Nittany Lions Dominate Buckeyes, 20–14," Penn State Athletics, November 19, 2011, https://gopsusports.com/news/2011/11/19/No_21_Nittany_Lions_Dominate_Buckeyes_20_14.aspx.

12. "Nittany Lions Earn Share of Leaders Division Title Despite Setback at No. 15 Wisconsin," Penn State Athletics, November 26, 2011, https://gopsusports.com/news/2011/11/26/Nittany_Lions_Earn_Share_of_Leaders_Division_Title_Despite_Setback_at_No_15_Wisconsin.aspx.

13. "Season Stats," Penn State Athletics, August 8, 2018, https://gopsusports.com/documents/2018/8/8/22779__m_footbl_2011_12_stats__season_stats_20111122aaa.pdf.

14. "Box Score," Penn State Athletics, Accessed August 18, 2020, https://gopsusports.com/documents/2018/8/8/22989__m_footbl_2011_12_box_score__stats_20120102aaa.pdf.

2014 Season

1. Alfred Santasiere. "Penn State Nittany Lions." In *New Era Pinstripe Bowl Official Game Program,* 150. 2014.

2. *Ibid.,* 151.
3. *Ibid.,* 152.
4. *Ibid.,* 154.
5. *Ibid.,* 156.
6. *Ibid.,* 158.
7. *Ibid.,* 160.
8. *Ibid.,* 161.
9. *Ibid.,* 162.
10. *Ibid.,* 164.
11. *Ibid.,* 166.
12. *Penn State Unrivaled.* Penn State University, 2014, DVD.
13. "Pinstripe Bowl—Boston College vs Penn State Box Score, December 27, 2014," Sports Reference, accessed August 18, 2020, https://www.sports-reference.com/cfb/boxscores/2014-12-27-penn-state.html.

2015 Season

1. Cheri O'Neill. "Nittany Lions 2015 Season Review." *71st Annual TaxSlayer Bowl Official Souvenir Program,* 46. 2015.

2. *Ibid.*
3. *Ibid.*
4. *Ibid.,* 48.
5. *Ibid.*
6. *Ibid.*
7. *Ibid.,* 50.
8. *Ibid.*
9. *Ibid.*
10. *Ibid.,* 54.
11. *Ibid.*
12. *Ibid.*
13. Doug Kelly. "Game of Epic Proportions." In *71st Annual TaxSlayer Bowl Official Souvenir Program,* 25. 2015.
14. *Ibid.,* 24.
15. "TaxSlayer Bowl—Penn State vs. Georgia Box Score—January 2nd, 2016," Sports Reference, accessed August 18, 2020, https://www.sports-reference.com/cfb/boxscores/2016-01-02-georgia.html.

2016 Season

1. Ming Wong. "Road to the Rose Bowl Game." *2017 Rose Bowl Game Program,* 70. 2016.

2. *Ibid.,* 71.
3. *Ibid.,* 72–74.
4. *Ibid.,* 76.
5. *Ibid.,* 77.
6. *Ibid.,* 78.
7. *Ibid.,* 80.
8. *Ibid.,* 82–86.
9. *Ibid.,* 88.
10. *Ibid.,* 89.
11. Michael Bradley. "Scouting Report." *2017 Rose Bowl Game Program,* 18. 2016.
12. *Rose Bowl Game Presented by Northwestern Mutual.* Team Marketing, 2017, DVD.
13. "Rose Bowl—USC vs Penn State Box Score, January 2, 2017," Sports Reference, accessed August 18, 2020, https://www.sports-reference.com/cfb/boxscores/2017-01-02-penn-state.html.

2017 Season

1. *2017 PlayStation Fiesta Bowl Media Guide,* 36. 2017.

2. *Ibid.,* 37.
3. *Ibid.,* 38.
4. *Ibid.,* 39.
5. *Ibid.,* 40.
6. *Ibid.,* 41.
7. *Ibid.,* 42.
8. *Ibid.,* 43.
9. *Ibid.,* 44.
10. *Ibid.,* 45.
11. *Ibid.,* 46.

12. *Ibid.*, 47.

13. *Ibid.*, 32–34.

14. *Ibid.*, 1.

15. *47th Annual PlayStation Fiesta Bowl.* Team Marketing, 2018, DVD.

16. "Fiesta Bowl—Washington vs Penn State Box Score, December 30, 2017," Sports Reference, accessed August 18, 2020, https://www.sports-reference.com/cfb/boxscores/2017-12-30-penn-state.html.

2018 Season

1. Sam Gardner, et al. "Penn State University Season in Review." *2019 VRBO Citrus Bowl Official Game Program, 90.* 2018.

2. *Ibid.*

3. *Ibid.*, 92.

4. *Ibid.*

5. *Ibid.*, 95.

6. *Ibid.*

7. *Ibid.*, 97.

8. *Ibid.*, 98.

9. "Citrus Bowl—Kentucky vs. Penn State Box Score, January 1, 2019," Sports Reference, accessed August 18, 2020, https://www.sports-reference.com/cfb/boxscores/2019-01-01-penn-state.html.

2019 Season

1. E.J. Smith and Zach Berman. "NFL Draft: Penn State Quarterback Trace McSorley Drafted by Baltimore Ravens in Sixth Round, Ryquell Armstead by Jacksonville Jaguars." *The Philadelphia Inquirer.* April 27, 2019. https://www.inquirer.com/eagles/nfl-draft-trace-mcsorley-ryquell-armstead-penn-state-temple-football-20190427.html.

2. Tom Fornelli. "Former Penn State quarterback Tommy Stevens transferring to Mississippi State." CBS Sports. May 17, 2019. https://www.cbssports.com/college-football/news/former-penn-state-quarterback-tommy-stevens-transferring-to-mississippi-state/.

3. *Penn State Cotton Bowl Media Guide, 30.*

4. *Ibid.*, 31.

5. *Ibid.*, 32.

6. *Ibid.*, 33.

7. *Ibid.*, 34.

8. *Ibid.*, 35.

9. *Ibid.*, 36.

10. *Ibid.*, 37.

11. *Ibid.*, 38.

12. Associated Press. "Penn State's Clifford Leaves Ohio State Game With Leg Injury." November 23, 2019. https://www.usatoday.com/story/sports/ncaaf/2019/11/23/penn-states-clifford-leaves-ohio-state-game-with-leg-injury/40693813/.

13. *Penn State Cotton Bowl Media Guide*, 40.

14. *Ibid.*, 41.

15. Michael Bradley. "Scouting Reports." *Cotton Bowl: Official 2019 Game Program, 19.* 2019.

16. *Penn State Cotton Bowl Media Guide*, 15.

17. Bradley, 24.

18. *Ibid.*, 19.

19. Jimmy Burch. "Memphis and Penn State to Tangle for the First Time in the 84th Classic." *Cotton Bowl: Official 2019 Game Program,* 12–14. 2019.

20. *84th Goodyear Cotton Bowl Classic: The Official Complete Game Broadcast.* Team Marketing, 2020, DVD.

21. "Cotton Bowl—Memphis vs. Penn State Box Score, December 28, 2019," Sports Reference, accessed August 18, 2020, https://www.sports-reference.com/cfb/boxscores/2019-12-28-penn-state.html.

Lists

1. "Penn State Nittany Lions Football Record by Year," Sports Reference, accessed August 18, 2020, https://www.sports-reference.com/cfb/schools/penn-state/.

2. *Ibid.*

3. *Penn State Cotton Bowl Media Guide,* 26. 2019.

4. "Trace McSorley College Stats," Sports Reference, accessed August 18, 2020, https://www.sports-reference.com/cfb/players/trace-mcsorley-1.html.

5. "Todd Blackledge College Stats," Sports Reference, accessed August 18, 2020, https://www.sports-reference.com/cfb/players/todd-blackledge-1.html.

6. "Kerry Collins College Stats," Sports Reference, accessed August 18, 2020, https://www.sports-reference.com/cfb/players/kerry-collins-1.html.

7. "Michael Robinson College Stats," Sports Reference, accessed August 18, 2020, https://www.sports-reference.com/cfb/players/michael-robinson-1.html.

8. "Daryll Clark College Stats," Sports Reference, accessed August 18, 2020, https://www.sports-reference.com/cfb/players/daryll-clark-1.html.

9. "Chuck Fusina College Stats," Sports Reference, accessed August 18, 2020, https://www.sports-reference.com/cfb/players/chuck-fusina-1.html.

10. "Wally Richardson College Stats," Sports Reference, accessed August 18, 2020, https://www.sports-reference.com/cfb/players/wally-richardson-1.html.

11. "Tony Sacca College Stats," Sports Reference, accessed August 18, 2020, https://www.sports-reference.com/cfb/players/tony-sacca-1.html.

12. "Tom Shuman College Stats," Sports Reference, accessed August 18, 2020, https://www.sports-reference.com/cfb/players/tom-shuman-1.html.

13. "Chuck Burkhart College Stats," Sports Reference, accessed August 18, 2020, https://www.sports-reference.com/cfb/players/chuck-burkhart-1.html.

14. "Christian Hackenberg College Stats," Sports Reference, accessed August 18, 2020, https://www.sports-reference.com/cfb/players/christian-hackenberg-1.html.

15. "Sean Clifford College Stats," Sports Reference, accessed August 18, 2020, https://www.sports-reference.com/cfb/players/sean-clifford-1.html.

16. "Galen Hall College Stats," Sports Reference, accessed August 18, 2020, https://

www.sports-reference.com/cfb/players/galen-hall-1.html.

17. "Anthony Morelli College Stats," Sports Reference, accessed August 18, 2020, https://www.sports-reference.com/cfb/players/anthony-morelli-1.html.

18. "John Shaffer College Stats," Sports Reference, accessed August 18, 2020, https://www.sports-reference.com/cfb/players/john-shaffer-1.html.

19. "Curt Warner College Stats," Sports Reference, accessed August 18, 2020, https://www.sports-reference.com/cfb/players/curt-warner-1.html.

20. "Ki-Jana Carter College Stats," Sports Reference, accessed August 18, 2020, https://www.sports-reference.com/cfb/players/ki-jana-carter-1.html.

21. "John Cappelletti College Stats," Sports Reference, accessed August 18, 2020, https://www.sports-reference.com/cfb/players/john-cappelletti-1.html.

22. "Larry Johnson College Stats," Sports Reference, accessed August 18, 2020, https://www.sports-reference.com/cfb/players/larry-johnson-1.html.

23. "Saquon Barkley College Stats," Sports Reference, accessed August 18, 2020, https://www.sports-reference.com/cfb/players/saquon-barkley-1.html.

24. "D.J. Dozier College Stats," Sports Reference, accessed August 18, 2020, https://www.sports-reference.com/cfb/players/dj-dozier-1.html.

25. "Franco Harris College Stats," Sports Reference, accessed August 18, 2020, https://www.sports-reference.com/cfb/players/franco-harris-1.html.

26. "Lydell Mitchell College Stats," Sports Reference, accessed August 18, 2020, https://www.sports-reference.com/cfb/players/lydell-mitchell-1.html.

27. "Curtis Enis College Stats," Sports Reference, accessed August 18, 2020, https://www.sports-reference.com/cfb/players/curtis-enis-1.html.

28. "Evan Royster College Stats," Sports Reference, accessed August 18, 2020, https://www.sports-reference.com/cfb/players/evan-royster-1.html.

29. "Blair Thomas College Stats," Sports Reference, accessed August 18, 2020, https://www.sports-reference.com/cfb/players/blair-thomas-1.html.

30. "Matt Suhey College Stats," Sports Reference, accessed August 18, 2020, https://www.sports-reference.com/cfb/players/matt-suhey-1.html.

31. "Tony Hunt College Stats," Sports Reference, accessed August 18, 2020, https://www.sports-reference.com/cfb/players/tony-hunt-1.html.

32. "Journey Brown College Stats," Sports Reference, accessed August 18, 2020, https://www.sports-reference.com/cfb/players/journey-brown-1.html.

33. "Bobby Engram College Stats," Sports Reference, accessed August 18, 2020, https://www.sports-reference.com/cfb/players/bobby-engram-1.html.

34. "O.J. McDuffie College Stats," Sports Reference, accessed August 18, 2020, https://www.sports-reference.com/cfb/players/oj-mcduffie-1.html.

35. "DaeSean Hamilton College Stats," Sports Reference, accessed August 18, 2020, https://www.sports-reference.com/cfb/players/daesean-hamilton-1.html.

36. "No. 1 At Last! Gregg Garrity Scores the Winning Touchdown for Penn State." *Sports Illustrated,* January 10. Cover page.

37. "Jimmy Cefalo College Stats," Sports Reference, accessed August 18, 2020, https://www.sports-reference.com/cfb/players/journey-brown-1.html.

38. "Chris Godwin College Stats," Sports Reference, accessed August 18, 2020, https://www.sports-reference.com/cfb/players/chris-godwin-1.html.

39. "Deon Butler College Stats," Sports Reference, accessed August 18, 2020, https://www.sports-reference.com/cfb/players/deon-butler-1.html.

40. "David Daniels College Stats," Sports Reference, accessed August 18, 2020, https://www.sports-reference.com/cfb/players/david-daniels-2.html.

41. "Joe Jurevicius College Stats," Sports Reference, accessed August 18, 2020, https://www.sports-reference.com/cfb/players/joe-jurevicius-1.html.

42. "Jordan Norwood College Stats," Sports Reference, accessed August 18, 2020, https://www.sports-reference.com/cfb/players/jordan-norwood-1.html.

43. "Shane Conlan College Stats," Sports Reference, accessed August 18, 2020, https://www.sports-reference.com/cfb/players/shane-conlan-1.html.

44. "Mt. Rushmore Archives," Big Ten Network, accessed August 18, 2020, https://btn.com/tag/mt-rushmore/.

45. "Paul Posluszny College Stats," Sports Reference, accessed August 18, 2020, https://www.sports-reference.com/cfb/players/paul-posluszny-1.html.

46. "LaVar Arrington College Stats," Sports Reference, accessed August 18, 2020, https://www.sports-reference.com/cfb/players/lavar-arrington-1.html.

47. "Catching Up With…" *The Morning Call,* accessed August 18, 2020, https://www.mcall.com/news/mc-xpm-2008-09-15-4193395-story.html.

48. "Mt. Rushmore Archives," Big Ten Network, accessed August 18, 2020, https://btn.com/tag/mt-rushmore/.

49. "Jack Ham (1990)—Hall of Fame," National Football Foundation, Accessed August 18, 2020, https://footballfoundation.org/hof_search.aspx?hof=1864.

50. "Courtney Brown College Stats," Sports Reference, accessed August 18, 2020, https://www.sports-reference.com/cfb/players/courtney-brown-1.html.

51. "Sean Lee College Stats," Sports Reference, accessed August 18, 2020, https://www.sports-reference.com/cfb/players/sean-lee-1.html.

52. "Navorro Bowman College Stats," Sports Reference, accessed August 18, 2020, https://www.sports-reference.com/cfb/players/navorro-bowman-1.html.

53. "Tamba Hali College Stats," Sports Reference, accessed August 18, 2020, https://www.sports-reference.com/cfb/players/tamba-hali-1.html.

54. "Pete Giftopoulos College Stats," Sports Reference, accessed August 18, 2020, https://www.sports-reference.com/cfb/players/pete-giftopoulos-1.html.

Appendix A

1. *Penn State Cotton Bowl Media Guide*, 8. 2019.

Appendix C

1. *2019 Penn State Cotton Bowl Media Guide*, 44–48. 2019; "Cotton Bowl—Memphis vs. Penn State Box Score, December 28, 2019," Sports Reference, accessed August 18, 2020, https://www.sports-reference.com/cfb/boxscores/2019-12-28-penn-state.html.

Appendix D

1. *2019 Penn State Cotton Bowl Media Guide*, 46. 2019; "Cotton Bowl—Memphis vs. Penn State Box Score, December 28, 2019," Sports Reference, accessed August 18, 2020, https://www.sports-reference.com/cfb/boxscores/2019-12-28-penn-state.html.

Appendix E

1. Louis Prato. *The Penn State Football Encyclopedia*, 547–651. Champaign: Sports Publishing, 1998; "College Football Statistics and History." Sports Reference, accessed August 21, 2020. https://www.sports-reference.com/cfb/.

Appendix F

1. Louis Prato. *The Penn State Football Encyclopedia*, 547–651. Champaign: Sports Publishing, 1998; "College Football Statistics and History." Sports Reference. Accessed August 21, 2020. https://www.sports-reference.com/cfb/.

Appendix G

1. Louis Prato. *The Penn State Football Encyclopedia*, 547–651. Champaign: Sports Publishing, 1998; "College Football Statistics and History." Sports Reference, accessed August 21, 2020. https://www.sports-reference.com/cfb/.

Bibliography

Bannon, Peter, Joseph Bannon, and Adrian Pratt. *Restoring the Pride: Penn State's 2005 Championship Season,* ed. Robert Heisse. Champaign, IL: Sports Publishing, 2005.

Bauer, David. *Sports Illustrated Presents: That Perfect Season, Penn State 1994.* New York: Time, 1995.

Bilovsky, Frank. *Lion Country: Inside Penn State Football.* West Point, NY: Leisure Press, 1982.

Brush, Daniel, David Horne, Marc Maxwell, and Jared Trexler. *Penn State Football: An Interactive Guide to the World of Sports.* New York: Savas Beatie, 2009.

Contz, Bill. *When the Lions Roared: Joe Paterno and One of College Football's Greatest Teams.* Chicago: Triumph, 2017.

Denlinger, Ken. *For the Glory: College Football Dreams and Realities Inside Paterno's Program.* New York: St. Martin's Press, 1994.

Doster, Rob, ed. *Gameday Penn State Football: The Greatest Games, Players, Coaches and Teams in the Glorious Tradition of Nittany Lion Football.* Chicago: Triumph, 2007.

Fitzgerald, Francis. *Greatest Moments in Penn State Football History.* Louisville: AdCraft Sports Marketing, 1996.

Fitzpatrick, Frank. *The Lion in Autumn: A Season with Joe Paterno and Penn State Football.* New York: Gotham Books, 2005.

Hyman, Jordan. *Game of My Life, Penn State: Memorable Stories of Nittany Lions Football.* Champaign, IL: Sports Publishing, 2006.

Johnson, Randy. *Hail to the Lions! Salute to a Championship Season.* Birmingham, AL: EBSCO Media, 1995.

Missanelli, M.G. *The Perfect Season: How Penn State Came to Stop a Hurricane and Win a National Championship.* University Park: Pennsylvania State University Press, 2007.

Naylor, Rex. *The Forgotten Seasons: Penn State Football 1977-1978.* N.p.: Naylor Publishing, 2018.

O'Brien, Michael. *No Ordinary Joe: The Biography of Joe Paterno.* Nashville: Rutledge Hill Press, 1998.

Panaccio, Tim. *Beast of the East: Penn State vs. Pitt.* West Point, NY: Leisure Press, 1982.

Paterno, Joseph, and Bernard Asbell. *Paterno by the Book.* New York: Random House, 1989.

Prato, Lou. *Game Changers: The Greatest Plays in Penn State Football History.* Chicago: Triumph, 2009.

———. *100 Things Penn State Fans Should Know and Do Before They Die.* Chicago: Triumph Books, 2015.

———. *The Penn State Football Encyclopedia.* Champaign, IL: Sports Publishing, 1998.

Rappoport, Ken. *Penn State Nittany Lions: Where Have You Gone?* Champaign, IL: Sports Publishing, 2005.

———. *Tales from Penn State Football.* Champaign, IL: Sports Publishing, 2007.

Richeal, Kip. *Welcome to the Big Ten: The 1993 Penn State Football Season.* Champaign, IL: Sagamore, 1994.

Index

289